Objects with Perspective

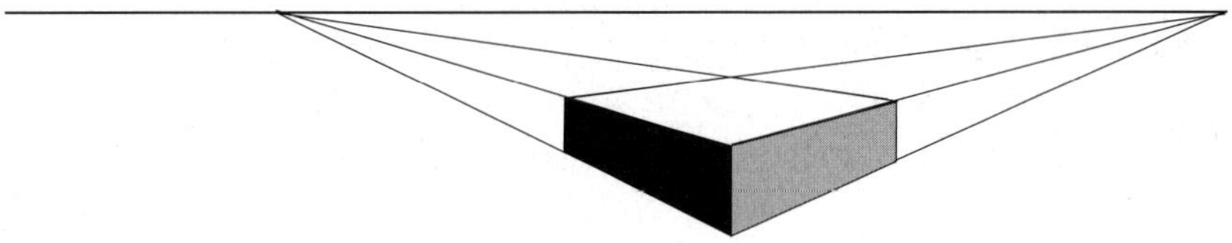

Objects with Perspective

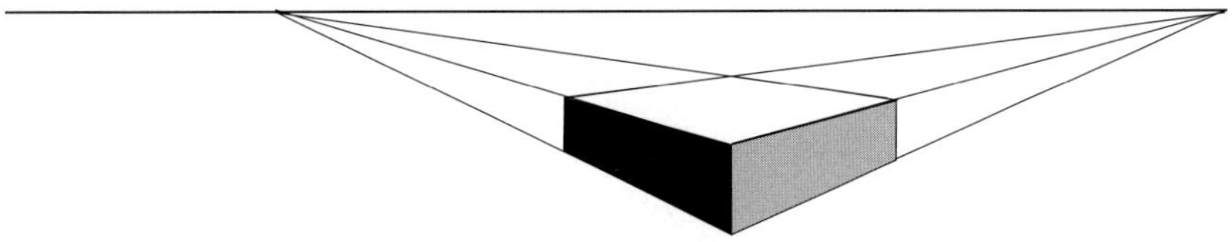

Waltraud Häckl, Editor

Contributors:

M. Sim, N. Simon, P. Kist, E. Essenius, I. Szántó

DUP Satellite / 2004

DUP Satellite is an imprint of

Delft University Press
P.O. Box 98
2600 MG Delft
The Netherlands
Telephone: + 31 15 2785678
Telefax: + 31 15 2785706
E-mail: Info@Library.TUDelft.NL

ISBN 90-407-2464-4

Printed in The Netherlands

Contents

Preface

I. Intended Audience

This book is an introduction to the object model Perspective-DB©. The model is mainly designed to support the life-cycle of large and comprehensive information systems. The life-cycle consists of design, implementation, exploitation, maintenance and evolution. Such information systems impact a broad spectrum of persons in the organization [Cattell and Barry, 2000]. An important aspect of Perspective-DB is that it is a versatile tool that can be used by all people involved in the successful introduction, incorporation and maintenance of an information system within an organization. This includes directors, managers, consultants, system administrators, end-users and customers.
The common denominator that enables all persons involved with the information system to communicate with each other in a clear common language is the object model. The object model of Perspective-DB and its conceptual modeling capability is described in the first part of the book.
The second part of the book is intended for the end-users, it describes the novel interactive characteristics of the object model.
The third part which is intended for developers, explains the textual representation of the object model. The final part is important for information system administrators as it describes how the textual representation is used as a powerful data exchange format.
Throughout the book, both the end-user and developer views of the object model are explained. The book is therefore a useful introduction for people interested in developing systems with Perspective-DB. The book is also useful for those who are not involved with Perspective-DB based systems directly because the object model reaches beyond the type of database management system. The concepts can be applied to model a wide spectrum of applications.
The book requires no previous knowledge of software engineering, be it programming or information system engineering. The object model is based on a few intuitive and well-known concepts from daily life. The reader is not led into a world of bits and bytes and algorithms, but into the world of objects. The reader is shown how it is possible to re-use the existing way we think about things in the real world by describing them in terms of objects, of the information these objects contain and how these objects interact. The model is natural and intuitive since it contains well-known principles we encounter in real life such as object existence, object hierarchies and object inheritance. The model has a simple yet powerful schematic representation.

II. Perspective-DB in a Nutshell

Perspective-DB Object Model

Objects are analogous to real-life things both tangible and abstract. For example, a person, a room, a building, an organization. As in real-life, objects are constructed from simpler objects, and relate to other objects. Simpler objects describe the properties of composite objects. In the same way that real-life things are active, objects are also active, they can carry out operations that can change their own state and indirectly that of other objects. Object existence is an important daily life concept we use for reasoning because it determines the scope of an object's life-time. For example, when we think about a room we take for granted that its building exists, and if the building were destroyed, then the room, of course, would cease to exist. We encounter various object hierarchies as well. For example, an organization is made up of departments and sections, and buildings are made up of levels and rooms. Inheritance likewise is a natural phenomenon; homo Sapiens `is a` mammal and so inherits the properties of mammal.

Perspective-DB Object Database Management System
From early on, emphasis was put on the graphical representation philosophy of Perspective-DB and this has a major impact on the model. The idea is that the object model is not only a tool for analysts, designers and developers, but is just as valuable for the end-user to help him/her to navigate through a complex system without becoming disoriented, while providing a representation that is inherent to the application at hand and based on the type of action to be performed. The object model is completely incorporated in the Object Database Management System (ODBMS)[1]. The ODBMS forms the foundation upon which specialized systems can be built. These properties of the object model are retained in the specialized systems that also profit from the wide range of general services. Combined with the Perspective-DB development system (Perspective CASE)[2] it is a powerful platform that enables even small companies to produce large and complex information systems that up till now have usually only been within the reach of companies that can afford high development costs.

III. Structure of the Book

The book is roughly divided into the following parts:

- Introduction to the Field, Case Study and Related Work
  In the introduction the reader is given a short explanation on the basic principles of Perspective-DB, which is placed in the context of the requirements of information systems and related work in the field. The universe of discourse of a hospital administration system is used as a case study throughout the book[3].

- Schematic Object Model The opening chapters explain the object model using the schematic representation as the communication vehicle.

- Developers and End-user Views
  The schematic representations for developers and end-users is introduced and then applied to the case study in order to consolidate how to do conceptual modeling with Perspective-DB. The Hospital system is simple yet covers many aspects of design. Readers who are not directly involved in using the system can achieve a fair level of conceptual modeling based solely on the schematic representation and this case study.

- Using the Textual Object Model for Meta Data Design
  The reader is introduced to the basics of the textual representation of the object model. Thereafter, the representation is applied to show how it is used to define the structural and behavioral aspects of the Hospital system, the so-called Meta data. This part explains how the schematic representation is converted to the textual format that is actually used to realize the system.

- Schematic and Tabular User Interface
  The reader is introduced to the schematic and tabular interactive interface. Using the case study hospital system, the user is shown how to navigate the object base, create and manipulate the objects. This part is necessary for end-users and persons who frequently need to communicate with the end-users.

---

[1]The object model continues to evolve; this book however, is purposefully restricted to incorporated elements.

[2]Organizations interested in developing applications with Perspective-DB ODBMS can send an e-mail to info@bitbybit-is.nl or surf to www.bitbybit-is.nl.

[3]The case study is based on an application developed for educational and training purposes. Organizations interested in using this application are requested to send an e-mail to info@bitbybit-is.nl for more details.

- Using the Textual Object Model for GUI and Language Design
  The TOML representation is applied to show how it is used to define the GUI and the language visible to the end user in the Hospital system.

- Using the Textual Object Model for Data-Exchange (Query)
  The textual representation also forms the basis for data exchange. This file-based exchange format enables the populating and extracting of data from the object base.

- System building aspects of the Model
  This explains the concepts of how a system is constructed using partitioning, vertical partitioning by means of levels and horizontal partitioning by means of modules, and how this is achieved seamlessly within the constructs of the object model.

- Relation to Standards
  This provides the reader mainly with a comparison of Perspective-DB with an international object database standard and intends to provide a setting for this model in the context of mainstream object database modeling.

IV. Content of the Book

Schematic Object Model

- Chapter 2 explains how real-world things are mapped to objects, and introduces the basic characteristics of objects. The reader becomes familiar with a small number of simple constructs which used together form basic objects, the foundation for the object model. A case study showing how to build a small component is used to help to aid comprehension of the material.

- Chapter 3 extends the basic object with additional characteristics in order to achieve a so-called first order object. An important extension is the object's capacity to interact through relationships. First-order objects are suitable for modeling at a conceptual level and for designing large systems. They form the elementary object upon which the Perspective-DB Object Model is based. This chapter places the constructs of the basic objects in the context of the first order object, and deals with the various kinds of relationships. An important kind of relationship is ownership, because it determines for each object which other object is its owner. The owner is the only object allowed to create and eventually destroy that object.

- Chapter 4 extends the characteristics of first order objects by introducing the general concept of object identity. Object identity is necessary in order to unambiguously distinguish an object from all other objects in the object base, and to provide a systematic means to locate an object. The chapter goes on to deal with several variants of object identity, and explains how each one is used for a particular situation.

- Chapter 5 explains the schematic view of the developer and of the end-user and how these views complement one another to form a clear picture of the system. The developer view describes how the system is built and the end-user view describes the end-user interface.

Consolidating the Case Study

- Chapter 6 consolidates the case study of a small hospital application. It explains how the designer uses the object model to convert the system requirements into a system design and how the end-user uses the object model as a tool to understand the application. The developer and end-user views are used as the communication vehicle.

Using the Textual Object Model for Design - Meta Data

- Chapter 7 explains the complementary textual object model called the Textual Object Model Language (TOML), its syntax and usage as a means to describe applications. The TOML language is divided into several domains, each responsible for a particular task.
- Chapter 8 explains how the structure and behavior of objects is defined in TOML using the Meta domain.

Schematic and Tabular User Interface

An important feature of the interactive aspect of the object model is that it provides both schematic and tabular representations. These representations provide an equivalent form of navigating, viewing and manipulating the object base. Both interface representations can be manipulated simultaneously and interact with one another.

- Chapter 9 explains how to navigate and view objects in the object base using the schematic representation.
- Chapter 10 explains how the end-user uses the schematic representation to create and manipulate objects in the object base.
- Chapter 11 introduces the most important tabular view, called the Form and its use alongside the schematic representation. The chapter explains how the Form view represents an object and how it is used to view and manipulate the objects in the object base.
- Chapter 12 introduces other important tabular views and explains how the end-user uses these to view and manipulate the objects in the object base. The Overview shows the contents of a relation, the Association view shows the objects with which a particular object interacts, and the Query view returns a table containing the results of a request for particular information about objects.
- Chapter 13 explains how to formulate queries based on the query language of the object model.

Using the Textual Object Model for Design - GUI and Language

- Chapter 14 explains how the graphical specification of objects is defined in TOML using the Graphical domain.
- Chapter 15 explains how the objects are configured to represent the information in an appropriate natural language in TOML using the Language domain.

Using the Textual Object Model for Data-Exchange

The Textual Object Model Language is also used for importing objects into, exporting objects from, and manipulating objects in an object base. These activities are done in TOML using the Instantiation domain.

- Chapter 16 explains how the objects are created and manipulated in TOML using the Instantiation domain and how this representation is used to import and export objects.
- Chapter 17 explains how the import can be refined by using the Instantiation domain extended with a query facility (Set by Query). This provides more control over what information should be created and manipulated in the object base.

- Chapter 18 explains how the export can be refined by using the Instantiation domain extended with a query facility (Get by Query). This provides control over what information should be extracted from the object base.

Building systems

- Chapter 19 explains how, using particular object types, the object model is used to build systems. It explains the architecture of the Perspective-DB object management system, and three important principles of building complex applications: the first is building the system, layer upon layer; the second is dividing each layer into smaller modules each containing a limited number of objects, and the third is how the concept of inheritance is applied to re-use the definitions of objects to define other objects.

Relation to Standards

- Chapter 20 provides a means for the reader to relate Perspective-DB to other object models. The well known ODMG standard and the UML method are used as the means of comparison. The hospital case study is used to discuss the differences between the models and design methods and their advantages and disadvantages. The comparison provides a vehicle to argue the justification for an additional object model to exist beside the ODMG and UML.

Functional (Mathematical) Description

- The Appendix gives the reader an idea of how Perspective-DB can be described more formally by means of a mathematical model.

V. A Short History of Perspective-DB

The specification and design of the Perspective-DB object model began at Bitbybit Information Systems in 1992. It is based on the simple philosophy behind object technology: the definition and manipulation of computerized information can be abstracted from a level of bits and bytes to a level natural for human perception, namely objects that can store data, act, re-act and interact in much the same way as things do in real-life.

From the start the model has been driven by the requirements of a commercial system, and great care has been taken to extend the system to the needs of the users, while remaining true to the concepts of the model. The first system to be built on the Perspective-DB foundation was a planning system called Iris-Planning, which is a commercial product developed by Bitbybit Information Systems. It is constructed of three main subsystems: the first is the Perspective-DB ODBMS foundation, the second is an Organization Infrastructure System built upon the ODBMS which manages general aspects of the organization such as space management, structure of the organization, activity management etc. The third is the timetabling, reservation and registration system which communicates with the infrastructure system to provide powerful and comprehensive planning capability. The system was first used commercially to timetable in 1996. The product is now in use in many organizations.

The graphical interface became operational in 1997. Perspective-DB is probably the only system that provides the end-user with an interactive graphical object model as the foundation of the end-user interface.

Since the year 2001, Bitbybit Information Systems offers the Perspective-DB CASE product to other organizations. R&D collaboration with researchers from the Delft University of Technology has been an important factor in enhancing the quality of the model and the system based upon it. Bitbybit Information Systems (www.bitbybit-is.nl) is the proprietary owner of the object model and the ODBMS.

VI. Contributors

The major contributors to the development of the Perspective-DB model, ODBMS and to this book:

- Waltraud Häckl[4] - DELOBIS
  Waltraud holds a PhD in Process Engineering and a PhD in Computer Science. She was chair-holder of the Database Management Systems section at Delft University of Technology, specializing in object database technology, object modeling and alignment of business processes and supporting information systems. Waltraud is founder of DELOBIS, Delft, where Perspective-DB ODBMS is applied in developing comprehensive information systems. Waltraud wrote the preliminary version of this book based on various existing publications and internal documents produces by the major contributors during the design and development of Perspective-DB.

- Mattie Sim - Bitbybit Information Systems
  Mattie has a PhD in Electrical Engineering.
  Mattie is co-director and coordinates the company's activities and is involved in the R&D of Iris-Planning and the Perspective-DB.
  He has participated in European projects in the areas of Framework and Database Technology and has lectured on the subject of Object Database Management Systems at the Delft University of Technology. Mattie was responsible for revising the preliminary version, based on the comments of the board of reviewers of Delft University of Technology and the major contributors.

- Natalio Simon - Bitbybit Information Systems
  Natalio has a MSc in Electrical Engineering.
  Natalio is co-director and supervises the R&D of the Iris-Planning product. He is active in the area of Information Systems development based on Object Databases and Artificial Intelligence.

- Peter Kist - Bitbybit Information Systems
  Peter is a self-made, experienced programmer and software system developer.
  Peter is co-director and supervises the R&D of the Perspective-DB product.
  Peter has worked as an application developer and as a system designer specializing in Design Systems for engineering applications. He specializes in Object Database development.

- Edwin Essenius - Bitbybit Information Systems
  Edwin has a MSc in Electrical Engineering.
  Edwin is the main developer of Perspective's graphical user interface. He has several years experience in Object Design and Programming and in developing Graphical User Interfaces.

- Iván Szántó - Bitbybit Information Systems
  Iván has a MSc in Electrical Engineering.
  Iván has made major contributions to the design and implementation of the query module and functional description of Perspective-DB as part of his PhD research project [Szántó, 2004]. Previously, he worked as a systems engineer for Sun and he also has experience in the performance tuning of parallel queries for the Oracle RDBMS.

[4]Waltraud appears in Bibliography under her previous name, Gerhardt

VII. Acknowledgments

Thanks go to prof. dr. ir. T. (Theo) P. van der Weide, Katholieke Universiteit Nijmegen for his contribution to the functional description of the Perspective-DB and applied here to the Hospital case study in the Appendix.

Thanks go to all persons that have contributed to designing and developing Perspective-DB; special thanks go to ir. E. (Erno) Marks, ir. N. (Nils) P. van der Knaap and ir. R. (Rosa) M. Frederico da Silva.

Thanks go to all persons that have provided constructive end-user feedback to improve Perspective-DB; special thanks go to ir. T. (Torsten) Gerhardt and drs. L. (Lieske) Simon.

Thanks go to `Senter`, an organization of the Dutch Ministry of Economic Affairs, for helping with the financing of the Perspective-DB project[5]; special thanks go to dr. F. (Frans) B. Gerritse.

Thanks go to the `Faculty of Architecture` of the TU Delft, for commissioning the IRIS-Planning system, the first commercial application built on Perspective-DB; special thanks go to ir. C. (Kees) Daleboudt.

Thanks go to R. (Ruth) Taylor MSc. for correcting the English of the numerous versions.

Thanks go to ir. S. (Sander) van de Merwe for designing the cover.

Thanks go to L. (Lydia) M. ter Horst-ten Wolde, Senior publisher, Delft University Press for the assistance in publishing this book.

[5]TOK95069 titled *Object Management System*

List of Figures

Chapter 1

Introduction

1.1 Universe Of Discourse of the Case Study

The first step toward designing an information system is defining the boundaries of what the system should do. The description of this boundary is called the **Universe Of Discourse** or **UoD** for short. The UoD reduces the complexity of the real-world by removing all irrelevant detail.
The Hospital Case Study is an example of an application that is used throughout the book to explain the Perspective-DB object model. Here follows the motivation for the system followed by a summary of its UoD.
A research-bureau wants to make a database with information about hospitals in the region in order to monitor and control activities. The system has been ordered by a local council which decided to improve cooperation among hospitals and to get an overview of the hospital situation in general. It is used by the hospitals in that area. The hospitals have a joint office which administers the information system. Each hospital provides the administrator with up-to-date data. The system administers the departments, the employees, and patients of each hospital.

- The system should be able to enter and manipulate data on hospitals and if necessary delete data concerning a particular hospital. Each hospital has a unique name. Each hospital consists of departments, split into two groups: service which is directly responsible for the care of the patients and support which is responsible for the ancillary services required by the service departments; the departments being distinguished according to type. The bureau needs to add departments to a hospital, manipulate data on departments and if necessary delete data concerning a particular department.

- The service departments are split into two groups: wards and clinics. The wards contain in-patients who must have beds and stay overnight. Clinics handle out-patients who only come during the day for treatment. Each department has a maximum working capacity which may not be exceeded. The bureau also needs to know what the actual working capacity is. The capacities refer to the number of patients that the department can handle, and is currently handling. In the case of the support department, for example, the capacity for a kitchen implies the maximum number of persons it can feed, and how many it is currently feeding, etc. Examples of wards are Internal and Orthopaedic. Examples of clinics are Internal and General. A clinic can provide service to several Wards.

- There are two support groups: medical-support and general-support. Examples of general support are Laundry and Kitchen. Examples of medical support are Pharmacy and Operating-theater.

- The bureau manages a list of persons. It needs to add persons, manipulate data on persons and if necessary remove persons from the list. Various data on persons should be known, such as the name, address, gender, and telephone number.

- It is possible to keep track of the persons each section employs. Persons can be employed and discharged from a section. The bureau wants to ensure that a person does not exceed the number of hours agreed upon in the employment contract. The actual number of hours must also be maintained. A person may work for more than one department, or hospital, for a certain number of hours, within the limits of the employment contract. Each employee is identified by a code. A report can be kept on the progress of the employee.

- Each patient is identified by a code, and based on the insurance policy, it should be possible to categorize the patient i.e. class A or B. A short report is kept on each patient. A patient can receive treatment from several clinics, but may only be registered in one ward (a patient cannot occupy two beds). It is possible to keeps track of the patients that each service department (ward, clinic) handles. Patients can be checked-into or checked-out of a service department as long as the capacities are not exceeded. It is not necessary to track patients receiving service from a support department. Only the numbers of patients or persons serviced per department is important. It is necessary to keep track of the persons employed by a support department.

It is clear from the above description that the UoD is a simplification of the real-world because in reality there is a multitude of additional information concerning the running of a hospital. The UoD filters out all detail that is not pertinent to the goal the information system must achieve.
In chapter 6 you will find detailed information about all object types and their attributes.

1.2 Modeling of Information-Systems: Characteristics and Models

An **Information System**, commonly abbreviated to **IS** is a system composed of various components such as database management systems, application programs and user interfaces, which together provide the functionality that the various users of the system require.
An IS is usually constructed by using various general-purpose programs, which form the building blocks. These building blocks provide a lot of packaged functionality and also the means to build on top additional functionality required for the IS.
The central building block is the ODBMS. The other building blocks are generally required to fill in functionality that the ODBMS cannot provide. An ODBMS with more comprehensive services is likely to result in a more coherent IS that is easier to construct and maintain.

The ODBMS is a generic software system that is used as the foundation upon which a specific software system can be built. The main purpose of the ODBMS is to minimize the amount of effort required to design, build, maintain and evolve the specific system, by providing generic object management services. The ODBMS should capture the description of the UoD in an **object schema** using a formal notation, known as the **object model**. The ODBMS should realize the object schema and manage the data objects of the schema by applying the object model in the functional running specific system.

There are various criteria to measure the power of an ODBMS and this section is aimed at providing some background information concerning the relations between the lifetime aspects of an information system and the characteristics of an object model and the ODBMS.

1.2.1 Criteria for selecting an ODBMS

When selecting an ODBMS to be used as the foundation for an IS in a particular application domain, it is important to consider technical and applicability criteria that can be applied to the building-blocks used to build the system.
There are many criteria, here we emphasize several that are directly influenced by the modeling powers of the object model and the ODBMS which is providing the object model. Often the criteria do not stand alone, but are the result of combining existing criteria, therefore the following list is ordered accordingly:

- Service throughout the lifetime phases of the IS. The ODBMS should provide service and support to the IS during all stages:
  a) During the design of the IS the object model should help the designer to correctly reflect the information of the UoD and how it is to be manipulated.
  b) During construction of the IS the ODBMS should help the developer to ensure that the design is correctly realized in the IS applications.
  c) During exploitation the ODBMS should help to present the user with the data and functionality necessary for him or her to accomplish the task in a manner that reflects the UoD of that user.
  d) During the maintenance phase the ODBMS should help to localize the problems and minimize the risk of fixing these problems.
  e) During the evolutionary phase the ODBMS should help the designer to easily adapt the IS.

- Expressiveness of the UoD semantics. The UoD confines and expresses the information of the real or imaginary world that the IS is to manage. For the IS to manage this information data optimally, the UoD must be accurately and unambiguously modeled. Independent of all subjective aspects that are associated with the analysis of the UoD, the data model must be suitable to capture the meaning (semantic) of the UoD in terms of structure and behavior with the desired accuracy, meaning:
  a) The model should not break down when a high level of detail is required.
  b) The model should not break down when a high abstraction level is required.
  c) The semantic should not be lost when the model is realized.
  The database structures and operations should accurately reflect the intention of the design. The distortion is minimal when the designed structures and operations remain the same in the developed system (1 to 1, without transformation into another data model). This requires that the data model used for the design is the same as that of the ODBMS that realizes this design.

- Upholding data independence. It is important that the changes to one part of the system do not impact other parts of the system.

  An **entity** is a unique identifiable unit carrying semantics within the UoD. When using the model to describe the UoD, it is important to be able to describe objects as self-contained entities and to be able to relate these to other objects that together compose the UoD model. For example, it should be possible to describe a person and his or her characteristics as an entity (composed of sub-entities), as opposed to describing the birthdate of persons in one list and the addresses in another. This independence should also be reflected in the data structures used to realize these objects in the system. Various aspects of an object might be displayed to the user in the context of other information but the object model should uphold the concept of a general view-point, in database jargon called the "conceptual data schema". The conceptual data schema is a means to achieve this so-called data independence[1].

[1] See the ideas on the ANSI/SPARC 3-schema architecture.

The data are described (modeled) in as neutral a way as possible so that all applications belonging to the IS can interpret it correctly and the value of particular data need only have one so-called logical occurrence. For example, a particular date has only one occurrence. If the date changes, then all applications belonging to the IS will be aware of this change.

- Upholding data integrity. When using the object model to describe the UoD, it is important to be able to describe the rules and constraints that exist between objects of the UoD. In the realized system, data integrity implies that data is correctly described and stored in the database and also remains so during and after processing the data. The ODBMS achieves this by making use of the data model and applying generic database and application management operations that respect the object model.

  An important aspect of data integrity is existential dependency. Existential dependencies operate on objects that are strongly related (often hierarchically). For example: a room cannot exist without a level, which in turn cannot exist without a building. When the building is destroyed, the levels and their respective rooms must be destroyed as well, and vice versa, a room cannot be created if the building and its respective level do not exist.

- Reuse of data structures and functionality. Reuse implies that once a component used in the IS has been designed, realized and tested and is in good working order, it should be reused when required in any location in the IS. In addition to saving development costs, it is then safe to say that:
  a) The same functionality is truly the same, as opposed to two programs that are expected to provide the same behavior but which differ in various details due to the difference in programming.
  b) Maintenance and adaptations will occur in one location.
  c) The system architecture is simplified due to the fact that there are fewer parts and fewer dependencies.

- Structuring of the system architecture. The system architecture should be structured within clear parts. The IS should be based on and constructed of meaningful, informative and functional building blocks. Each block should form a separate unit representing a coherent meaningful part of the IS. Each part should have a well defined logical location within the IS's structure. Relations of the parts amongst themselves should be unambiguous. To realize this, the building blocks should be ordered in system layers with well defined semantics. Layers should be partitioned into modules, also with well defined semantics.

  Modules can be combined to form a more comprehensive whole based on the semantics of the modules. The inside semantics of each module should be influenced as little as possible by its relations to parts of other modules. This requirement should be recursively applicable i.e. to enable combining smaller parts (*components* in their own right) to form larger parts (also *components* in their own right) etc.

  Each module should reflect a different aspect of the UoD, to ensure that the various modules of an IS do not contain the same information. When they are joined together, the added value is ideally more than the sum of the individual parts. This depends on the manner in which the modules can be joined up so that they can relate to each other's data. The object model should be able to describe the various modules that form a layer. The ODBMS should support the construction of layers from modules.

- Scalability. This characteristic implies that the object model can be used to describe a variety of applications, each one represented by several modules, and which together compose the IS.

The IS ranges from small applications with simple schemas to very large ones with complex schemas. It should enable easy adaptation of the design so that the applications can grow and change through an evolutionary process. The ODBMS should be able to support the realization of small and large scale applications and their adaptations.

- Integration of various facets that comprise an IS. Some important design facets related to modeling to be considered are structural, behavioral, constraining, representational and natural language. A unified model should enable the description of as many aspects as possible. The ODBMS should enable the realization of these facets based on the description captured using the object model.

1.2.2 Relational Database Technology

This is a well thought-out and widely used technology with a sound underlying theoretical basis [Date, 1995]. The available data structure is a relation, represented as a table. Other structures are not possible. The content of a field in a table can only be atomic. An **entity type** is a template for a semantic categorization of entities. A table definition may represent all or a part of the structural aspects of an entity type from the UoD. Often, the relational community applies the term object to a row of a table. This is to suggest that a table definition is a kind of object type; a row then represents an instance of that type. However, when speaking about object modeling within the context of relational database technology, it is important not to forget the interpretation of the term object: the modeled object or instance is no longer a 1 to 1 model of the original entity because it had to be normalized to well-defined information units i.e. the relations and respective tables, due to the integrity constraints of the relational model. This fact would not lead to the loss of semantics if there were a modeling construct to express the original UoD semantics of the original entity explicitly, for example, through explicit marking of the various tables which belong to the original entity as well as the structural dependencies between each other i.e. the relationships and how these tables are logically related to each other, to model the semantics of the UoD entity.
Even so, with this relational interpretation of the object concept in mind, a row of a table reflects an instance of the object-type, as characterized by means of the table definition. An instance is uniquely identified i.e. distinguishable from other instances in the table, by means of the **primary key**. This is a column of a table or a combination of columns. These columns may only have one occurrence of these values i.e. the value must be unique.
Relationships between tables are represented by means of pairs of primary and **foreign keys**, indirectly. A foreign key is an attribute whose values are present as a value of the corresponding primary key. According to this definition, a primary key - foreign key pair describes the existential dependency between the instances. The instance of the primary key must first exist before the same value can be used for a foreign key, but because no other construct is available for expressing a relationship, relationships that do not need to uphold existential integrity must also be modeled in this way.
Because a field may only contain atomic values, a primary key - foreign key pair can only connect one instance with one or more other instances although several foreign key values can contain the same primary key value, therefore so-called 'many to many' relationships cannot be modeled directly. To express many to many relationships directly, it would be necessary for example for one field to contain an array of values, that is to say, the primary key values of the related instances. Let us consider modeling a patient being treated in several clinics, implying that a clinic treats a number of patients. In a relational data schema a table must be added that contains all the related pairs of patients and clinics one by one. This table is additional to the tables which model a clinic and a patient.

These aspects together limit the semantic expressiveness of the relational model. Other relevant aspects of the relational data model are:

An application can be viewed as a module, but there is no inherent modeling concept to define the boundaries of a module.
Some relational DBMS's allow applications functionality to be stored in procedures, which is a kind of semi-object approach concerning the behavioral part of an object model. However the stored procedures are not modeled via the data model and are not an integral part of it.
There is no inheritance concept which limits the re-use of the modeled objects across system layers.

Characteristics of the data model that are enforced by means of the normalization rules ensure that a table definition is clearly encapsulated as an integer unit of pieces of information that semantically belong together. In this way it ensures that a piece of information is defined only once in the so-called logical data schema.

Here lies the power of the relational model: the sound theoretical foundation of encapsulating integer information-units that can be related to each other using the integrity concept of primary key - foreign key. The limitation is that these information units are only presentable as tables, and that the foreign key value, like any field content, can only be defined on one primary key value. From this logical data schema the table definition can be derived that describes how the data can be used in the application, guaranteeing so-called data independence. For the derived so-called external data schemas the normalization rules are not applied. For example, the same data can occur multiple times in an external data schema. This is no problem in itself for data integrity, if all respective external schemas are derived from the common logical data schema, a so-called 'view'. In this case, the data values are copied to the application at the moment of their usage. This avoids replication of data and therefore ensures data integrity very simply. The different presences are virtual and it can be ensured that an update in one place becomes visible in all applications (views). This manner of working is applied by means of the so-called 3 schema (tier) architecture for databases (standard architecture). Two schema layers are already introduced with the logical data schema and the external data schemas (the application's data schema) A third schema layer concerns the aspects of physical implementation. The problem with this fine architecture is that in practice it is often not applied, mainly for performance reasons. Although the various applications differ in the physical realization of the database tables they must all use the same database management system concurrently and compete for the system resources. This requires not only an advanced generic database management functionality, resulting in complex, large database management systems, but slows down the performance of the competing applications at the same time. This often leads to a practice in which the various application programs which belong to the same IS logically and which would have to use the same database, are implemented as separate database systems, each one with its part of the *originally common* database. In case several of these applications are using the same data, these data are replicated in each database system in its own database. In order to avoid inconsistencies between the data in the different application databases, an update protocol is introduced.

As a result, the complexity of a number of separated database systems, rather than one IS with one physical database used by several applications side by side, becomes even higher. Maintenance, which is costly and error prone is a particular problem.
On the other hand, relational database systems are well tunable. They can be developed so that the greatest functionality can perform well in a given situation. However, this is often achieved at the price of inflexibility and complexity.

Client/Server architectures can be well realized. However, the potential of system architectures is limited concerning the aforementioned characteristics.

1.2.3 Use of Semantic and Object Models

In practice it has become common not to model applications realized with relational databases directly using the relational model. The conceptual design is done by means of a semantic data model [Elmasri, 89] or an object model [Cattell and Barry, 2000]. With these models it is possible to capture the semantics of the UoD more explicitly, rather than in terms of tables and primary key - foreign key pairs. It is widely believed that in this way the design quality can be raised in a simple manner, i.e. the correctness and completeness of the data can be better determined. Commonly used data models for this task are variations on the Entity-Relationship Model (ERM) [Batini et al.,1992] and to an increasing degree the Unified Modeling Language (UML) [UML].
Despite the differences between the ERM variants, these models all share the characteristic that data structures can be modeled but not behavior.
A data schema modeled by an ERM is represented graphically within a so-called ER diagram (ERD). Some ERM variants and other semantical data models can model generalization and specialization. Despite the fact that these terms are also applied to describe inheritance in object models, their actual intention of usage in a semantic data model is different from that of object models. These concepts have been developed in semantical data models to determine that certain entity types are semantical generalizations of other entity types and a generalization in the design can be substituted by one of its specializations. A specialization always adds characteristics or at least a restriction on values of attributes of a generalization; they specialize the meaning of the generalization.
Object models are intended to describe from which other object type a particular object type inherits its definition when using the terms generalization and specialization.
Some variants of the ERM offer existential dependency as a modeling construct by means of strong and weak entities and relationships. However, it is expected that the application developer ensures that data can only be imported and destroyed in the database in the prescribed order, following the existential dependency on the basis of the information in the ERD, by means of programs.
This is also mainly due to the fact that there are no longer readily available database management systems that support an ER database design directly.
An ERD must be transformed to a data schema and designed with a data model that can be supported by a database management system. Generally this is a relational system. There are several tools available for the transformation of a graphical design into a relational data schema. The tools also provide help to partially automate the transformation from an ER schema to a relational data schema.
ERM's do not support the modularity concept etc.

In addition to the object model, UML also possesses concepts for the design of the operation signatures and a number of ancillary models to design additional IS aspects, such as dynamical behavior of the application and control flows. Many of these ancillary models (now incorporated within UML) have been in existence for a long time and are included in UML in order to provide a complete toolkit of models for larger software systems. A problem here is that the various diagram-techniques do not work with the same precision i.e. on the same level of detail concerning the modeling of an object. Furthermore, the relationships between them are not supported directly. It is expected that the designer relates the various modeling aspects to form a whole, based on personal design experience. For example, the designer has to ensure that the definition of the structure and operations of a particular object, which is defined within a UML class diagram, is in accordance with the needs required within a sequence of UML collaboration diagrams.

Some of the models of UML are implemented in the design tool Rational Rose [Rational Rose]. It is quite easy to produce a graphical design as an object schema. Operations designs can be partially transformed to a program.

The structural part of an object schema can be transformed into a relational schema based on transformation rules. In principal these do not differ from the transformation rules of the ERM.

The incorporation of additional design aspects into UML makes it possible to describe a more complete picture of a UoD with UML than with ERM. But also here, the design of the UML object schema or class diagrams is not directly supported in the database management system, including object-oriented databases. The class diagram must be transformed into another schema which uses other modeling principles. Because there is no 1 to 1 mapping between these concepts and the UML concepts, semantics of the design are lost. The automatic conversion does not change this fact.

As opposed to the ERM, UML offers more detailed concepts to define an object schema. Firstly, it seems advantageous to describe the UoD in great detail. However, even when a semantically rich UML object schema i.e. class diagram is made, it is generally transformed into a semantically poor relational schema.
In both the ER and the UML class diagrams the semantic description remains a reference. It exists separately from the relational data schema, so that at a given stage in the life cycle of the database it is probable that the design semantic and the conceptual schema no longer match, assuming they did so in the first place. To avoid this problem the two schemas must be kept in sync; this is not an easy task to accomplish.

The UML package concept has the intention of modularization. The recommended concept for determining the package boundaries is the **logical horizon**. The designer must find an appropriately dominant object and its logical horizon e.g. patient or clinic in our hospital case study. This is where the combined multiplicity of the relationship (the correct term for cardinality used in UML) is 1 or 0. In other words, the place where either one or no instance of the related object can be present, determines the border of the package. The problem is that at the conceptual modeling level the multiplicity is a weaker modeling concept than at the application level: A multiplicity of "multiple" in a conceptual schema can be reduced to 1 in an external schema (an application schema). Then the boundary of the application can be established with the logical horizon, but not the modularization of the conceptual schema.
In fact, UML does not intend to distinguish between conceptual and external schema levels.
UML supports inheritance, and concepts for re-use of data and functionality are readily available.
UML is discussed further in Chapter 20.

1.2.4 Object Database Management Group (ODMG)

The ODMG development began in 1993 with the goal of achieving a standard for object data models. Early on the group also established a cooperation with OMG (Object Management Group), which promotes object technology in general. The standard proposal of ODMG starts out from the view that the object specification must fulfill the requirements of the application. An object schema is therefore not intended as a conceptual schema such as intended in the 3 schema architecture, but as an external schema. The database is physically constructed just as it is defined in the application schema.
Here the object databases try to prevent the various transformations between the schemas as in the classical approach. At the same time they have a major disadvantage: data independence does not play a role. For example, data independence implies that dates are only defined once in the logical/conceptual data schema and are derived in the external schemas. The same object must be redefined in each database application; there is no common intersection in the case where several applications use the same data. There is nothing to enforce a common conceptual schema. Data integrity is maintained in the scope of one application but not over several.

In order to achieve that kind of data integrity, additional tools must be used such as transaction server etc. The problem here is that there are no means available to enforce mutual coordination. The system designer and developer could apply different models and methods and it depends on their experience as to how consistently they go about the work. A common case of incompatibility is between the database designer and the application designer.
Modularity within an application in ODMG is not important. The semantic expressiveness of the model is aimed at the accurate definition of an application suitable for one database. There are various database management systems which already support parts of the concept. An ODMG schema can reasonably be implemented in a number of ODBMS's. The inheritance concepts of ODMG are very detailed. There is a difference between structure and behavior inheritance. They support complex concepts of re-use of structure and functionality.
ODMG is discussed in more detail in Chapter 20.

Chapter 2

The Perspective-DB Object Model Foundations

2.1 The Object Base as a Model of a Universe of Discourse

Here we introduce some basic definitions used throughout the book. These definitions are analogous to definitions used in object modeling `in principle`. However, there are differences in the interpretation of terms and also additions to and subtractions from known object models, e.g. UML. We therefore recommend studying the definitions carefully in order to understand this book.

An **object** is a unique identifiable unit carrying semantics which can be expressed in a formal way by unambiguous characteristics.

An **object base** is used to store objects, if necessary persistently[1], with the purpose of offering:

- information carried by the objects to several types of human users, and
- objects of the object base to various applications, other objects and software systems in general which in turn, can process the objects for their own purposes.

We call the various consumers of objects of an object base, users.
A **Universe of Discourse** or UoD for short is the limited field of interest of the users of a particular object base. It is a part of a real or imaginary world or a mix of both as explained in 1.1.

We use the term object base only for the structured collection of those objects needed to fulfill the requests of its users concerning their UoD.
A structured collection means the objects have to be associated with each other in terms of the semantics of the UoD and the functionality they offer to their users (and to each other).

The semantics of the object base have to be a model[2] of the UoD. The functionality has to exploit the semantics in an unambiguous way.

An **object schema** defines the semantics and functionality of an object base that models the UoD. An object schema consists of objects that define other objects.

[1] Persistent implies that if the running application stops, the information is not lost because a copy of the information exists on a persistent information storage device, commonly in file format on a hard disk.

[2] A model is a simplified description of a system used in explanations, calculations, etc. (Oxford Advanced Learners Dictionary).

An object base consists of objects.

An object base is generally defined by several object schemas. Each of these object schemas describes several aspects (points of view) of the UoD at several levels of detail.

An **object model** is a collection of constructs that enable one to express the semantics and functionality of a UoD by means of an object schema.

Summary:

> An object model provides the constructs to define object schemas.
> An object schema defines an object base from a particular point of view.
> An object base is a model of a UoD.

An **object base management system** is a structured collection of objects that enable and support the definition and manipulation of object bases.
In principle, the object base management system is also built from objects that conform to the same object model as the object bases and applications that it manages[3].
An **Application** encapsulates an object base into one single object that fulfills the principle needs of various users. Applications can be associated with each other for the purpose of fulfilling user requests on several object bases.

We use the term **developer** for a person who specifies the object schemas and applications.
We use the term **user** as aforementioned.
We use the term **end-user** for a person who uses applications.

2.2 The Road Map Metaphor

A cartographer applies a legend (set of generic constructs) according to a set of rules to produce a road map. All cartographers will produce a similar map of a designated area if they use the same constructs in a similar way. As a result, a car driver can interpret the map of `any` designated area `regardless of` the publisher.
The constructs express a generic and canonical representation of a designated area i.e. a model of the area.
A map is a graphical schematic representation that utilizes common human perception capacities concerned with understanding related constructs, i.e. a schema of the area. It is actually an object schema, since it describes objects of the UoD of a geographical area.

A set of generic constructs of a comprehensive `graphical` object model can be compared to the legend of a road map. An object base developer can apply the graphical object model, according to the generic object model rules, to produce a canonical object schema that can be interpreted by colleagues and other users. You can compare the users with motorists reading a map to find their way through an area. By analogy, the end-users have to find their way through the application.

If we analyze how a road map works, we see that there are several levels of definition. For example, the construct Road has a graphical notation defined in the legend.

[3]Preliminary work of the contributors on the concepts of an object base management system prior to the Perspective-DB ODBMS has been published in [Sim, Gerhardt, Kist and Simon, 1994] and [Sim, 1993]

When looking at a particular map, we see many occurrences of the Road construct.This indicates an important modeling principle, the differentiation between the type of an object and an object instance which is an occurrence of the type.
Most object models have a graphical notation beside the textual. At this point we are not interested in whether both notations are equivalent. We are primarily interested in the following aspect of the graphical notation;
the state-of-the-art object models are able to produce static schematic definitions i.e. they describe the object types. Additionally object models offer (more or less passive) structural schematic presentations (e.g. as trees) of the object instances. They show which instances belong to a particular object type. Those tree-presentations are similar to those used in MS-Windows, for example, to represent directory and file organization.

With such static schematic presentations users can get descriptions of the object base and using these, inform themselves about the object base. However, they are not capable of manipulating (e.g. create, delete, modify, query) objects by directly exploiting the schematic presentation(s). To do this, they need other means accessible to the users through applications only[4].
Using applications in such a traditional way does not exploit the full potential offered by object modeling.
A step in the right direction is when operations described in the schema can be executed in the schema. In this case the schema not only defines the object base but is also used to manipulate the running application.
This has several advantages:

- The user need not deal with different presentations of the same objects.
- The user can use the knowledge about how the objects are defined and relate to each other directly during operation. The user always sees the objects in context.
- Once the user understands the presentation constructs, he/she can operate any application defined with the same object model.

In fact, only when the last aforementioned advantages are guaranteed, does the road map metaphor fit.
Remember, anybody can `use` any road map of an arbitrary area as long as the map producers use the same legend. Analogously, anybody can `use` any application as long as the application is produced using the same object model.

Perspective-DB applies this analogy and to our knowledge, is the only object model and management system able to do so.
To achieve this, the graphical object model is extended with the dynamic behavior of the application. As a pre-condition, the object model provides constructs to unify the notation of object definitions and the presentation of objects contained in the object base. As a result, the user view of an object schema is the GUI (Graphical User Interface) of the application in an interactive operating mode.

The examples used throughout the Chapter are based on the Hospital Case Study introduced in 1.1.

[4]Different applications usually present the same object types in a way different from each other and from the schematic presentation.

2.3 Object Type

Objects are categorized in object types and object instances.
To define an object base, types of objects are described instead of describing each object instance separately:
Let us take for example the objects *Karen Fisher* with the following characteristics `Name:` *Karen Fisher*, `Birth-date:` *1949-01-23*, and `Address:` *45 Waldegrave Rd. Bickley* and the object *Betty Lasker* with the following characteristics `Name:` *Betty Lasker*, `Birth-date:` *1955-05-24*, and `Address:` *2 South Lane Waterloo.* Both objects share the characteristics Name, Birth-date and Address.
We see that these objects are characterized in a similar way semantically and mean a Person. Therefore, `Person` is the object type of the object instances *Karen Fisher* and *Betty Lasker* in this case.
You can deduce from this example that:

- The name of the object type gives the general meaning of the object type, e.g. object type `Person` is a human being; an individual with distinct characteristics[5].
- The characteristics describe an interpretation, provided by the designer(s) of the object type when choosing the characterizing properties they consider relevant from the large pool of potential properties, e.g. `Name`, `Birth-date`, `Address` characterize `Person`, and not `Name, Height, Weight`.

The interpretation by the designer(s) is not arbitrary. It has to ensure that information about an object type is expressed as needed by users.

Once the object type is characterized it is assumed that its name is a synonym for the collection of characteristics in the context of the object base.
Therefore `Person` and the collection (`Name, Birth-date, Address`) have the same semantics.

To summarize, an **object type** is defined by the collection of its characteristics, and an object type receives a name.

Graphical notation:

An object type is represented by a (finely outlined) rectangle, see Figure 2.1.
There is a default for the size of the rectangle; the size is configurable.
The default color code of the rectangle's background beige.

The name is placed inside the rectangle by default or beside it (when it is drawn very small).

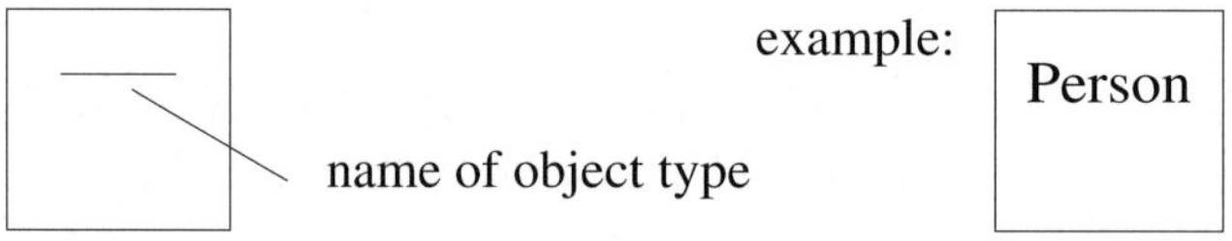

Figure 2.1: Object type

Example: Object type Person.

[5]Oxford Advanced Learners Dictionary

2.4 Instance

Any object fulfilling the definition of an object type is an **instance** of that object type. The object *Karen Fisher* is an instance of object type `Person` if the object *Karen Fisher* is characterized by `Name`: *Karen Fisher*, `Birth-date`: *1949-01-23*, and `Address`: *45 Waldegrave Rd. Bickley.* It fulfills the object type definition (`Name, Birth-date, Address`) of the object type `Person`.

Integrity rule:
An object is an instance of precisely one object type.

Integrity rule:
An instance can be created if and only if its object type exists.

Graphical notation:

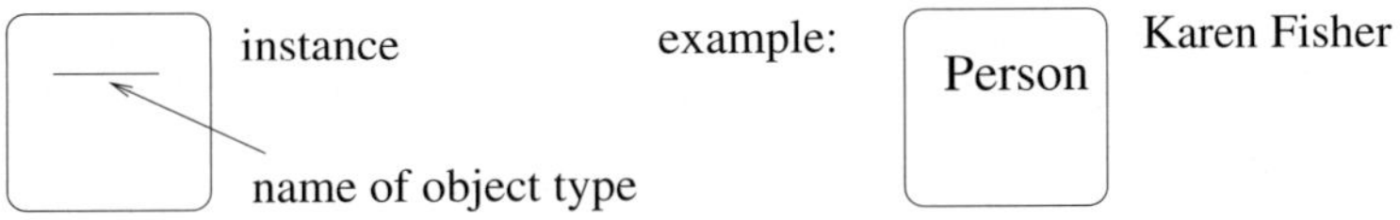

Figure 2.2: Object instance

An instance is represented as a rectangle with rounded corners, see Figure 2.2. Its template is the graphical notation of the object type.

2.5 Implementation and Interface Modeling

The fundamental object types and constructs[6] are elementary building blocks to build more complex object types. In the introduction to Perspective-DB we mentioned that the object base management system is also built from objects that conform to the same object model as the object bases and applications it manages. This is possible because the object model unifies the constructs necessary to build programs and to do conceptual object modeling. This means that people developing systems at all levels can also use the model. The object instances are physical entities[7] that interact with each other. They reside in object pools inside the computer. They are created, destroyed, and manipulated. The objects present themselves to the end-user through an interface that removes unnecessary details. For example, it is possible to use the model to define various libraries of objects with general purpose tasks.
However, in this book we do not focus on the implementation level of system development (how the objects we deal with are constructed inside). We assume that object types exist which enable one to describe things at an interface level (how we see an object we are using). This implies being able to describe the UoD at the appropriate semantic level and not needing to build everything from scratch. The reason we have chosen to introduce the foundation first, is that it is important to understand that the object types and constructs used for modeling at the level of UoD are composite object types constructed from simpler object types. There is no breakdown of concept between the interface and implementation levels. It is a continuum, therefore the terms interface level and implementation level modeling are relative.

[6]Well known examples of constructs are literals such as string and integer.

[7]We consider them physical entities because they exist as segments of memory allocated in the memory of the computer.

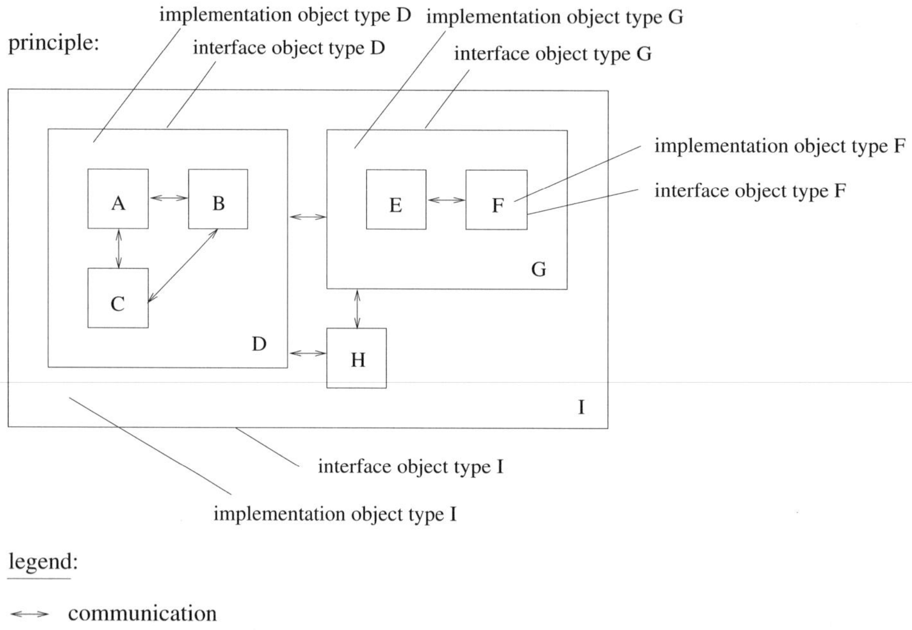

Figure 2.3: Principle of relativity of interface and implementation level (not formal notation)

Figure 2.3 illustrates this relativity. The object types `A, B and C` compose object type `D`. The composition of `A, B` and `C` builds the implementation of object type D. The object types `A, B` and `C` are not visible at the interface of object type `D`. The object types `E` and `F` build the implementation of object type `G`. Object type `G` together with `D` and `H` build the implementation of object type `I`. If a user deals with the interface of `I`, the user will not see the object types `A - H`.

2.6 Fundamental Object Types and Constructs

There are several elementary kinds of object types for making structural combinations between object types. These are `Literal, Array, Reference` and `Operation`. There are several kinds of constructs for combining object types. These are **Membership** and **Inheritance**.

The following describes characteristics of fundamental object types and constructs:

- Behavior: The operations which are offered at the interface of the object type or by the construct.
- Cardinality range: A constraint for the permitted numbers of components of the particular object type.
- Cardinality: The actual number of components.
- Range: A constraint for the permitted object types which may be a component of the particular object type.
- Value range: A constraint for the permitted range to which the values of the object type may belong, e.g. any integer between 0 and 10000.

The constructs are used to build such object types from fundamental constructs which have the properties that an application developer and end-user will be interested in. These characteristics will enable such users to describe and exploit the semantics of the UoD.

2.6.1 Literal Object Type

In general, the purpose of a literal is to store a single value, e.g. a `character`, an `integer`, a `float`, a `double`, a `string` (of characters) etc. Examples are the `character` *a*, the `integer` *2346*, the `float` *23.46*, the `double float` *23.467893* etc.

A literal has the following characteristics:

- **Behavior:**
  Each literal type has various operations for manipulating the value and enabling interaction between instances of the corresponding type. Examples: value assignment and comparison, and for numerical literals, mathematical functions such as addition and subtraction.
- **Object Type range:**
  The type of value it stores. Examples are as above.
- **Value Range:**
  Permitted values that the literal instance may store. The range for characters could be all the characters of an alphabet or several, or only the upper cases or the lower cases, or an enumeration out of the characters of an alphabet e.g. (*A, a, B, b, C, c, X, x, Y, y, Z, z*) or of several alphabets etc. The range of integers could also be the range of the integers supported by the operating system , or a limitation based on the permitted values in the UoD e.g. *-20000* until *+50000*, or an enumeration of particular permitted values, e.g. (*-5, -2, 1-6, 11, 17*) etc.

See Figure 2.4. The example shows the `literal integer` *2346*.

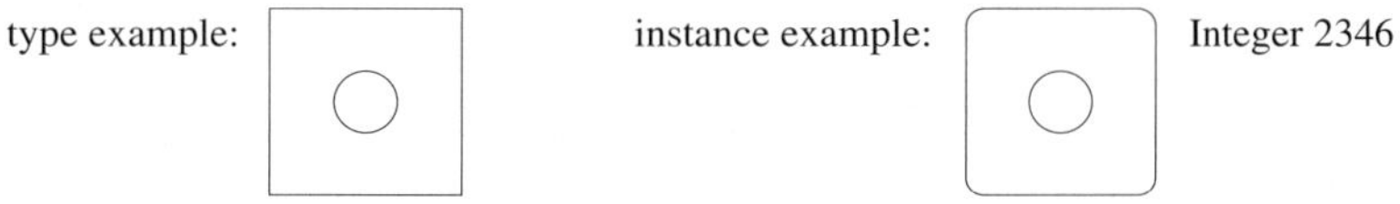

Figure 2.4: Example for literal

2.6.2 Reference Construct

The **reference** construct defines a pointer to an object type. A reference instance points to an object instance, see Figure 2.5.

A reference has the following characteristics:

- **Behavior:**
  Assigning, removing and reassigning a location[8] as value. Dereferencing the value, i.e. getting the object instance it refers to.
- **Cardinality range:**
  The cardinality range is 1 meaning it must always point to an instance, or 0,1 meaning it can be empty. Empty means there is no reference to a particular instance.
- **Cardinality:**
  The cardinality of a reference instance is 0 if empty, otherwise 1.

[8]The location of an object is the address where the object resides in the memory of the computer.

- **Cardinality range:**
  The cardinality range is 1 meaning it must always point to an instance, or 0,1 meaning it can be empty. Empty means there is no reference to a particular instance.

- **Cardinality:**
  The cardinality of a reference instance is 0 if empty, otherwise 1.

- **Object Type range:**
  To which object type the reference can point. For example, integers only.

- **Value Range:**
  To which instances within the given object type the reference can point. For example, integers between *-1000* and *+1000*.

In Figure 2.5, the reference points to the object type `Address`. `Address` is an object type already constructed by fundamental object types and constructs.

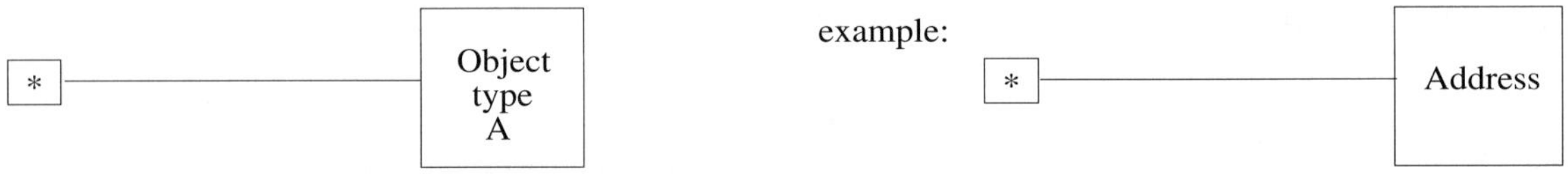

Figure 2.5: Example for reference

2.6.3 Array Construct

The **array** defines a sequence of instances[9] of the same object type.
An array has the following characteristics:

- **Behavior:**
  Various operations to traverse the elements, e.g. iteration forwards and backwards, direct access to an element by index or by its value.

- **Cardinality range:**
  The minimum and maximum number of elements, e.g. minimum is *1*, maximum *10*; the array must have 1 element and may have up to 10 elements.

- **Cardinality:**
  The actual number of elements. The array in Figure 2.6 has a cardinality of *4*.

- **Object Type range:**
  The object type of the elements. The array in Figure 2.6 has an object type range of Integer.

- **Value Range:**
  The value range of the object type the array holds. For the array in Figure 2.6, the value range could be (*1-10*), meaning all integers between 1 and 10.

[9]Each element in the array is an instance of the object type.

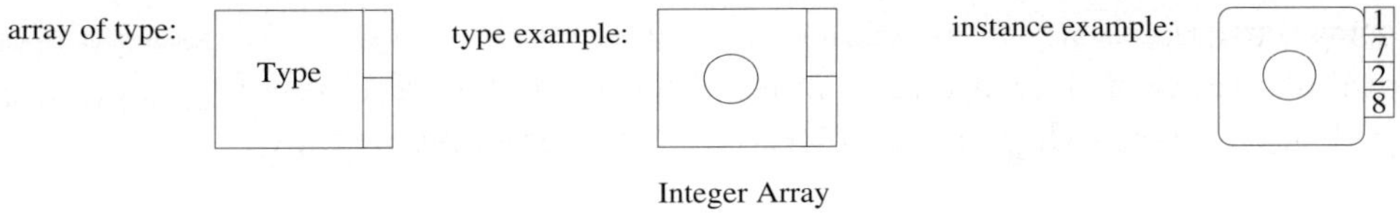

Figure 2.6: Example for array

2.6.4 Operation Object Type

The **operation** is an elementary kind of object type for defining the behavior of object types. An operation is a composed object type consisting in general of a list of object types called arguments, and a return object type. Also associated with the operation object type is a definition of what the operation should do when it is executed[10]. Executing an operation[11] implies that an instance of an operation object type processes values of the argument instances and returns an instance which is the result.

An example for an operation is computing a person's current age, given the birth-date, see Figure 2.7.
An operation has the following characteristics:

- **Behavior:**
  Arguments are object types and can be categorized as `input`, `output` or `input-output`. An **input** argument provides an input value to the operation. An **output** argument can be assigned as value by the operation. Arguments can be any object type, including operation types. An **in-output** argument does both. An operation can instantiate various object types during execution, including other operation types and its own. The operation of Figure 2.7 will have as input the person's birth-date and as output the person's age.

- **Cardinality range:**
  The minimum and maximum number of return values. The cardinality range is 0 and 1. The example operation has the cardinality range 1.

- **Cardinality:**
  It is 0 if the operation returns no object i.e. is void, and 1 if it does. The cardinality of the example operation is 1.

- **Object Type range:**
  The type of the returned object type. The object type range of the example is Float to represent a numerical value with a particular part of an hour, e.g. 32.5.

- **Value Range:**
  A subset of the allowed values of the returned object type. The operation can constrain the range. The example operation does not need a constraint of the range.

2.6.5 Membership Construct

Characteristics of an object type are called **members**. The ability to be a member is called **membership**. In general, members are also object types. They are 'glued' to the object type they characterize.

[10] For example consider the operation `Multiply_Integers`. Is has two arguments of type integer and a return value of type integer. The definition of the operation is that the result of multiplying the two arguments should be assigned to the return value

[11] The term `invoking an operation` is used alternatively.

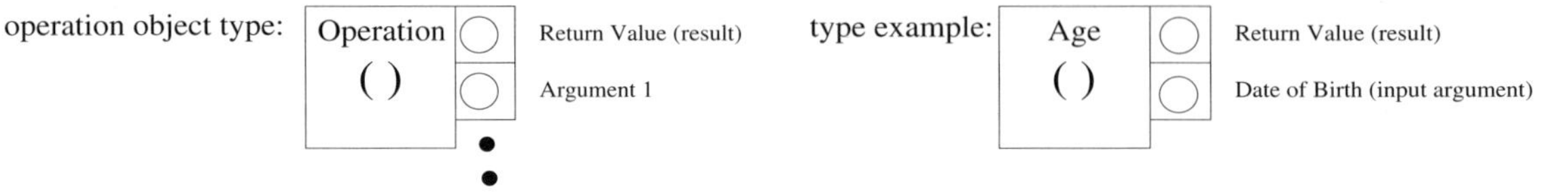

Figure 2.7: Example for operation

Therefore an object type plays the **role** of a member in other object types. Object types are constructed of members.
Figures 2.8 and 2.9 illustrate the principle.

We distinguish between the following (sub-) roles of members: **attribute, relation and operation**, see Figure 2.8.
Attributes and relation constitute the properties of the object type, i.e. define its **structure**. Operations define its **behavior**. These are further explained in the next chapter.
When a member object type itself contains members with several sub-roles, it has combined roles. Usually it is then given the role of its most dominant member with respect to its characterized object type. Therefore the role of a member is a relative term describing the primary task it fulfills in characterizing an object type.

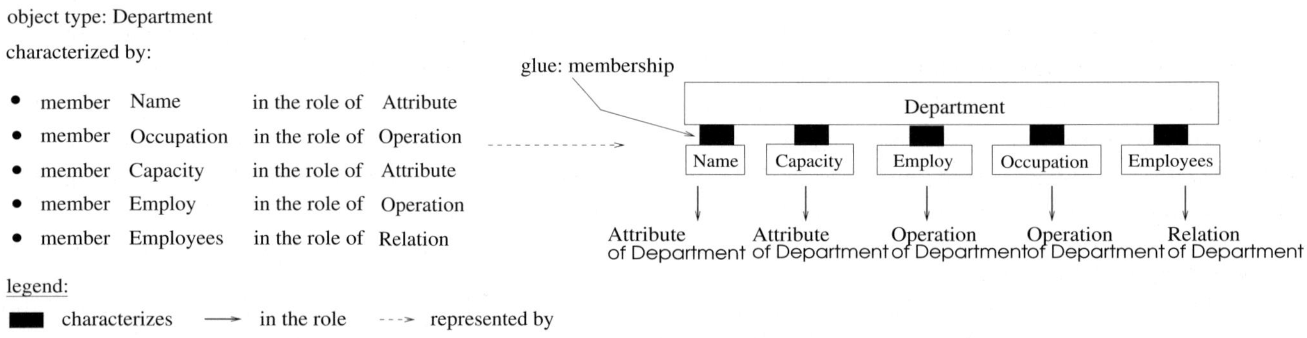

Figure 2.8: Roles of members (not formal notation)

Graphical notation:

A member is also represented by a (thin lined) rectangle.
Members are attached to the outside edge of the rectangle representing the object type with the exception of the generic operations (explained later) which are placed inside the rectangle.

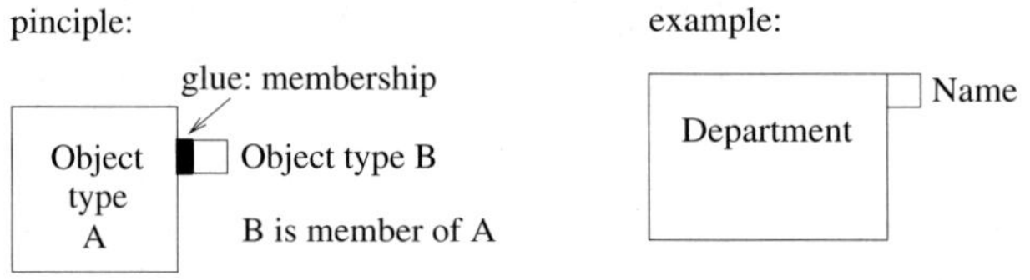

Figure 2.9: Principle and example of member (in the formal notation the glue is not shown).

Depending on the kind of member, a default symbol or a default color code is used to represent it. The symbols and codes are explained below together with the roles attribute, relation and operation.

Illustration of membership: the membership hierarchy is shown in Figure 2.10.

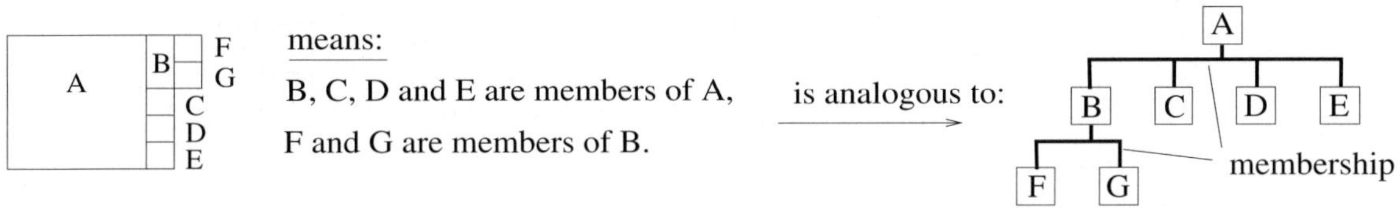

Figure 2.10: Illustration of the membership hierarchy (the figure on the right is not in formal notation)

The **membership hierarchy** provides the access path to a member. We write the name of the object type and the name of the member separated by a dot to specify a particular member of a particular object type in the textual notation. For example, `A.B.G` identifies member `G` of `B` which in turn is a member of `A`.
All members in the hierarchy contribute as a whole to the characterization of the root. In Figure 2.10 this is object type `A`.

2.6.6 Inheritance Construct

Inheritance is a construct that extends the membership construct. It enables the characterized object type, the **specialization**, to inherit the members of another object type, the **generalization**. The members of a generalization can be common to several specializations.
Inheriting the members of a generalization means that the specialized type `considers` the members of the generalized type to be its own characterizations. This implies that the specialization can access the members of the generalization directly[12]. Therefore the members of the generalization are parts of the **interface** of the specialization. The normal properties of membership remain. The specialization still considers the generalization to be an object type. The generalization remains an object type in its own right.

The object types in the inheritance hierarchy can be imagined as glued together as illustrated in the left part of Figure 2.12.

The figure emphasizes two perspectives on the inheritance hierarchy.

- The left part of the figure emphasizes the perspective of a specialization; the specialization is glued to its generalization in such a way that the members of the generalization are directly accessible at the specialization's interface, together with its additional members. There is no difference between the inherited and the added members if an observer looks only at the interface. The generalization is an internal member of the specialization, offering its members at the specialization's interface. At the same time, the generalization with its members is directly accessible.

- The right part of the figure emphasizes that a specialization must not repeat the definition of the member of its generalization. It virtually takes the member over from the generalization, where the inherited member is defined in reality. The generalization is an object type in its own right. This perspective describes how a specialization is constructed out of its generalization.

[12]This is the general concept. In fact, it is also possible to specify which members should be directly accessible and which not. The unaccessible members may still be part of the interface specification

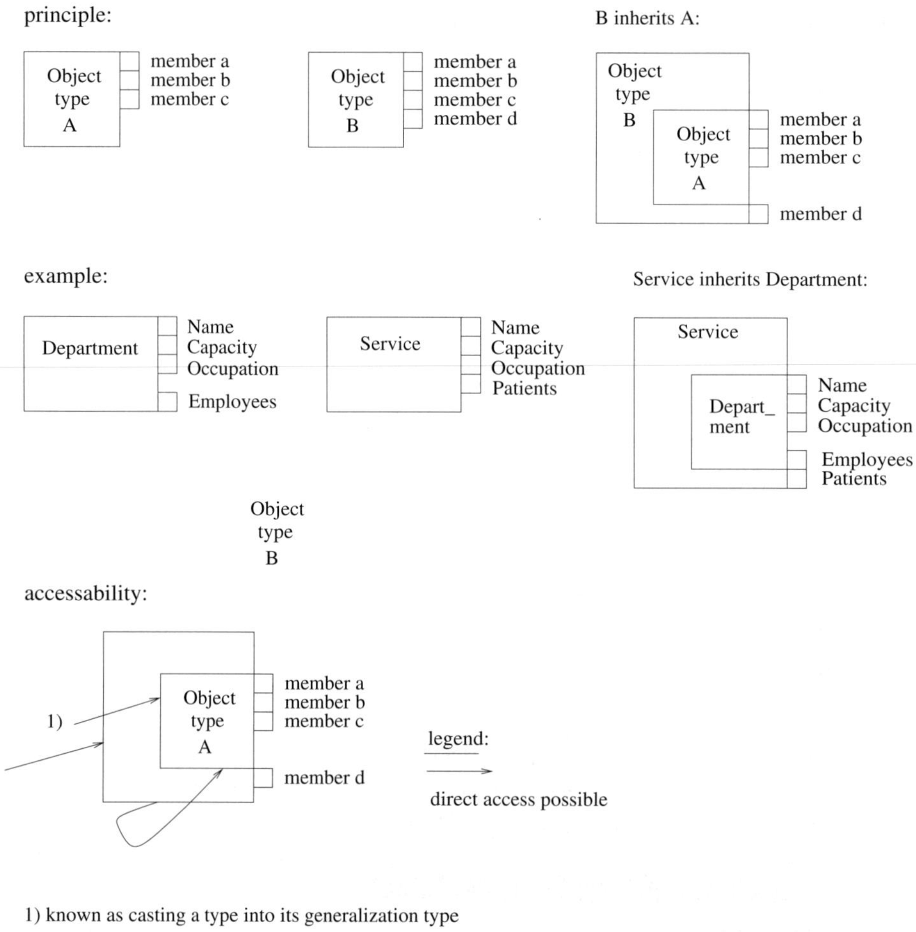

Figure 2.11: Principle and example of inheritance (in the formal notation the generalization is not drawn inside the specialization)

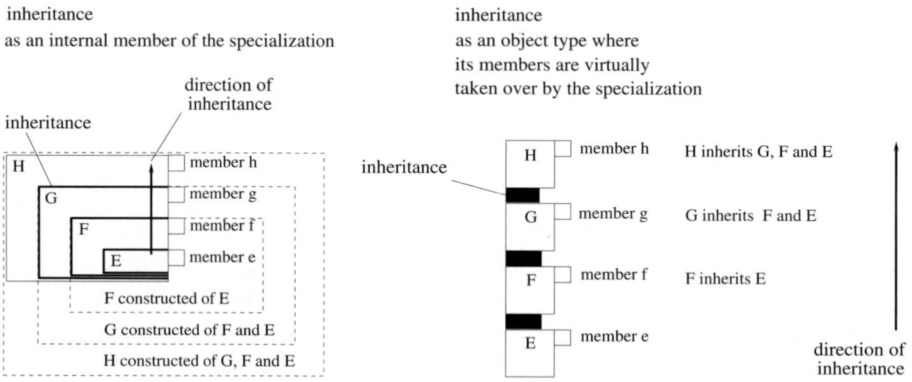

Figure 2.12: Two perspectives of the inheritance hierarchy (the figure on the right shows the formal notation of inheritance)

Graphical notation:

The graphical notation uses an abstraction of the presentation in Figure 2.12 depending on the viewpoint from which a user is observing the relevant object types.

2.6.7 Constructing Object Types Example

The following example explains a simplified implementation of an object type called `Linked_List` which can manage connections between instances. In reality such connections, formally called `relations`, are implemented in a more sophisticated way although the concept remains the same. The concept of relations is dealt with in the next chapter[13].

Figure 2.13 illustrates the following situation:

The object types `Department` and `Employee` are specializations of a generic object type, `Object`. The object type `Department` adds the members `Name, Capacity, Occupation`[14] and `Employees` to the inherited member Object_Type. The object type `Employee` adds the members `Code, Function` and `Hours` to the inherited member `Object_Type`.

The member `Department.Employees` refers to the object type `Employee`. Because one instance of `Department` can refer to more than one instance of `Employee` (semantics: one department has several employees), this member is constructed from more fundamental object types to be able to contain the references from one `Department` instance to several `Employee` instances. In this case, `Department.Employees`, is a `Linked_List` (for its symbol, see legend in Figure 2.13).

Figure 2.14 describes department `Surgery` with three of its employees. Each of the employees is referred from `Department.Employees`.

Now, we look at Figure 2.15.

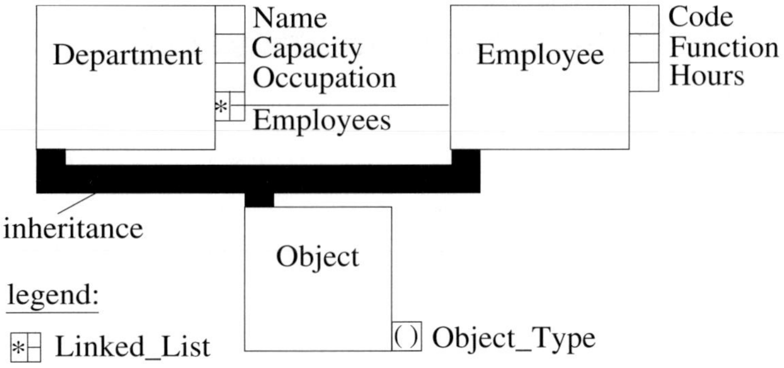

Figure 2.13: An example for constructing object types

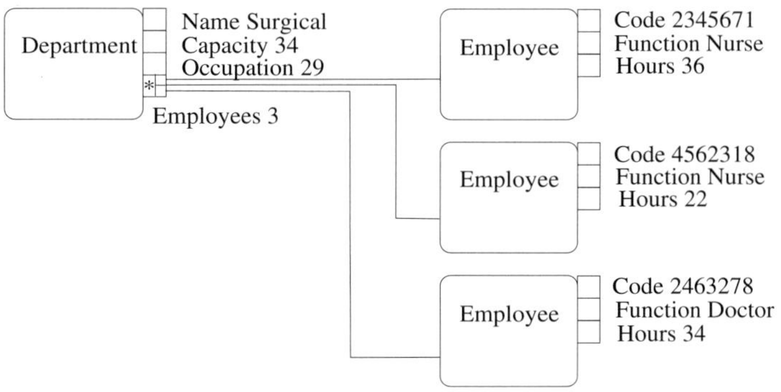

Figure 2.14: The example at instance level

[13]The construction of the linked-list is slightly technical and the reader can skip this section without loss of continuity. It is given here for completeness, to demonstrate how the same building blocks of the model can be applied at a detailed level of implementation (as opposed to models that can only be applied at the conceptual level).

[14]Throughout the book we use the term Occupation to denote the number of persons that currently occupy a department.

The object type Linked_List itself is also a specialization of Object.

The members it adds to the inherited Object_Type, are: the literal Number_of_Elements, the operations Insert_Object_At_Offset, Remove_Object_At_Offset and Get_Object_At_Offset and the reference First_Link. This reference refers to the object type Link. Link is also a specialization of Object. Link adds the following members to the inherited Object_Type: the operations Get_Object, Get_Next_Link and Get_Previous_Link and the references Previous_Link which refers to Linked_List or back to the object type Link, Next_Link which refers back to the object type Link and Object which refers to the object type Object.

The references which refer back to the same object type of which they are members are called **recursive**.
Figure 2.16 illustrates the Linked_List construction at instance level. Here we see the recursive references referring to the following instance of Link. Each instance of Link refers also to another Object instance. In the example such an object is an instance of Employee. This is possible because Employee is an Object (Employee is a specialization of Object).

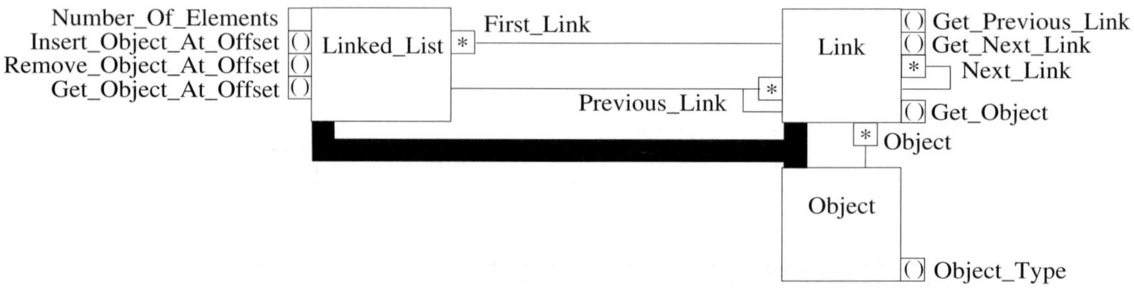

Figure 2.15: An example for constructing Linked_List

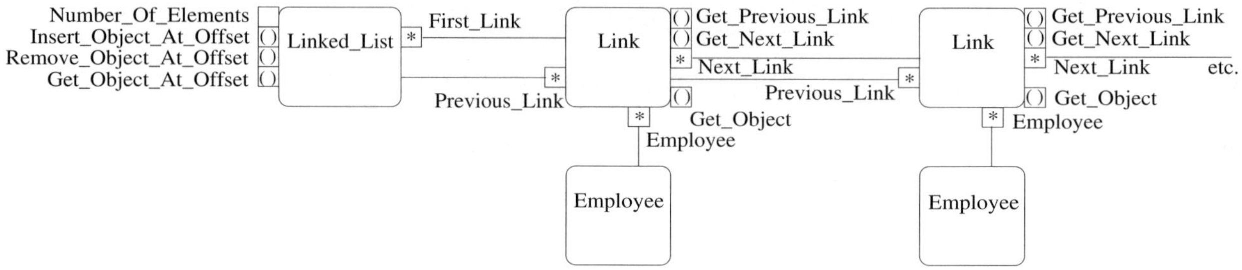

Figure 2.16: Linked_List at instance level

The object type Linked_List as described in Figure 2.15 is an implementation of Department.Employees of Figure 2.13. An application using the object types Department and Employee of Figure 2.13 will only see the member Department.Employees (its interface) but not how it is constructed (its members, its generalization).

Chapter 3

First Order Object Types: Membership

Since our focus in this book is modeling at application level we continue on the assumption that we are using an object type which possesses a set of characteristics necessary for modeling the UoD at a high abstraction level[1]. These objects are constructed using the building blocks as explained in 2.6. The construction process of these types is not described in this book because it is very detailed.

The characteristics of the object type must be suitable to express the semantics of the UoD in terms which are familiar to the human user.
This object type has evolved through an inheritance hierarchy in order to acquire its current interface. We categorize this type and its specializations as **first order** object types.

The examples used throughout the chapter are based on the Hospital Case Study introduced in 1.1.

3.1 Member Role: Attribute

In general, the purpose of the member attribute is to store values. An attribute is constructed from fundamental literal and array object types by applying inheritance and membership. It represents a semantic unit of information. `Examples` are the attributes `Name` and `Capacity` of object type `Department`.

An attribute has the following characteristics:

- **Behavior:**
  An attribute has various operations for manipulating the value and enabling interaction with other members of the same or different object type.

- **Object type range:**
  The object type range defines to which category of object types an attribute may belong.
  There are three basic categories of attributes: atomic, collection and composite:
  Atomic are attributes that can store integers, characters, strings, floating points etc.
  Collection are attributes that represent various sorts of lists, arrays, sets, bags etc.
  Composites are attributes that contain various members but do not represent a collection.

[1]As opposed to the linked-list example of 2.6.7 which is a very technical UoD.

For example, the attribute `Name` is an atomic attribute of the object type `Department` and a particular department is named *X-ray Lab*. `Name` is of object type String. A composite attribute is `Capacity`[2] of `Department`. `Capacity` has the members `Min_Capacity` and a `Max_Capacity` both of type Integer. The department named *X-ray Lab* has a `Min_Capacity` of 5 persons and a `Max_Capacity` of 10.

- **Value Range:**
  The value range defines those values which may be assigned to an attribute.
  `Example`: The name of a department of a particular hospital must come from the set of names. This can be expressed through an enumeration which contains the permitted names of departments at that hospital.
  Limiting the value range in this manner is not the only possibility. An alternative for example, is permitting all strings starting with an upper case, or all strings up to a particular length, or all strings starting with a particular letter combination, etc.

  Integrity rule:
  An attribute value has to be in accordance with the defined ranges.

  Integrity rule:
  An attribute value may be inserted if and only if the instance exists.

`Graphical notation:`

The member-rectangle for attribute contains the symbol circle or has the color code orange.
The attributes are placed around the rectangle of the object type, generally starting with the right side, then left, then top and or bottom. We recommend enlarging the object type rectangle if many attributes are to be placed. Although the object type takes up more space, it is more important to have an orderly and clear impression when you look at the schema.

- `Atomic attribute:`
  `Example`:

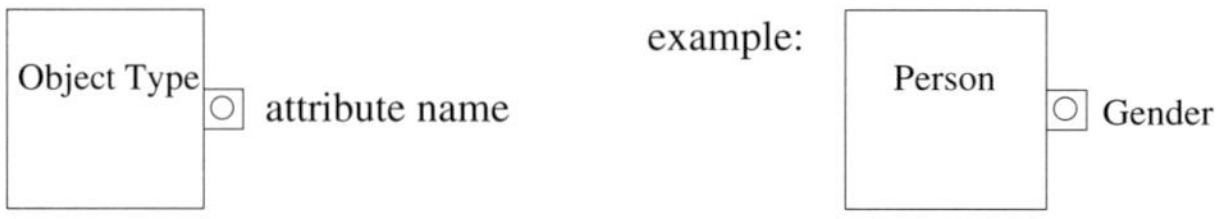

Figure 3.1: Atomic attribute

`Person.Gender`
This is an attribute where the range of values is generally limited. The range is an enumeration defined during the application development and need not be tailored to particular persons.

Further `examples` are:
`Patient.Category`
This is an attribute where the range is also limited but the limitations have to be adapted according to the real-world range of values in the object base.

[2]Actually in the Hospital Case Study it is not a composite but an integer representing the maximum capacity to simplify matters. However, it could very well be a composite as described here.

Hospital.Name
This is an attribute where the range of values is open; it is limited to the value range of the object type, here storing a string.

- Composed attribute:
  Example:

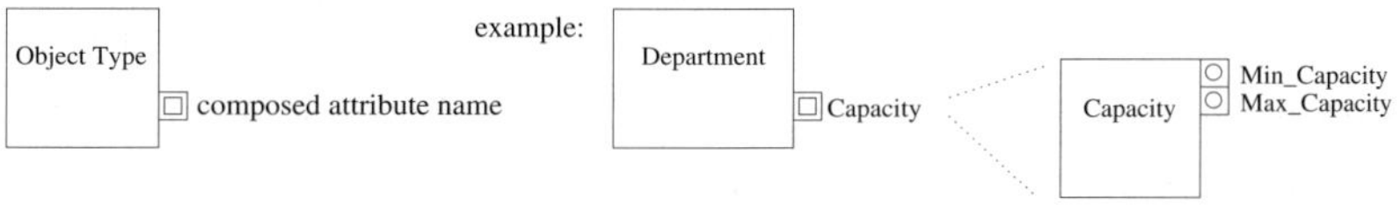

Figure 3.2: Composed attribute

Department.Capacity
The capacity-attribute pops up if it is activated. If the attribute is not activated it hides its members.
The third part of the figure shows the popped-up attribute Capacity. Now all its members are accessible in the same way as any individual member.

- Media type:
  Media types are actually composite attributes, however they overrule the normal behavior of a composite type and display the intended media value in the most appropriate way.

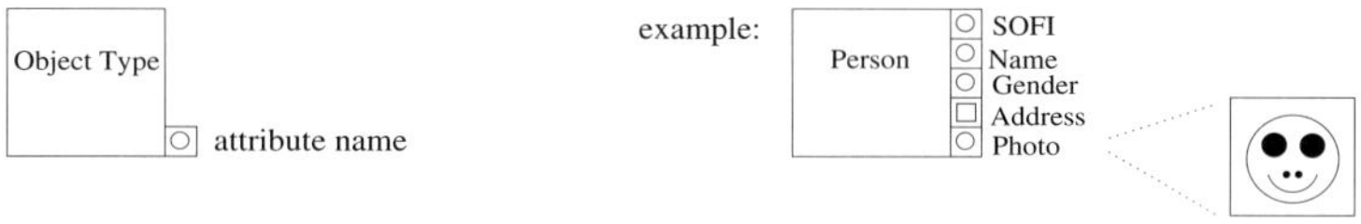

Figure 3.3: A media type attribute

Example:
Person.Photo:
This attribute contains a photo.
The third part of the figure shows the window displaying the photo popped-up after the attribute is activated.

Some other examples are:
Hospital.Video
This attribute contains a video.
When the attribute is activated a video pops up and can be played.
Patient.Report
This attribute contains a text-file presenting a medical report about a patient.
When the attribute is activated a file pops up inside a text-editor.

3.2 Member Role: Relation

3.2.1 General Introduction

In general, the purpose of the member relation is to store a collection of references to instances. A relation is an object type characterizing its owner by associating the owner object type to one or more object types.
The name of the relation is generally the name or role of the object type it refers to in singular or plural form.
`Examples` are `Employees` of `Department`, `Departments` of `Hospital` and `Children` of `Person`.
The characteristics of a relation specialize the characteristics of the fundamental object types reference and array. The characteristics of the constructs membership are applied.

A relation has the following characteristics:

- **Behavior:**
  Navigating and iterating the references; assigning, removing and reassigning a reference.
- **Cardinality range:**
  The cardinality range gives the possible number of references in the collection. It defines how many instances of the associated object type(s) its owner instance can be associated with regarding this relation. The range can be given as a minimum and a maximum number, only the maximum number (the minimum defaults to 0), or as `many` denoting an unlimited maximum.
- **Cardinality:**
  The cardinality is the current number of references in the collection of an instance.

Examples will be given within the following part of the section about relationship type.[3]

3.2.2 Relationship Type

Relations and a connector compose a relationship type.
A **connector** represents the link between the associated object types.

A **relationship type** represents an association between object types. This can be an association with other object types outside the considered object type or with the considered object type itself (recursive relationship type).

A **relationship** is an instance of a relationship type.

`Examples` are shown in Figure 3.4 to 3.9. The examples will be explained in the following sections.
`Integrity rule:`
`A relationship may be created if and only if the instances of the associated object types already exist and the relationship type exists.`

A relationship type has the following characteristics:

- **Direction:** A relationship type can be uni- or bi-directional.

[3]`Graphical notation:` The member-rectangle for relation contains a symbol or has the color code *yellow*.
The symbol depends on the category of the relation and the cardinality range. We will introduce it together with the cardinality range and refine it during the explanation of the relation categories.

Uni-directional:
A uni-directional relationship type implies that only one of the object types possesses the relation member. Since only one type has the collection of references to the other, it is not possible to access the former object type from the latter, i.e. the relation works only one way[4].
The term reference is commonly used to imply the uni-directional relationship type with cardinality one[5].
Bi-directional:
A bi-directional relationship type implies that both object types possess the relation member. Since both object types have the collection of references to each other, it is possible to access each object type from the other, i.e. the relation works both ways.
The term relationship type is commonly used to imply the bi-directional case.

`Examples`:
A hospital has an address. It may be important to know the address of a hospital but not to know which hospital belongs to a particular address.
The relationship type between hospital and address in this case is uni-directional.
In this example the address can be accessed through the hospital, i.e. a relation `Hospital.Address` exists but the hospital cannot be accessed through the address, i.e. a relation `Address.Hospital` does not exist[6].

Suppose that various clinics co-operate with various wards. In this case, it must be possible to find out which clinic co-operates with which wards and vice versa. Therefore the relationship type is bi-directional. In this `example` both the relations `Clinic.Wards` and `Ward.Clinics` exist.

`Graphical notation:`

`Uni-directional:`
The relationship type is represented as the relation of the one associated object type and the line connecting it to the other object type, see Figure 3.4. The representation for instances is the same.
`Bi-directional:`
The relationship type is represented as the relations of the associated object types and the line connecting them, Figure 3.5. The representation for instances is the same.

- **Cardinality range:**
The cardinality range of a relationship type is composed of the cardinality ranges of the participating relations. `Example: Ward.Clinics` and `Clinic.Wards`.
The cardinality range of this relationship type is many to many. The use of plural for both relations indicates that one ward co-operates with one or more clinic(s), one clinic co-operates with one or more ward(s).

[4] A simplified construction of this type is described in 2.6.7.
[5] The construction of this reference is built using the reference in 2.6.2 but is more complex.
[6] In the Hospital case study, the relation is actually bi-directional and is called `Addresses` because a hospital normally has several addresses.

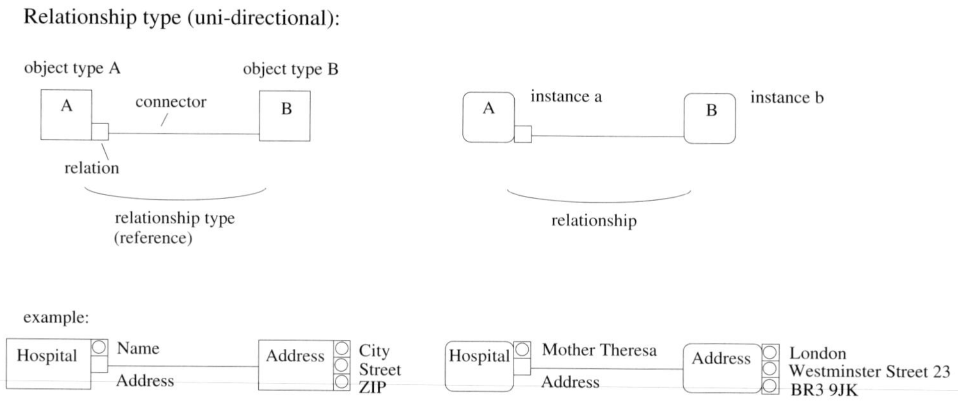

Figure 3.4: An uni-directional relationship (type)

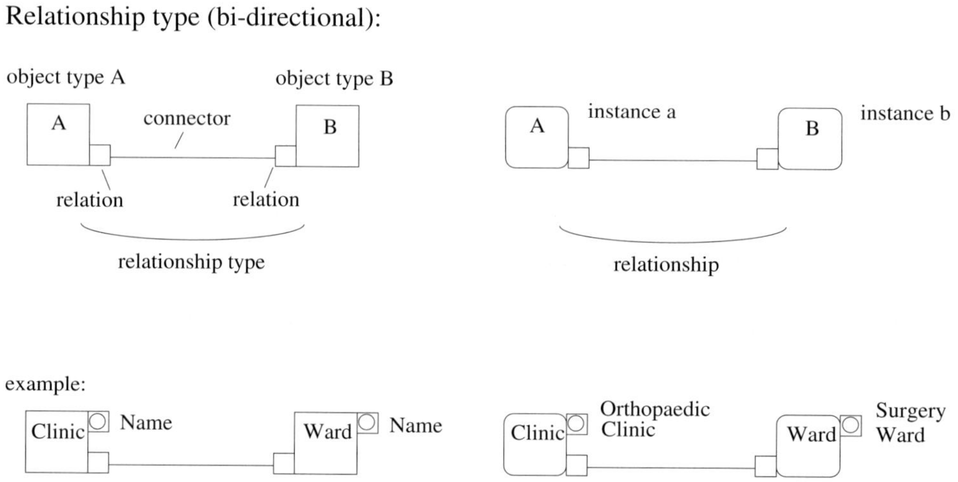

Figure 3.5: A bi-directional relationship (type)

`Graphical notation:`

The cardinality range of a relationship type is presented by:

- the name of the relation in either singular or plural form,
- the symbol for the cardinality range of the relation.

The symbols of Figure 3.6 are used to give the cardinality range. In the case of a uni-directional relationship type the same symbols are used, but only in the one relation.

- **Cardinality:**
  The cardinality of a relationship type indicates the number of instances actually associated with each other in a relationship of the considered relationship type.
  Figure 3.7 shows the semantics of cardinality range in the case of a bi-directional relationship type.

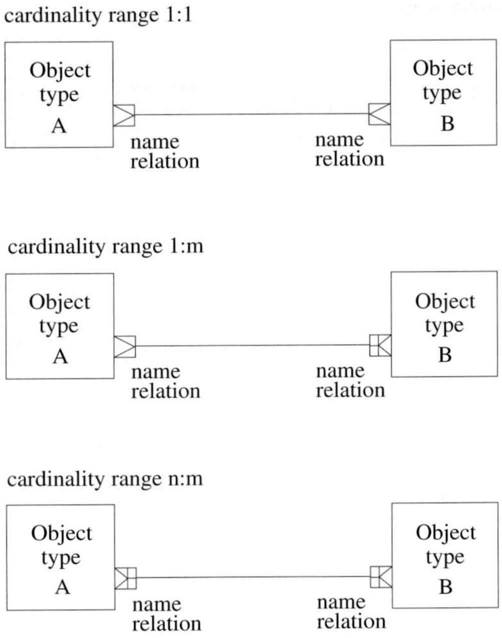

Figure 3.6: Cardinality range conventions

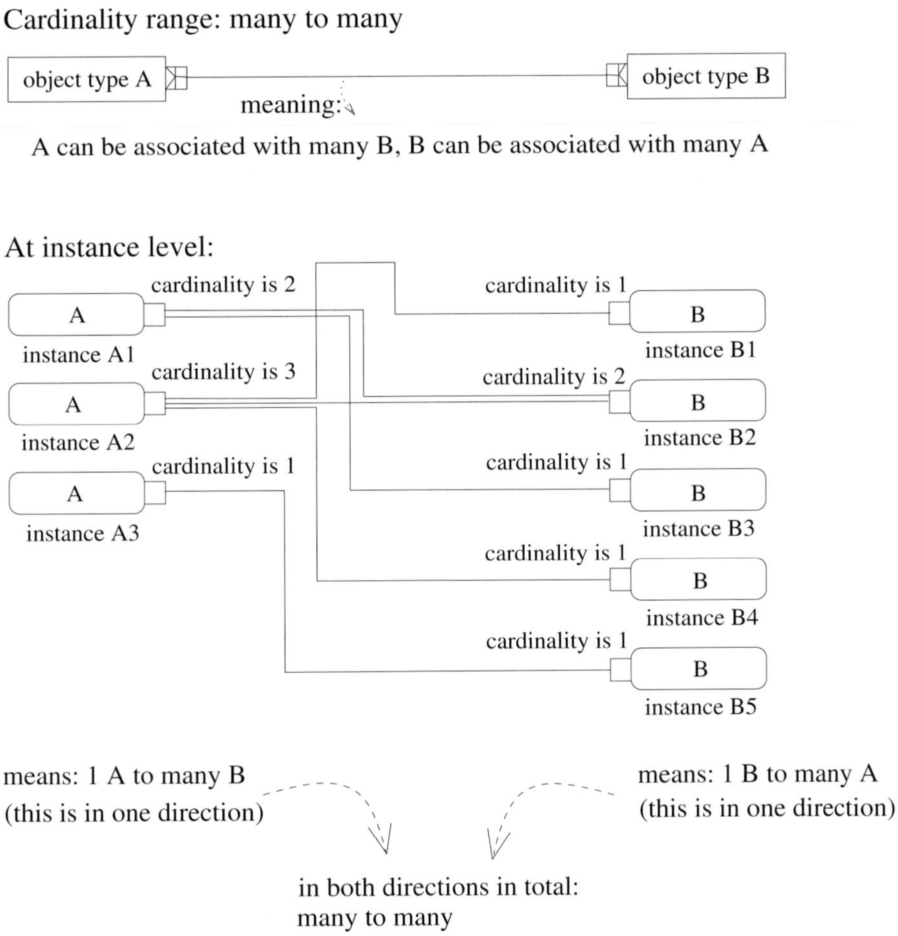

Figure 3.7: Semantics of cardinality, bi-directional relationship type

Graphical notation:

The cardinality of a relationship is represented by a number beside the relations, denoting the number of instances in the relations, (visible if the relevant object types are activated within the schema).
`Example`: 5 clinics co-operate with a particular ward. The second of the 5 clinics is the actual instance, meaning it is being accessed at this moment.

Figure 3.8 illustrates that `Clinic` *Orthopaedic* relates to five `Ward` instances and the second instance (*Surgery*) is being accessed; on the other side `Ward` *Surgery* relates to 4 `Clinic` instances and the first (*Orthopaedic*) is being accessed.

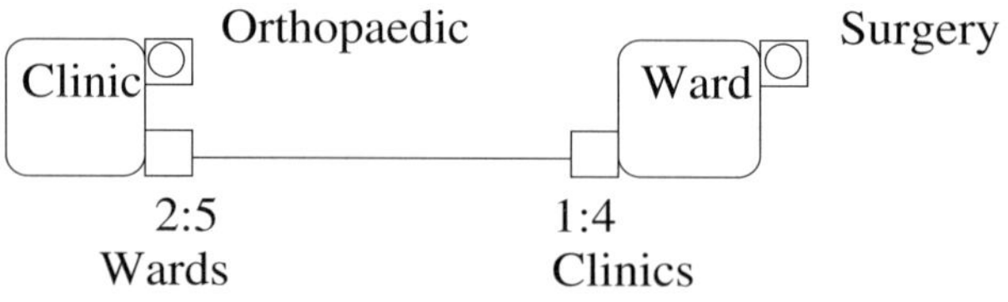

Figure 3.8: Representation of the cardinality

- **Value range:**
  The value range of a relationship type lists the object types that can be associated with each other.
  The value range of the co-operating wards and clinics is object type `Clinic` on one side and object type `Ward` on the other.

3.2.3 Recursive Relationship Type

A recursive relationship type has the same object type at both ends of the relationship.
`Example:` Suppose that we want to model which persons are the children of which parents. In this case, object type `Person` is associated with itself, meaning a particular person is a parent of another person, and a particular person is a child of another person, see Figure 3.9. At instance level, different instances of the same object type are associated with each other.
The example describes a bi-directional recursive relationship type. A recursive relationship type can be uni-directional also.

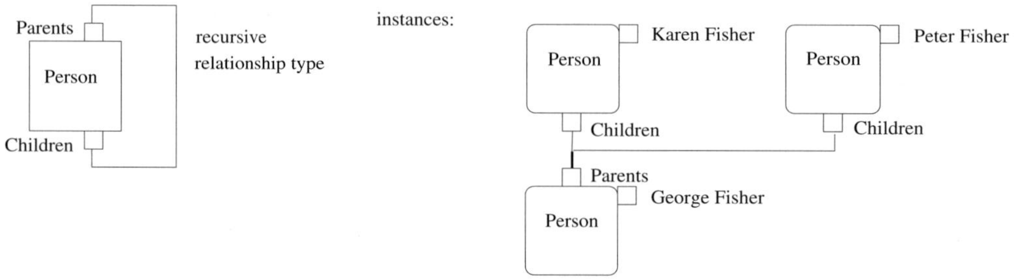

Figure 3.9: A recursive relationship type (bi-directional)

`Graphical notation:`

The connector associates two relations of the same object type in the case of a bi-directional recursive relationship type. It connects a relation of the object type and the object type itself in the case of a uni-directional recursive relationship type.

3.2.4 Relationship Member

Relationship types may have members. They are called **relationship members**. Normally these members are attributes, hence the term **relationship attribute**.
A relationship member is used when the information it contains is only relevant when instances are related through the relationship. This guarantees that the information will only exist when meaningful.

`Graphical notation:`

The relationship member is attached to the connector by default or associated by a small connector line, depending on the space available in the object schema.

Figure 3.10 shows an `example` of the following situation with regards to person roles in a hospital; a person may have several roles, e.g. as employee or as patient. Within a particular role the person has a status. Concerning the role as patient, the status carries information about health insurance status; concerning the role as employee, the status contains information about the kind of employment, i.e. full-time or part-time.
The status is not a member of `Employee` because an employee instance might exist without a relation to a person, e.g. a vacancy. In this case the status is irrelevant. The status is also not a member of `Person` because a person may possibly have several roles.

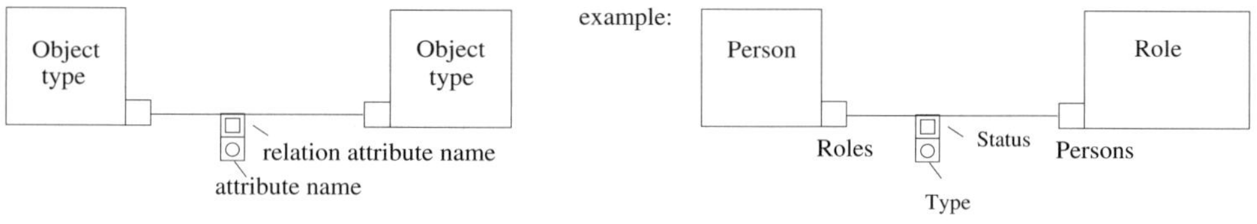

Figure 3.10: A relationship member

Relationship members have the same properties as members in general.
In the example of Figure 3.10 we consider the relationships extending from an instance of `Person.Roles`, that of several roles a particular person has. The same is valid in the other direction. We have to consider the relationships extending from one instance of `Role.Persons`, thus the several persons having the same role, e.g. nurse.
Two cases can be distinguished:

- **Private:** Any relationship extending from one relation instance has its own relationship member.
  For `example`: The Person named *Fisher* is a `Patient` in the `Ward` *Orthopaedic* with `Status` type *First Class* and also a `Patient` in the `Clinic` *Surgery* with the `Status` type *Second Class.*

- **Shared:** All relationships extending from one relation instance share the same relationship member.
  For `example`: The `Person` named *Johnson* is a part-time `Employee` working in `Ward` *Orthopaedic* and in the `Clinic` *Surgery.* Since the `Status` type is `shared`, the value *Part Time* applies to both. If the `Status` type is modified to *Full Time*, it will apply to both.

Whether a relationship member is `private` or shared is configurable. There is no symbol for expressing the difference.

3.2.5 Ownership Relationship Type

Relationship types are categorized as **ownership** and **non-ownership**. Non-ownership, explained below, is also called **Secondary**.
Ownership between object types is expressed through the hierarchical ownership relationship type. In general, ownership relationship types bind the owned object types to the `owner` object type with a *rope*.

Ownership expresses and maintains **existential dependency** between instances of the related object types:

The owned object instance can only be created and can only exist as long as its owner exists and will be destroyed when its owner is destroyed.
An object type is owned by another if its instances are existentially dependent on instances of that object type.

For `example`, a department of a hospital is existentially dependent on the existence of the hospital itself. The hospital is the owner of its departments. This dependency is represented as ownership relationship type between the object type `Hospital` and the object type `Clinic`.

An ownership relationship type has the following characteristics:

- An instance has one and only one direct owner instance. A clinic is owned by a particular hospital, for example.
- The ownership is transitive.
  A certain instance of an object type is owned by an instance of each of the object types transitively above it in the hierarchy, starting with the root object type (the most abstract object type in the ownership hierarchy).
  When using the term owner we usually mean the direct owner.
  A hospital is the direct owner of its clinics. A clinic is the owner of its employees. Transitively, a hospital is also the indirect owner of the employee-occupations of its clinics. The situation is illustrated in Figure 3.11.

The relation that an instance is owned by is called the `owner_relation`. `Hospital.Clinics` is the `owner_relation` of the instances of `Clinic`.

Ownership can be recursive.
When a certain object type is owner and owned for the same ownership relationship type, this means that a certain instance of that object type owns other instances of the same object type. An `example` of a recursive ownership relationship type could be: `Department` owned by `Department`, see Figure 3.12[7] meaning that a particular department has dependent departments, in this case sub-departments. The sub-departments cannot exist without the existence of the owning department.

[7] In the Hospital Case Study departments do not own departments to simplify matters. However it could very well be done as described here.

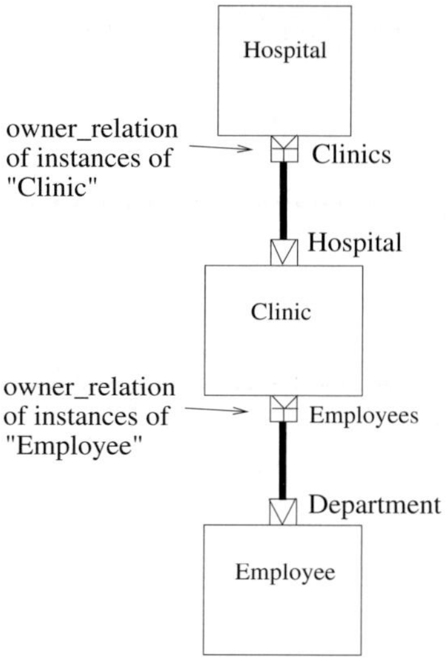

Figure 3.11: Example of an ownership relationship type

`Integrity rule:`
`Every object type belongs to an ownership-hierarchy`[8]`.`
`Integrity rule:`
`An instance may belong to one and only one ownership-hierarchy.`
`Integrity rule:`
`An owned instance can be created and destroyed only from its owner instance via its owner_relation.`

An owner instance is also called the **creator** of its owned instances.

`Graphical notation:`

`Placement convention:` the owned object types are placed below their owner.
The relations should be placed as follows:
- the relation on the owner object type at the lower side of the rectangle in the middle
- the relation on the owned object type at the upper side of the rectangle in the middle

`Symbols:`
- the relation at the owner side has the same symbol as explained for the cardinality range according to the cardinality range of the relation, see Figure 3.6
- the relation at the owned side has the same symbol as for the `1-cardinality` range, but facing the other way around[9], i.e. to the owned object type relation at the upper side of `Clinic` and at the upper side of `Employee`, see Figure 3.11.

`Thickness of the connector:`
Lines thicker than the connector line for the secondary relationship type, e.g. 10 pixels.

The conventions can be seen in Figure 3.11 and Figure 3.12 is an example of a recursive ownership type.

[8] Object type `Manager` is the root object of an object hierarchy. An object type can have several owner object types.

[9] This is to give an additional sense of direction. The convention is that in the schema, the owner type is always placed above the object types that it owns, however there are exceptions where it is convenient to place both types side by side. It helps orientation in the case of a recursive relationship.

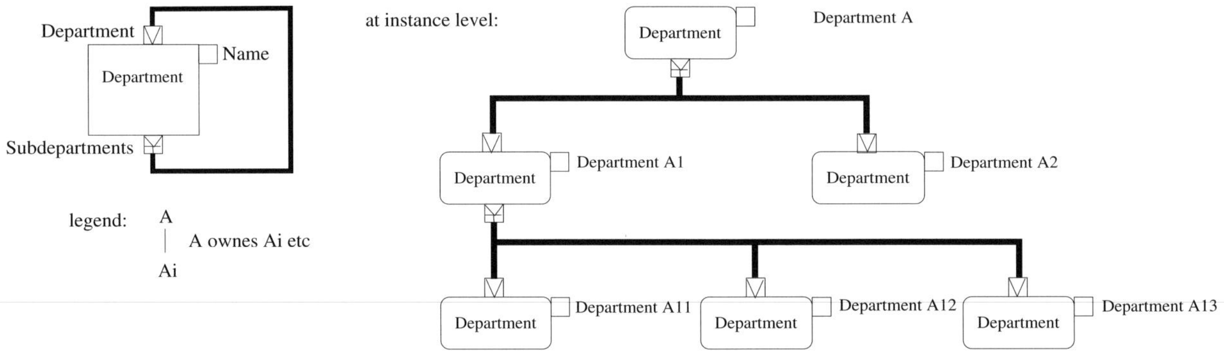

Figure 3.12: An example of a recursive ownership relationship type

Heterogeneous relationship: An ownership relationship is heterogeneous if the owner relation can relate to instances of two or more object types. An example of this is shown later on in section 4.6.2.

3.2.6 Secondary Relationship Type

Between objects, relationship types may exist which express semantics that differ from those of ownership.
Secondary relationship types can associate object types from several abstraction levels of the same ownership hierarchy, either the same branch or different branches of it, as well as of different ownership hierarchy.
For `example`, if a particular ward cooperates with a particular clinic, this is represented by a secondary relationship type between the object types `Ward` and `Clinic`. The semantics of the relationship type is content driven; we interpret it as `Ward` cooperates with `Clinic`. See Figure 3.13.

```
Integrity rule:
Secondary relationships do not have impact on the integrity rules of the ownership
hierarchies to which the object types belong.
```

`Graphical notation:`

Placement convention: there are no special placement conventions, but the placement should be realized so that the connector can be drawn as simply as possible and with as few crossings with other connectors as possible.
Symbols for the cardinality range: see Figure 3.6.
Thickness:
the finest lines in the object model, e.g. 1 pixel.

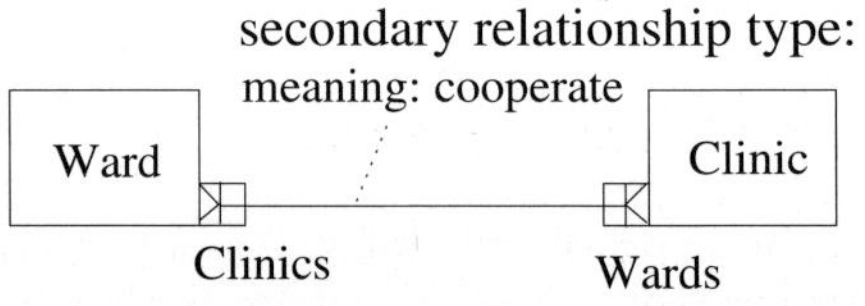

Figure 3.13: An example of a secondary relationship type

We can now make the example of Figure 3.9 more precise: the relationship type between Person.Children and Person.Parents is a secondary relationship type with the cardinality range: many children may belong to a parent. Maximally 2 persons[10] may be parents of a child.

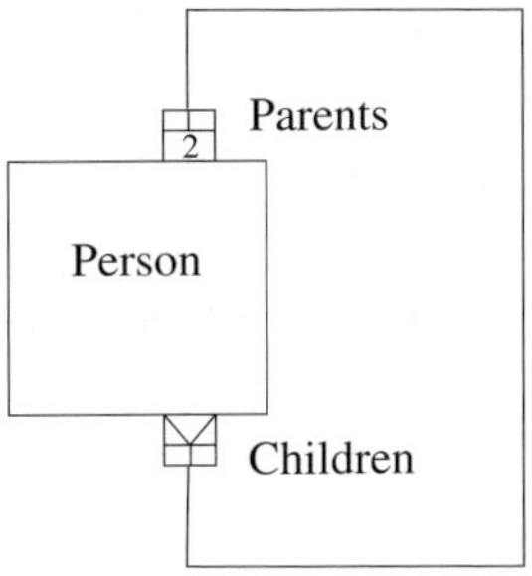

Figure 3.14: A secondary recursive relationship type

Heterogeneous relationship: A secondary relationship is heterogeneous if either the source or target relation[11] can relate to instances of two or more object types.An example of this is shown later on in section 5.3.1.

3.3 Member Role: Operation

An operation is an object type which characterizes another object type by means of processing particular activities on the object type it characterizes and on other object types. Examples are Employee.Hours where the actual number of hours has to be computed from the number of working hours, and Department.Check_In where a patient has to be registered in a department of a hospital. The characteristics of an operation use the characteristics of the fundamental object types operation, literal and array.

Operations are categorized as generic and specific.

3.3.1 Generic Operation

A generic operation is an operation shared by each object type in the object base in principle. Perspective-DB currently supports the following generic operations for each object type:

- Operations to view information:
  - Obtain help
  - Produce a form showing (the members of) a certain related instance
  - Produce an overview of all instances with their properties related through a certain relationship type
  - Produce an overview of all related instances
  - Produce a hierarchical overview of all directly and indirectly owned instances

- Operations to insert or remove information:
  - Create new instances
  - Destroy instances

[10]In a real system this value would be higher in order to take step-parents into account as well.
[11]Actually both the source and target relations can participate in a heterogeneous relationship.

- Insert relations
- Remove relations
- Modify values
- Copy instances
- Move instances

- Operation to export information:
  - Export information, contained in a `media type attribute`, to other databases or vice versa
- Operation to find a particular instance:
  - Get a particular instance of an object type that contains a given value

`Graphical notation:`

The member-rectangle for the generic operations contains an upper case letter indicating the functionality. The color code is *light gray.*
The placement of the generic operations on the object type surface cannot be changed, even if some are not used. For these operations, `not` changing the placement is much more important than for other members. The generic operations are used in almost every object type and the user is familiar with the placement.

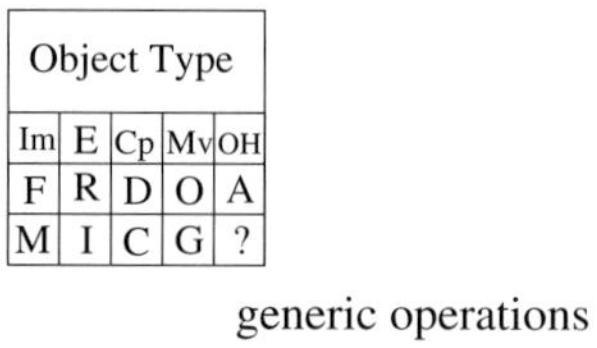

Figure 3.15: Generic operations

`Example Ward`, see Figure 3.16:

F (Form): presents a form view of the selected related instance of `Ward` showing all members (with the same color code as in the model notation)
M (Modify): enables the modification of the attribute values of the actual instance of `Ward`
E (Export): enables the export of media types, where instance values are physically stored, to files outside the object base. If that is not a Perspective-DB object base the operation can be applied to the attribute `Video`
R (Remove): enables the removal of a secondary relationship instance, here outgoing from the relations `Clinics` and `Supports`
I (Insert): enables inserting a secondary relationship instance, here to the relations `Clinics` and `Supports`
D (Destroy): destroys instances from the owned object types, here from `Employees` and `Patients`
C (Create): creates instances in the owned object types, here in `Employees` and `Patients`
O (Overview): generates a tabular overview of those instances related to a particular ward, which belong to a selected relation of `Ward`, here `Clinics`, `Supports`, `Employees`, `Patients` and `Hospital`
G (Get): gets an instance which is related to the actual instance of `Ward`, here from `Clinics`, `Supports`, `Employees`, `Patients` and `Hospital`

A (Association): generates a tabular view of all instances related to the actual instance of `Ward`, and is a list of the related instances from `Ward`, here from `Clinics`, `Supports`, `Employees`, `Patients` and `Hospital`
The list can be asymmetric due to the different number of related instances in the related object types
? (Help): enables help information about the `Wards` and all its members
Mv (Move): moves an owned object to another owner
Cp (Copy): copies an owned object, to the same or a different owner
OH (Ownership Hierarchy): generates a tabular view of all the ownership hierarchies starting from the invoked object as root

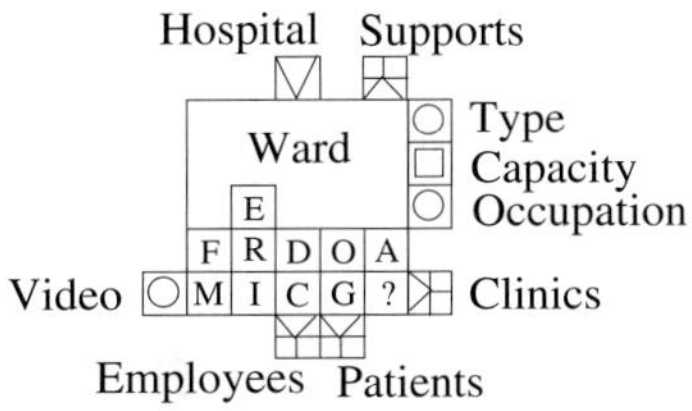

Figure 3.16: Example `Ward`

3.3.2 Specific Operation

A specific operation is an operation which is specific for the object type of which it is a member.

The member-rectangle for the specific operations contains the symbol `()` due to its equivalence to the function-symbol. The color code is *pink*.

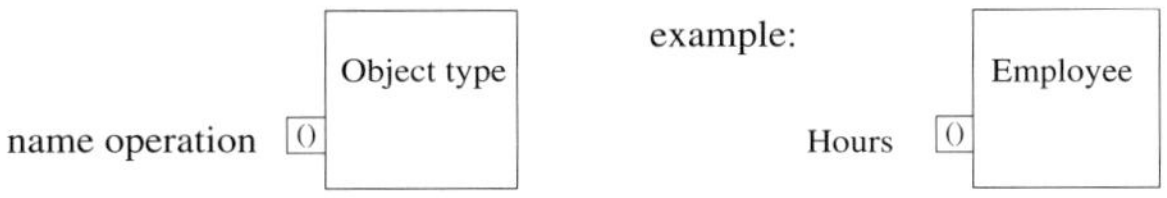

Figure 3.17: Specific operation

`Example:`
`Clinic.Employ`
This operation registers a person as employee of the clinic.
`Example:`
`Employee.Hours`
This operation computes the number of hours an employee actually works.

3.3.3 Invoking an Operation

An operation has a somewhat different nature from other object types. This is because its purpose is to manipulate one or more instances. An operation is activated by *asking* the owner object instance of that operation to execute the operation. This is called **invocation** of an operation. The executing operation can in turn call upon the instances it manipulates to invoke other operations. In fact an operation can call itself, if necessary. Such operations are called **recursive** operations. Each time an operation is invoked it is instantiated in the volatile memory of the computer.

The instantiation contains information necessary for the processing. When the operation instance terminates it is automatically destroyed. Because an operation invocation only exists during processing, it is not saved persistently as is the case with other types. An operation is also not considered to be a first order object type, rather a member of a first order object type.

Another property of object type operation is that in the role of member of an object type it can be overruled in specialized object types. This implies that it is possible to retain the operation name, its return and argument object types, yet change its computation in a specialized object type if desired.

3.4 First Order Inheritance

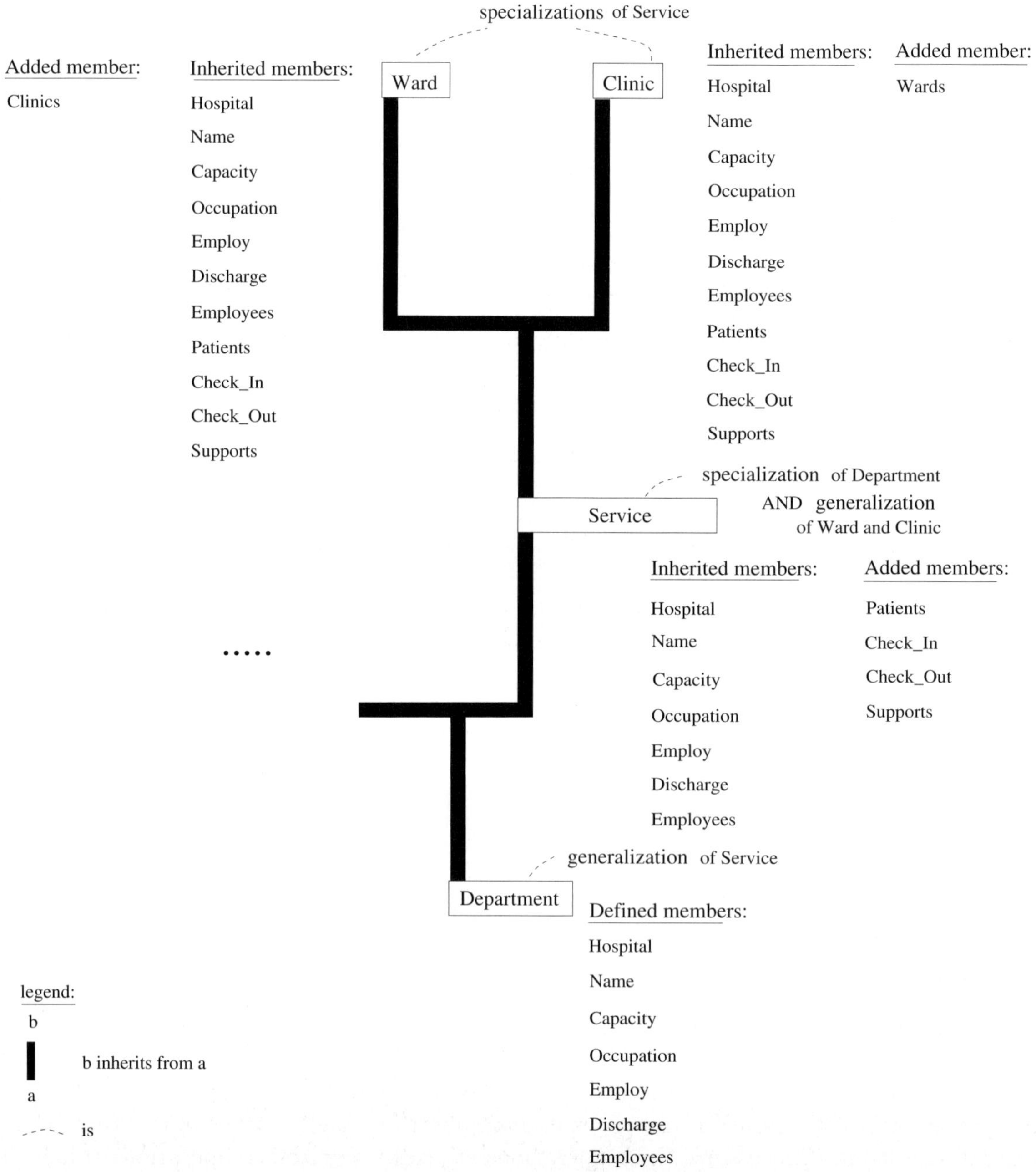

Figure 3.18: Example of an inheritance hierarchy

Several object types may have the same members.
We say that they share common members. `Wards, Clinics, Medical Support` departments and `General Support` departments share the following members: `Name, Capacity, Occupation, Employ, Discharge, Employees, Hospital`.
The object types are specializations of the generalization which defines the shared members. `Department` is the generalization object type of `Ward`, `Clinic`, `General_Support` and `Medical_Support`.

Inheritance has already been introduced as a fundamental construct for constructing composite object types from fundamental object types. We now elaborate on this construct.

The fact that a particular object type is a generalization of a particular object type is expressed through the generalization/specialization hierarchy. This hierarchy is used to define the direction of inheritance. For our purposes, the terms generalization/specialization hierarchy and the inheritance hierarchy are considered to be the same. We prefer the term inheritance hierarchy.

A generalization does not inherit from itself. There is no recursive inheritance.

Specializations may add new member definitions to those they inherited. Patients are treated in a ward. Thus, `Ward` has additional members concerning patients, e.g. `Patients`, `Check_In` and `Check_Out`.

`Patients` are also treated in clinics. `Clinic` adds similar additional members to Department as `Ward`. From this we conclude that we can introduce a generalization to `Clinic` and `Ward` defining their additional shared members, e.g. `Patients`, `Check_In` and `Check_Out`. We name the generalization object type `Service`. But that generalization has to inherit the members of a Department. Thus it is also a specialization, namely of the generalization `Department`.
The example is presented in Figure 3.18.
This figure shows the perspective on inheritance where the members are `taken over` transitively, as seen on the right side of Figure 2.12. It is necessary to make this explicit where the members are defined.

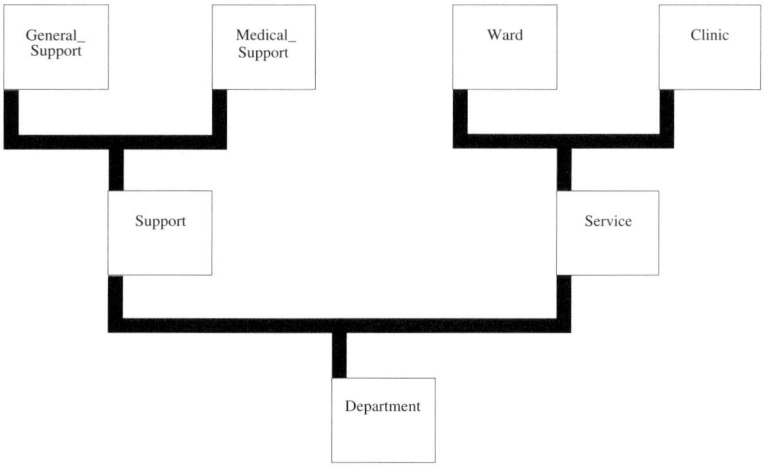

Figure 3.19: Example of an inheritance hierarchy: Departments of a hospital

A specialization may also modify characteristics of the inherited members:

- `an attribute:` the cardinality range, the range of data types, and the value range can be limited
- `a relation:` the cardinality range and the direction can be limited e.g. instead of the upper limit *many* for the cardinality the number *25* is defined, or instead of a bi-directional relationship type a uni-directional relationship type is allowed
- `an operation:` the implementation can be overwritten (known as polymorphism).

We summarize:
The root of the hierarchy is the most common object type definition of the hierarchy. It defines the members shared by all the other object types in the inheritance hierarchy.
The specializations which make up the leaves of the hierarchy inherit all the member definitions and the limitations from the entire branch of the hierarchy starting from the root.

An inheritance hierarchy has the following characteristics:

- The inheritance is transitive.
  The members which an object type inherits do not have to be defined again within the type definitions of the specialization objects.

- The inheritance is compulsory.
  A particular object type may ignore a member it inherits but it is there[12].

- The inheritance is polymorphic.
  Characteristics of a member which an object type inherits may be overwritten with more specific members.

`Integrity rule:`
Any object type may inherit its generalization from one and only one object type directly.

The integrity rule means that `multiple inheritance` is not permitted[13]

The base object type of all first order objects in Perspective-DB is `OMS_Object`. The reason for the prefix *OMS* (Object Management System) is explained in Chapter 19 on system building.
A generalization can have more than one specialization. In this case, the line is split to connect them with the common generalization, see Figure 3.18. The generalization/specialization hierarchy between `Service` and `Ward` and `Clinic` opens two branches, one for each specialization.

`Graphical notation:`

`Placement convention:` the specialization object types are placed above their generalization object type.
The connector has a fixed placement on the rectangle of the object type:
on the generalization side first left position, top of the rectangle
on the specialization side first left position, bottom of the rectangle.

`Symbols:`
The connector line, its position and thickness.

[12]Where the member is defined as `private` it is there, but the specialization is not aware of its presence.
[13]multiple inheritance is technically possible but experience has shown that the advantage of multiple inheritance is offset by the additional complexity it introduces.

`Thickness:`
The thickest line used in the object model, a little smaller than 1 grid unit, e.g. 18 pixels.
See also Figure 3.19.
Figure 3.19 shows an inheritance hierarchy of the departments of a hospital as follows:

Object type `Department` is the generalization for

- `Support`
- `Service`

`Support` is the generalization for

- `General_Support`
- `Medical_Support`

`Service` is the generalization for

- `Clinic`
- `Ward`

`Remarks to inheritance of operations:`

- Generic operations:
  Each object type inherits these operations from the base object type `OMS_Object`.
- Specific operations:
  These operations are inherited from the generalization just as any other member.

Overruling generic operations is possible but this should be done with caution. Generic operations should be overruled when integrity conditions have to be added.

Chapter 4

First Order Object Types: Identification

4.1 Semantic & Syntactic Identification

To make objects distinguishable from each other, objects have to be identifiable. An object is identifiable if there is something which makes it unique when compared with other objects. Identification provides a means to make an object unambiguously recognizable and denotable. The property "uniqueness" has to be guaranteed within a particular scope of the object e.g. its owner, the object base or the application. Furthermore, the property has to be guaranteed from the object's creation to its destruction.
Identification of objects occurs on a semantic or a syntactic basis.

4.1.1 Semantic Identification

Identification on a semantic basis means that the identification of an object is associated with the meaning of the object. An object is recognizable by a user through its characteristics or a particular part of its characteristics. A user will unambiguously refer to an object through the semantic identifier. Further, the placement of an object within an object schema and also how it is to be processed is based on its semantics.

4.1.2 Syntactic Identification

Identification on a syntactic basis means that an identifier exists for each object which is part of the object definition and known to the system which manages the object. The management system can find and access the object based on this identifier and it can refer to the object through this identifier. The identifier has no semantics and it will never change even when all characteristics of the object have been changed. This identifier is a system internal identifier.
To help understand the difference let us take the example of identifying cities. The terms *London Paris* and *New York* have special meanings and we can immediately place these objects in a particular context. However, these cities may also be identified by a global position based on longitude and latitude coordinates, i.e. a number. The first is a semantic and the latter a syntactic identifier.
For object bases and their applications both semantic and syntactic identification categories are necessary:

- The first, to make sure that a particular object can be used by a human user and by an application if the object has to be recognized by its semantics.

- The second, to make sure that a particular object can be managed by the system independently of the object's state and context i.e. its semantics.

The semantic based identification is explained below as we wish to explain the design and use of object bases and applications.

4.2 Object Type Identification

An object type is semantically identified by its name. `Hospital` and `Department` are names of object types.
Names of object types must be unique within the application.
The name can be extended with the layer name. Layers and modules will be introduced later. Through this extension the object type identification can be unique within a particular information system involving several applications.

The identification of an instance happens according to the existential dependency defined by the ownership hierarchy to which an instance belongs. We distinguish between local and global identification. Key and Alias are local identifiers and Canonical-ID, Short-ID and Truncated-ID are global identifiers.

The examples used throughout the chapter are based on the Hospital Case Study introduced in 1.1.

4.3 Instance Key Identification

An instance is locally identified semantically by its **key**. Local means within the scope of its owner_relation.

A key is an attribute with the following characteristics:

- The key achieves uniqueness by a unique value of the key attribute in the scope of its owner_relation.

  `Example:` An object type `Clinic` is owned by `Hospital`. The owner_relation is `Clinics`, a relation of the object type `Hospital`. The key attribute of the object type `Clinic` is `Name`. Local uniqueness is achieved when all clinics of the same hospital, e.g. *Elizabeth*[1], have another value for `Name`. For example, one has the name *Surgery*, another *Orthopaedic*; two *Orthopaedic* clinics in the *Elizabeth* hospital are not possible in this case.
  However, there could be clinics with the same name *Orthopaedic* in several hospitals, e.g. *Elizabeth* and *Mother-Theresa*. The two `Clinic` instances belong to two different instances of *Hospital*: *Elizabeth* and *Mother-Theresa*. Each clinic instance is unique within the scope of its owning hospital instance. see Figure 4.1. *Elizabeth* could have a ward and a clinic with the same name, *Orthopaedic* for example.

- The key property of an attribute will be inherited.

- It is normally forbidden to modify the value of a key. Nevertheless, Perspective-DB permits the modification of key values. The reasons are that in real life situations the person inserting the value is likely to make typing errors, and an unforeseen situation might arise requiring a change of value.

[1] Throughout the book we use Elizabeth rather than Elizabeth Hospital, the same applies to Mother Theresa Hospital etc.

Perspective-DB checks that the key value is not already being used to identify another instance of the same owner in the following cases: a new instance is inserted, or the key value of an existing instance has to be modified. The modification will be valid immediately in each view[2] of the object because all views are synchronized. It will also be valid in each secondary relation in which the object is participating.
N.B.; there is a system internal identifier whose value is not changeable. The system can manage the value change through this internal identifier.
The key is used to identify the instance, therefore modifying the key can cause complications where the key is used as a reference in an external system.

In Perspective-DB only atomic attributes are permitted as keys to avoid unnecessary complexity.

The key is normally the attribute a user uses for direct access to the object. The user knows the value of that attribute in principle and uses this knowledge to find a particular object with that key value.

`Graphical notation:`

The key attribute is placed at the top right corner by default. The name of the key attribute placed in a fine-lined rectangle, see Figure 4.2.

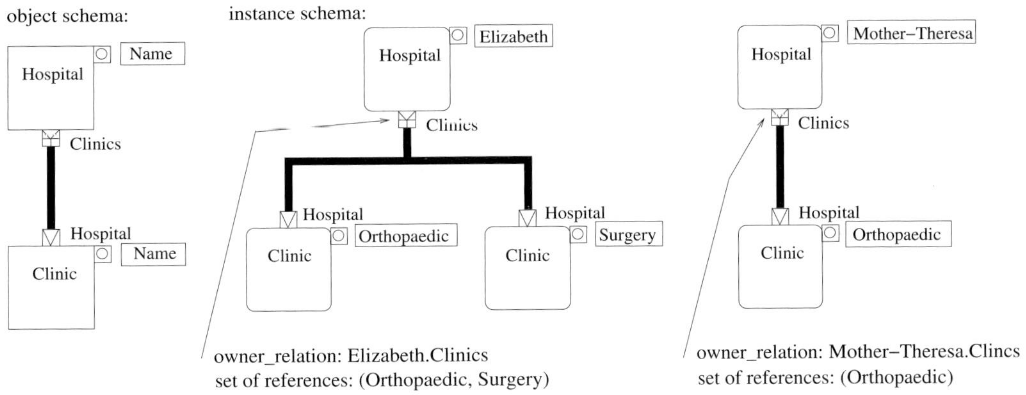

Figure 4.1: Illustration of local uniqueness achieved by the key

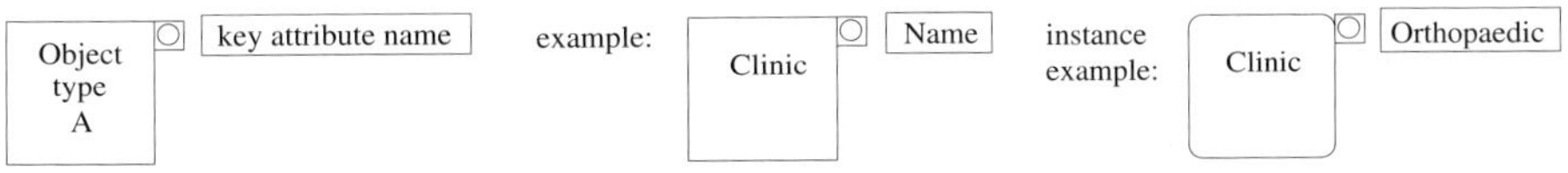

Figure 4.2: Placement of key

4.4 Instance Alias Identification

Keys may represent a property which is existent in the Universe of Discourse, or a key attribute may be introduced as an `artificial` property to offer the uniqueness in a simple manner, e.g. if an attribute combination only can offer the unique identification property within the scope of the `owner relation`.

[2]Here, we mean a view in the GUI if the same object is visible in more than one place, e.g. in the schema and in a table.

Sometimes the values of the chosen artificial key attribute are not sufficiently semantic for the various users. Take the `example` of `Persons` in an organization. For administrative reasons persons belonging to an organization need to be identified by unique serial numbers to guarantee correct processing and correct conveying of information between various information systems. Therefore the key is most likely to be a number. However the end-user of a particular information system prefers to identify the persons by their names. To enable this another attribute can be used as an **alias** for the key in listings etc. The alias is an arbitrary (also atomic) attribute which functions as a nick-name. A constraint on the alias is that it must not conflict with another alias or key within the same `owner relation`. This ensures that the system can at all times identify the object by its key or by its alias so that both are legitimate local identifiers.

4.5 Instance Canonical-ID Identification

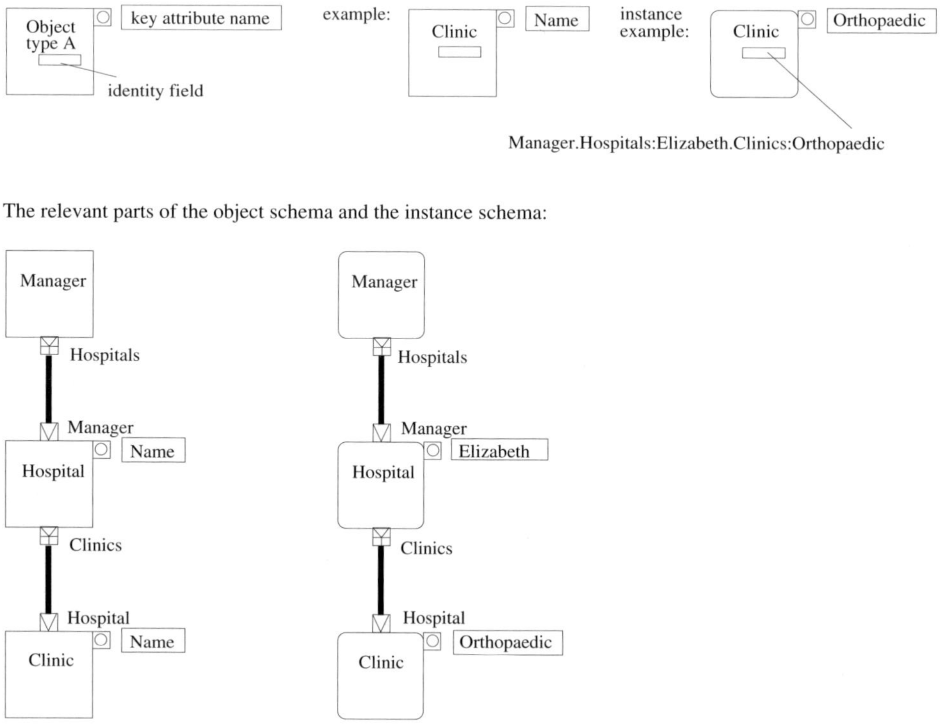

Figure 4.3: Placement of identity

Instances are globally identified by an identification path. The identification path is called the `identity` of an instance.
`Global` has to be understood as `application wide` at this point.
For the identity the ownership hierarchy is used. The identity `follows` this hierarchy.
The identity of an instance is the path
`Key_value(of_the_root_instance).Owner_relation_name1:Key_value1.`
`Owner_relation_name2:Key_value2` etc. until the key of the intended instance is reached.
We call this identification path the canonical form.
The first key is always the key value of the root instance of the ownership hierarchy. See Figure 4.4.

Objects with the keys
Manager.Hospitals:Elizabeth.Clinics:Orthopaedic and
Manager.Hospitals:Mother-Theresa.Clinics:Orthopaedic are two semantically based globally unique identified instances.

`Graphical notation:`

The global identity is placed automatically in the identity field in a running application, see Figure 4.3. This is an ancillary service of Perspective-DB for the interactive object schemas represented as graphical user interfaces. For example, it is possible that only part of the ownership hierarchy is visible on the screen where the user is interacting at a particular moment. To prevent the user having to scroll across the screen to know the identity of a certain instance, the path is given at the location where the actual activities happen i.e. at the surface of the object type.
In a static object schema e.g. on paper, it is not necessary to give the identity in this way because the object types and the instances are presented separately. The key values are given only in an instance schema. If the instance schema is also static, it is not necessary to give the identity path within the objects. The entire ownership hierarchy is always visible and the instance's location is immediately recognizable, see Figure 4.4.

Figure 4.4 represents the path for the identity using the ownership relationship type.

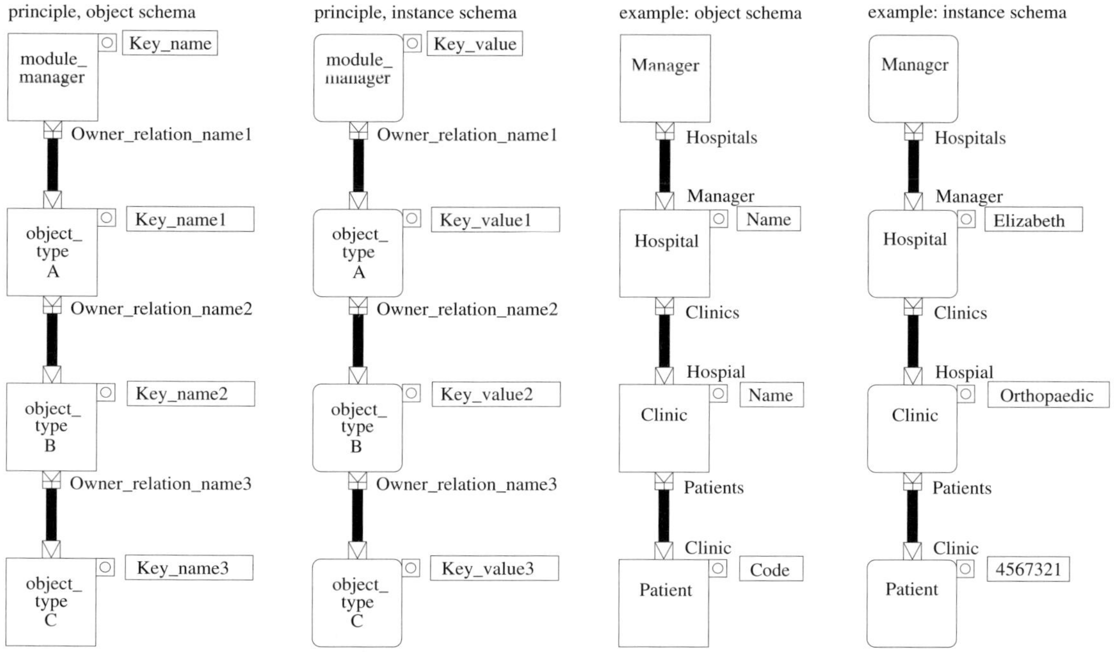

Figure 4.4: Illustration of the path for global identity of an object type instance

Figure 4.5 illustrates the identity using the ownership relationship type in the case of two branches.

4.6 Instance Short-ID Identification

To simplify the use of ownership relationship types the following categorization of the ownership relationship type is made:

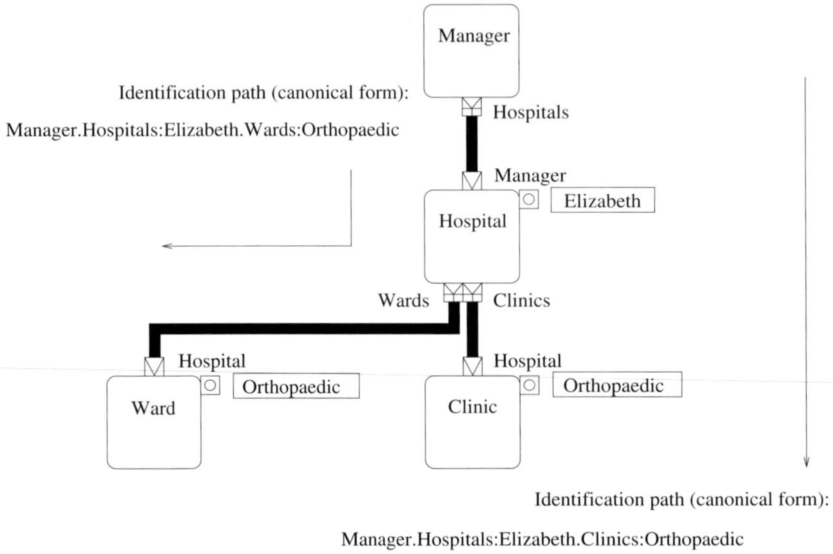

Figure 4.5: Illustration of uniqueness through the identification path

4.6.1 Default Ownership

A Default ownership is a particular branch in the ownership hierarchy which is the most dominant, i.e. which will be used most. The identification of instances within such a branch can use a short form for the notation.
The short form is
`Key_value(of_the_root_instance).Key_value1.Key_value2.Key_value3` etc. until the key of the intended instance is reached, see Figure 4.6.
The `owner_relation_names` are known automatically when the ownership relations are configured as Default.
The short-cut works also in the case of a split ownership relationship type[3].
`Example:` `Hospital` owns the object types
`General_Support` and `Medical_Support`. The short-cuts for the situation of figure 4.7 are *Manager.Mother-Theresa.Laundry* and
Manager.Mother-Theresa.X-ray.

```
Integrity rule:
Any ownership hierarchy may have one and only one Default branch.
```

Figure 4.6 illustrates the principle.

4.6.2 Primary Ownership

The rest of the ownership hierarchy. The canonical form of the identification path has to be given to identify an instance.
Identity paths for the `example` of Figure 4.6:
For the Default ownership: *Manager.Elizabeth.Surgery*
For the Default ownership at the beginning and the Primary ownership for continuation: *Manager.Elizabeth.Clinics:Orthopaedic*

[3] *Supports* is configured as Default solely to illustrate that a short-cut can be applied to a split relationship. In fact, *Wards* is the Default.

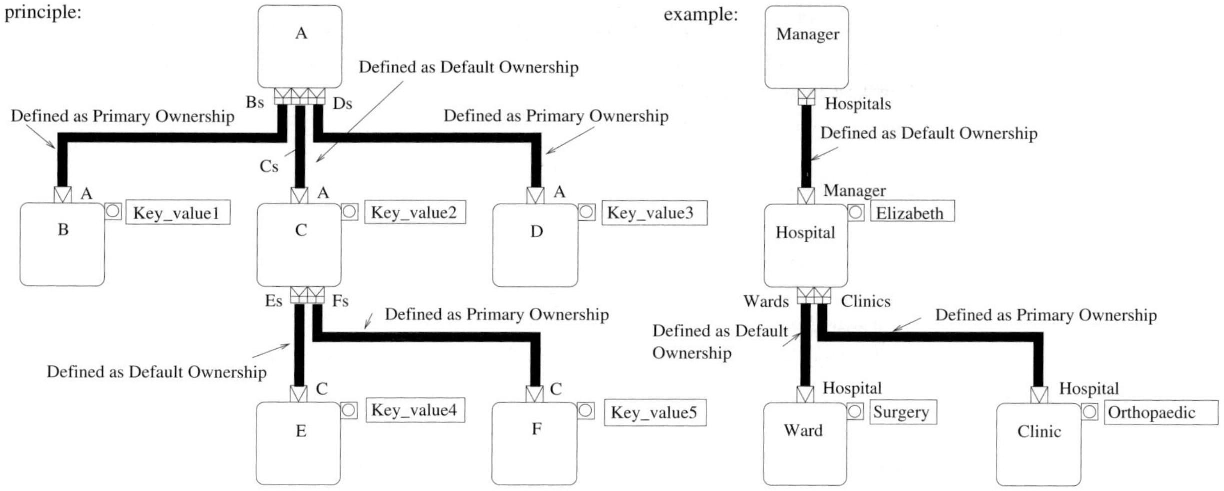

Figure 4.6: Principle of defining Primary and Default Ownership

It is common to position the default branch in the center because it is the most dominant.

Heterogeneous relationship: The relationship from `Hospital.Supports` to `General_Support.Hospital` and `Medical_Support` is heterogeneous, because `Hospital` can contain numerous instances of both types in the relation `Supports`.

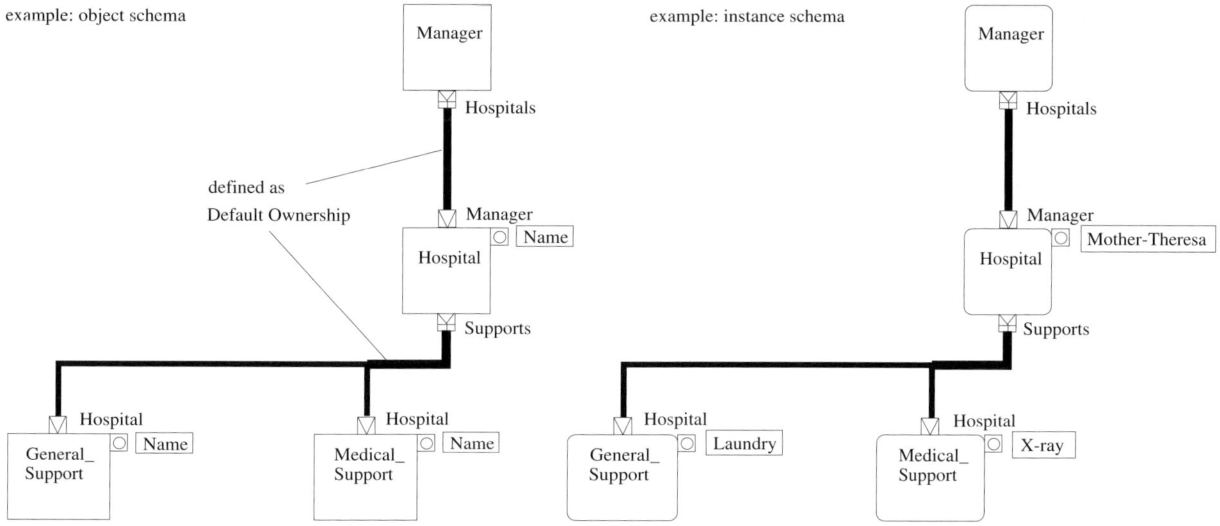

Figure 4.7: A split Default Ownership hierarchy

4.7 Instance Truncated-ID Identification

Take the `example` of telephone numbers to understand the principle of Truncated-IDs. When dialing locally, we use a short number. When dialing outside the district, we need to prefix a district number, and when dialing abroad we need in addition to prefix a country number. The Truncated-ID which works on the same principle implies that when an object needs to be identified within a particular context it is enough to provide sufficient identity to locate the object.

This ID is identical to the complete ID, with one or more of the keys beginning with the root, truncated. Depending on whether the object is along a default ownership path or not, the Truncated-ID can be in the Canonical-ID form or the Short-ID form.

4.8 Member Identification

4.8.1 Local Member Identification

At `object type level` *local* means uniqueness in the scope of the object type.
The local identification of a member happens according to the existential dependencies defined by membership. The local member identification is given by `object_type_name.member_name`, e.g. the member `Capacity` of `Clinic` is uniquely identified by `Clinic.Capacity`.
At `instance level` *local* means uniqueness in the scope of the instance.
The local member identification is given by `key_value.member_name`; `key_value` is the key of the instance.

`Example`: The member `Capacity` of the instance `Orthopaedic` of the object type `Clinic` is uniquely identified by *Orthopaedic.Capacity*.
If the member is a composite, its members are given in line, separated by a dot .

`Example`: `Clinic.Capacity.Max_Capacity` and `Orthopaedic.Capacity.Max_Capacity`, see Figure 4.8[4].

4.8.2 Global Member Identification

At `object type level` the global identification is the same as the local because the object type name is globally unique (at this point global means in the scope of the application as mentioned above).
At `instance level` the global identification of a member is given through the combination of the identity of the instance and the member name concatenated to the identification path and separated by a dot.

`Example` of the canonical form:
Manager.Elizabeth:Capacity, see Figure 4.8.

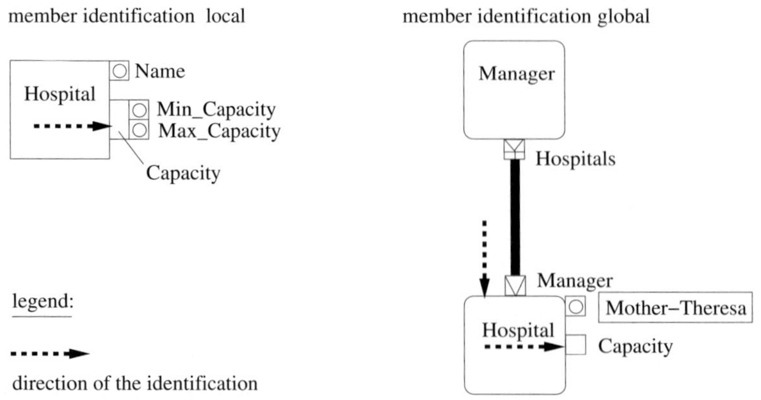

Figure 4.8: Illustration of the identification path of a member

[4]As previously mentioned, in the Hospital Case Study, Capacity is actually not a composite but an integer, for simplicity.

4.9 Context Dependence of Semantics

We illustrate the consequences of the ownership hierarchy and of the identification within this hierarchy for the semantics of the objects through the following example:
We consider the ownership relationship types between `Hospital.Wards`, `Ward.Hospital` and between `Ward.Employees` and `Employee.Ward`. Figure 4.9 the left part shows the ownership hierarchy in the object schema (the object types); the right part shows the instance schema.

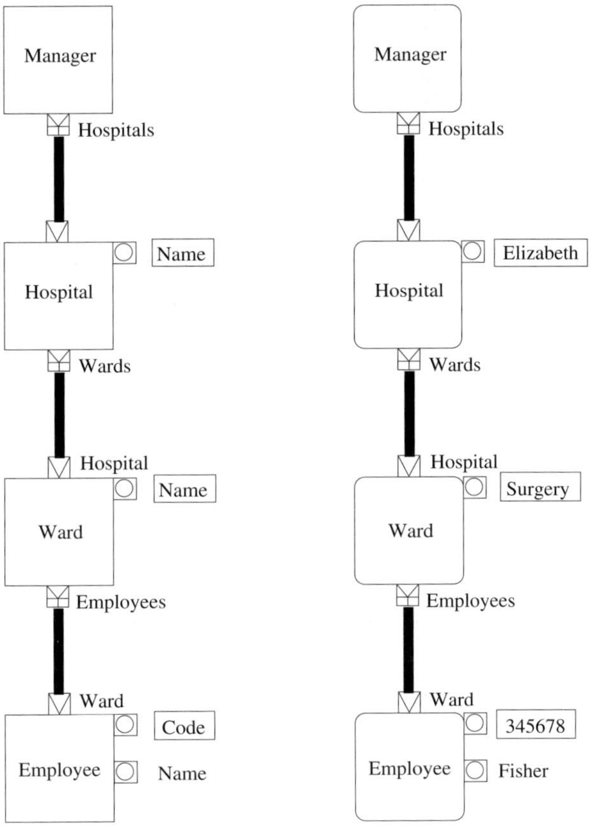

Figure 4.9: An instantiated ownership hierarchy

The ownership relationship type applies existential dependencies between owning and owned instances as mentioned above. What does this mean explicitly?

In the first place, an instance of type `Hospital` has to exist. This instance will be created by the manager which we shall not consider.
The `Hospital` instance represents a particular hospital, e.g. *Elizabeth.*

Elizabeth hospital has several wards among them *Surgery.*
This is expressed thus: the instance *Surgery* of `Ward` is owned by the instance *Elizabeth* of type `Hospital`. The instance `Surgery` has to be created out of *Elizabeth* hospital.

Now the created instance *Surgery* of `Ward` can be considered: *Surgery* has a number of employees, among them *Fisher* having the `Employee.Code` *345678.*
This is expressed thus: the instance *345678* of `Employee` is owned by the instance *Surgery* of `Ward`.
The instance *345678* must be created and deleted out of *Surgery.*

It is important to understand that we build a hierarchy of related instances, as illustrated in Figure 4.9. The upper instances own the lower. It is always clear which instance is owned by which.

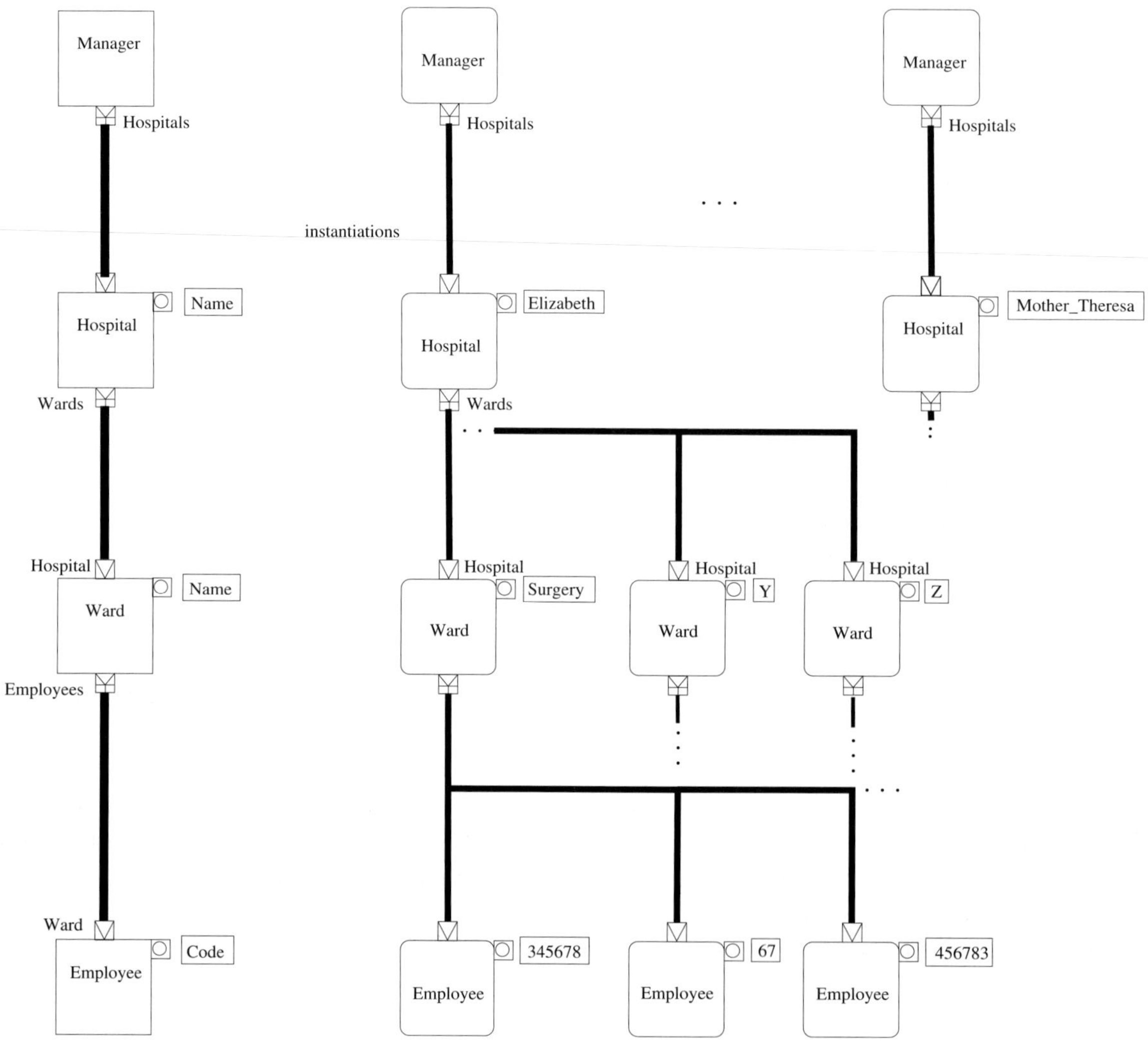

Figure 4.10: More details of the instantiated ownership hierarchy

This approach has consequences for the semantics of the objects. With the ownership hierarchy, we build a semantic context of the objects. To illustrate what is meant, consider the small hierarchy we can build with the three instances of Figure 4.9. In Figure 4.10 the same example is shown but with more details concerning other instances.

We consider the hierarchy starting with *Fisher*, `Employee.Code` *345678*.
The instance `Employee.Code` *345678* has three meanings depending on the context.

1. If we only see the last object type of the ownership hierarchy, and here it is the instance `Employee.Code` *345678*, the meaning is: *Fisher*. We find the name through the value of the attribute `Name` for the instance `Employee.Code` *345678*.

2. If we extend the context to the owner instance of `Employee.Code` *345678*, we consider *Surgery.Employees:345678*. The meaning is: *Fisher* is an employee of *Surgery*.

3. If we extend the context further to the owner instance of *Surgery.Employees:345678*, we consider *Elizabeth.Wards:Surgery.Employees:345678*. The meaning is: *Fisher* is an employee of the surgical ward of *Elizabeth* hospital.

Now we start the consideration at the root instance:

- From the root we go down the hierarchy to: *Elizabeth* hospital.
- We extend the context through the relation *Elizabeth.Wards* and one of the references contained in the set of references within *Elizabeth.Wards*: `Surgery`. The meaning is then: *Elizabeth* with its surgical ward.
- We extend the context through the relation `Ward.Employees` and one of the references contained in the set of references within `Ward.Employees`: *345678*. The meaning is: *Elizabeth* hospital with its surgical ward with its employee *345678* (*Fisher*).

We can imagine the observations here described as zooming in or out of a particular object, here the instance *Elizabeth* of object type `Hospital`.
The ownership hierarchy represents a *refinement* of the root object with respect to those objects which are existentially dependent on it.
We can access all the refined objects too by *going down* the hierarchy (zooming in). *Going up* the hierarchy (zooming out) means accessing a larger grain object.

Perspective-DB maintains the ownership hierarchy automatically. The system's understanding of ownership relationships has the following consequences:

As soon as *Elizabeth* hospital is accessed Perspective-DB gets the tree of instances constituted by the ownership hierarchy beneath. Now we can *walk through* the hierarchy by choosing one of the references contained in the owner-relation and repeating the process on that selected object etc.
Therefore, we will not get *Surgery* ward of *Mother-Theresa* hospital by accident if we are busy with *Surgery* ward of *Elizabeth* hospital.

4.10 Perspective-DB Legend

The important constructs of the first order object model have now been explained. We now summarize the graphical representation of the Perspective-DB object model in the following legend, see Figure 4.11.
We refer to object schemas, represented by the notation of this legend as canonical schemas.

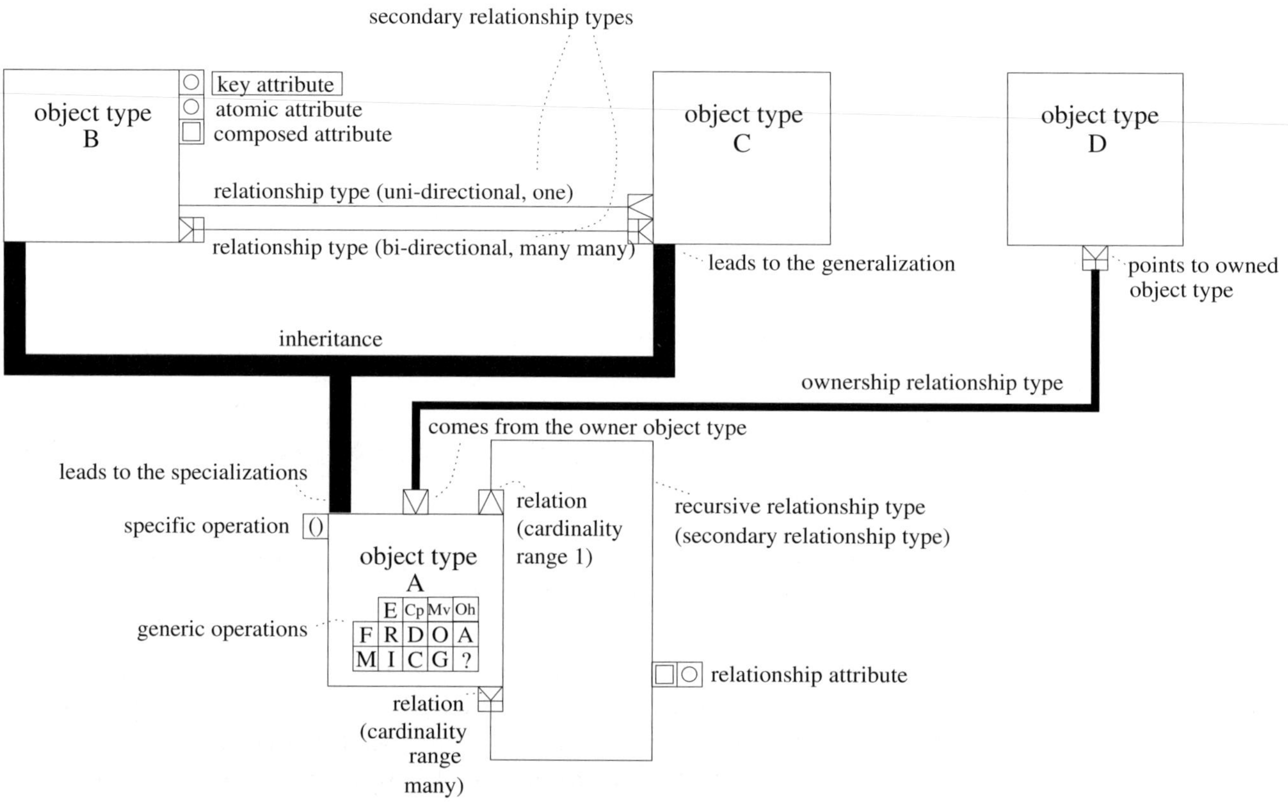

Figure 4.11: The Perspective-DB graphical object model legend

Chapter 5

User Views of the Object Model

5.1 Developer and End-User Views of a Layer

A **View** focuses an object schema to suit the observation point of a particular type of user. A different observation angle shows different aspects of the object schema. A view can also present the same aspects using different appearances. For example, suppose we are observing instances of object types. We can view these in canonical schematic form or in tabular form.
In Chapter 2 Section 5 we explain the terms implementation modeling; how the objects we deal with are constructed inside, and interface modeling; how we *see* an object we are using. An application layer (the system built on top of the ODBMS, see Chapter 19) is represented in two main views: the **Developer View** which is the view of the implementation and the **End-user View** which is the view of the interface.
The Developer and End-user Views are synonyms for the **Implementation** and **Interface Views**. The reason for using the terms Developer and End-user is because they reflect the role of the persons who deal with these views. The end-user only needs to deal with the Interface View. The developers deal with both views. They must always understand the end-user's point of view because this is what drives the development and defines the specification for what the application should do.
An illustration of these two views of a module is given in Figure 5.1. The end-user's angle shows what is happening on the surface, and the developer's angle shows what is happening inside. The two views keep the development and using aspects of the application separated. The same object model applies to both views.

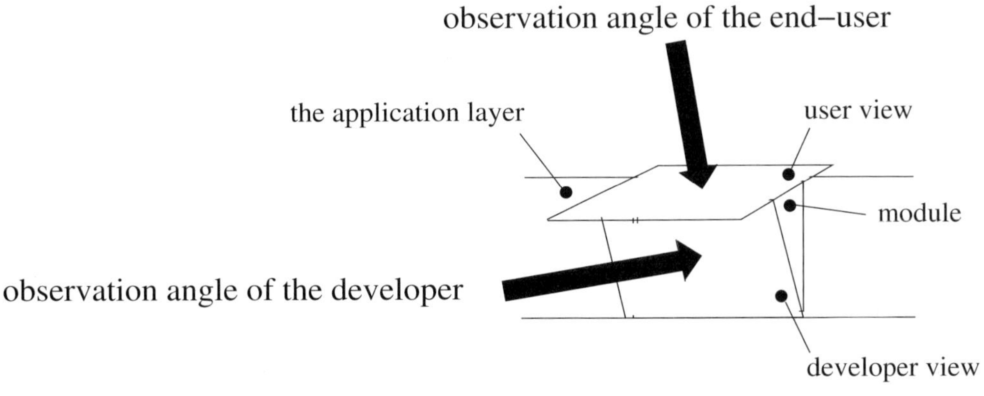

Figure 5.1: Illustration of the developer and the end-user view

In the following we explain the two views in more detail and show consequences for the graphical representation of the object schema within both views.

5.1.1 Role of the Developer View

The developer view describes how the application is constructed:

- The inheritance hierarchies, starting with the most generic object types and leading up to the object types visible to the end-user. The inheritance hierarchy crosses several layers.
- The members of each object type in the hierarchy are specified. The member is not repeated in specializations unless there is a change. In the case of attribute members this implies a change in the range of the values; in the case of relation members, a change in the configuration of the connectivity; in the case of operations, a change in the functionality.

The examples used throughout the chapter are based on the Hospital Case Study introduced in 1.1.

5.1.2 Role of the End-User View

The end-user view describes the object types visible at the interface:

- Instances of these object types are created, manipulated and destroyed. When looking from above one can observe all the interface object types at the top of each inheritance hierarchy. To understand this better, imagine the left side of Figure 5.2 projected on the front side of Figure 5.1 and the right side of Figure 5.2 projected on the the top side of Figure 5.1.
- All inherited members are present in the interface object types. Therefore an end-user observes the inherited attributes, operations, and relations with their connectors without seeing where they originate.

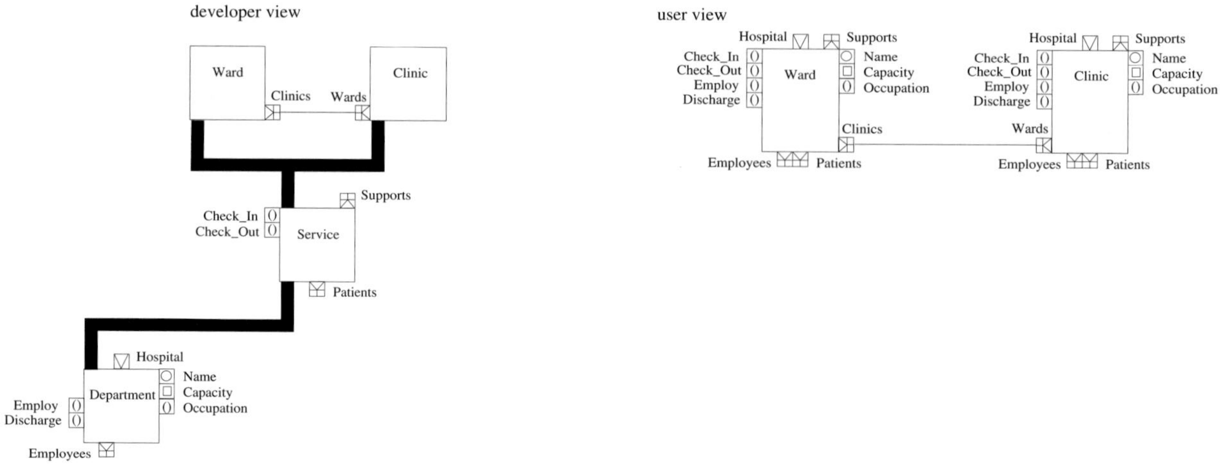

Figure 5.2: Presentation of members in the developer view (left) and in the end-user view (right)

5.2 Presentation of Members

Illustrated in Figure 5.2. The left side of the figure shows a part of the developer view containing the inheritance hierarchy branch from `Department` to `Ward` and `Clinic`. The right side of the figure shows the user view.

The developer view describes the inheritance order, the user view describes the result; what can be observed at the interface of the highest specialization. Figure 5.2 also shows the secondary relationship type between `Clinic` and `Ward`. This is a relationship type between the most specialized object types of the inheritance hierarchy branch shown. In this simple case there is no difference in the appearance of this relationship type in the developer or user views. More intricate cases of relationship types are considered in the following section.

5.3 Presentation of Relationship Types

When a relation member is defined in a generalization it is duplicated in each specialization of the user view, as is the case for any member. In addition the connectors are duplicated too. This is necessary to capture all the occurrences of the relation type. Duplication can occur on one side or on both sides. A duplication causes a split in the connector. In the following section we provide `examples` with secondary relations and in the following section, with ownership relations.

5.3.1 Secondary Relations

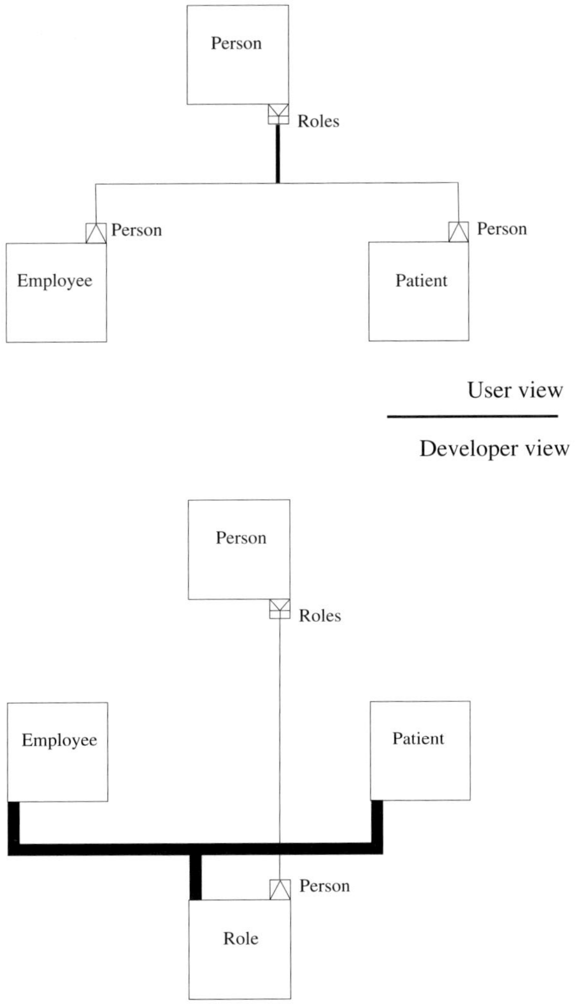

Figure 5.3: Presentation of a secondary relationship with a split on one side

Split on one side
In Figure 5.3 it is modeled that persons can play the role of patient and employee. The developers view shows that the relation `Person` is defined in object type `Role`. The end-user view shows that the relation `Person` occurs twice, inherited by `Patient` and `Employee`. The relation `Roles` of object type `Person` occurs only once in the user view because it is defined in the same object. The `example` shows that the connector-line splits at one end. The different thicknesses of the connectors in the user view make it clear that person instances connect to patient and employee instances, but patient and employee instances cannot connect to each other.

Conventions:
1. At a splitting point you have to continue on a connector of a different thickness from the connector you are coming from.
2. Depending on where you start, the thickness of the connectors must either constantly increase or decrease.
3. The number of splitting points in a relationship type should be minimal. The minimum is reached if none of the splitting points can be deleted without introducing ambiguity in deciding the flow of a relationship.

Heterogeneous relationship: The relationship from `Person.Roles` to `Employee.Person` and `Patient.Person` is heterogeneous, because `Person` can contain numerous instances of both types in the relation `Roles`.

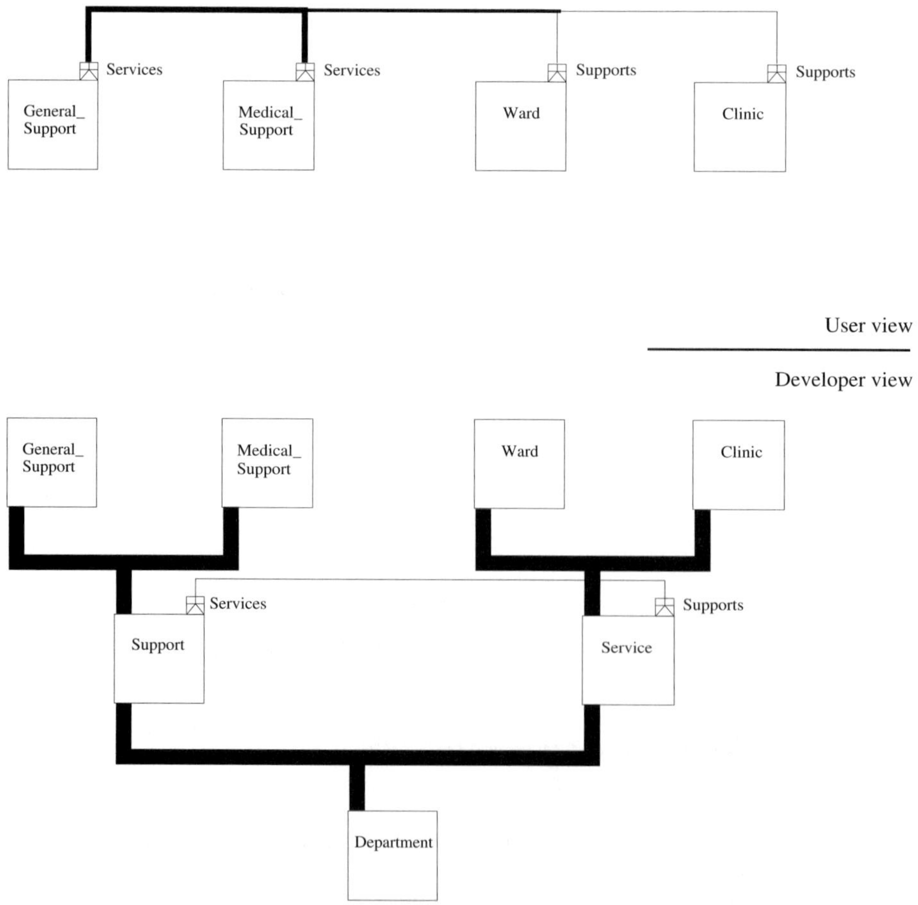

Figure 5.4: Presentation of a secondary relationship with a split on both sides

Split on both sides
Figure 5.4 shows an inherited secondary relationship type duplicated in the user view. The departments are specialized in support and service departments. Support departments are specialized further in general and medical support departments. Service departments are specialized further in wards and clinics. Support and service departments are related to each other. The interpretation of this relationship type is: support departments, such as laboratory, provide support to service departments, such as surgical.
The `example` shows that the connector-line splits at both ends. The reason is that both `General_Support` and `Medical_Support` provide services to `Ward` and `Clinic`. At instance level, `Medical_Support` instance *Laboratory* provides service to `Clinic` instance *Surgery* and *Orthopaedic*. Moreover, `General_Support` *Kitchen* also provides service to *Surgery* and *Orthopaedic*. The different thicknesses of the connectors in the user view make it clear that service instances can only connect to support instances.

Heterogeneous relationship: The relationship from `Ward.Supports` to `General_Support.Services` and `General_Support.Services` is heterogeneous.
The relationship from `Clinic.Supports` to `General_Support.Services` and `General_Support.Services` is also heterogeneous[1].

5.3.2 Owner Relations

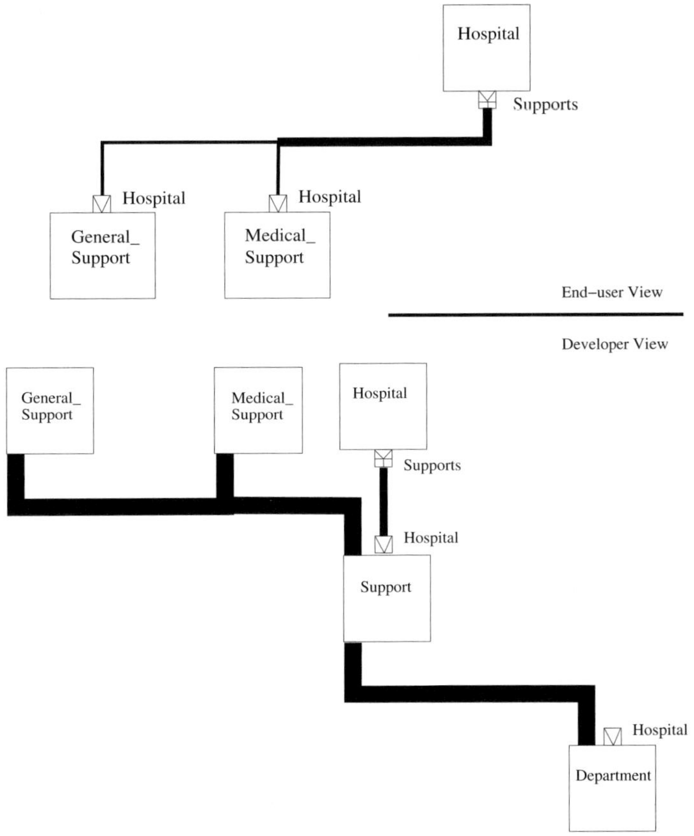

Figure 5.5: Presentation of a split at the owned side

[1]In this case this has been achieved using one relation in the generalization object-type `Support` and in the generalization object-type `Service`. Using the same relation in the generalization is compact and enhances reuse, however, the same result could be achieved by defining the relations `Services` and `Supports` separately in the specializations.

Split at the owned side

Figure 5.5 shows that between General_Support and Medical_Support at the owned end of the ownership relationship type and Hospital at the owning end, only one ownership relationship type exists. *Going along* the connector with Hospital.Supports as source, you come to the splitting point where two connector lines diverge, each with a different thickness from the one you came from. This means you can take either one of them to end up at one of the target ends. *Going along* the connector with e.g. General_Support.Hospital as source you come to the splitting point where two connector lines diverge. One of them has the same thickness as the one you came from. That connector line is therefore forbidden for continuing your trip. It would lead you back to a source end (also an owned relation). The other connector line has a different thickness which permits you to continue your trip. It will lead you to a target end (the owner relation).

Note that in the developer view the relation Hospital has been duplicated in object type Support because it describes that object type Hospital is connected to Support via the relation Supports. In the object Department it is not yet known where relation Hospital connects.

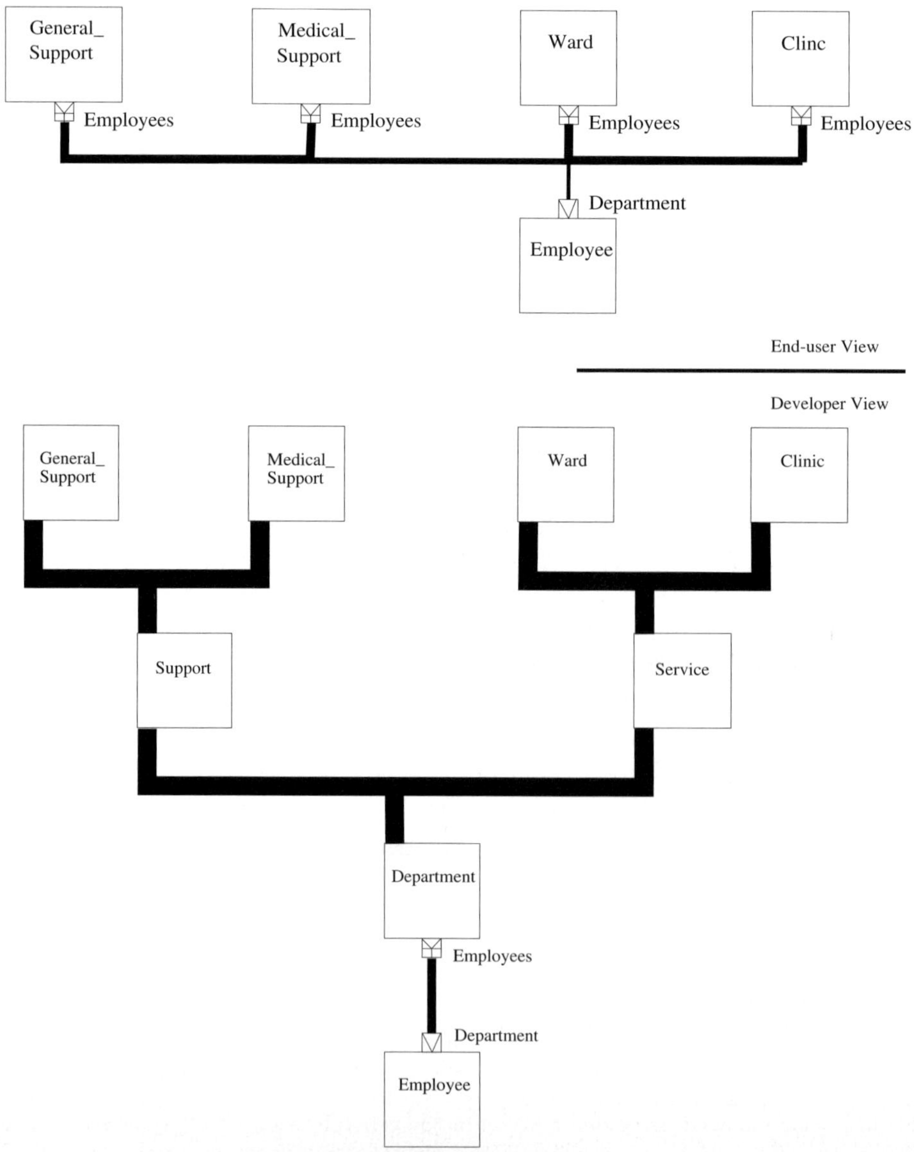

Figure 5.6: Presentation of a split at the owner side

Split at the owner side
Figure 5.6 shows that `Department` owns `Employee`. The developer view describes that the four specializations of `Department` inherit the ownership with `Employee`. Therefore, in the user view the split end of the relationship type is at the owner side.

In the ownership hierarchy of Figure 5.6 the several branches represent the same ownership relationship type. At instance level, an owned instance has only *one* owner instance. That owner instance can be of one of the (specialized) owner object types. An employee instance is owned by an instance of `General_Support` *or* `Medical_Support` *or* `Ward` *or* `Clinic`.

5.4 Splitting versus Adding Relations

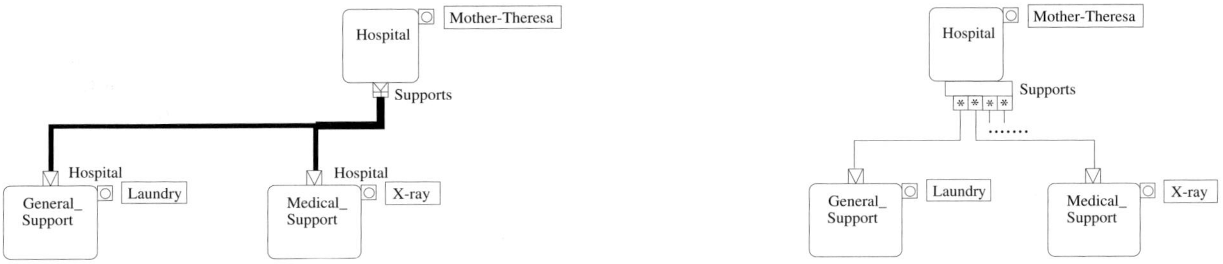

Figure 5.7: An example of a set of references contained in a relation instance, developer view (left) and end-user view (right)

It is clear from the previous section that a **source** relation connects to several **target** relations and vice-versa. This raises the question: *when is it better to define a new relation as opposed to re-using and thereby splitting a relation?*

5.4.1 A Case of Splitting

The left side of Figure 5.7 is an `example` of Figure 5.5 at instance level. The ownership hierarchy of Figure 5.5 between `Hospital` and `General_Support` and `Medical_Support` is an example of a split ownership relationship type. Both support department object types share the relation `Hospital.Supports`. The instances owned by a particular hospital, `e.g.` *Mother-Theresa* refer in this situation to the same set of references within the shared relation instance *Mother-Theresa.Supports*. This is possible because it is guaranteed that there is no other instance of both specialized object types having the same key value as here, having the same department name.
On the right side of Figure 5.7 the relation `Supports` is blown-up to show what goes on inside the relation; it shows a collection of references in the form of a list to the `Support` instances of type `General` and `Medical`.

Consequences:
1. This configuration implies that it is not possible to have an instance of type `General` and an instance of type `Medical` with the same key.
2. It is not possible to distinguish the two types based on access to the relation `Supports`. Suppose it is desirable to access only instances of type `General`. In this case it is necessary to iterate the list and filter the type `General` from the type `Medical`.
3. If the number of `Support` instances is very large the list will be very long. This can have a negative impact on the performance of the system.

Design Decision:
The reason for choosing to re-use the relation was based on the assumption that these consequences are not relevant in this case. Re-use reduces the number of design components and complexity of the application and is therefore preferred.

5.4.2 A Case of Adding

Let us now study the ownership situation between the owner `Hospital` and the owned object types `Clinic` and `Ward`, see left side of Figure 5.8. In the Universe of Discourse, clinics and wards cooperate. Cooperating clinics and wards usually belong to the same hospital. The `Wards` and `Clinics` are separate relations of object type `Hospital`.

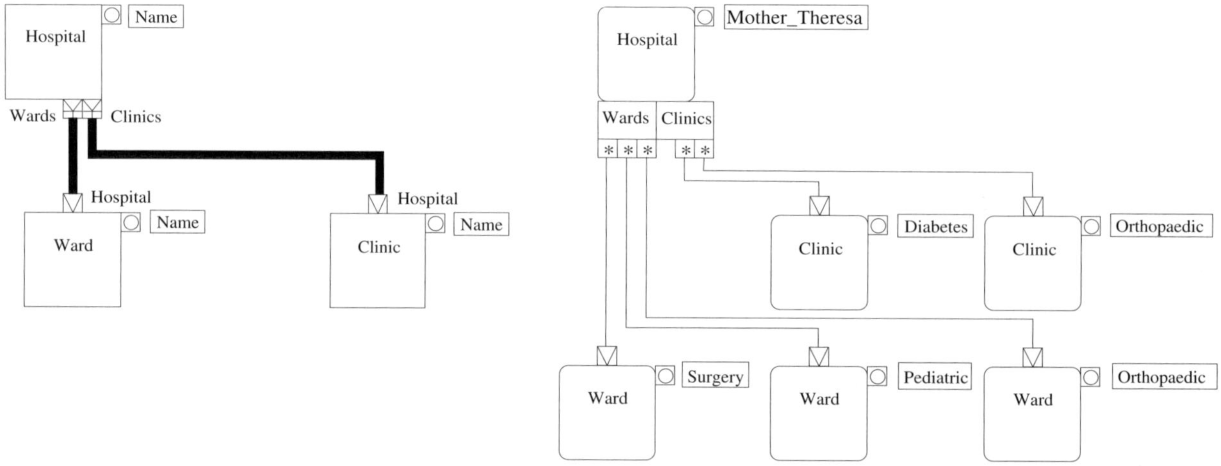

Figure 5.8: An example where one branch of the ownership hierarchy would cause problems, developer view (left) and end-user view (right)

Consequences:
1. Since instances of each type have a different owner relation it is possible to give clinics and wards identical keys. For `example`, we can name both clinic and ward *Orthopaedic*, as shown in the right side of Figure 5.8.
2. Whenever information relating only to ward is required, we can access `Wards` without needing to filter out instances of type `Clinic`.
3. We have two smaller collections making iteration and management of the collections more efficient.

Design Decision:
The reason for choosing to add a relation was based on the assumption that these consequences are relevant in this case.

5.4.3 Secondary relationship types

The uniqueness of key does not play a role in the decision process, however the quantity and filtering criteria do.
The relation instance always contains the list of references to the related instances (at the other side of the relationship type). There is always only *one* list for any relation instance, independent of how often the connector line is split up. The reason being that the split relationship type is in fact only one relationship type.

Chapter 6

Applying the Views to the Case Study

6.1 Introduction

This case study shows how to design a simple application with the Perspective-DB object model.

The UoD of the case concerns a hospital information system as described in 1.1.
We first present the end-user's specifications, followed by an explanation of the design process for production of the end-user schema shown in Figure 6.1. We repeat this process for the developer's view.

6.2 The End-user View

6.2.1 The End-user View Specification

- `Hospital`: a hospital registered in the information system.
  - It has one or more `Clinics`, `Wards`, `Medical Support` and `General Support` departments.
  - It has a unique `Name`, and at least one `Address`.
  - It has `Video` which produces a picture of the hospital.
- `Ward`: a department of a `Hospital` treating in-`Patients` and offering beds to its `Patients`.
  - It can co-operate with one or more `Clinics` of the same or other hospitals.
  - It can also co-operate with one or more `Medical Support` and `General Support` departments of the same or other hospitals.
  - It has a `Name`.
  - It has a `Video` that produces a picture of the `Ward`.
  - It has a `Capacity` defining the maximum number of treatment places (beds).
  - It has a number of `Patients`.
  - The `Patients` remain overnight.
  - It has a number of `Employees`.
  - It can compute the actual `Occupation` of its treatment places.
  - It checks-in and checks-out `Patients`.
  - It hires and discharges `Employees`.

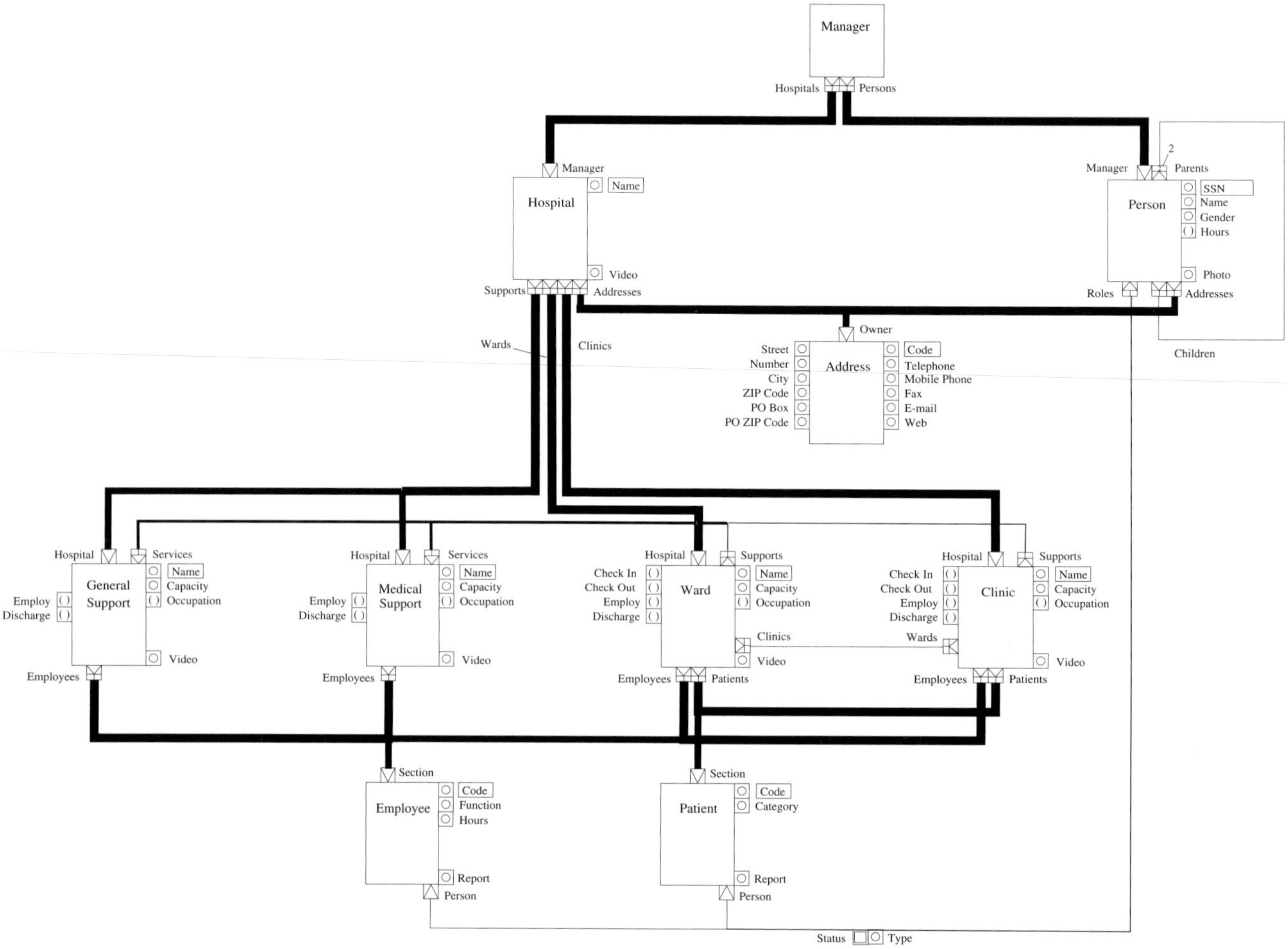

Figure 6.1: The end-user view of the Hospital case

- `Clinic`: a department of a `Hospital` treating out-`Patients`.
  - It can co-operate with one or more `Wards` of the same or other hospitals.
  - It can also co-operate with one or more `Medical Support` and `General Support` departments of the same or other hospitals.
  - It has a `Name`.
  - It has a `Video` showing the clinic.
  - It has a `Capacity` defining the maximum number of treatment places.
  - It has a number of `Patients`.
  - The `Patients` arrive for their treatment and depart the same day (beds are not required).
  - It has a number of `Employees`.
  - It can compute the actual `Occupation` of its treatment places.
  - It checks-in and checks-out `Patients` and hires and discharges `Employees`.
- `Medical Support`: a department of a `Hospital` offering medical services to other departments, `e.g.` medical lab services, X-ray services etc.
  - It can co-operate with one or more `Wards` and `Clinics` of the same or other hospitals.

- It has a `Name`.
- It has a `Video` showing the department.
- It has a `Capacity` defining the maximum number of support places.
- It can compute the actual `Occupation` of its medical support places.
- It has a number of `Employees`.
- It hires and discharges `Employees`.

- `General Support`: a department of a `Hospital` offering general services to other departments including general services to `Patients` and `Employees`, such as catering.
  - It can co-operate with one or more `Wards` and `Clinics` of the same or other hospitals.
  - It has a `Name`.
  - It has a `Video` showing the department.
  - It has a `Capacity` defining the maximum number of support places.
  - It can compute the actual `Occupation` of its general support places.
  - It has a number of `Employees`.
  - It hires and discharges `Employees`.
- `Employee`: a work position at a `Ward, Clinic, Medical, and General Support`.
  - Employee is hired and discharged by the `Ward, Clinic, Medical Support` and `General Support` departments where he/she works.
  - Employee has a `Code`, a `Function`, the number of `Hours` the person is employed for, and a `Report` about skills etc.
  - Employee has a `Status` describing whether the person works full-time or part-time.
- `Patient`: a person who receives treatment from a `Ward` or a `Clinic`.
  - Patient is checked-in and checked-out by the `Ward` or `Clinic` where he/she is treated.
  - Patient has a `Code`, a `Category` in accordance with the kind of his/her health insurance, and a `Medical Report`.
  - Patient has a `Status` describing the kind of health insurance which he/she has.
- `Person`: a person who is employed by or treated at one or more `Hospitals`.
  - Person has a `Social Security Number`, a `Name`, a `Gender`, a home and at least one `Address`.
  - A `Photo` is available of the `Person`.
  - In the case that the person is employed at any of the hospitals, the total number of `Hours` the person is employed can be computed.
  - In the case of a minor, the system registers who the person's parents are.
  - A person can be treated by one ward only at a time.
- `Address`: an address of a `Hospital` or `Person` which has the following members.
  - `Code`; to distinguish the type of address, e.g. home or work.
  - `Street`; name of the street.

- Number; house number.
- City; name of the city.
- ZIP Code; postal code of the city and street.
- PO Box; post office box.
- PO ZIP Code; zip code of the PO Box.
- Telephone; main phone number.
- Mobile Phone; of contact person.
- Fax; main fax at the location.
- E-mail; main e-mail at the location.
- Web; main web site at the location.

6.2.2 Designing the End-user View Schema

We shall now apply the graphical object model to map the specification to a schema.

Structure

- Ownership hierarchy:
  - The root of the hierarchy begins with the module manager Manager.
    This manager is the owner of the whole ownership-hierarchy and is responsible for all objects in the Hospital-module. The manager, which is the sole root object of the hierarchy, is already instantiated.
  - The manager is the owner of the object types: Hospital and Person.
  - Hospital is the owner of the object types: General Support, Medical Support, Clinic, Ward and Address.
  - Clinic, Ward, General Support and Medical Support own Employee.
  - Clinic and Ward own Patient.
  - Person and Hospital are the owners of Address.

  The relationship types are bi-directional, so we can interpret the schema from the side of the owned object types as well. For illustration, Employee is owned by Clinic, Ward, General Support and Medical Support.

- Attributes:
  - Hospital has the attributes Name (key) and Video.
  - Person has the attributes SSN[1] (key), Name, Gender and Photo.
  - Ward, Clinic, General Support and Medical Support have the attributes Name (key), Capacity and Video.
  - Employee has the attributes Code (key), Function, Hours and Report. Hours gives the number of hours a person may work for a particular department.
  - Patient has the attributes Code (key) and Report.
  - Address has the attributes Code (key), Telephone, Mobile Phone, Fax, E-mail, Web, Street, Number, City, ZIP Code, PO Box and PO ZIP Code.

[1]Social Security Number (National Insurance Number in the UK).

- Secondary relations:
  - The relationships `General Support.Services - Ward.Supports`, `General Support.Services - Clinic.Supports`, `Medical Support.Services - Ward.Supports`, and `Medical Support.Services - Clinic.Supports` represent co-operation. This relationship is split at both ends and has cardinality range *many:many*.
  - The relationship `Ward.Clinics - Clinic.Wards` represents co-operation. The relationship has cardinality range *many:many*.
  - The relationship `Person.Parents - Person.Children` is used to associate a child with its parents. The cardinality range is *2:many*. This relationship is recursive.
  - The relationship `Person.Roles - Employee.Person` and `Person.Roles - Patient.Person` represent the roles of a person within hospitals. The relationship is split at one end. The relation `Person.Roles` is shared by `Employee` and `Patient`. The cardinality range is *many:1*.
- Relationship attribute:
  - The relationship `Person.Roles - Employee.Person` and `Person.Roles - Patient.Person` has a relationship attribute: `Status`. The status of the person is the type of insurance in the case of a patient and the type of employment in the case of an employee.

Behavior

- Specific operations:
  - `Person` has the operation `Hours`. This computes the number of hours a person is occupied in all employee roles in various departments of various hospitals.
  - `Ward, Clinic, General Support` and `Medical Support` have the operation `Occupation`, in order to calculate the number of patients being served. In the case of a `General` and `Medical Support` the `Occupation` calculates the number of patients of all the `Wards` and `Clinics` it serves[2].
  - `Ward, Clinic, General Support` and `Medical Support` have the operation `Employ`, in order to register a person as employee.
    The `Employ` operation takes the `Person.SSN` of a selected person instance, the `Employee.Code` of the new employee and the `Hours` the new employee works as input arguments[3]. The owner instance of the operation creates an instance of `Employee` with the given `Code`, sets `Employee.Hours` to the given `Hours`, and relates the new `Employee` instance to the given `Person` instance through the relationship `Employee.Person - Person.Roles`.
  - `Ward, Clinic, General Support` and `Medical Support` have the operation `Discharge`, in order to remove an employed person.
    The `Discharge` operation takes the `Employee.Code` of a selected employee instance. The owner instance of the operation destroys the instance of `Employee` with the given `Code` which causes the relation between the `Employee` instance to the given `Person` instance through the relationship `Employee.Person - Person.Roles` to be removed.

[2]Not to be confused with the attribute `Capacity` which limits the number of patients that can be served.

[3]The new employee instance does not yet exist, but the arguments Code and Hours can still be entered because the object Employee switches to the role of object type, rather than object instance.

- `Ward, Clinic` have the operation `Check In`, in order to register a person as patient.
  The `Check In` operation takes the `Person.SSN` of a selected person instance and the `Patient.Code` of the new patient as input arguments. The owner instance of the operation creates an instance of `Patient` with the given `Code` and relates the new `Patient` instance to the given `Person` instance through the relationship `Patient.Person - Person.Roles`.
- `Ward, Clinic` have the operation `Check Out`, in order to release a person as patient.
  The `Check Out` operation takes the `Patient.Code` of a selected patient instance. The owner instance of the operation destroys the instance of `Patient` with the given `Code`, which causes the relation between the `Patient` instance to the given `Person` instance through the relationship `Patient.Person - Person.Roles` to be removed.

• Creation and destruction of instances:

  - The sole instance `Manager` can create and destroy instances of type `Hospital` and `Person`, using the generic operations `Create` (**C**) and `Destroy` (**D**).
    The connection is made between `Manager.Hospitals` and `Hospital.Manager` as well as between `Manager.Persons` and `Person.Manager`.
  - A `Hospital` instance can create and destroy instances of type `General Support, Medical Support, Clinic` and `Ward` using the generic operations `Create` and `Destroy`. The connection is made or removed between `Hospital.Supports` and `General Support.Hospital` or `Medical Support.Hospital` and also between `Hospital.Wards` and `Wards.Hospital` and also between `Hospital.Clinics` and `Clinics.Hospital`.
  - Instances of type `Clinic, Ward, General Support` and `Medical Support` cannot create and destroy instances of type `Employee` using the generic operations `Create` and `Destroy`. This is done using the specific operations `Employ` and `Discharge`.
  - Instances of type `Clinic` or `Ward` cannot create and destroy instances of type `Patient` using the generic operations `Create` and `Destroy`. This is done using the specific operations `Check In` and `Check Out`.

• Insertion and removal of relationships:

  - To register that the instance *Orthopaedic* of type `Clinic` co-operates with the instance *Surgery* of type `Ward` the generic operation `Insert` (**I**) in either `Ward` or `Clinic` is used.
    To end their co-operation the generic operation `Remove` (**R**)is used. The connection is made between `Clinic.Wards` and `Ward.Clinics`.
  - To register that the instance *Surgery* of type `Ward` requires services from the instance *Laundry* of type `General Support` the generic operation `Insert` in `Ward` is used.
    To end their co-operation the generic operation `Remove` in `Ward` is used. The `Insert` and `Remove` operations are only applicable from `Ward`. The connection is made between `Ward.Supports` and `General Support.Services`. The same applies to Inserting and Removing between `Ward` and `Medical Support, Clinic` and `General Support` and `Clinic` and `Medical Support`.
  - Instances of type `Employee` cannot `Insert` or `Remove` a `Person` using the the generic operations `Insert` and `Remove`. This is done using the specific operations `Employ` and `Discharge`. The same applies to `Patient`. For the same reason instances of type `Person` cannot `Insert` or `Remove Employees` and `Patients`.
  - To associate a child with its parent the instance of type `Person` that is the child and the instance of type `Person` that is its parent are related using the generic operation `Insert`. The `Insert` can be applied via `Parent.Children` for the parent or `Person.Parents` for the child. The same applies for `Remove`.

6.3 The Developer View

The end-user's view shows the interface of the system. The developer's view shows the implementation of the system. The focus of the latter is therefore on the inheritance hierarchy of the object-types and where the members are defined. It is only necessary to add information to the developer's view that cannot be derived from the user-view.

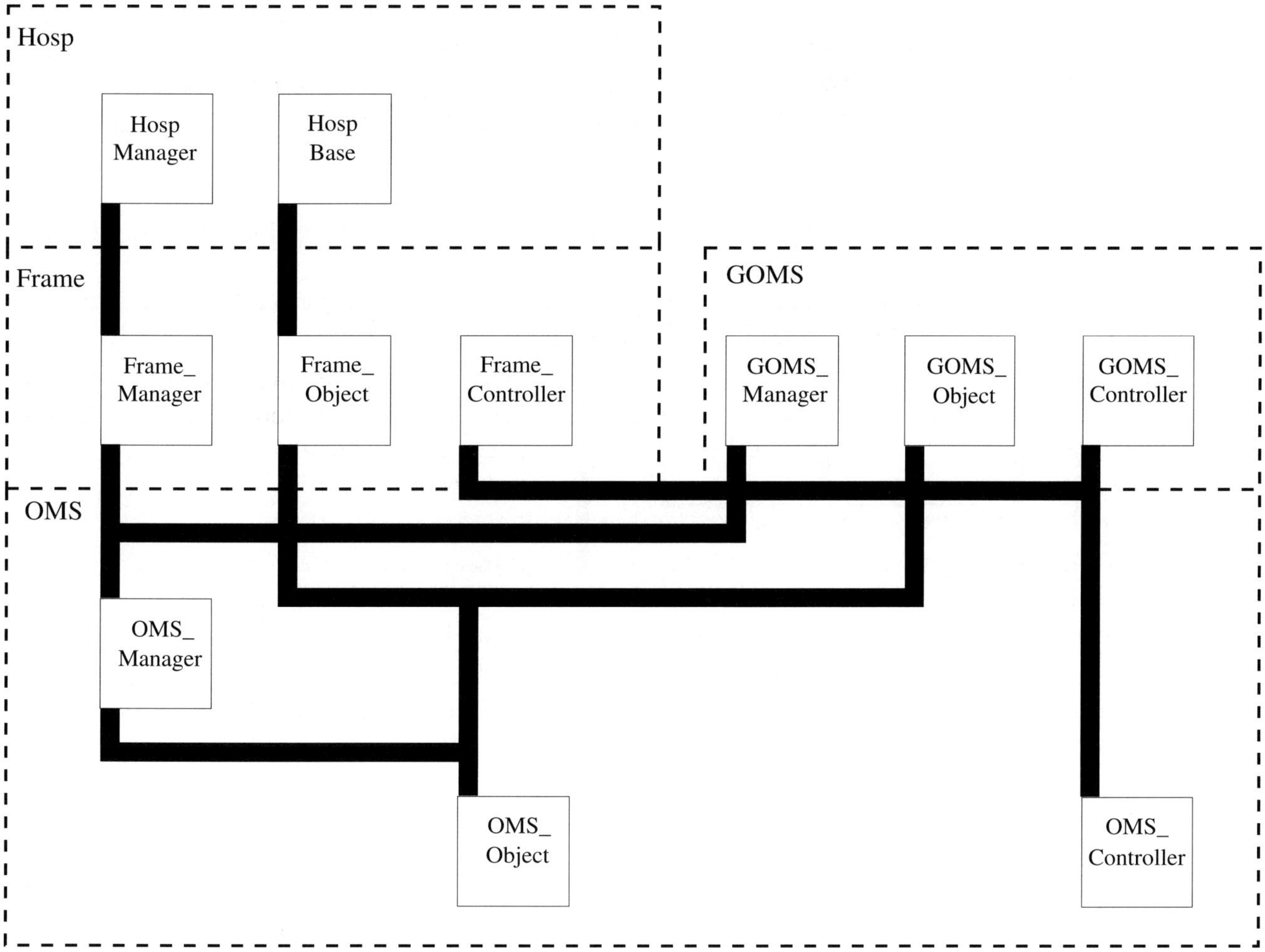

Figure 6.2: The foundation of the hospital system

6.3.1 The Foundation

The developer must determine on what layer to place the foundation of the system. The hospital system is a simple application therefore it is sufficient to define the system in one layer, using one module. This is shown in Figure 6.2. `Hospital` is built on the `Frame` layer which is the highest layer of functionality provided by the Perspective-DB system. The foundation of hospital consists of the object types `Hosp_Base` and `Hosp_Manager`. `Hosp_Base` is a specialization of `Frame_Object` and `Hosp_Manager` is a specialization of `Frame_Object_Manager`. See Chapter 19 and Figure 19.3 for information on system building object types.

Figure 6.3 shows the developer's object schema of the `Hospital` system. In the developer view it is practical to use an **object type reference**.

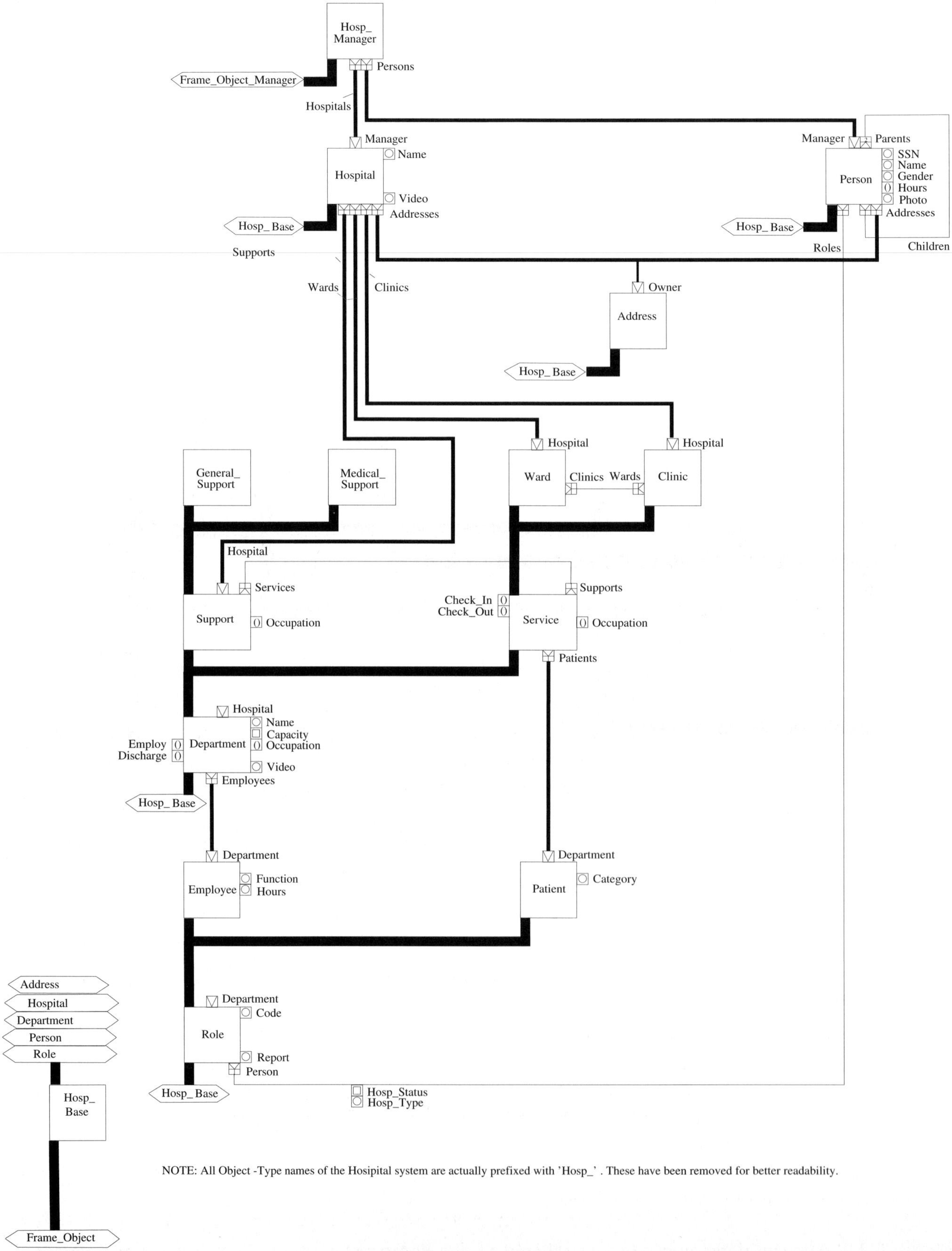

Figure 6.3: The developer view of the Hospital case

This construct enables reference to a particular object type without having to show its definition in order to avoid repetition of drawing the object type. In the schematic it is represented by a hexagon containing the name of the object type referred to. For example, Hosp_Manager has the object type reference Frame_Object_Manager as its base type, which means: Hosp_Manager inherits Frame_Object_Manager.

6.3.2 Inheritance Hierarchy

The rule of thumb during design is to avoid repetition of types and members by applying inheritance to obtain re-use. This means that the developer should strive to introduce generalized types to accommodate members that can be shared.

- Hosp_Base is the generalization of Department, Hospital, Person, Role and Address[4]. Defining a base class for the module is good practice because it provides a point in the system hierarchy from where it is possible to identify object types as belonging to hospital, i.e. they are all specializations of Hosp_Base. Moreover, it is possible to add common structure and behavior for all the object types in the module.

- Frame_Object_Manager is the generalization of Hosp_Manager. The model requires each module to have its unique manager object type. The manager instance forms the entry point to all instances in the module and contains specific management functionality for the module.

- Address appears in the end-user schema, so it is not necessary to repeat the description of its members.

- Hospital appears in the end-user schema.

- Department is the generalization of Support and Service. It adds members common to all four end-user department types as follows:

  The attributes Name, Capacity and Video.

  The special operations Employ and Discharge.

  The ownership relation (owner-side) Employees.

  The ownership relation (owned-side) Hospital which is not connected, because the owner relation is determined in its specializations.

  The operation Occupation, which is a stub since the functionality calculating occupation is determined in the specializations.

- Support is the generalization of General_Support and Medical_Support.

  It adds the secondary relation Services.

  Its relation Hospital is connected to relation Hospital.Supports.

  It overrules the operation Occupation to suit support departments. The calculation is based on the total number of patients in all service departments that are served[5].

[4]All object type names of the Hospital system are actually prefixed with 'Hosp_' which is the abbreviated name of the system. For example the object type Person is actually named Hosp_Person. This is important to identify to which part of a complex system an object type belongs and to avoid naming collisions between object types in different sub-systems. The system prefix has been removed for better readability.

[5]Not to be confused with Capacity which limits the total amount of persons that can be served.

- `Service` is the generalization of `Ward` and `Clinic`.

  It adds the secondary relation `Supports`.

  It adds the operations `Check_In` and `Check_Out` needed by `Service` types.

  It overrules the operation `Occupation` to suit service departments. The calculation is based on the number of patients treated by the department.

- `Ward` appears in the end-user schema.

  It adds the secondary relation `Clinics`.

  Its relation `Hospital` is connected to relation `Hospital.Wards`.

- `Clinic` appears in the end-user schema.

  It adds the secondary relation `Wards`.

  Its relation `Hospital` is connected to relation `Hospital.Clinics`.

- `General_Support` is in the end-user schema.

- `Medical_Support` is in the end-user schema.

- `Role` is the generalization of `Employee` and `Patient`. It adds members common to both end-user role types as follows:

  The attributes: the key `Code` and `Report`.

  The secondary relation `Person`.

  The ownership relation (owned-sited) `Department`. This relation is not connected because the owner relation is determined in its specializations.

- `Employee` appears in the end-user schema.

  It adds the attribute `Function` and `Hours`.

  Its relation `Department` connects to `Department.Employees`.

- `Patient` appears in the end-user schema.

  It adds the attribute `Category`.

  Its relation Department connects to `Service.Patients`.

- `Person` appears in the end-user schema and adds as follows:

  The attributes: `SSN, Name, Gender` and `Photo`;

  The special operation `Hours`.

  The ownership relation (owned-side) `Manager`.

  The ownership relation (owned-side) `Addresses`.

  The secondary relation `Roles`.

  The recursive secondary relationship type between `Person.Parents` and `Person.Children`.

- `Relation_Attribute` is the generalization of `Status`. `Relation_Attribute` is an object type defined in layer VOMS of Perspective-DB.

  The relationship type between `Person.Roles` and `Role.Person` is characterized by the attribute `Status` which adds the attribute `Type`.

6.3.3 Design Decisions

- The main purpose of the type `Department` is to accommodate the relations `Hospital` and `Employees` and the operations `Employ` and `Discharge` shared by the four end-user specializations.

- The purpose of the distinction between `Service` types and `Support` types is due to the relationship `Support.Services - Service.Supports`, the fact that methods `Check_In` and `Check_Out` and the relation `Patients` only apply to `Service` types and to overrule the `Occupation` calculation.

- The purpose of the general type `Role` is to provide a place for the relations `Department` and `Persons` that are shared by the types `Employee` and `Person`.

- A possible enhancement to the design is to create a general type for `Hospital` and `Person` because they both have a relation `Manager` and `Addresses`.

6.3.4 Comparing Developer and End-user Views

- The developer view contains all the object types found in the end-user view, as expected.

- The end-user view only shows the leaf object types of the hierarchy, because these are the tangible object types the end-user can manipulate. The developer view shows all relevant object types that contribute to the leaf object types. For `example`, the end-user view does not show that `Employee` and `Patient` are `Roles` of a `Person`.

- In the end-user view the members are all represented clustered in the leaf object types. In the developers view the members are shown in the object type where they are added. They are not redrawn in specialized types unless their meaning is overruled.

- In the end-user view the relations are explicitly defined between the leaf object types. In the developer view the relations are defined between the generic types and are redrawn only if the connectivity is overruled.

- The members that appear in the end-user view are positioned as in the developer view. For example, take the member `Capacity` in `Department` in the developers view. The same member appears in the same position in its specializations in the end-user view. Another example is the relationship `Clinics` and `Wards` in `Ward` and `Clinic`.

- The positioning of the object-types remains consistent between the developers and end-user view. In the developer's view not only is the object-type inheritance hierarchy taken into consideration but also the object-type ownership hierarchy. For `example`, the object-types `Hosp_Manager`, `Hospital` and `Ward` appear at the same height and level in both views. When differences are unavoidable due to the different objectives of the end-user and developer views, they are minimized.

- General design rules are also upheld. For example, the crossing of lines is minimized. This cannot be avoided completely because of other design rules, such as keeping members in permanent positions. In addition, the lines are drawn either horizontally or vertically because diagonal lines put extra strain on the viewer. The ownership hierarchies are kept vertical with owners always above owned object types, and owner relations centered when possible. Care is taken that the names of object types and members conform to the naming conventions. For `example`, `General_Support` as opposed to *GeneralSupport*.

Prefixing of object types with the layer name (in the developer view) is important, even in this simple case, in order to avoid name conflicts with object types in underlying layers, and to identify clearly the layer to which an object type belongs. Care is taken to distinguish clearly between owner and non-owner relations.

- The developer is given insight into the implementation of the object type, i.e. to the inheritance tree to a depth necessary to carry out the implementation of the application.

6.4 The Instantiation View

The object base changes with each operation performed by the application as instances are created and destroyed, relations between instances inserted and removed and the values of attributes modified.

The instantiation schema is therefore a snap-shot of a selected part of the application. Figure 6.4 shows a part of the instantiation object schema of the `Hospital` system.
The instantiation schema is useful in case studies aimed at verifying whether the Universe of Discourse maps correctly into the object base and application in detail. Several scenarios, each with a small amount of representative data are sufficient to check the quality of the object base design. During the study it helps to lay the end-user view beside the instantiation view to simulate what happens in the instantiation view when a particular operation is invoked, when a relationship is navigated, and when a particular query is processed. The simulated actions must succeed, otherwise the design has to be adapted.
The schema in Figure 6.4 is an example of a scenario concerning information on two hospitals. `Hospital` has two instances: *Mother-Theresa* and *Elizabeth.*

`Person` has four instances: *123456, 123457, 345123, 789234* (the Social Security Numbers).

Mother Theresa hospital has the address: *code Main. Person 123456 address: code Main.*

Mother Theresa hospital has two general support departments: *Laundry* and *Kitchen.* It also has two medical support departments: *X-Ray* and *Blood-Lab.* The four support departments have a common owner relation. A limitation is that it is not possible to have a general and medical support instance with the same name (the key), because each must be unique in the scope of their owner.

Mother Theresa hospital has three wards: *Surgery, Pediatric, Orthopaedic.* It has one clinic: *Orthopaedic.*

Wards and clinics have a separate owner relation which means that a ward and a clinic of Mother Theresa hospital can have the same name (name is the key).

The *Blood-Lab* supports the wards *Surgery, Pediatric* and *Orthopaedic* as well as the *Orthopaedic* clinic.

Ward *Surgery* has three employees: *code 0003, 0007* and *0023.* All three employees are already existing persons, see the relations `Employ.Person` and `Person.Roles` for persons *123456, 123457,* and *345123.*

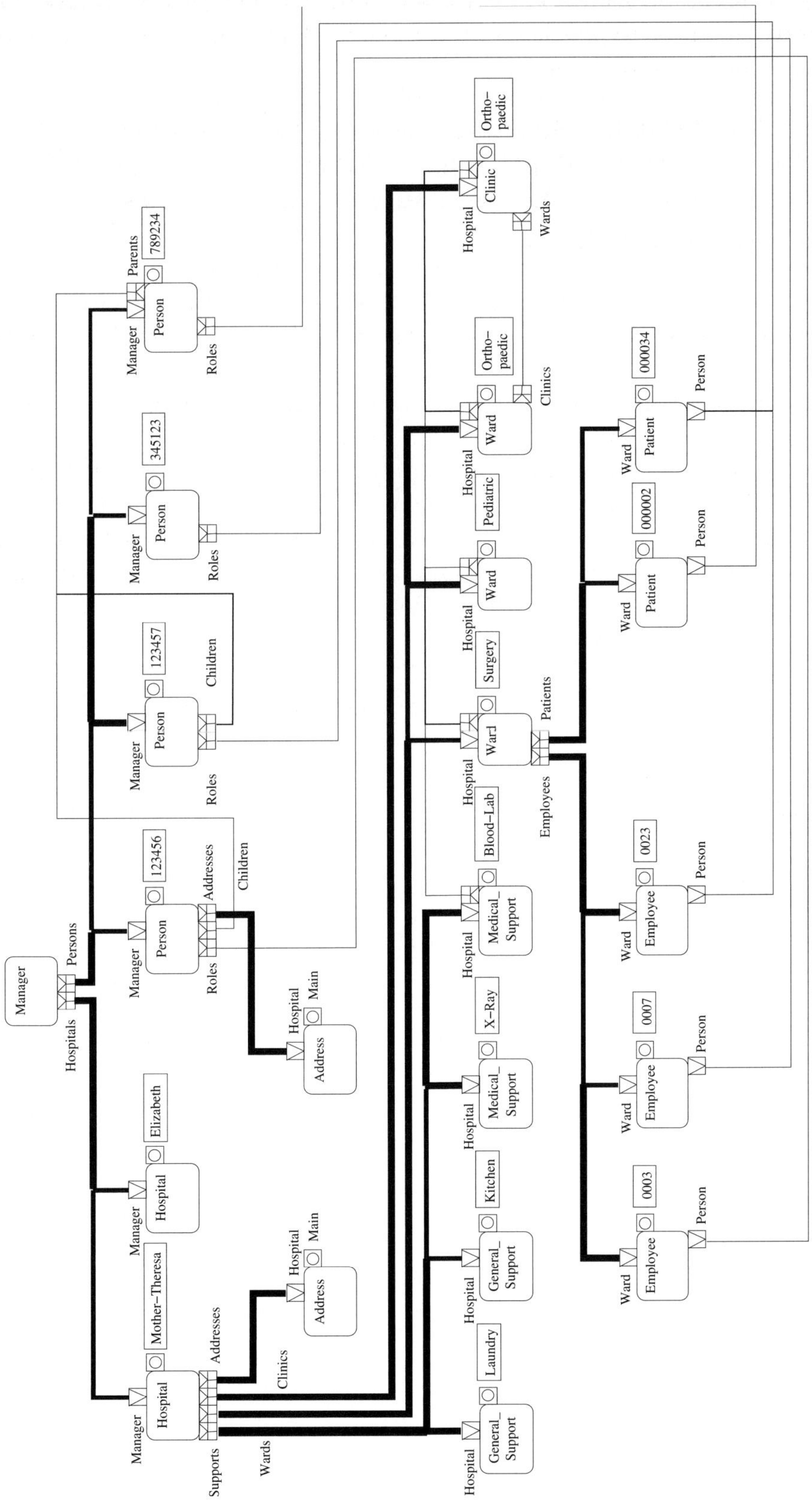

Figure 6.4: The instantiation view of the Hospital case

Ward *Surgery* has three employees: *code 0003, 0007* and *0023.* All three employee roles belong to already existing persons, see the relationships `Employ.Person` and `Person.Roles` for persons *123456, 123457,* and *345123.*

Ward *Surgery* has two patients: *000002* and *000034.* The two patient roles belong to already existing persons, see the relations `Patient.Person` and `Person.Roles` for persons *345123* and *789234.* Person *345123* has two roles, as patient and as employee. `Roles` is a secondary relation for patients and employees, therefore patients and employees can have the same key values.

Person *789234* is the child of persons *123456* and *123457.* The parents share a (secondary) relation `Person.Parents`. This does not cause problems, because the parents always have different key values.

Chapter 7

Textual Object Management Language

7.1 Standard File Import/Export

In the section on `VOIS` services in Chapter 19, a short explanation is given on persistence management. Persistence ensures that objects residing in the object heap of the running application can be saved to files and likewise, such files can be loaded in the running application to restore the objects. The `TOML` (Textual Object Management Language) is the standard format used for capturing system information in files.
In the section on `OS` services in Chapter 19, a short explanation is given on the `OML manager`. The manager is responsible for the conversion between the file information and the object heap. It interprets the information in the `TOML` file and passes it on to a controller in each layer.
In the section on layer components in Chapter 19, a short explanation is given on the various domains. The `TOML` format recognizes four domains: `metadata`, `language`, `graphics` and `instantiation`.

- The **metadata** domain contains structure, behavior, constraints and integrity information.
- The **language** domain contains the translations necessary to present the textual information in various natural languages.
- The **graphics** domain configures the appearance of the user-interface.
- The **instantiation** domain enables the creation and manipulation of various object instances required for a running system to be operational. The object instances of the application are saved in the `Run_Site` (Chapter 19, Framework Management) persistent database versions in this format.

Each module in the layer has a set of TOML files, one file per domain.

7.2 The OML-Tree

Figure 7.1 shows the import (on the left) and export (on the right) in more detail. The OML manager manages its own object heap called the OML-Tree. What is special about the OML-Tree is that it is constructed of instances of one type only, the **OML_Object**.
The root of the "OML-Tree" is "OML-Manager". An `example` of an OML-Tree is shown in 7.2.

When a file is imported it is parsed by the OML-Parser. It interprets the file content and with assistance of the OML Manager, converts this content to an OML-Tree. Once the OML-Tree has been built, the Controller converts the instances in the OML-Tree into objects of various types according to the schema.

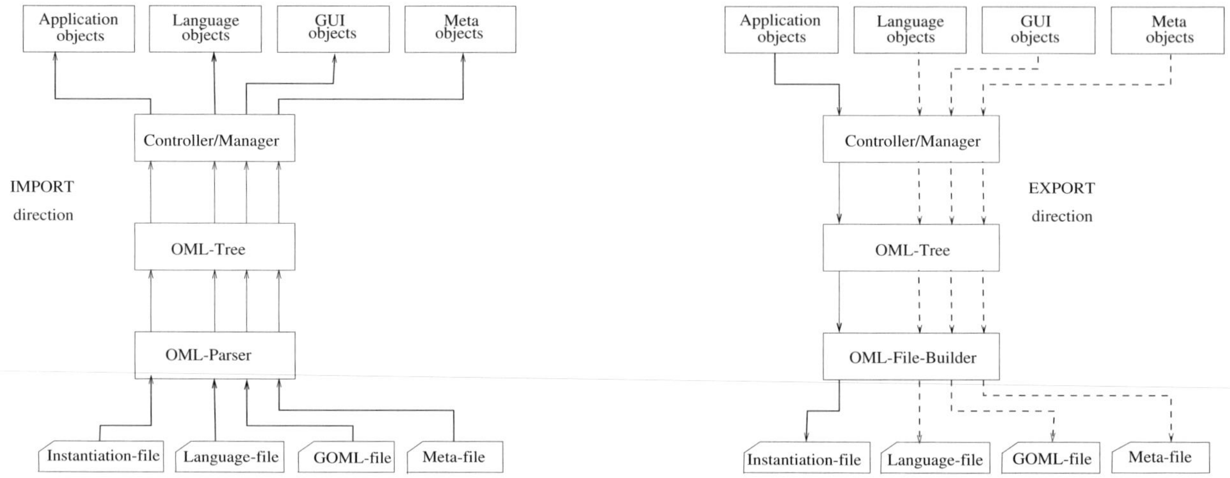

Figure 7.1: OML_object default processing flow

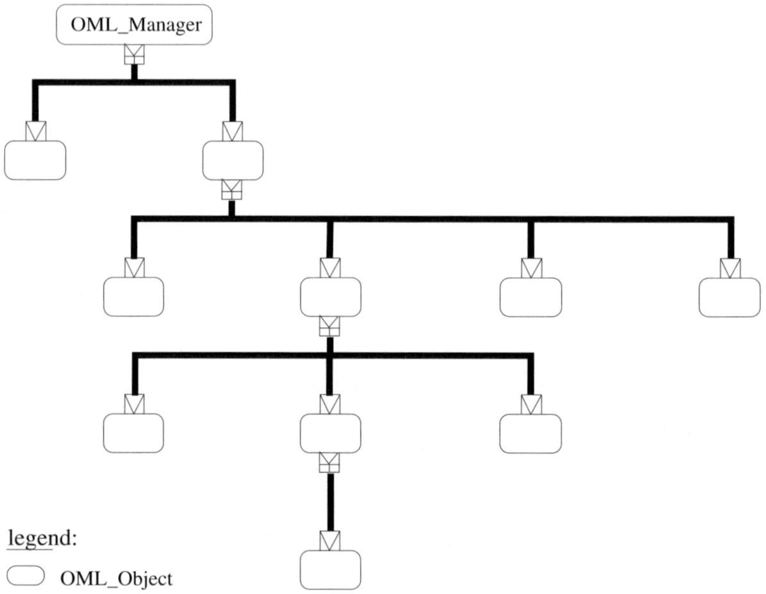

Figure 7.2: Example of an OML-Tree (Instantiation View)

When a module is exported its instances are first converted into an OML-Tree. An OML-File-Builder object then saves the OML-Tree instances in a file in TOML format. The stippled arrows indicate that objects of these domains are not normally exported because they are usually put into the TOML files by the application developer.

7.3 The OML Object

The OML-Object type is shown in 7.3.

`The attributes of OML object are:`

- `Key`: the means for the unique identification of an object relative to its owner. The content of the other members determines which values the `Key` can get and how the key is to be interpreted.

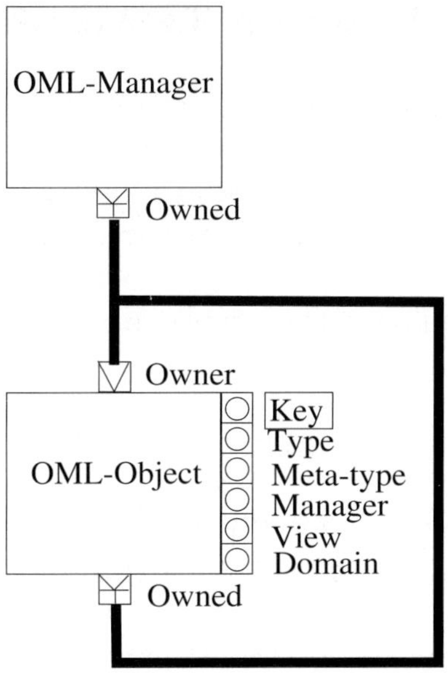

Figure 7.3: Members of OML Object

- `Type`: used to define the type of the object. In some cases it is also used as a general value field. The content of the other members determines which values the `Type` can get and how it is to be interpreted.

- `Metatype`: a categorization of object types in accordance with their role within the context. For each `Metatype` certain `Types` are pre-defined. Others may be defined by the developer.

- `Manager`: administers and handles the object in accordance with its `Domain, View,` and `Metatype`. For each `Manager` certain `Metatypes` are pre-defined.

- `View`: a categorization of the presented characteristics of an object type (the characteristics which can be described, observed and manipulated in this view). The semantics of the categorization depends on the `Domain`.

- `Domain`: the various domains have been listed previously.

`Example` of the OML_Object instance with the following values:

`Key`: *Mother-Theresa*
`Type`: *Hospital*
`Metatype`: *Object*
`Manager`: *Hospital_Controller*
`View`: *Instance*
`Domain`: *Instantiation*

This OML_Object instance contains information on the instance with key *Mother-Theresa*, of object type `Hospital` managed by the Hospital controller.
`The relations of OML object are used to create an OML-Tree:`

- `Owner`: Refers to the `OML_Object` owner.

- `Owned`: Refers to the `OML_Object` instances owned by this object.

7.4 Mapping the OML-Tree to a TOML File

The TOML format is a textual representation of an OML-Tree. Each OML object is represented by six fields called the header, and a body. The body begins with { and ends with } and may contain other OML objects. Each field is the content of a member of the OML object. The member name is implicit and determined by the position. The order starts with `Key` on the left and ends with the `Domain` on the right.

Therefore the TOML format for the previous example is:

```
Mother-Theresa Hospital Object Hospital_Controller Instance Instantiation { }
```

The { } implies that this object does not own any others, i.e. the body is empty.

Supposing *Mother-Theresa* has a `Ward` *Surgery*, then we can add this as follows:

```
Mother-Theresa Hospital Object Hospital_Controller Instance Instantiation
 {
   Wards:Surgery Ward Object Hospital_Controller Instance Instantiation { }
 }
```

Wards:Surgery indicates that the instance *Surgery* is owned by *Mother-Theresa* via the relation `Wards`. Note that the closing curly bracket of instance *Mother-Theresa* now appears after its owned object *Surgery*, i.e. the body of *Mother-Theresa* now contains Surgery.

The OML-Tree corresponding to the TOML syntax of this example is shown in Figure 7.4.

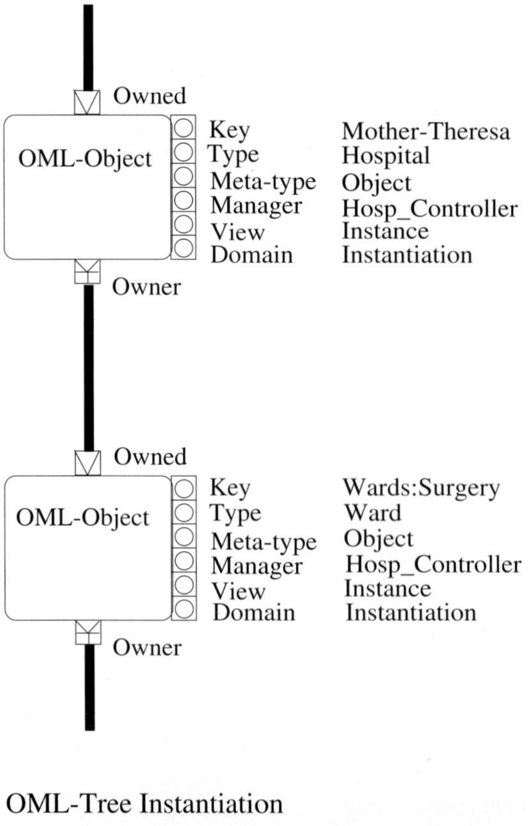

Figure 7.4: Partial OML-Tree (Instantiation View) and TOML syntax

Various syntax constraints and rules need to be observed in TOML format.

Here are two:

- Space sensitivity:
  Any attribute value of an OML object (its `Key` and signature) must be separated from the next in the textual syntax by at least one space.
  If a field must contain a space, it can be given by using quotes encapsulating the value containing the space character.

- The OML tail rule:
  If part of the tail of an owned object matches the tail of its owner, the tail of the owned object may be omitted.

Here is an example using both rules:

```
Mother-Theresa Hospital Object Hospital_Controller Instance Instantiation
 {
   Wards:Surgery Ward { }
   Persons:687245 Person
    {
      Name "Smith Jones" Member { }
    }
 }
```

Due to the tail rule, *Wards:Surgery Ward* will expand automatically to include *Object Hospital_Controller Instance Instantiation.*
We have added the `Person` with `Key` *687245* (which is its `SSN`). Name is also a member of object type `Person`. Its value is *Smith Jones.* The quotes indicate that the field contains several words. The `Metatype` is *Member.* Due to the tail rule, the controller, view and domain need not be given as they are the same as the owner's.

Chapters 8, 14, 15 and 16 are dedicated to the TOML syntax of one domain.

Chapter 8

The Meta Domain

The `Meta TOML` is the textual equivalent of the schematic developer view. Throughout this chapter the corresponding schematic is illustrated beside the textual definition.
The `Meta` domain has two views, **Structure** and **Behavior**.

8.1 View: Structure

The `Structure View` specifies the static aspects of object types.
The `Manager` values for the `Structure View` are the controller names. For `example` VOIS_Compiler and OMS_Controller are the controllers (super managers) of the VOIS and OMS layers. The manager values can be aliased, for example: VOIS and OMS. These controllers belong to the foundation layers of Perspective DB explained in Chapter 19.

8.1.1 Defining an object type

An object type has the `Metatype` value *Class* which is an alias for object type. The term *Class* stems from the terminology traditionally used in object-oriented programming languages.

```
Person Person Class VOIS_Compiler Structure { }
```

Figure 8.1: Defining an object type

The left side of Figure 8.1 shows the `Meta TOML` definition of an object type. The right side shows the analogous graphical representation of the definition (developer's view). The `Type` always states the name of the object type.
The `Key` gets the same value as `Type` as there is no other appropriate value.

8.1.2 Adding members

General
The `Type` specifies the object type of the member.
The `Key` specifies the name of the member.

```
Person Person Class VOIS_Compiler Structure
 {
  SSN VOIS_String Class { }
  Name VOIS_String Class { }
  Gender int Literal  { }
  Photo OMS_Image_File Class { }
  Manager VOMS_Relation Class { }
  Roles VOMS_Relation Class { }
  Parents VOMS_Relation Class { }
  Children VOMS_Relation Class { }
  Addresses VOMS_Relation Class { }
  Hours Hours () { }
 }
```

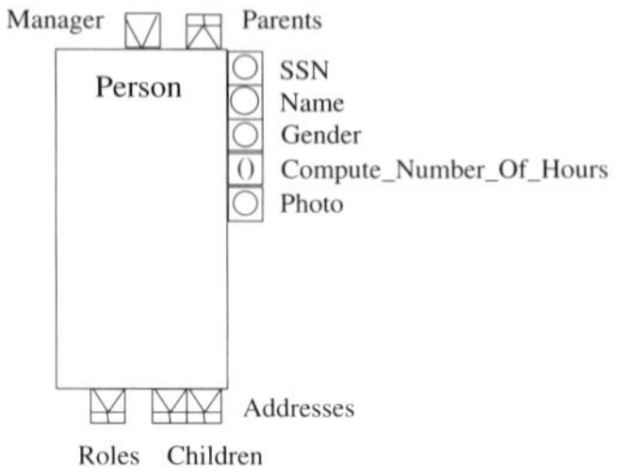

Figure 8.2: Adding the members of an object type

Figure 8.2 illustrates how to add the member definitions to the object type. The members of an object type are defined within the body of the `Meta TOML` object owner (the object type).

- `SSN, Name, Gender` and `Photo` are attributes, defined using a variety of `Metatypes` and `Types`. These will be explained in the following subsections.
- `Manager, Roles, Parents, Children` and `Addresses` are relations. A relation is always of `Type` VOMS_Relation. Whether it is an ownership or secondary relation is a matter of configuration (to be explained later).
- `Hours` is an operation (in the Hospital case study abbreviated to `Hours`). An operation is always of `Metatype ( )`. The `Type` is the name of the operation.
  The `Key` gets the same value as `Type` (there is no other appropriate value).

Metatypes and Types for attributes

- `Metatype` *Class*. `Examples` for `Type` values are:

  VOIS_String: a string stored in ASCII format, is a pseudo-literal

  OMS_Image_File: a photo or image stored e.g. in JPG format

  OMS_Video_File: a video stored e.g. in MPG format

  OMS_Text_File: text stored e.g. in ASCII format
- `Metatype` *Literal*: the attribute is a literal. `Examples` for `Type` values are:

  char: a character

  int: an integer
- `Metatype` *Auto*: is used if the system can automatically derive the `Metatype` of a `Type`. In this case, VOIS_Compiler substitutes the right metatype automatically.
  Most literals, pseudo-literals and return types of operations will be substituted using *Auto*.
  `Type` is the attribute type, *e.g. int*.
- `Metatype` *: the attribute is a pointer to an object of the specified type.
  `Type` is the referred object type, *e.g. Type char* implies this attribute is a pointer to a character.

8.1.3 Defining inheritance

```
Person Person Class VOIS_Compiler Structure
{
  Hosp_Base Hosp_Base Isa VOIS_Compiler Structure { }
  SSN VOIS_String Class VOIS_Compiler Structure  { }
  ......
}
```

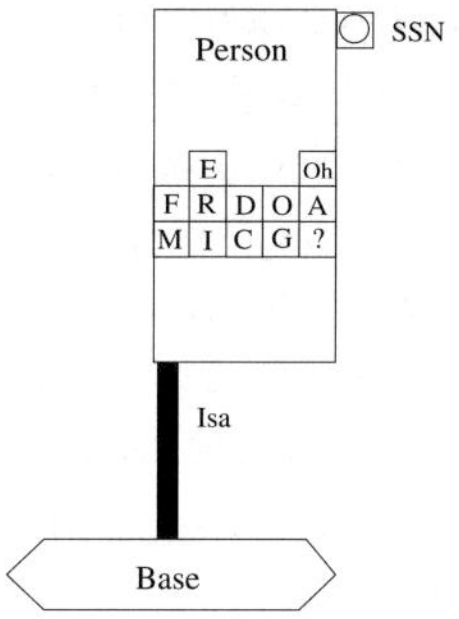

Figure 8.3: Defining inheritance

The `Metatype` *Isa* is used to indicate the generalization object type. Isa is always defined in the specialization object type in order to specify from which object type it inherits its initial members.

The `Type` describes the name of the generalization object type.
The `Key` gets the same value as `Type` (because there is no other appropriate value).

The `example` in Figure 8.3 indicates that `Person` is a specialization of `Hosp_Base`. Via `Hosp_Base` it transitively inherits the characteristics of the first First Order object type, `OMS_Object`, such as the generic operations, `Insert`, `Remove` etc.

8.1.4 Defining operations

```
Person Person Class VOIS_Compiler Structure
{
  .......
  Hours Hours () VOIS_Compiler Structure
   {
    return_type int Auto VOIS_Compiler Structure { }
   }
}
```

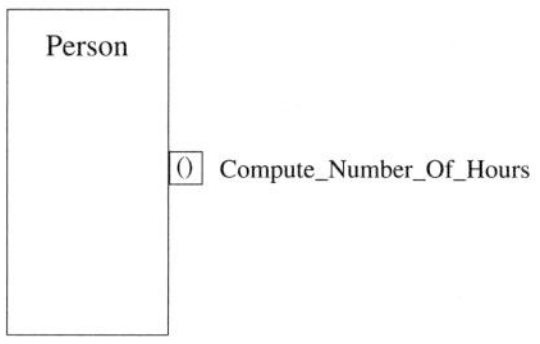


```
Department Department Class VOIS_Compiler Structure
{
  .......
  Employ Employ () VOIS_Compiler Structure
   {
    return_type OMS_Execution_Result Auto VOIS_Compiler Structure { }
    SSN char * VOIS_Compiler Structure { }
    Code char * VOIS_Compiler Structure { }
    Hours int Literal VOIS_Compiler Structure { }
   }
  .....
}
```

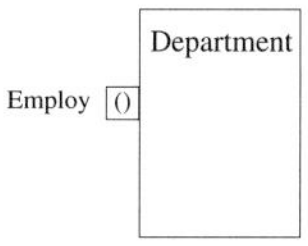

Figure 8.4: Defining the body of an operation

The upper part of Figure 8.4 shows the definition of the operation `Hours` which is a member of object type Person. It has a return value but no arguments.

The lower part of the same figure shows the definition of the operation `Employ` which is a member of object type `Department`.
Its behavior is known from the examples in Chapter 10. An elementary explanation of operations is given in Chapters 2 and 3.
The `Type` is the name of the operation.
The `Key` gets the same value as Type (there is no other appropriate value).

The `body` contains the input- and the output-arguments of the operation.
The members in the body of an operation are defined in the same way as members in an object type. They are ordered as follows: the first member is the return_type of the operation; the arguments follow, specified in the logical order of the argument value collection.
In the `example` of the operation `Employ`, the person to be employed has to be specified first (member `SSN`); then the instance of the role `Employee` gets a key value (member `Code`); then the limitation on the number of hours the employee may work (member `Hours`).
The arguments of an operation can be collected from the the same or other object types (the next chapter explains how this is specified). The attribute names of the relevant members are given as the `Key` values of the arguments. For `example, SSN, Code` and `Hours` in the lower part of Figure 8.4.
The `Key` of the first argument, the return type, is always named `return_type`. The `Type` is the argument's object type , e.g. in the upper part of Figure 8.4 an integer.
When the return value only needs to indicate whether the operation succeeded or failed, it is common to use the literal type OMS_Execution_Result (which has the range OK or ERROR), as shown in the lower part of the figure. The `Metatype` is usually Auto.

8.1.5 Defining a relation attribute

```
Status Status Class VOIS_Compiler Structure
{
  OMS_Relation_Attribute OMS_Relation_Attribute Isa { }
  Hosp_Type char * { }
}
```

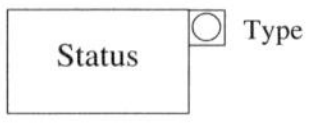

Figure 8.5: Defining a relation attribute

A relation attribute inherits its characteristics from OMS_Relation_Attribute. Its members may be defined as members of an object type, with the limitation that it is not a First Order object. Figure 8.5 shows the definition of Status with its attribute named Type.

8.1.6 Defining a multi-media object

```
    OMS_Image_File OMS_Image_File Class Compiler Structure
(1) {
      OMS_File OMS_File Isa { }
    }

    Person Person Class Compiler Structure
(2) {
      Photo OMS_Image_File { }
      ........
    }
```

Figure 8.6: Defining a multi-media object

Multi-media attributes are defined in several object types of the case study, e.g. `Video` in `Department`. Figure 8.6 shows the definition for a still image object (e.g. JPG format). All multi-media attributes inherit their generic behavior from OMS_File (Mark 1)[1].
The media object type can be a member of a first order object type, in this example, the member Photo of Person (Mark 2).

8.2 View: Behavior

The Behavior view specifies the dynamic aspects of objects.
The `Manager` field values can be OMS and Relation. The Relation Manager is used for configuring information in the body of a relation (see 8.2.6). In the other cases of behavior definition, the Manager is OMS.

8.2.1 Indicating the key attribute of an object type

```
    Person Person Class VOIS_Compiler Structure
     {
       SSN VOIS_String Class VOIS_Compiler Structure { }
(1)    Primary SSN Key OMS Behavior { }
       .....
     }
```

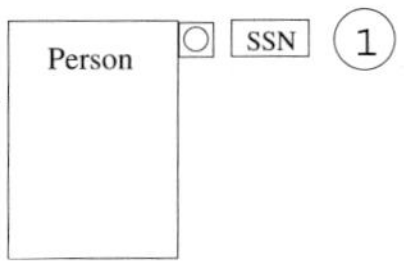

Figure 8.7: Indicating the key attribute

Figure 8.7 shows how to indicate the key attribute of an object type (Mark 1). In the graphical representation the attribute's name is enclosed by a rectangle.
The `Metatype` field value is *Key*. The `Type` value gets the name of the key attribute. *Primary* is the `Key` field value[2].

8.2.2 Setting the range of an attribute

```
    Person Person Class VOIS_Compiler Structure
     { .....
       Gender int Literal VOIS_Compiler Structure
        {
(1)       Simple "Equals: 1 0 2" Range OMS Behavior { }
        }
       .....
     }
```

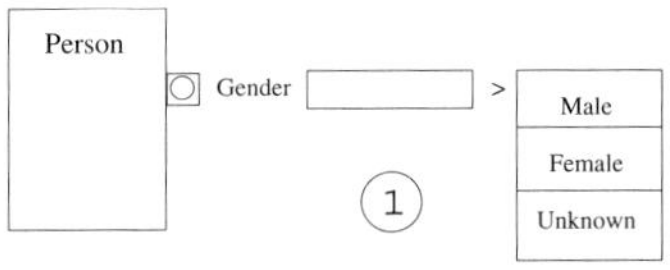

Figure 8.8: Setting the range of attributes

Figure 8.8 shows the range definition for Gender of Person (Mark 1). This limits the value that can be assigned to the attribute to one of the values within the range definition.

The `Metatype` of a range expression is *Range*. The `Type` value is the range setting. The range setting begins with a key word that defines the kind of range followed by a :. The permitted key word depends on the attribute type such as illustrated with the examples for integer and character.

[1]This is already defined in layer OMS and therefore does not need to be redefined in the application.

[2]Secondary is used to denote that the attribute is part of a compound key. A compound key is constructed from the values of several attribute, one being the Primary and the rest Secondary.

- `Type` value is *int*:
  Possibilities are Equals, Not-Equals, Greater, Greater-Equals, Smaller, Smaller-Equals, Between and Between-Equals.

- `Type` value is *char*:
  Possibilities are Equals and Not-Equals.

The `Key` values are *Simple* for an atomic attribute and *Multiple* for a composed attribute (the attribute itself has members).

As illustrated in Chapter 10, the end user can iterate over the range and select an appropriate value. As a result of the definition in Figure 8.8 the user can iterate the values in the value field of the attribute `Gender`. The definition implies that `Gender` is an atomic attribute. Three values are possible to specify the gender of a person. *Equals* indicates that it has to be one of the values. The first value present in the range (1 in this case) is recognized by the system as the default, when relevant. The user will not see a number because the number is mapped in the Language TOML domain to an expression with a semantic the user understands (1, 0, 2 are mapped to Male, Female, Unknown respectively). The range values as shown in the figure on the right are visible on demand in the interactive user schematic.

8.2.3 Configuring the location of on-line system documentation (Help)

```
Hosp_Manager Hosp_Manager Class VOIS_Compiler Structure
 {
   ......
  Design_Path "Perspective:Hospital.Hospital" Member OMS Behavior { }
   .....
 }
```

Figure 8.9: Configuring the location of on-line information (Help)

The documentation consists of a tree of directories and files in HTML format, with various entry points. It is possible to define the file system location (path) of an entry point for a particular system or module. This path is used by the generic operation Help to locate the appropriate help document. The `Metatype` is *Member*.
`Type` is given in the form: "Product name: Layer-name.Library-name.Module-name".

- Product-name: is the name of the product (system).

- Layer-name: is the name of the layer (subsystem) within the product.

- Module-name: is the name of the module within the given library.

`Key` is *Design_Path*.

In the example in Figure 8.9 the product is named Perspective, the layer, Hospital and the module, Hospital.
It is sufficient to define the Product-name in the base manager of a system, with the exception of documentation which deviates from the normal location.

```
Person Person Class VOIS_Compiler Structure
 {
   .....
   Manager VOMS_Relation Class VOIS_Compiler Structure
    {
(1)   Hosp_Manager.Persons Connects_From Relationship OMS Behavior { }
    }
   Roles VOMS_Relation Class VOIS_Compiler Structure { }
   Parents VOMS_Relation Class VOIS_Compiler Structure
    {
(2)   Person.Children Connects Relationship OMS Behavior { }
    }
   Children VOMS_Relation Class VOIS_Compiler Structure { }
   ......
 }
```

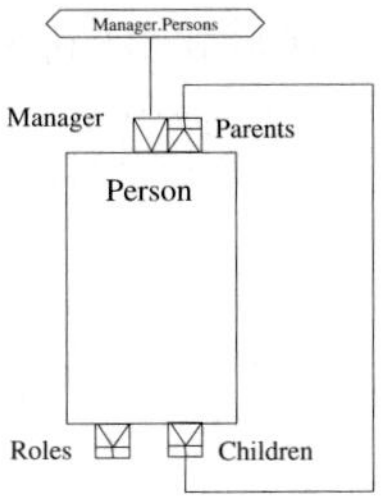


```
Role Role Class VOIS_Compiler Structure
 {
   .....
   Person VOMS_Relation Class VOIS_Compiler Structure
    {
(3)   Person.Roles Connects Relationship OMS Behavior { }
    }
   .....
 }
```

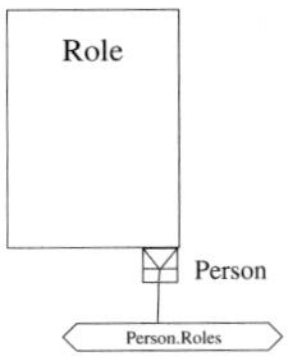


```
Service Service Class VOIS_Compiler Structure
 {
   .....
   Supports VOMS_Relation Class VOIS_Compiler Structure
    {
(4)   Support.Services Connects_To Relationship OMS Behavior { }
    }
    .....
 }
```

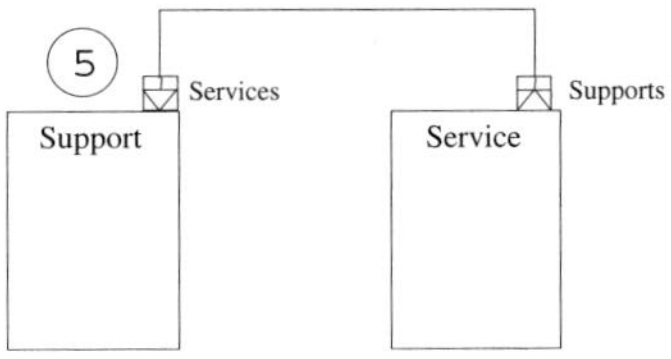

Figure 8.10: Configuring the connectivity of relations

8.2.4 Configuring the connectivity of relations

Within a relation (the source) it is possible to configure the connection to relations on the other side (targets). Such a connectivity configuration is called a connector. In the case of a recursive relationship type, the source and the target are different relations within the same object type.
The connectivity need only be configured on one side.
The `Metatype` is *Relationship*.
The `Type` value defines the kind of connectivity desired.

- *Connects*: A relationship may be inserted and removed from a relation on both sides of the connection.

- *Connects_To*: A relationship may be inserted and removed only from the side on which it is defined.

- *Connects_From*: A relationship may be inserted and removed only from the opposite side on which it is defined.

The Key is given in the form: object_type name.relation name.

- object_type name: is the name of the object_type on the opposite side of the relationship type.
- relation name: is the name of the relation on the opposite side.

Figure 8.10 illustrates how the relations Manager, Roles, Parents and Children define the connection to the opposite relations.
The connector between Manager.Persons and Person.Manager is defined in Person.Manager (Mark 1). This is an ownership relation, how to configure the owner is dealt with later.
The recursive relationship type between Person.Parents and Person.Children is defined via the connector in Person.Parents (Mark 2).
The connector between Role.Person and Person.Roles is defined in Role.Person (Mark 3); for this reason the relevant definition in Role is added to the figure, see the middle part.
The lowest part of the figure shows the definition of a connector with the Type value Connects_To (Mark 4). In this case, relationships may be inserted and removed only from Service.Supports, not from Support.Services, see Mark 5. The object types Support and Service are generalizations. In the case study Ward and Clinic services may register their cooperation with General and Medical supports.

8.2.5 Defining an ownership relationship type

```
Person Person Class VOIS_Compiler Structure
 {
   ....
   Manager VOMS_Relation Class VOIS_Compiler Structure
    {
      Hosp_Manager.Persons Connects Relationship OMS Behavior
       {
(1)      Owned Primary Ownership OMS Behavior { }
       } (2)     (3)
    }
   ....
 }
```

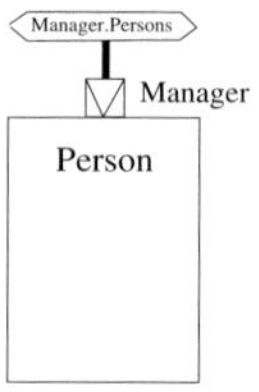


```
Hosp_Manager Hosp_Manager Class VOIS_Compiler Structure
 {
   ....
   Hospitals VOMS_Relation Class VOIS_Compiler Structure
    {
      Hospital.Manager Connects Relationship OMS Behavior
       {
(4)      Owner Default Ownership OMS Behavior { }
       } (5)     (6)
    }
   ....
 }
```

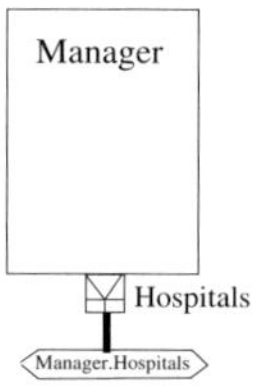

Figure 8.11: Defining ownership

The definition that a relation is an owner or is owned (belongs to an ownership relationship type) is given in the body of the connector[3].

[3]The connector was introduced in an abstract fashion in section 3.2.2. Here we are dealing with how to define the properties of the connector.

The Metatype is *Ownership*, the Type is *Primary* or *Default* and the Key is *Owned* or *Owner*.

Figure 8.11 shows two examples. In the upper, the primary ownership between Manager.Persons and Person.Manager is configured (Mark 1). The default (dominant) ownership between Manager.Hospitals and Hospital.Manager is configured in the lower (Mark 4)[4]. The default ownership is defined here in the connector of the relation Manager.Hospitals; which indicates that the connector belongs to an owner relation (Mark 5). In the case of Person.Manager the connector belongs to an owned relation (Mark 2).
The default ownership branch is the relationship type between Manager.Hospitals and Hospital.Manager (Mark 6). The ownership relationship type between Manager.Persons and Person.Manager is primary (Mark 3).

8.2.6 Defining the cardinality of a relation

```
Person Person Class VOIS_Compiler Structure
 {
   .....
   Manager VOMS_Relation Class VOIS_Compiler Structure
    {
(1)  Cardinality many Cardinality relation Behavior { }
     Hosp_Manager.Persons Connects Relationship OMS Behavior
      {
       Owned Primary Ownership OMS Behavior { }
      }
    }
   Roles VOMS_Relation Class VOIS_Compiler Structure
    {
(2)  Cardinality 1 Cardinality relation Behavior { }
    }
   Parents VOMS_Relation Class VOIS_Compiler Structure
    {
(3)  Cardinality many Cardinality relation Behavior { }
     Person.Children Connects Relationship OMS Behavior { }
    }
   Children VOMS_Relation Class VOIS_Compiler Structure
    {
(4)  Cardinality 2 Cardinality relation Behavior { }
    }
   ......
 }

Role Hosp_Role Class VOIS_Compiler Structure
 {
   .....
   Person VOMS_Relation Class VOIS_Compiler Structure
    {
(5)  Cardinality many Cardinality relation Behavior { }
     Person.Roles Connects Relationship OMS Behavior { }
    }
   .....
 }
```

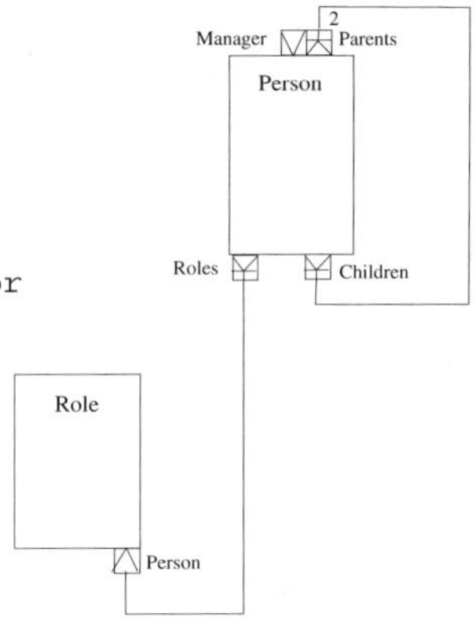

Figure 8.12: Defining cardinality

Defining the cardinality range may be done in the same way for ownership and for secondary relations. The Metatype value is *relation*. The Type value is one of the cardinality range types, e.g. *many* or *1*.

[4]See also section 4.6.

Cardinality is the Key value as there is no other appropriate value.

In the examples of Figure 8.12 the cardinality definitions for the relations are as follows: The Manager can manage several Persons (Mark 1). A Child (Mark 4) can have a maximum of two Parents and a Parent can have several Children (Mark 3). A Person can have several Roles (Mark 5), and a Role belongs to one Person (Mark 2).

8.3 OML Tail Rule Example

The following example illustrates the effect of the tail rule for the Meta-domain. Figure 8.13 shows the definition before applying the tail rule.

```
Person Person Class VOIS_Compiler Structure
 {
   Hosp_Base Hosp_Base Isa VOIS_Compiler Structure { }
   SSN VOIS_String Class VOIS_Compiler Structure { }
   Name VOIS_String Class VOIS_Compiler Structure { }
   Gender int Literal VOIS_Compiler Structure
    {
     Simple "Equals: 1 0 2" Range OMS Behavior { }
    }
    Photo OMS_Image_File Class VOIS_Compiler Structure { }
    Manager VOMS_Relation Class VOIS_Compiler Structure
     {
      Cardinality many Cardinality relation Behavior { }
      Hosp_Manager.Persons Connects Relationship OMS Behavior
       {
        Owned Primary Ownership OMS Behavior { }
       }
     }
    .....
    Hours Hours () VOIS_Compiler Structure
     {
      return_type int auto VOIS_Compiler Structure { }
     }
 }
```

Figure 8.13: Before applying the tail rule

After applying the tail rule, see Figure 8.14:

8.4 Combining the configuration elements

The corresponding schematics for the following examples can be extracted from the developers view Schematic 6.3 in Chapter 6.
Figures 8.15, 8.16, 8.17 and 8.18 illustrate how inheritance of the Meta TOML affects the configuration of object types.

```
Person Person Class VOIS_Compiler Structure
 {
  Hosp_Base Hosp_Base Isa { }
  SSN VOIS_String { }
  Name VOIS_String { }
  Gender int Literal
   {
    Simple "Equals: 1 0 2" Range OMS Behavior { }
   }
   Photo OMS_Image_File { }
   Manager VOMS_Relation
    {
     Cardinality many Cardinality relation Behavior { }
     Hosp_Manager.Persons Connects Relationship OMS Behavior
      {
       Owned Primary Ownership { }
      }
    }
   .....
   Hours Hours ()
    {
     return_type int auto { }
    }
 }
```

Figure 8.14: After applying the tail rule

Figures 8.15, 8.16, show the configuration of `Department` and its specializations `Support` and `Service`. Figure 8.17 shows the `General_Support` object type, one of the specializations of `Support` department. Figure 8.18 shows `Ward`, one of the specializations of `Service` department.

```
Department Department Class VOIS_Compiler Structure
 {
  Hosp_Base Hosp_Base Isa { }
  Name VOIS_String { }
  Capacity int Literal
   {
    Simple "Between-Equals: 1 9000" Range OMS Behavior { }
   }
  Video OMS_MPEG_File { }
  Employees VOMS_Relation
   {
    Cardinality 1 Cardinality relation Behavior { }
   }
  Occupation Occupation ()
   {
    return_type int auto { }
   }
  Employ Employ ()
   {
    return_type OMS_Execution_Result auto { }
    SSN char * { }
    Code char * { }
    Hours int Literal { }
   }
  Discharge Discharge ()
   {
    return_type OMS_Execution_Result auto { }
    Code char * { }
   }
  Primary Name Key OMS Behavior { }
 }
```

Figure 8.15: Example department and its specializations: Part a

```
Service Service Class VOIS_Compiler Structure
 {
  Department Department Isa { }
  Supports VOMS_Relation Class
   {
    Cardinality many Cardinality relation Behavior { }
   }
  Patients VOMS_Relation Class
   {
    Cardinality 1 Cardinality relation Behavior { }
   }
  Check_In Check_In ()
   {
    return_value OMS_Execution_Result auto { }
    SSN char * { }
    Code char * { }
   }
  Check_Out Check_Out ()
   {
    return_type OMS_Execution_Result auto { }
    Code char * { }
   }

 }
```

Figure 8.16: Example department and its specializations: Part b

```
General_Support General_Support Class VOIS_Compiler Structure
 {
  Support Support Isa { }
  Hospital VOMS_Relation Class
   {
    Cardinality many Cardinality relation Behavior { }
    Hospital.Supports Connects Relationship OMS Behavior { }
     {
      Owned Primary Ownership { }
     }
   }
 }
```

Figure 8.17: Example inheritance general_support department

```
Ward Ward Class VOIS_Compiler Structure
 {
   Service Service Isa { }
   Hospital VOMS_Relation Class
    {
     Cardinality many Cardinality relation Behavior { }
     Hospital.Wards Connects Relationship OMS Behavior
      {
       Owned Default Ownership { }
      }
   Clinics VOMS_Relation Class
    {
     Cardinality many Cardinality relation Behavior { }
     Clinic.Wards Connects Relationship OMS Behavior { }
    }
 }
```

Figure 8.18: Example inheritance ward

Chapter 9

Schematic Interaction: Navigation

9.1 Mapping of Instances on the Object Schema

Until now we have dealt with the three static views of the object schema, the End-users, Developers and Instantiation schemas. In the case study we used these static schemas for modeling purposes. With several additions, the static End-user schema is transformed into an interactive GUI that can be used to manipulate the system and the object base it maintains. The capability of Perspective-DB object model and system to incorporate the GUI is a novel feature. Another model and system that incorporates the GUI is described in [van der Wolf, 1993], a framework design system for CAD, based on the semantic model described in [ter Bekke, 1992]. It is based on the concept that the end-user defines a query using the schema, which is executed and the result is displayed in tabular form. In Perspective-DB, the objects are accessed directly in the schema using the principle of navigation. In [van der Wolf, 1993] the schema and system are used to model and manage design metadata respectively, so called "large-grain data", whereas the Perspective-DB schema and system are intended to model and manage both large- and fine-grained data respectively (e.g. the design data as well).
Figure 9.1 shows the Interactive Schematic view of the hospital case study.
To achieve the match of instance presentations with the object type presentations in the object schema, the graphical presentation of object schema is extended with space for:

- The object ID: the object ID is placed on the face of the object-type, below the type name. It displays the key value of the instance, and expands with a mouse click to display the complete ID.
- The attribute values.
- The argument values and the return value of operations; various operations require the collection of argument values prior to execution and the return value of the operation must be displayed.
- The cardinality range and actual cardinality of relations; an additional numerical value, the cardinality index, tells which instance in the relation is currently being displayed. For example, the person named Fisher is female, with SSN 345678, has 2 parents, 1 child and is employed (see the top right of Figure 9.1).

9.2 Navigation

Navigation enables the end-user to **access** selected instances by traversing step by step through the object base from one instance to another. Traversal is done by means of **navigation paths**.

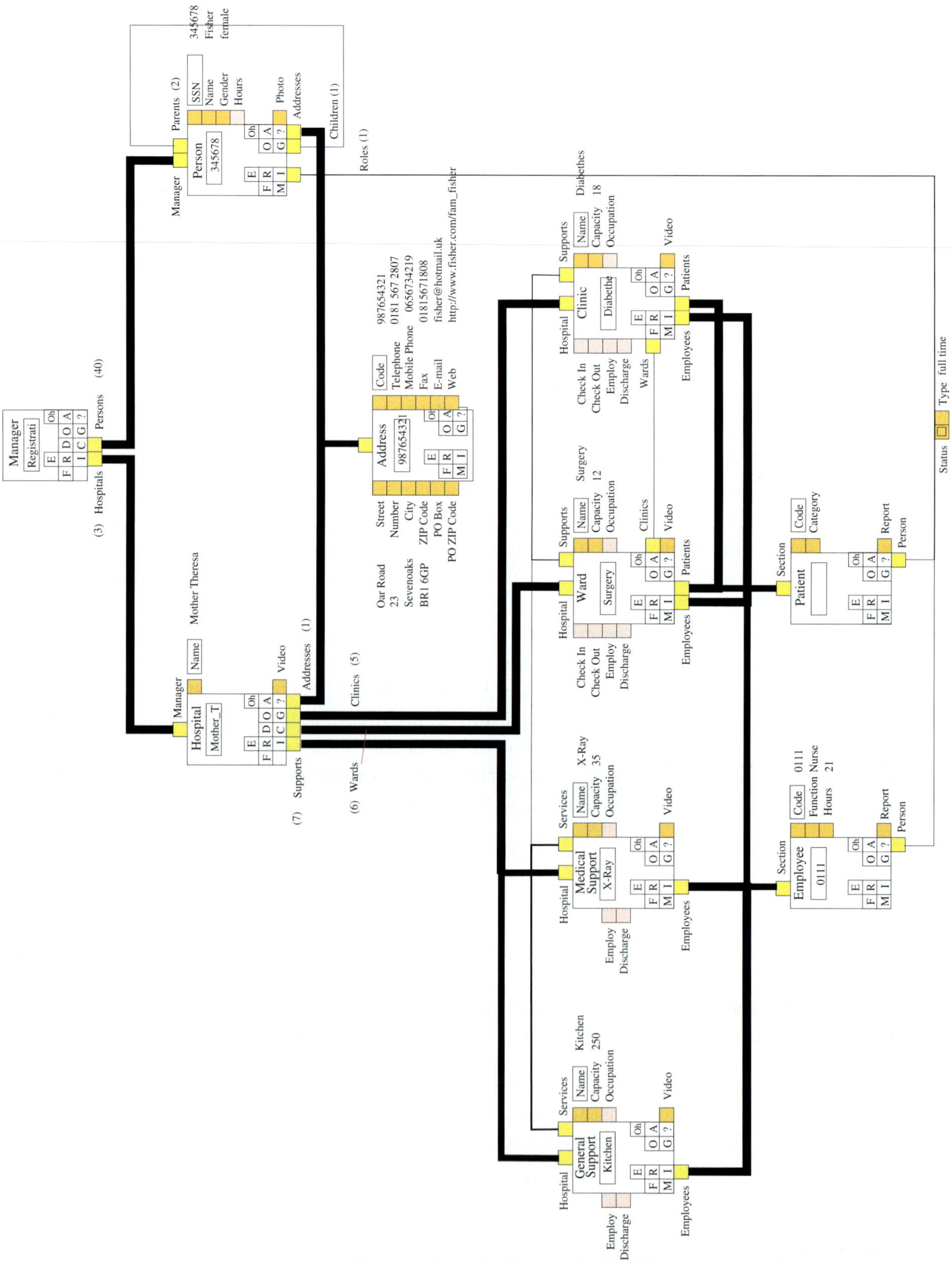

Figure 9.1: Instances within the user view

A navigation path is a collection of object types, relations, and connectors that together form a contiguous route in a consistent direction. Instances along the navigation path are **accessed**. Accessed instances are displayed. The end-user can traverse both ownership and secondary relations.
The end-user can clearly distinguish the navigation path because the relations involved have a different color. The user can constantly create new navigation paths and cancel existing ones. Perspective-DB accesses the managers automatically to ensure that each module has a starting point for navigation. The color coding for manipulating relationships is as follows: When the relationship is not active, the relation is yellow and the connectors are black. When the user selects a relation, it turns brown indicating it is active, and the connector coupled to it turns blue indicating that it is active too. A green connector implies that the user must select one connector out of several options (for example to choose between `Medical` and `General Support`).

9.2.1 Navigating an ownership relationship type

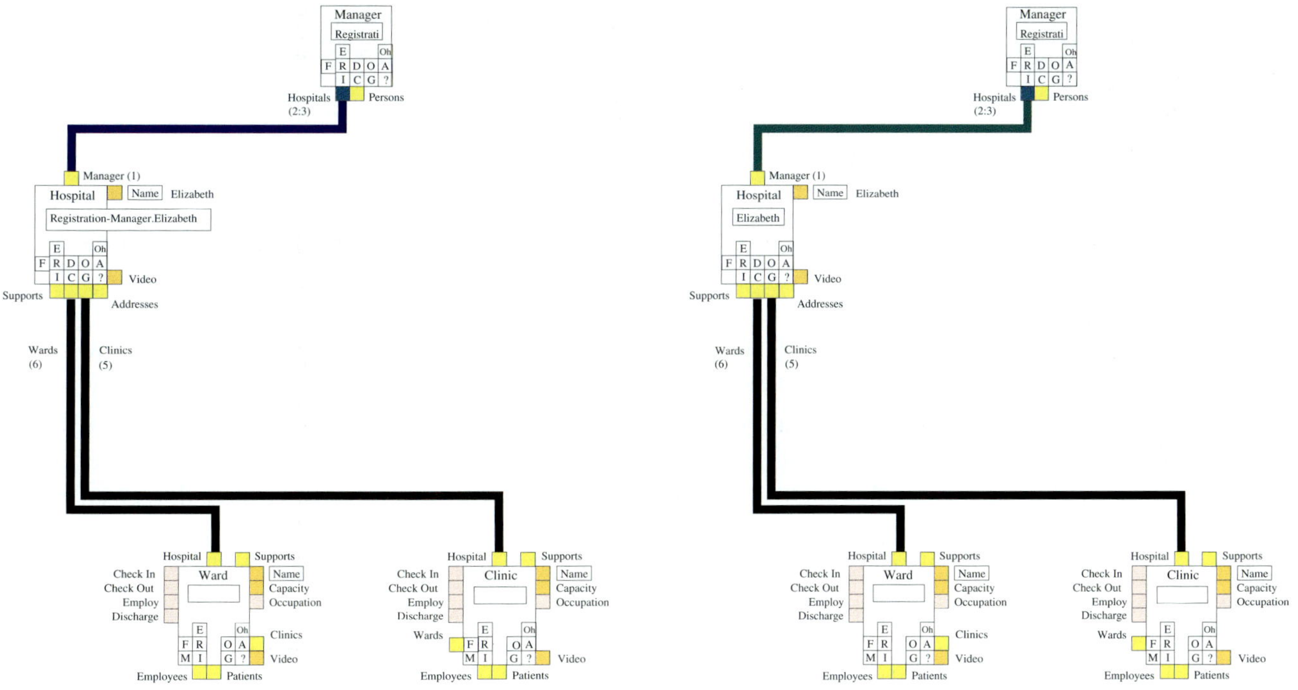

Figure 9.2: Navigating an ownership relationship type - 1

Navigation starts at the root of an ownership hierarchy. The desired ownership relation is activated at the manager object type by clicking the relation (with the left mouse button). The activated relation turns gray, the connector turns blue, and the first instance in the relationship is displayed. To find a particular instance the user can iterate the instances in the relationship until the desired instance is accessed.
Iteration is done by using the middle or right mouse buttons while clicking the relation or the connector. The middle button iterates backwards to the previous, and the right button forwards to the next.

The displayed instance can be recognized by the values of its members such as the key value and the ID[1].

[1]Normally the ID field shows the key. The user can get the ID by positioning the cursor in the ID field, and pressing the right mouse key.

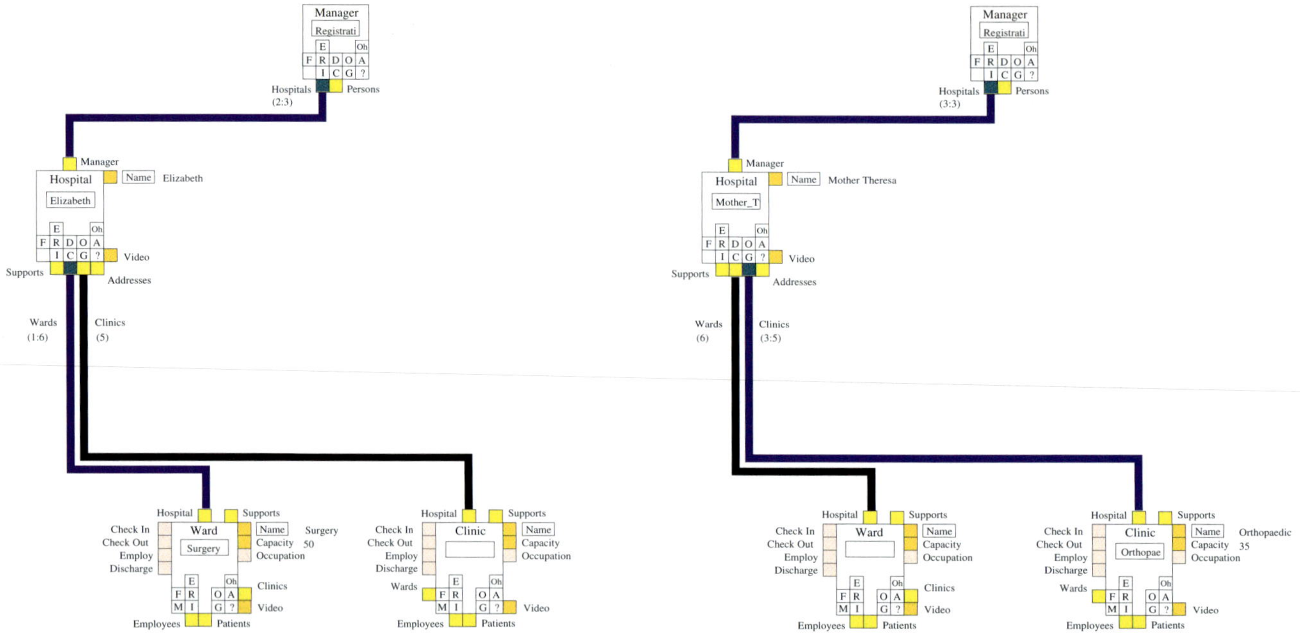

Figure 9.3: Navigating an ownership relationship type - 2

An `example` is shown in the left side of Figure 9.2, see the ownership relationship type between `Manager` and `Hospital`.

During the iteration over the activated relationship type, the cardinality presentation shows two numbers, separated by a ":". The number on the right is the cardinality (see Section 3.2.2). The number on the left is the index of the instance currently accessed. In the End-user view, we use the term cardinality to denote the actual number of instances present in the relation, not to be confused with the term cardinality (range) used in the Developers view and meta data, which determines the maximum number of instances allowed in the relation. The index is a useful reference point during iteration. The index of an instance might change when an additional instance is inserted and the relationship is ordered, e.g. to keep alphabetical order[2].
With the actions illustrated in Figure 9.2, left figure, the user navigates from the manager to the *Elizabeth* hospital, see cardinality index (2:3).

A relationship in the navigation path can be deactivated by clicking the relation or the connector. If the connector is selected (clicked) the relation remains active and the connector turns green (implying it is not active but is selectable), see the right side of Figure 9.2 (iterating the relation will have no effect)[3].
An accessed instance can be the starting point for further navigation, or can be manipulated, e.g. to execute an operation.
Figure 9.3, the left side, illustrates how to navigate from *Elizabeth* hospital to one of its wards, in this instance the ward *Surgery*. The navigation is as follows: click the desired owner relation (`Ward`) and iterate to the instance (with `Name` *Surgery*, cardinality index (1:6)).

[2]The relation is a set of object references, therefore the index is actually the position of the reference to the accessed object.

[3]The reason why it is possible to deactivate the connector, while the relation remains active is that in the case of a heterogeneous relationship the connector leading from the active relation will have several branches. It is possible to have one, several or all branches active (colored blue). The user can then deactivate and activate branches at will while the relation remains active.

The right side of Figure 9.3 illustrates how to navigate to the *Orthopaedic* clinic of the *Mother-Theresa* hospital. First, the *Mother-Theresa* hospital is activated, starting by activating the owner relation `Hospitals` of `Manager` (relation turns gray), iterating over its instances until *Mother-Theresa* hospital is accessed (see also: cardinality index (3:3)). Then, the owner relation `Clinics` of *Mother-Theresa* hospital has to be activated (clicking turns it gray) and iterated until the desired instance of `Clinic` is accessed (here, `Name`: *Orthopaedic*, cardinality index (3:5)). It is impossible to reach the clinic *Orthopaedic* belonging to *Mother-Theresa* hospital from the hospital instance *Elizabeth* directly.
The ownership relationships are always visible so that the user can clearly see the object hierarchies. In addition to iterating the relation to access an object, an alternative way is **access by index**. This is useful in the case of a relation with many object references. When the relation is active, the end-user can select the cardinality field and directly type in the index number. The object with the corresponding reference is then accessed.

9.2.2 Navigating a secondary relationship type

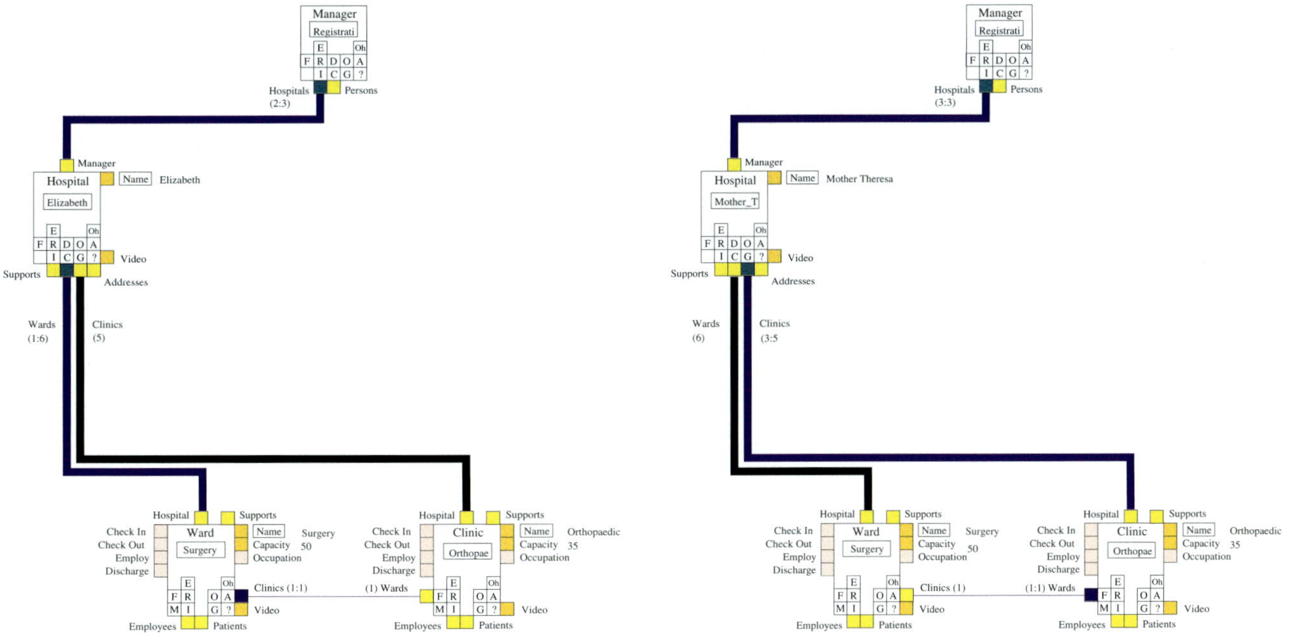

Figure 9.4: Navigating a secondary relation

Secondary relationship connectors are not visible in the user view when not active. When a secondary relation is activated, the connector becomes visible.
If the name of the relation appears at the place where the connector line should appear, the name will temporarily shift its position slightly.
The dynamic behavior of secondary relations and connectors is the same as in the case of an ownership relationship type.

Figure 9.4 illustrates the navigation through the secondary relationship type between `Ward` and `Clinic`.
This navigation is used to find out e.g. with which clinics a particular ward cooperates or vice-versa. In the example it implies the clinics that cooperate with the ward *Surgery* of the *Elizabeth* hospital. For this reason the secondary relation (`Clinics`) of ward *Surgery* (of *Elizabeth* hospital) is activated. The cardinality range (1) implies that *Surgery* ward of *Elizabeth* hospital cooperates with only one clinic, which means the iteration is limited to this one instance.

As soon as we iterate, the related instance at the other end of the secondary relationship will be accessed by Perspective-DB. In this example, it is clinic *Orthopaedic* of *Mother-Theresa* hospital.
The right side of the figure shows the same activity but from the other side of the secondary relationship. Orthopaedic clinic of *Mother-Theresa* hospital is accessed first, then `Wards` is activated. *Surgery* ward of *Elizabeth* hospital is found to be related.

Choices can now be made which are comparable to the case of ownership relationship type instances: the accessed instance can be used:

- as the starting point:
    - for further navigation deeper or higher in *its* (branch of the) ownership hierarchy or
    - for following a further secondary relationship
- to exploit the accessed information

9.2.3 Navigating a split at the target relationship type

When the relation is split, the connector line turns blue up to the splitting point. The split connector parts turn green indicating that the user can make a selection. When the user clicks the desired connector it turns blue. The others remain green indicating that they too can be selected.

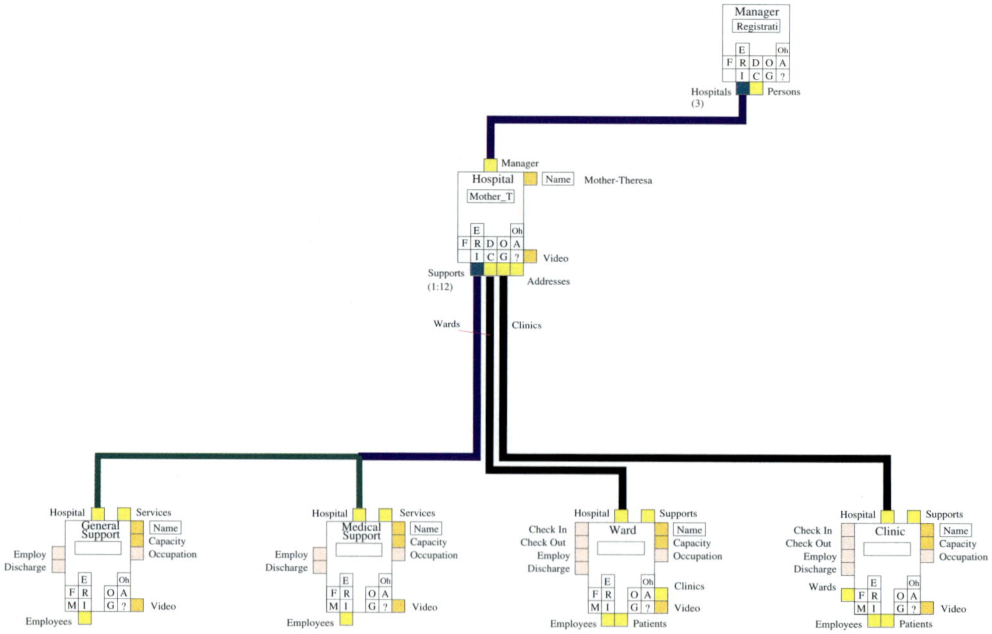

Figure 9.5: Navigating a split at the target relationship type, the split connector part is ready for selection

If the relationship is split at the target side, the connector parts beyond the splitting point are colored green to indicate that one has to be selected. This part of the relationship remains inactive until one of the split parts is selected.
Figure 9.5 illustrates this situation: `Supports` of *Mother-Theresa* hospital is activated.

There are two object types related to `Hospital.Supports` and there are 12 instances for *Mother-Theresa* hospital, see cardinality value (1:12). The connector to the `Support` departments can only be activated up to the splitting point. Beyond it, one part has to be selected. This is indicated by the two connector parts being green up to their target relations.

An instance can be accessed as follows:

- Select one of the connector parts by clicking. The connector turns blue. If this leads to another split, the process is repeated until the active connector reaches a relation.
- Iterate the relationship.

In Figure 9.6 the connector part to general support *Kitchen* is selected. The connector line turn blue (to indicate this). The non-selected connector part remains inactive (green).

When iterating, instances of type `Medical_Support` are skipped and only instances of type `General_Support` are shown. The cardinality index will skip positions accordingly.

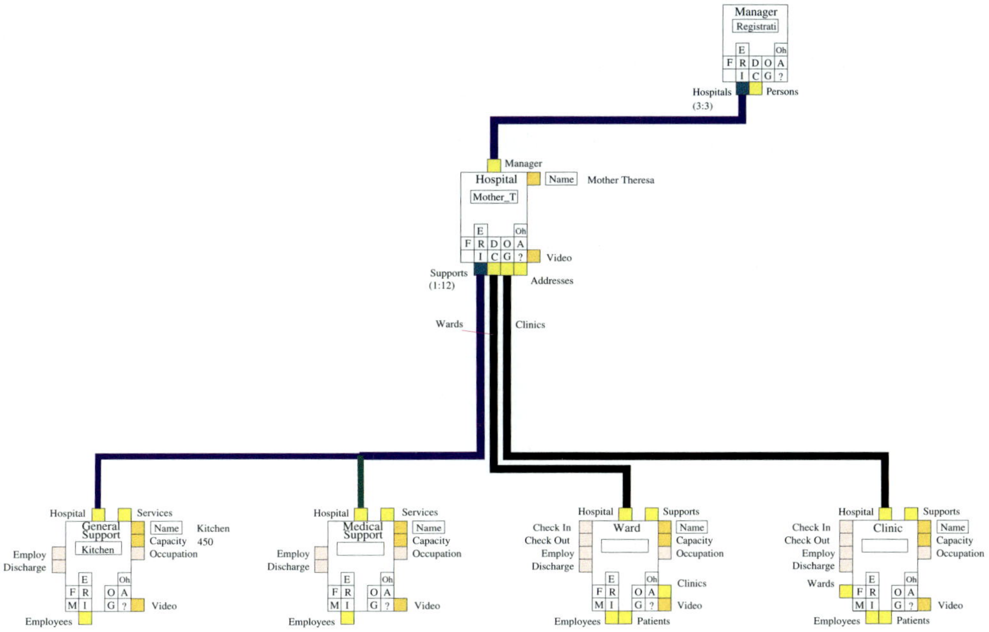

Figure 9.6: Navigating a split at the target relationship type; one of the connector parts is selected

Figure 9.7 shows what happens when the other part of the connector to a medical support (in this case X-Ray) is activated. The first part to the general support instance remains active (blue). The current instance is activated in the selected object type (`General_Support`), while the instance in the previously active type (`Medical_Support`) disappears. When iterating, the next instance appears in the corresponding object type and the previously active instance disappears, i.e. only one instance is active per iteration.

9.2.4 Navigation through a split at the source relationship type

If a relationship is split at the side where the navigation starts, Perspective-DB selects the navigation path along the connector parts leading to the target automatically, i.e. the connector parts from other sources do not get activated or become selectable.

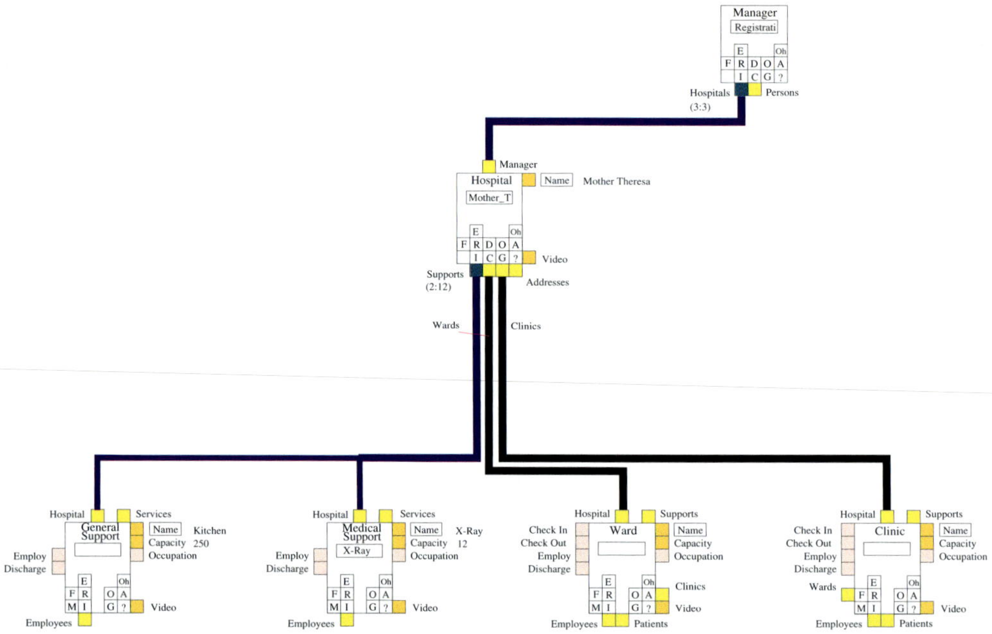

Figure 9.7: Navigating a split at the target relationship type; the other connector part is selected

It is useful to alternate the navigation path by deactivating one connector and activating another.

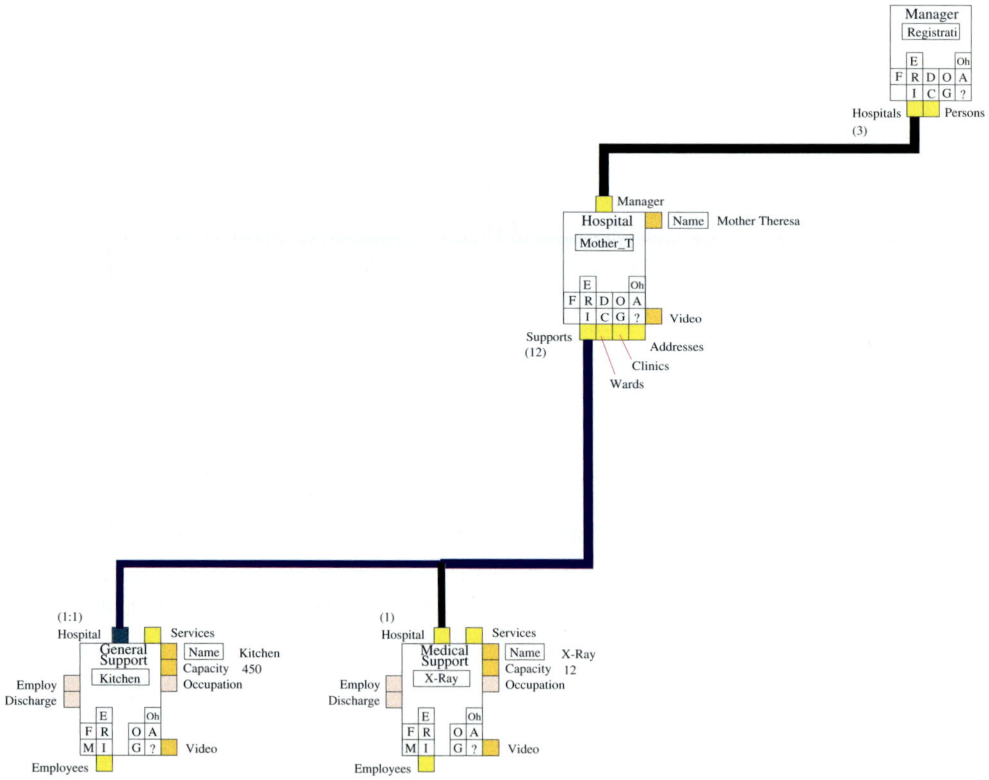

Figure 9.8: Navigating a split at the source relationship type; only one connector part is activated - 1

Figure 9.8 shows the navigation from the owned relation `Hospital` of general support *Kitchen* to its hospital *Mother-Theresa*.

As soon as `Hospital` of *Kitchen* is activated, the connector to *Mother-Theresa* becomes active. The connector part from medical support remains inactivate, as expected. The same happens in the case of the owned relation `Hospital` of medical support, e.g. *X-Ray*, being activated (`Hospital` of general support is de-activated). The connector part from general support remains inactive as illustrated in Figure 9.9.
Actually, at the meeting point the two paths join to become one.

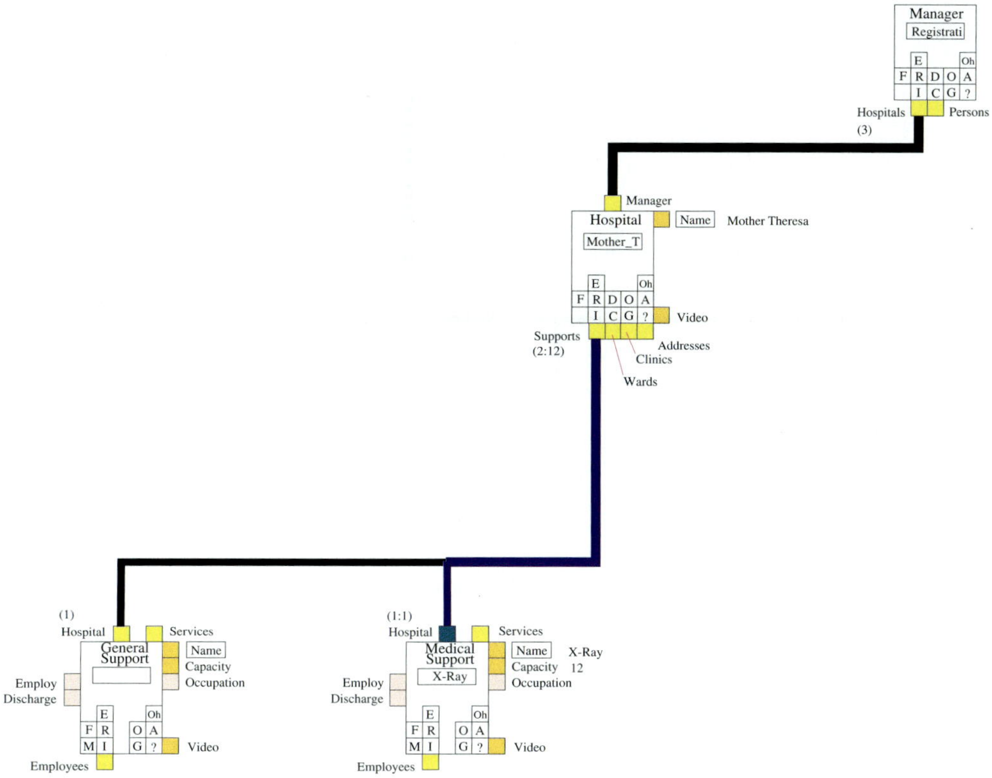

Figure 9.9: Navigating a split at the source relationship type; only one connector part is activated - 2

As soon as the relations `Hospital` of both general support and medical support are activated, Perspective-DB activates the respective part of the connector to the owner hospital as illustrated in Figures 9.10 and 9.11.

Figure 9.10 illustrates how Perspective-DB reacts to the situation proposed in Figure 9.9. In addition to the activated owned relation `Hospital` of *X-Ray*, the owned relation `Hospital` of *Kitchen* is now activated. This makes sense if information from both support department object types is needed simultaneously. In this case `Hospital` of general support is clicked. The connector part to the relation `Supports` of `Hospital` turns green (selectable), while the connector part from medical support remains blue (is active).
When the connector part between `General Support` and `Hospital` is activated by clicking, it turns blue and the former blue part turns green i.e. the connector part from `Medical Support` to `Hospital`. This is illustrated in Figure 9.11. The instance of medical support is now the actual instance owned by *Mother-Theresa* hospital; an instance of `Medical Support` can now be selected as the following actual instance owned by *Mother-Theresa* hospital.

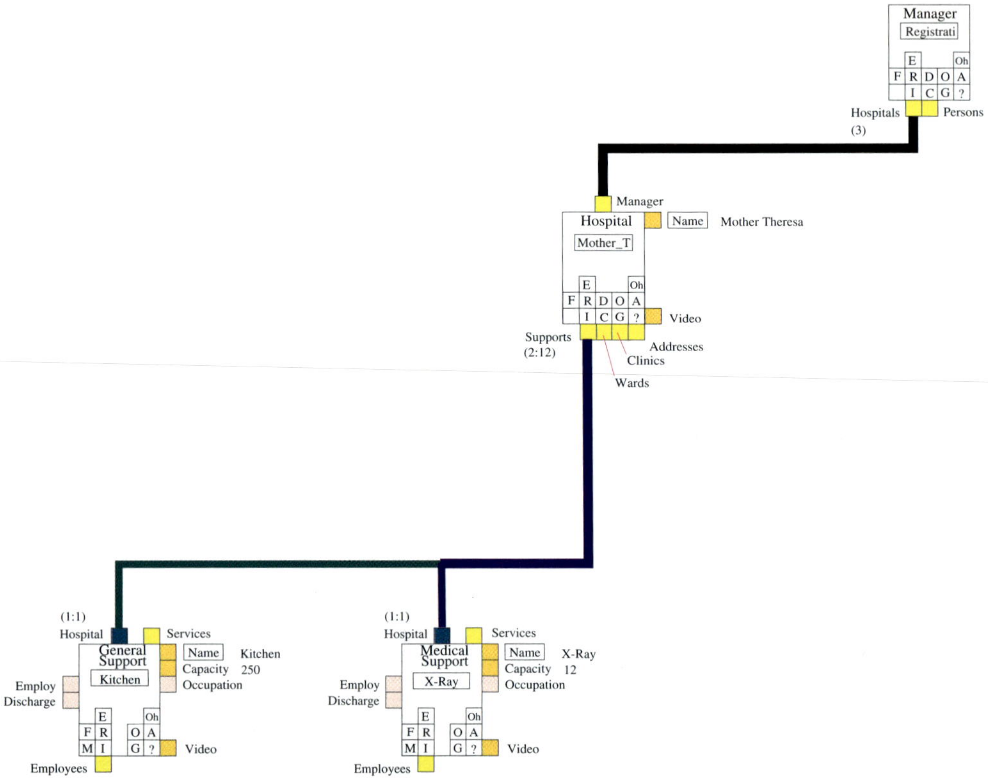

Figure 9.10: Navigating a split at the source relationship type; the second connector part can be activated

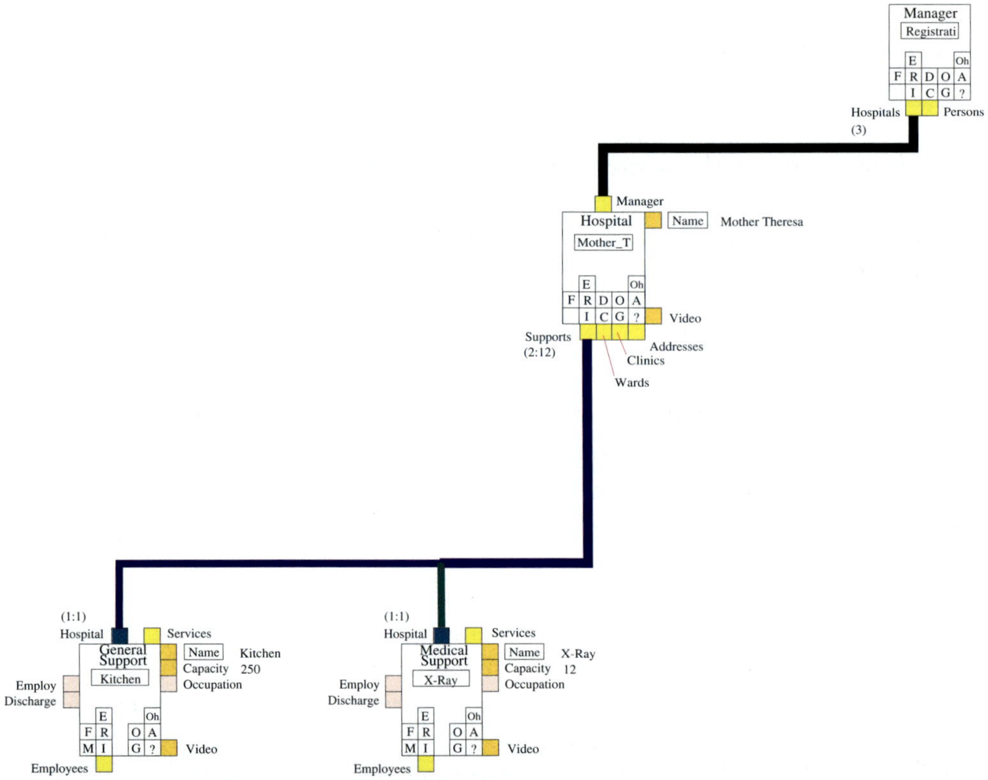

Figure 9.11: Navigating a split at the source relationship type; the second connector part is activated, the first can also be selected

Chapter 10

Schematic Interaction: Instantiation and Manipulation

10.1 Operations to Instantiate and Maintain an Object Base

The object base can be instantiated and manipulated in several ways:

- **File import**: loading prepared files in `TOML` instantiation format. This is an effective means of populating an object base.
- **Remote invocation**: another application invokes operations.
- **Schematic end-user interaction**: the operation members of accessed objects can be invoked.
- **Tabular end-user Interaction**: the object base is represented in various tabular formats that behave in accordance with the object model, including invocation of operations.

The user can combine schematic and tabular interaction which are tightly integrated. In general, the schematic is more effective for navigation and orientation, while the tables are more effective for rapidly modifying values of instances. The choice of what to use when depends on the task at hand and personal preference.

10.1.1 Creation of an Instance

The Figures 10.1 and 10.2 show how to create an instance using the schematic user view.

The creation of an instance is as follows:

- Access the owner instance.
- Activate its generic operation `C` (create).

  - The owner's selectable owning relations turn green indicating that the user has to choose one[1].
- Select the desired relation by clicking.

  - The selected relation turns blue, the selectable object types turn green.

[1] If there is only one owning relation, it turns blue indicating that it is selected.

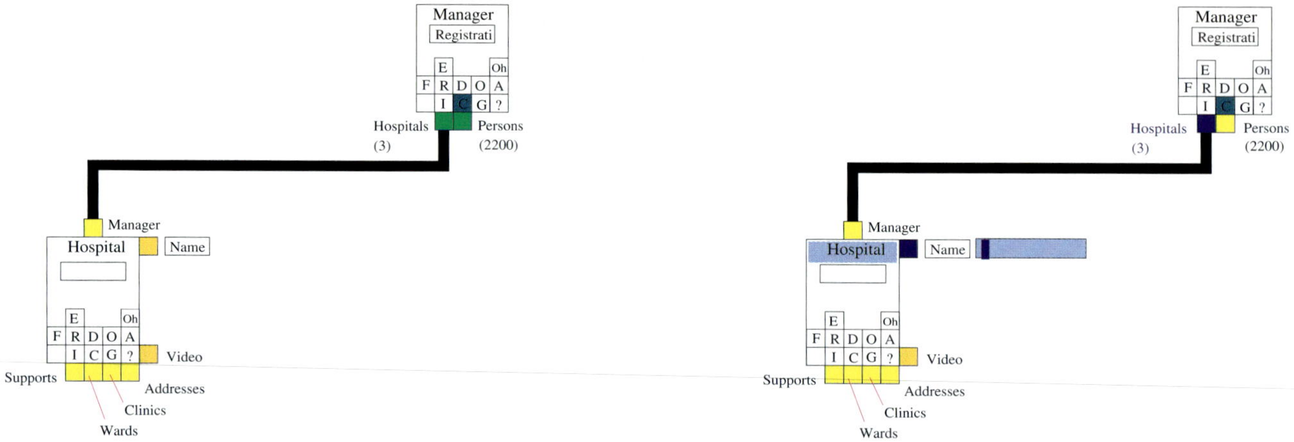

Figure 10.1: Creation of an instance; after activating the `Create` operation (left side) and selecting an owner relation (right side)

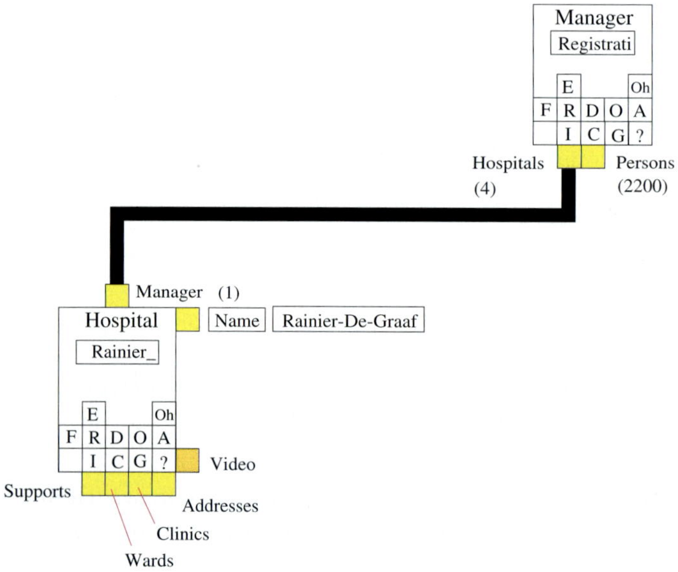

Figure 10.2: After creation of a new hospital instance

- Select the desired object type to be created[2].
  - The key attribute of the instance being created also turns blue.
- Fill in the value for the key.
- Press `ENTER`.
  - The new instance is created and the cardinality increases by 1.

The example illustrates the creation of a new hospital instance. At first the generic operation `C` (creation of an instance) is activated in the manager. This is illustrated on the left side of Figure 10.1. The two owner relations of `Manager` turn green meaning one of them has to be selected. By clicking the relation, `Hospitals` is selected.
The name of the object type `Hospital` and the value field of the key turn light blue, meaning it is ready to accept the key value of the new instance.

[2]In the case that there is only one object type on the other side it turns blue indicating it is selected.

At the same time the selected owner relation, the name of the active owner relation and the present cardinality value turn blue. In the example the relation `Hospitals`, its name and cardinality value *(3)* turn blue. See Figure 10.1, right side.
After inserting the key value (the name of the new hospital) the new instance is created. In Figure 10.2, the name *Rainier-De-Graaf* appears in the identity field. The cardinality value of the owner relation `Hospitals` increases to *(4)*. Perspective-DB will verify whether the key value remains unique in the scope of the owner relation, see Chapter 4 for more information. The attributes of the created instance are set to initial values.

10.1.2 Destruction of an Instance

Figures 10.3 and 10.4 show how to destroy an instance.

The actions for destroying an instance are as follows:

- Access the instance to be destroyed[3].
- Access the owner instance.
- Activate its generic operation `D`[4].
  - Its selectable ownership relations turn green.
- Select the desired relation by clicking.
  - The selected relation turns blue.
  - The identity field of the selected instance turns light blue.
- Press `ENTER`.
  - The cardinality decreases by 1.

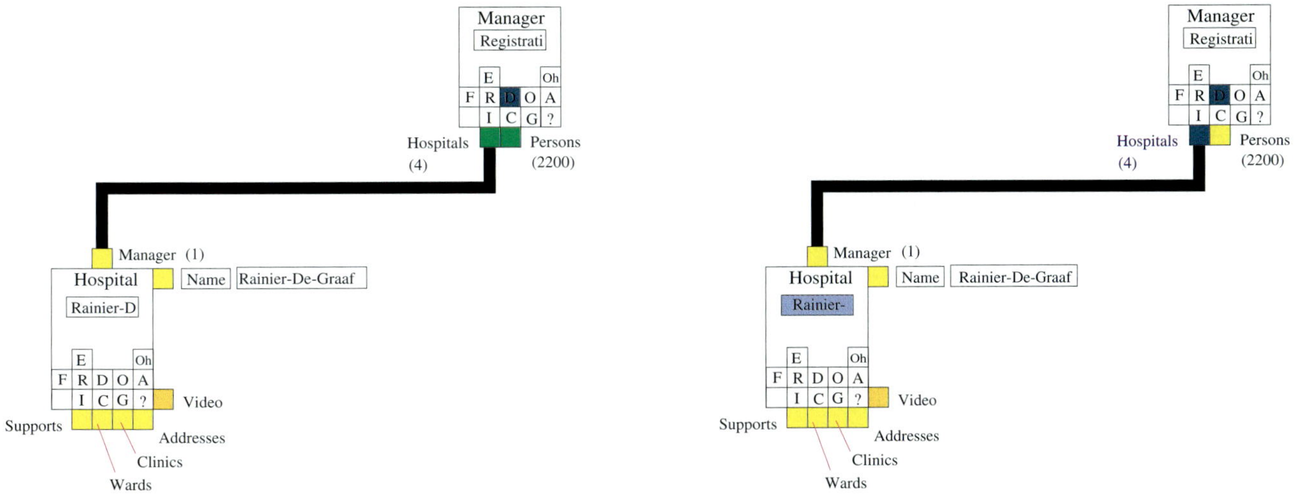

Figure 10.3: Destruction of an instance after activating the Delete operation (left side) and selecting an owner relation (right side)

[3]It is also possible to activate the destroy method and select the owner relation first. In this case, the destroy method is pending and a navigation is allowed in order to access the instance to be destroyed.

[4]If necessary you can check its global identity by clicking the field with the right mouse button.

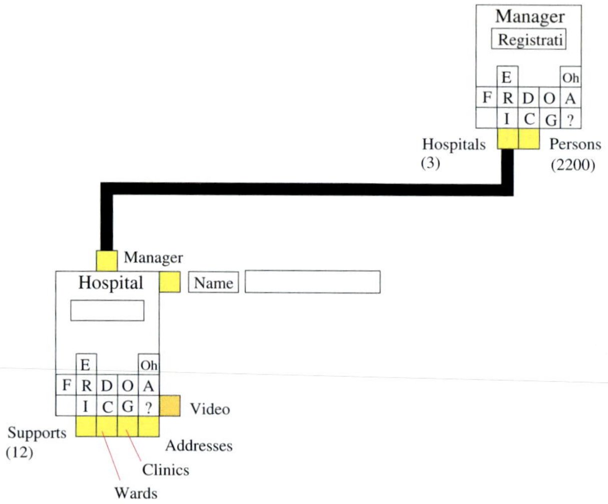

Figure 10.4: Destruction of an instance; after destruction of an instance

The example illustrates the destruction of the hospital instance *Rainier-De-Graaf*. At first the generic operation `D` (destruction of an instance) has to be activated in the manager. This is illustrated on the left side of Figure 10.3. The two owner relations of Manager turn green, implying that one of them has to be selected. **`Hospitals`** is selected in this example and turns blue and the ID field of object type Hospital turns blue indicating the instance in access is selected to be destroyed[5].
This is illustrated in Figure 10.3, right side. If the instance to be destroyed is in access (recognizable by name, identity and cardinality index), the destruction is executed when `ENTER` is pressed. The cardinality decreases to *3*, see Figure 10.4.

10.1.3 Enter and Modify values of Instances

Figures 10.5, 10.6 and 10.7 show how to enter and modify attribute values of an instance.
The generic operation **`Modify`** is used to enter and modify an attribute value. Entering the key value with **`Create`** is an exception.
Entering and modifying an attribute value of an instance is as follows:

- Access the instance where attribute values are to be entered or modified.
- Activate the generic operation `M` in the instance.
  - The selectable attributes turn green.
- Select the desired attribute by clicking.
  - The selected attribute turns blue.
  - The value field turns light blue.
  - Enter the value.
- Press `ENTER`.

The **`example`** on the left side of Figure 10.5 illustrates that the instance must first be accessed. In it, attribute **`Capacity`** of *Surgery* ward of the *Elizabeth* hospital is being modified.

[5]Alternatively, it is possible to iterate to the intended instance after invoking the destroy operation and selecting the owner relation. To start the iteration, the user selects the owner relation once more. The relation turns gray and the connector blue, indicating that the relation is active and iteration is possible.

The right side of the figure illustrates the behavior after activating the generic operation `M` (Modify). The activated operation button turns gray while the selectable attributes, including the name field of the key attribute turn green.

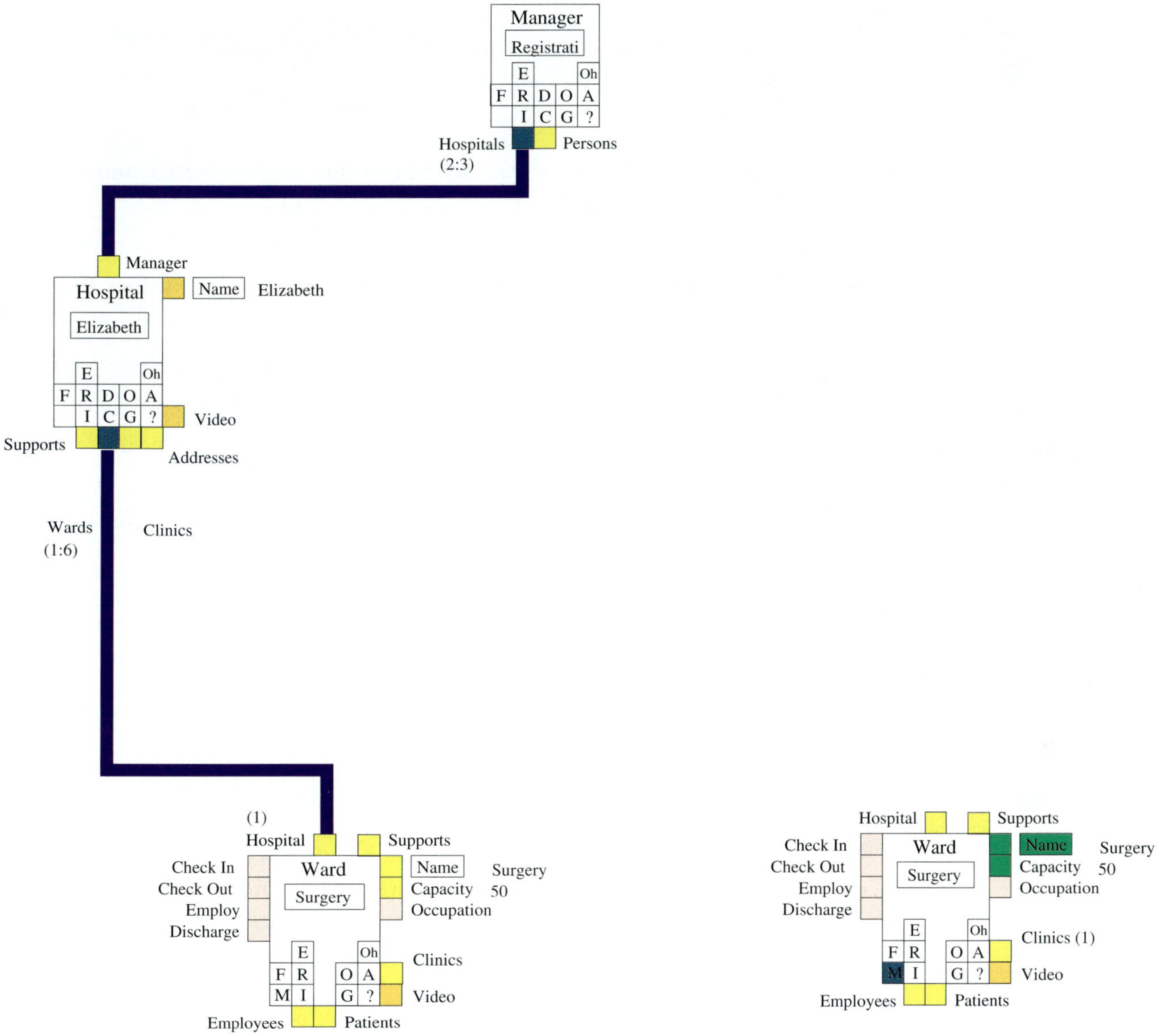

Figure 10.5: Enter and modify values of an instance; the instance is accessed (left side), the Modify operation is activated and the selectable attributes are indicated by the color green (right side)

The left side of Figure 10.6 shows the situation after selecting the attribute `Capacity`. The attribute itself turns blue, the value field turns light blue with a blue cursor placed in it[6]. The old value is still visible. The value will be overwritten by the new. The right side of the figure shows the instance after modifying the attribute value (then pressing `ENTER`).

Modifying Ranged Values

If an attribute has a predefined limited range of values, the permitted value can be found by iterating in the value field using the right (forwards) or middle (backwards) mouse button. When a ranged attribute is selected, a > appears beside the blue colored value field.

[6]The other attributes will resume their normal color.

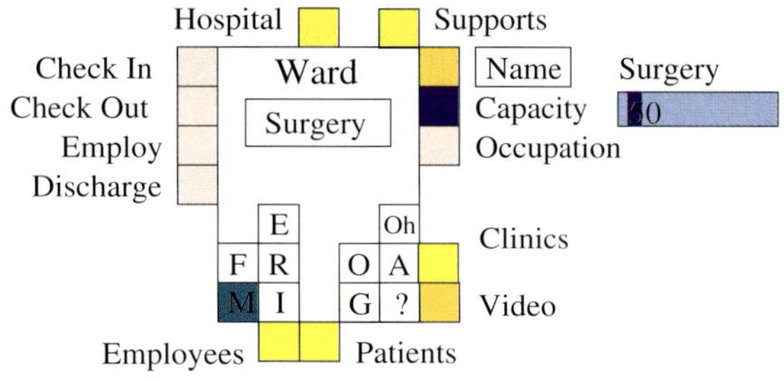

Figure 10.6: Enter and modify values of an instance; the attribute has been selected and can be modified (left side), the value is modified (right side)

The value domain is pre-defined by the application developer. Perspective-DB refuses values that are not in the range.

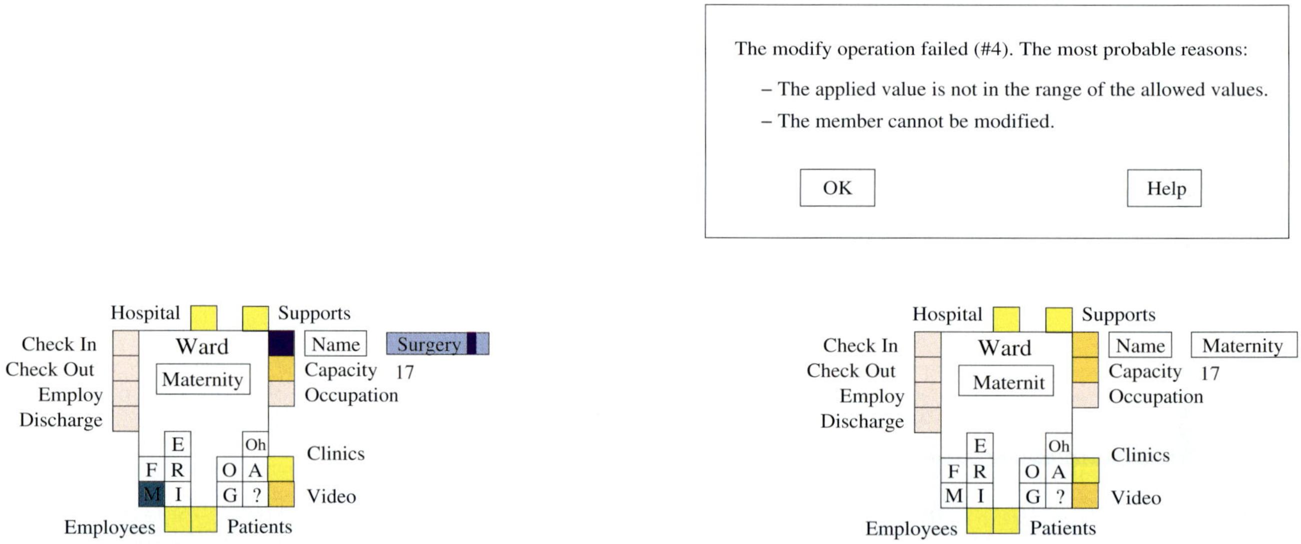

Figure 10.7: Result of entering an already existing key value

Figure 10.7 illustrates the reaction of Perspective-DB when the key value is modified to an illegal value. Suppose the user wants to rename *Maternity* ward *Surgery*. *Maternity* ward is in access. The generic operation `M` is activated and the key attribute is selected. The value *Surgery* is entered for a ward of *Elizabeth* hospital[7] and `ENTER` is pressed (see left side). A window pops up with an explanation for refusing the operation. In this case the first reason applies: the key value *Surgery* is no longer in the range of allowed values because it already exists as a ward of *Elizabeth* hospital[8].

10.1.4 Get a Particular Instance into Access

When iteration requires too much effort due to a large number of instances, the generic operation `G` (`Get`) can be used to search for an instance having a particular attribute value.
The first instance with the corresponding value is brought into access. If more than one instance has the same value, repeating the `Get` operation will access the next one.

Figures 10.8, 10.9 and 10.10 show how to get an instance.

[7] No > token appears at the end of *Surgery* because the range of names is unlimited.
[8] It is possible to modify the value of the key as long as it is not the key of another instance in the same relation.

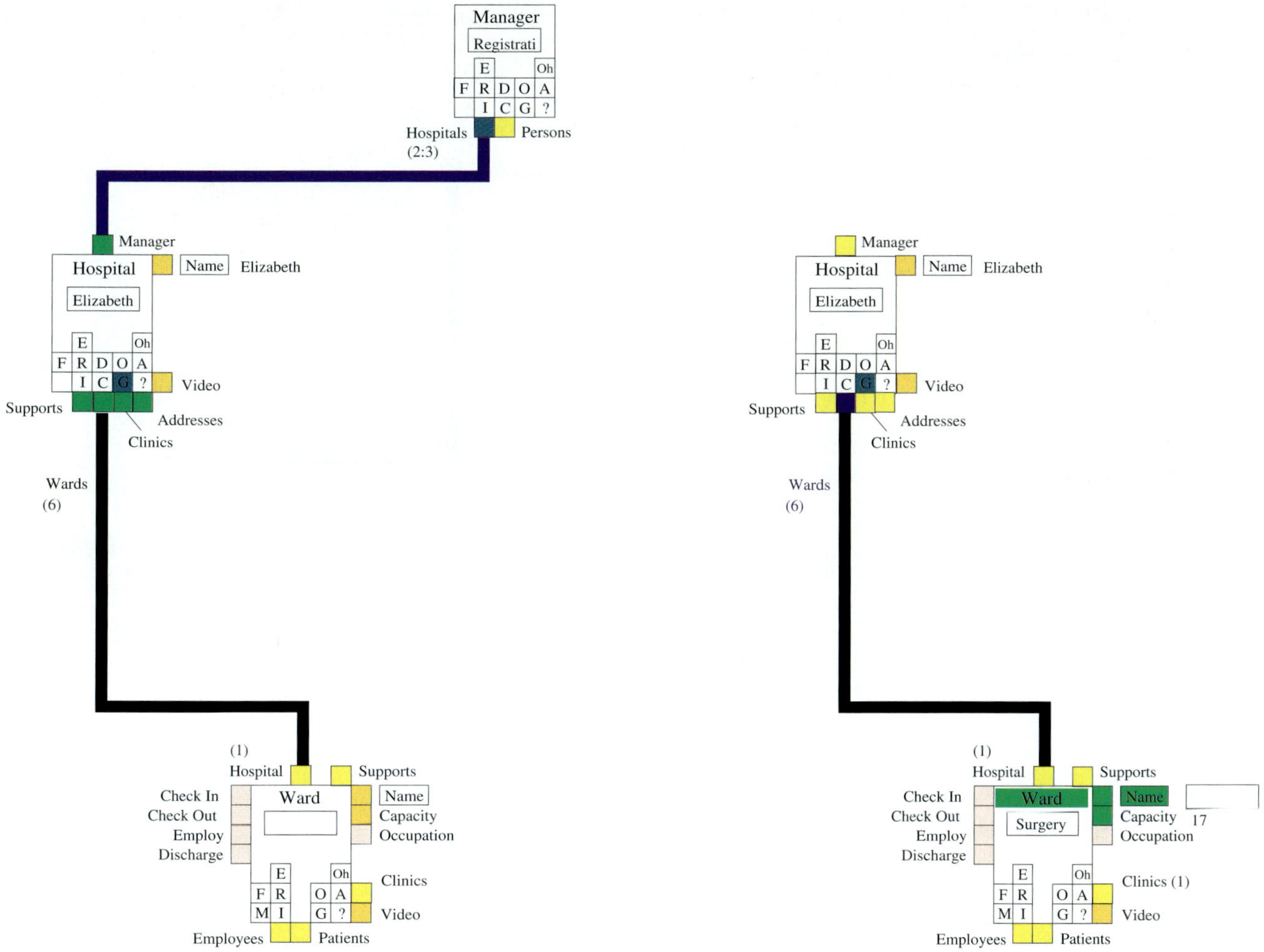

Figure 10.8: Get an instance - 1

The left side of Figure 10.8 illustrates the activation of `G` (`Get`) in the *Elizabeth* hospital. The ownership connector between Manager and *Elizabeth* hospital is still blue from the previous iteration to *Elizabeth* hospital. As soon as `G` is activated, all selectable relations turn green, including the owned relation Manager as in this case. The user has to select the relation to which he/she wishes to apply the `Get` operation. The right side of the figure shows that `Wards` is selected. The owner relation Wards turns blue, including its name and the cardinality value. The name of the object type Ward[9] and the selectable attributes are green. The user has to select the attribute to which he/she wishes to apply the `Get` operation.
In the `example`, `Get` is applied to the key attribute, see Figure 10.9. The user selects the key attribute shown on the left side (there is currently no instance in access). Then the user enters the intended name of the `Ward`, *Pediatric*, as shown on the right[10]. After inserting the value for the `Get`, `ENTER` is pressed.
The gotten instance ward *Pediatric* is now in access as shown in Figure 10.10.

Perspective-DB knows a short-cut for `Get`. A precondition is that a navigation path between the source (where the `Get` is performed) and target object types is active.

[9]If the user selects the name, the ID field turns blue and the user can enter the ID of the object required.
[10]The user can either type in the intended name, or select it by iterating the list of instances, see the > sign beside the key value field.

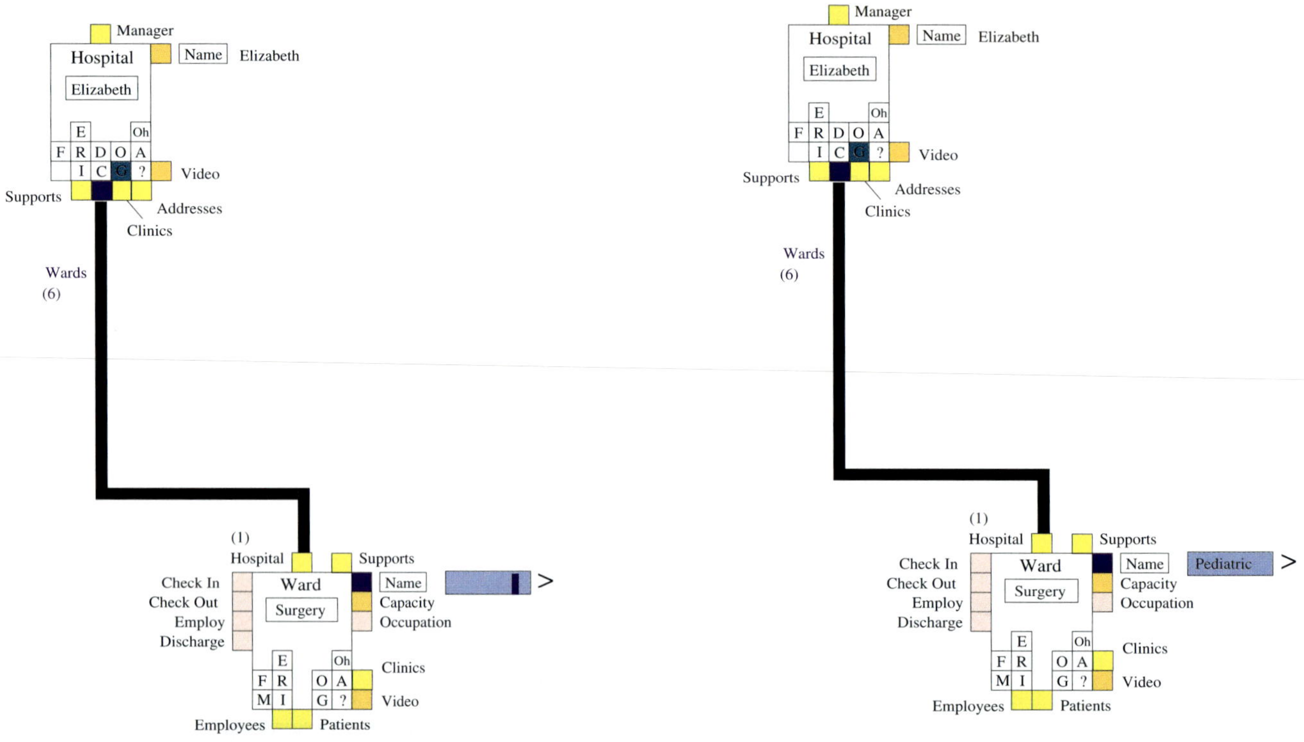

Figure 10.9: Get an instance - 2

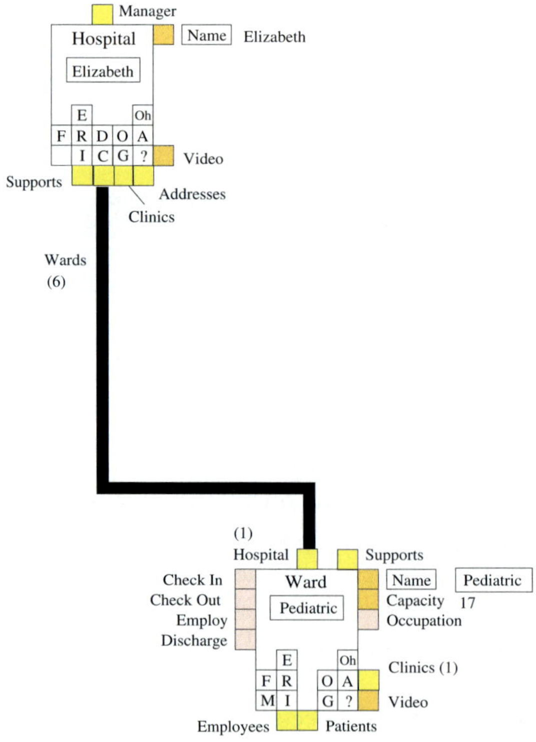

Figure 10.10: Get an instance; the result

Placing the cursor on the chosen attribute and pressing the `control-key` and the left mouse key simultaneously causes the member and the value field to turn blue.

The selection value can be entered and confirmed with `ENTER`. Instance(s) which fulfill the selection criterion can then be brought into access one by one by repeating the procedure. Figures 10.11 and 10.12 illustrate this short-cut.

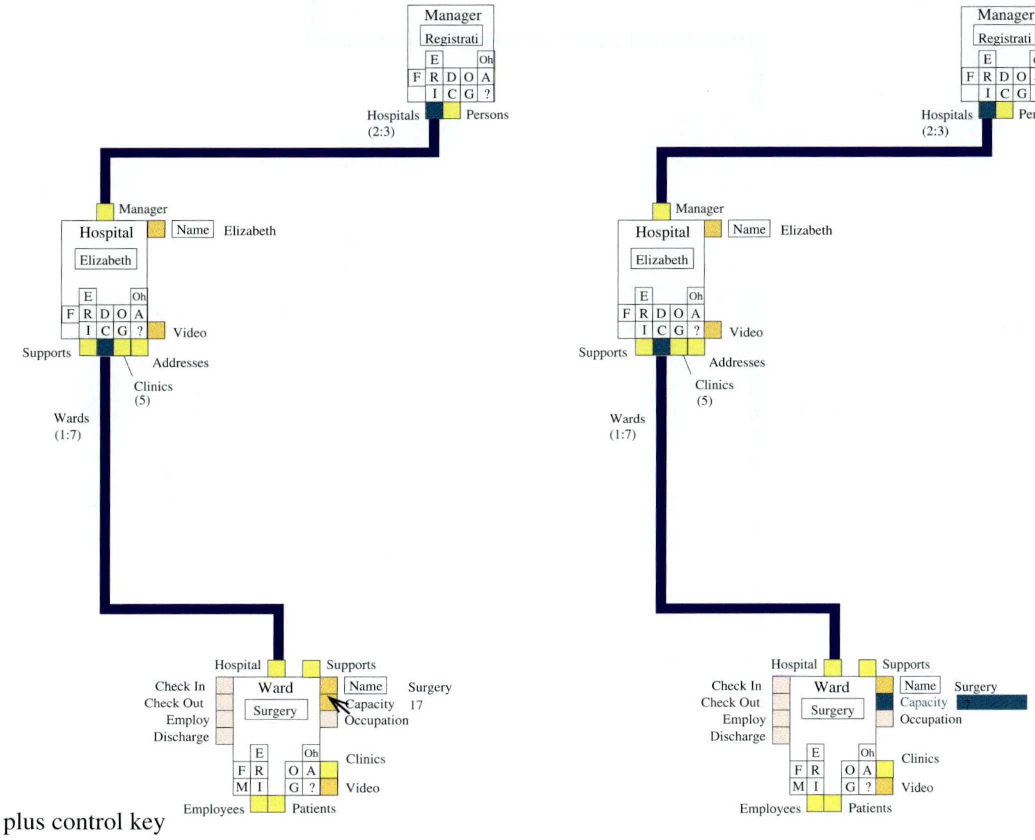

Figure 10.11: Short-cut for getting an instance

Figure 10.11 on the left shows that `Ward` of *Elizabeth* hospital is the actual object type. The goal is to find wards of *Elizabeth* hospital which have a capacity of *7*. For this reason, the mouse cursor is located on `Capacity`. As soon as the key `Control` is pressed, `Capacity` member and its value field turn gray. The value *7* is entered and confirmed, see Figure 10.11, right side. Figure 10.12 shows the actual instance of ward with the capacity *7*. To find the next instance with the same capacity, the short-cut `get` is repeated.

10.1.5 Insert in a Secondary Relationship

The actions for inserting a secondary relationship between two instances are as follows:

- Access the instance on the source side where a secondary relationship is to be inserted.
- Activate the generic operation `I` in the instance.
  - The selectable relations turns green.
- Select the desired relation by clicking.
  - The relation turns blue.
  - The name and the cardinality value turn blue.
  - The identity field of the target object type turns light blue.

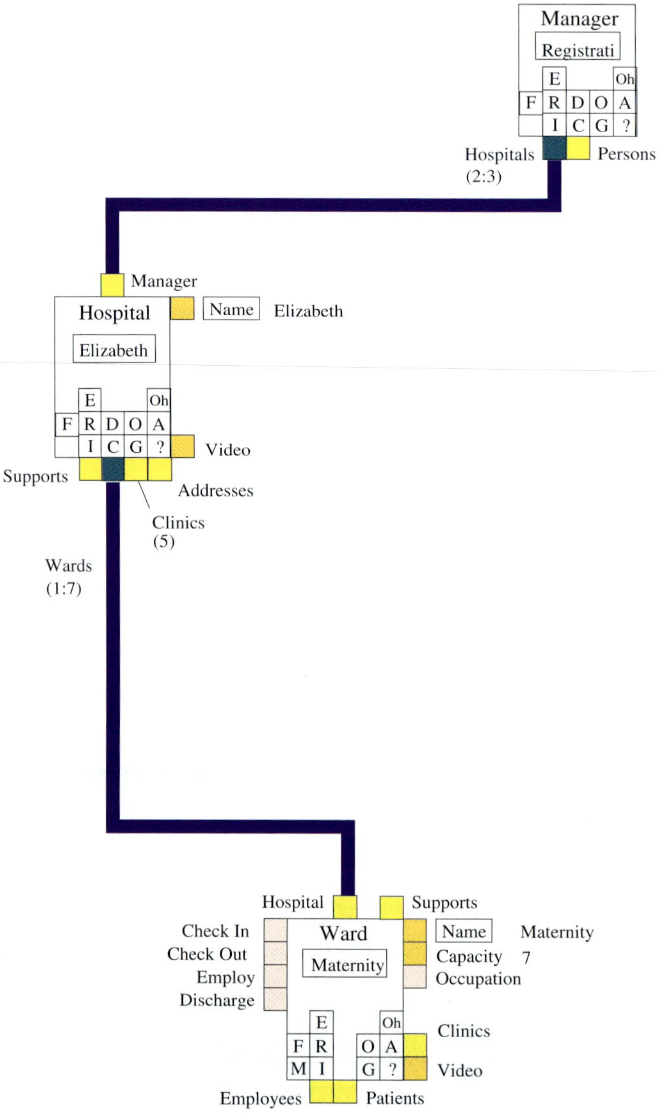

Figure 10.12: The instance in access

- Select the target instance by accessing it.
- Press `ENTER`.
  - The cardinality increases by 1.

Figures 10.13, 10.14, 10.15 , 10.16 show how to insert a secondary relationship.

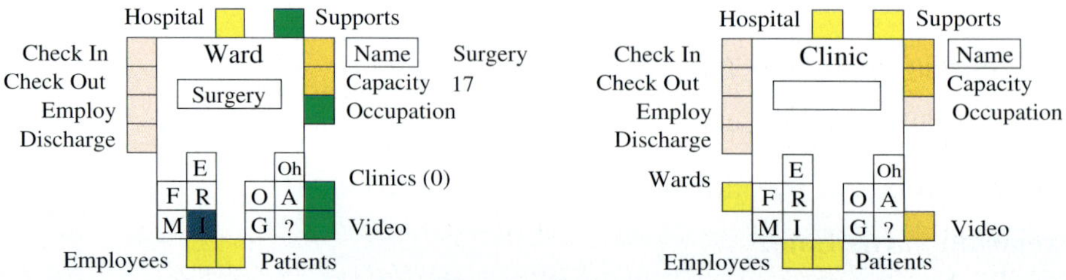

Figure 10.13: Insert a secondary relationship; the operation is activated

Figure 10.13 shows ward Surgery (of *Elizabeth* hospital) as the accessed source instance. The generic operation `I` (`Insert`) is activated. The selectable secondary relations and `Video` turn green.

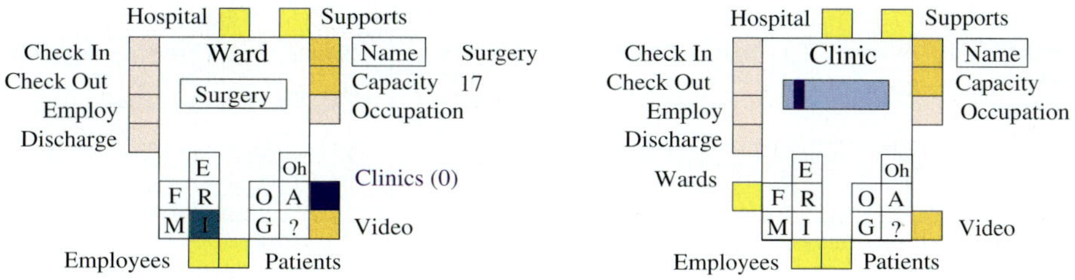

Figure 10.14: Insert a secondary relationship; the relation is selected

Figure 10.14 shows the situation after selecting `Clinics`. The relation `Clinics`, its name and cardinality value turn blue. The identity field of the object type `Clinic` turns light blue. An instance to be chosen will be related to ward *Surgery.Clinics*.

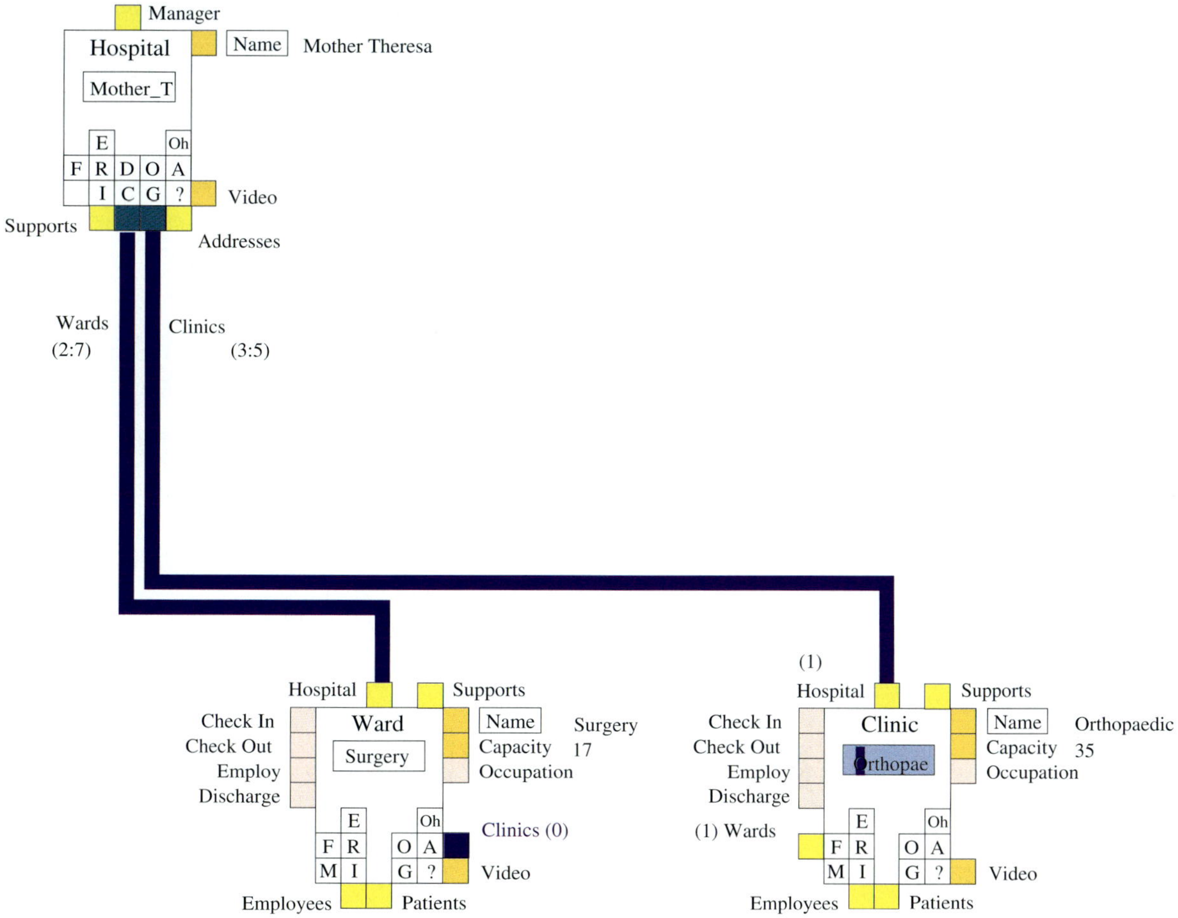

Figure 10.15: Insert a secondary relationship; select the relation at the target side

Figure 10.15, illustrates how to navigate to the instance that is to be related to ward *Surgery.Clinics*. In the example, clinic *Orthopaedic* of *Mother-Theresa* hospital is the target. First, *Mother-Theresa* hospital is accessed, then *Orthopaedic* clinic, see the blue ownership relation and connector.

The required instance (here *Mother-Theresa*'s *Orthopaedic* clinic) is selected and the insert operation is completed by pressing ENTER to confirm that the source and target instances in access are to be related.

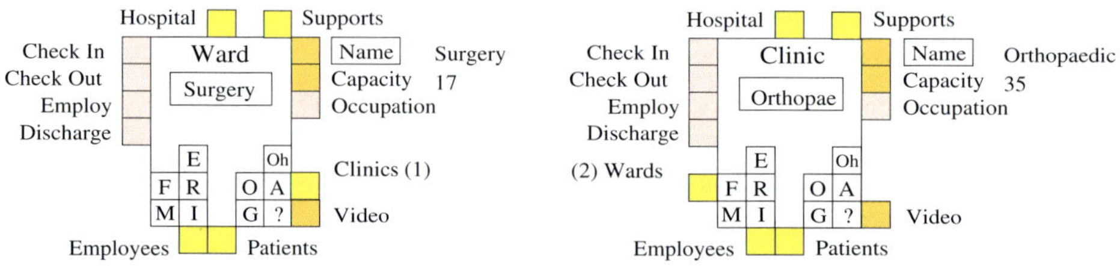

Figure 10.16: Insert a secondary relationship; the relationship is inserted

The result of the insertion is shown in Figure 10.16. The cardinality values of both relevant relations are incremented by 1, compare Figures 10.15 and 10.16. It is now possible to navigate this relationship.

10.1.6 Remove a Secondary Relationship

The actions for removing a secondary relationship between two instances are as follows:

- Access the instance where a secondary relationship is to be removed.
- Activate the generic operation R in the instance.
  - The selectable relations turn green.
- Select the desired relation by clicking.
  - The relation turns blue.
  - The identity field of the target instance turns light blue.
- Select the instance to be removed (by iterating the relation)[11].
- - Press ENTER.
  - The cardinality will be decremented by 1.

Figures 10.17, 10.18, 10.19 , 10.20 show how to remove an instance in a secondary relation.

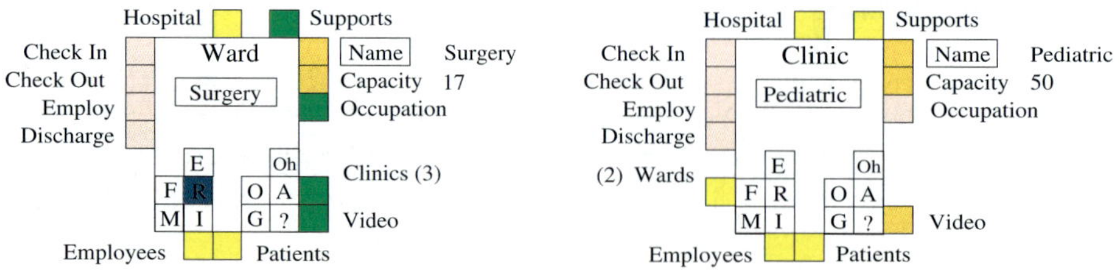

Figure 10.17: Remove a secondary relationship; the operation is activated

Figure 10.17 shows ward *Surgery* (of *Elizabeth* hospital) is the accessed source instance. The generic operation R (Remove) is activated. The selectable secondary relations turn green.

Figure 10.18 shows the situation after selecting Clinics. The relation Clinics, the relation name and the cardinality value turn blue.

[11]Alternatively, the user can first access the instance to be removed and then invoke the remove operation.

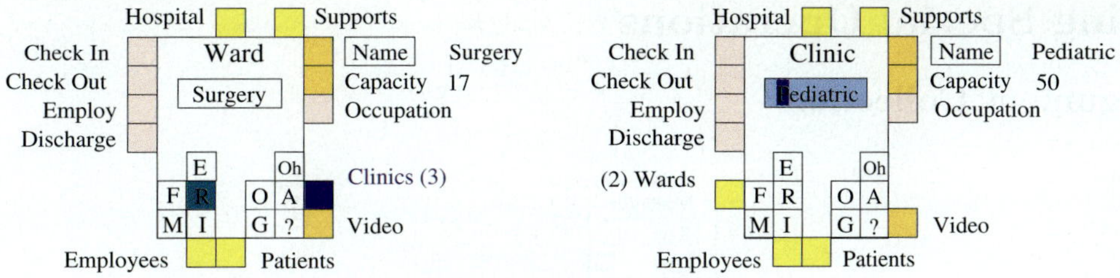

Figure 10.18: Remove a secondary relationship; the relation is selected

The identity field of the object type `Clinic` turns light blue. A blue cursor indicates that an instance can be selected. Presently, the *Pediatric* clinic is accessed. By iterating the relation `Clinics`, the instance *Orthopaedic* is accessed.

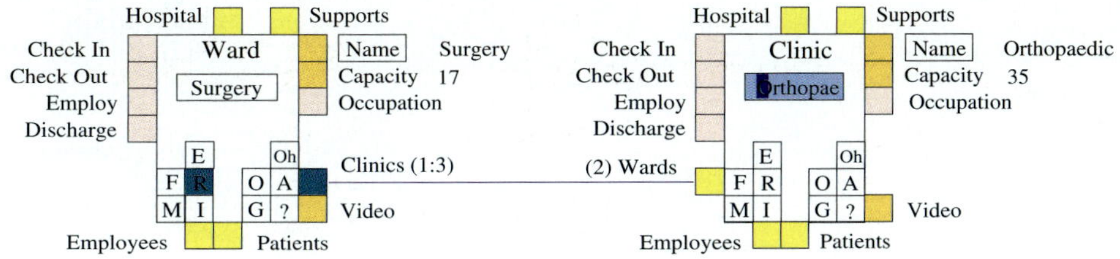

Figure 10.19: Remove a secondary relationship; iterating through the existing relationships

In Figure 10.19 the relationship between ward *Surgery.Clinics* and clinic *Orthopaedic.Ward* is activated. The remove operation can be completed by pressing `ENTER` to confirm.

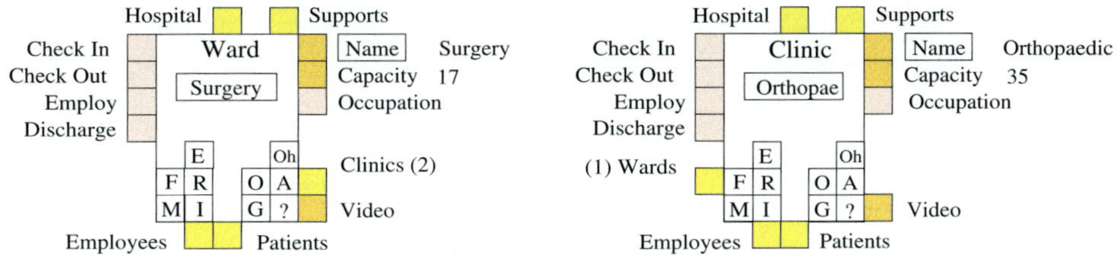

Figure 10.20: Remove a secondary relationship; the relationship is removed

Figure 10.20 shows the result of the remove operation, the cardinality values of the relations `Surgery.Clinics` and `Orthopaedic.Wards` are decremented by 1. The user has deactivated the relation `Clinics`.

10.2 Using Special Operations

10.2.1 Argument Collection

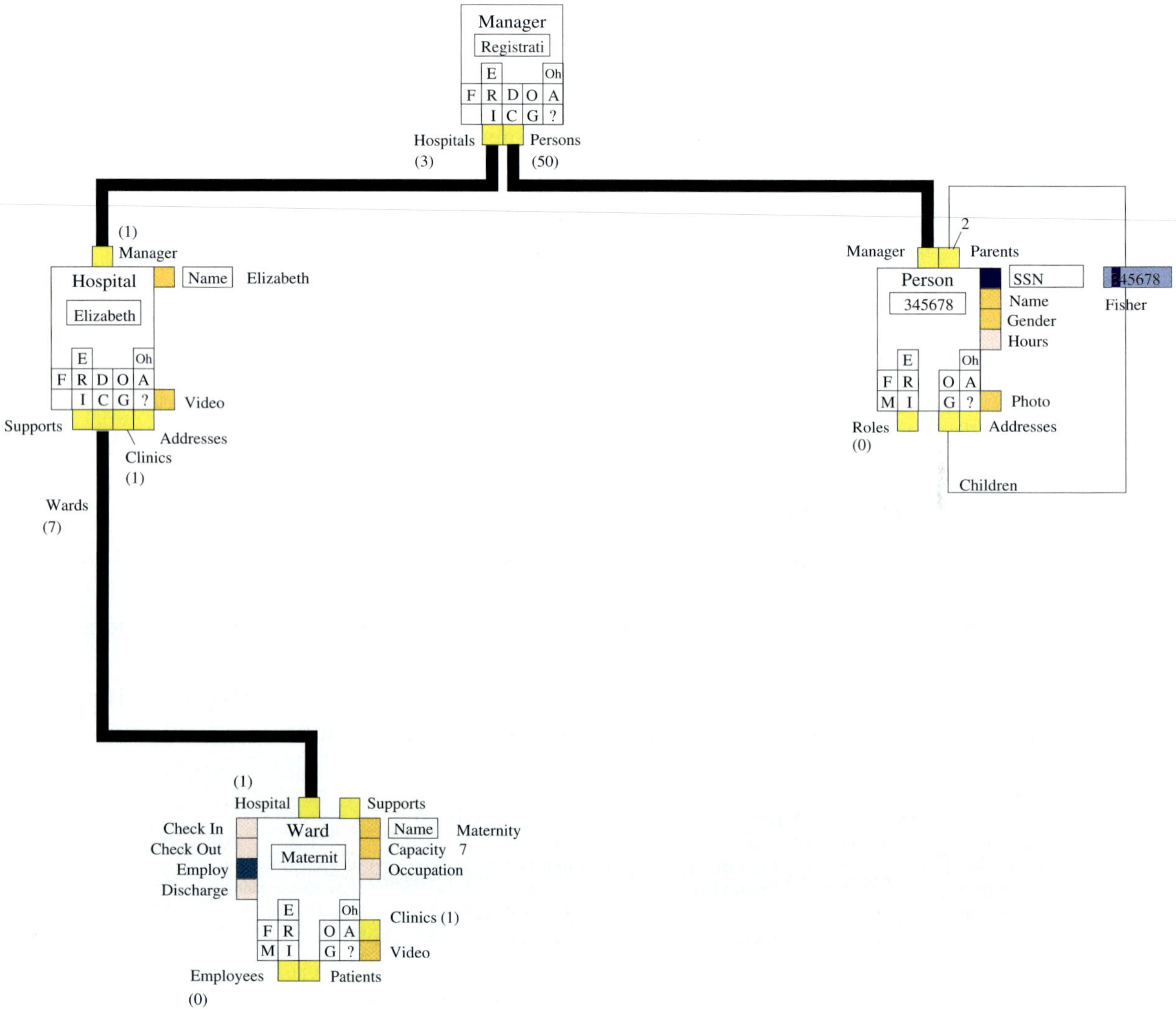

Figure 10.21: Activating a special operation

Some special operations do not need arguments. They will be invoked after they have been activated with a mouse click. The result is given in a **return value**, similar to an attribute value, in the field beside the operation-member rectangle.

Other special operations need arguments. The arguments for operations are collected along a **collection path**.

During the argument collection, the user is guided by the system through switching the relevant instance member to blue and positioning the (blue) cursor in the value field. When more than one argument is needed, Perspective-DB indicates this in the defined logical collection order.

When the collection of arguments requires a selection (because there are alternatives), either one or several object types, instances or members of an instance become selectable, depending on the situation. In situations where the system requires input from the end-user, various methods can be used. The end-user can insert a value using the keyboard. Alternatively the end-user can copy the value from another instance (found for example by navigation or query) using "drag and drop".

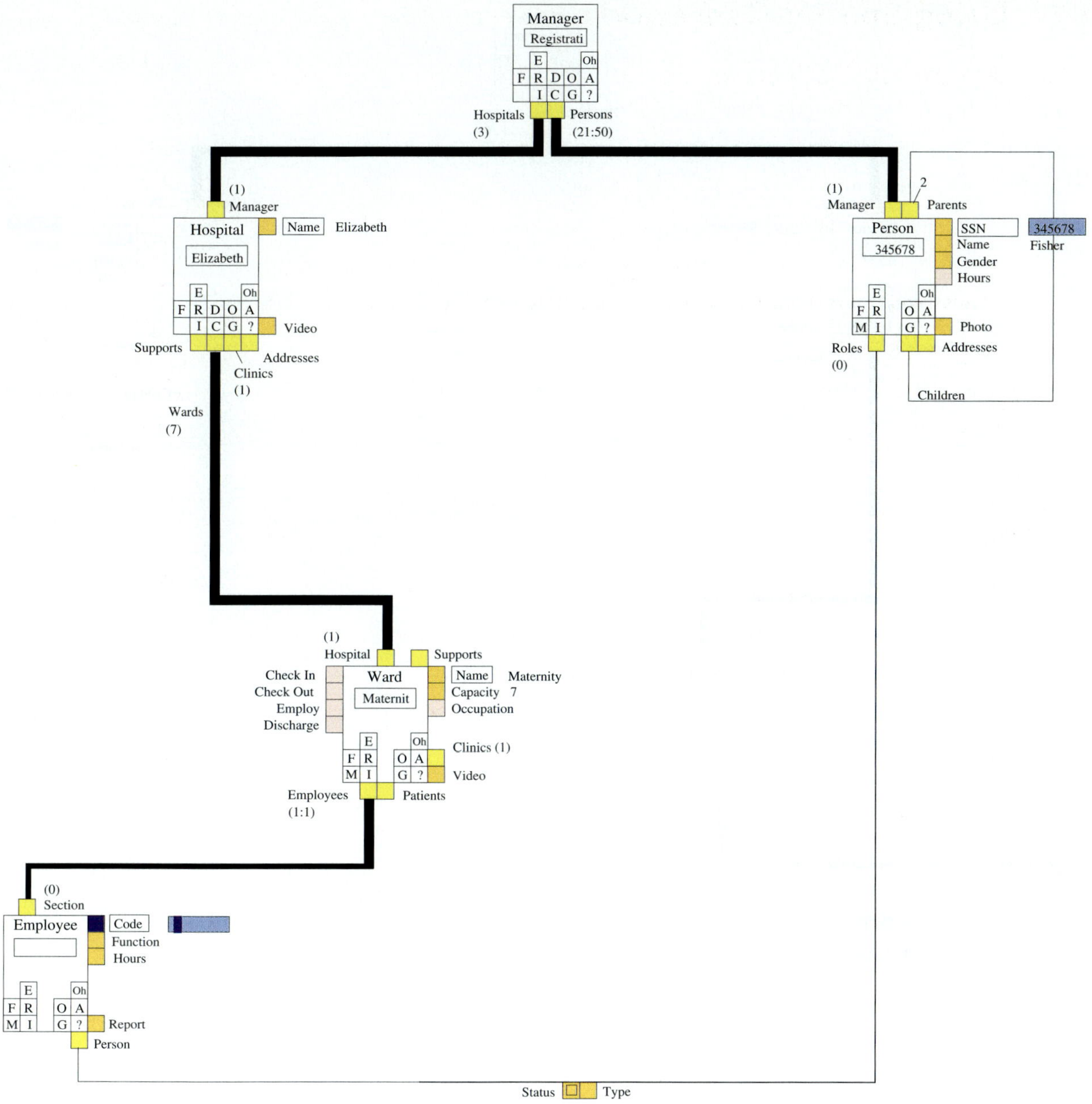

Figure 10.22: Collecting arguments for processing the operation - 1

The end-user can also iterate the list of possible values in the selected value field itself[12] and then select the one required.
When the sequence of the collection depends on the value of the former argument, Perspective-DB manages the argument collection as follows:
When an operation with serval arguments is invoked, the arguments of that operation are collected sequentially. Based on the input of a single argument, one or more object types, instances, or members in the collection path can be activated or de-activated according to the information given in earlier arguments.

[12]The existence of a list of possible values generally applies to attributes that have a value domain that is ranged.

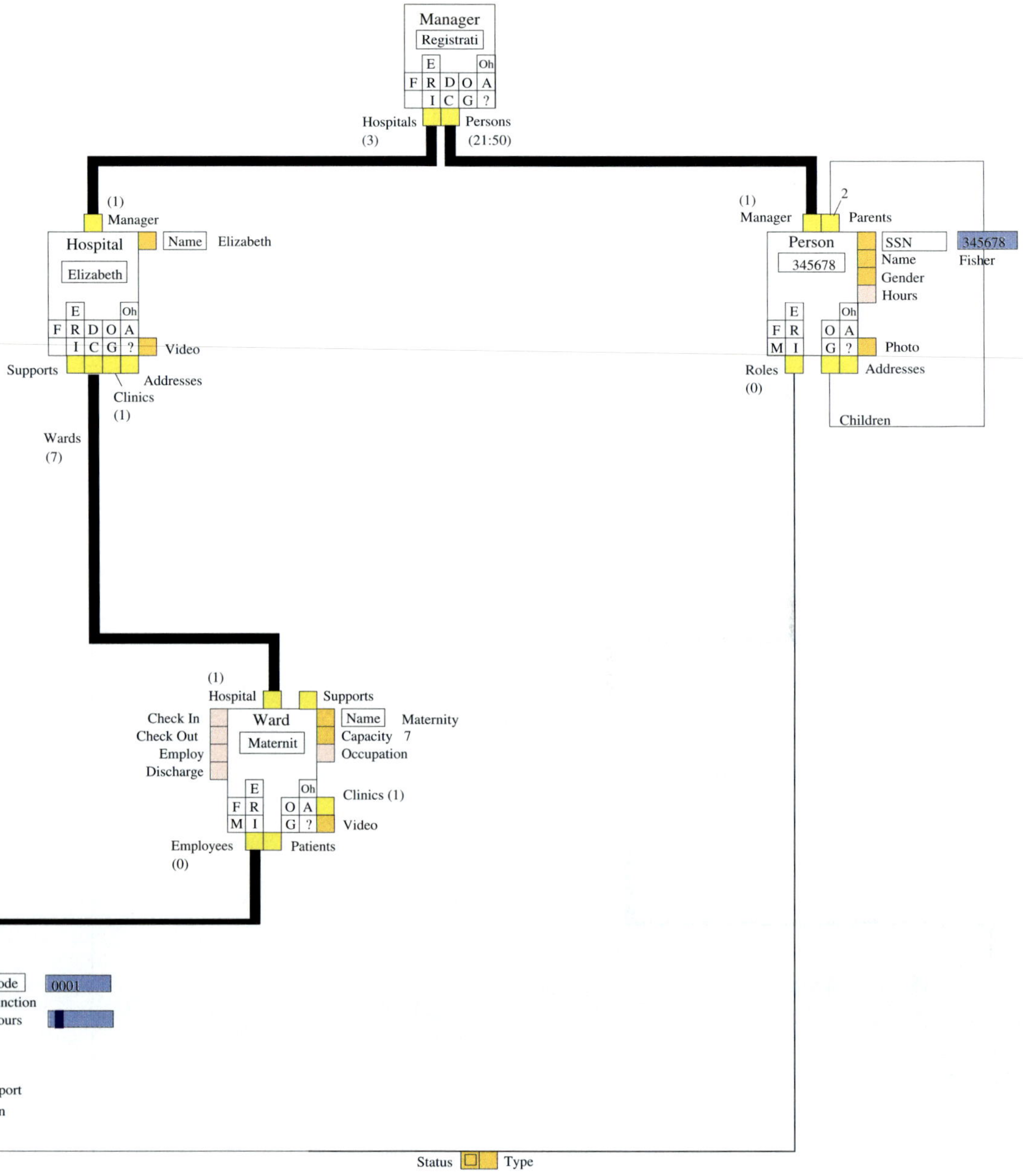

Figure 10.23: Collecting arguments for processing the operation - 2

Figure 10.21 illustrates activating a special operation, in this example employ a person in ward Maternity of *Elizabeth* hospital. The special operation `Employ` is activated. The member turns gray. The processing of this operation needs arguments from other instances[13]. In the example, the first argument is the key of the person to be employed. Thus, the key value of `Person` turns blue. A cursor is placed in the attribute value field, indicating that a value is expected. In this particular case only a `SSN` (Social Security Number) can be entered which already exists. It is not possible to employ a person who is unknown in the application. Thus, the right person has to be brought in access at first, then the key value has to be entered by pressing `ENTER`. Here, the person with the `SSN` *345678* is employed.
Figure 10.22 shows the argument collection.

[13]The system starts the argument collection procedure directly after the operation is activated.

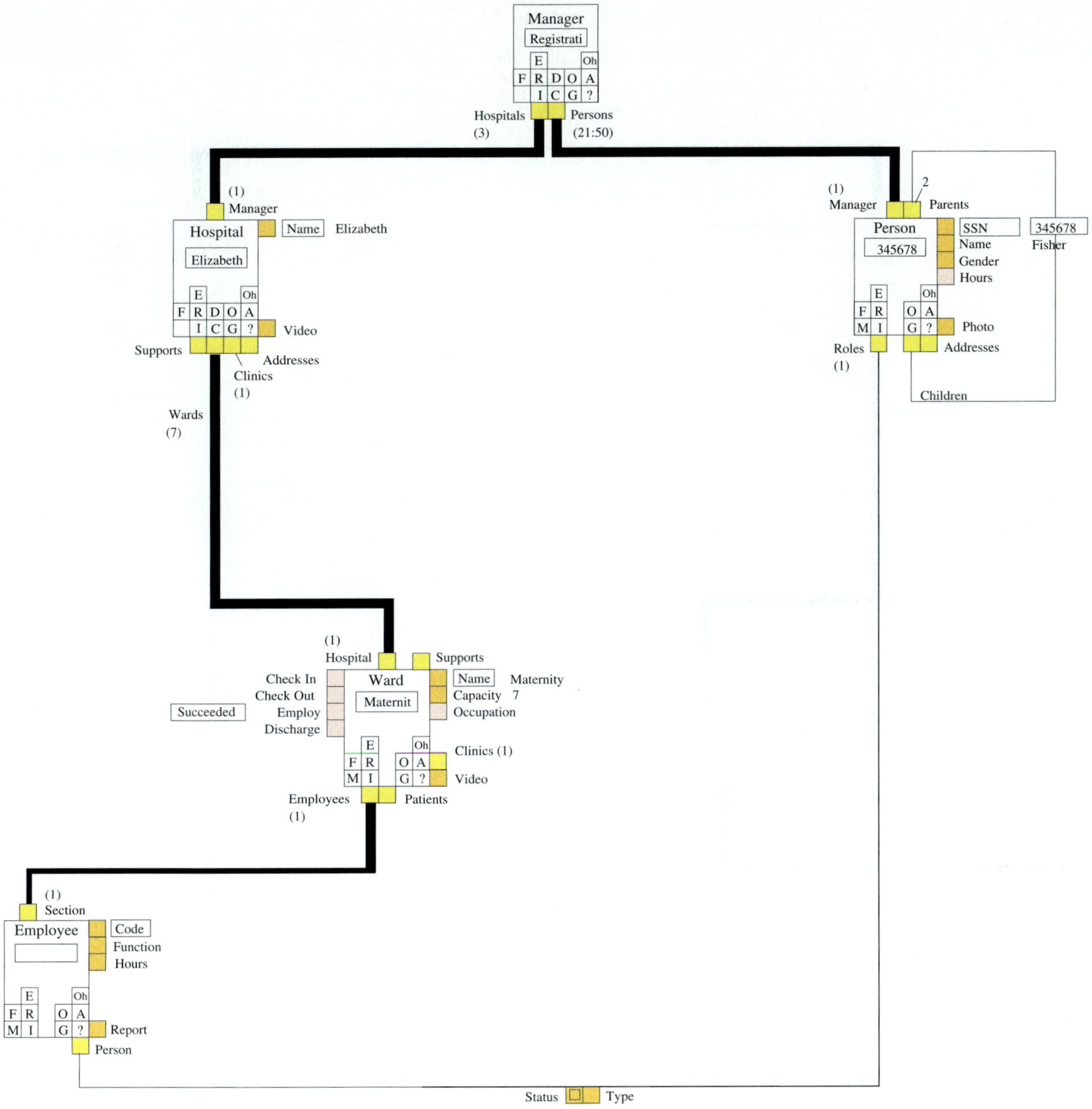

Figure 10.24: The operation succeeded

The person with `SSN` *345678* is accessed and the key value is entered as the first argument. The value field and member remain blue, but the cursor is no longer visible because it now focuses on the next argument to be collected. The key attribute and value of `Employee` turn blue, see Figure 10.23. A cursor placed in this value field indicates that a code has to be inserted. The value is then confirmed with `ENTER`.
Thereafter, the next argument, `Hours` turns blue, indicating that an integer defining the number of hours is to be inserted. This is the last required argument, so that confirming the input with `ENTER` completes the operation.

Figure 10.24 shows the situation after the operation is processed successfully, see the information beside the `Employ` operation. Before activating the operation, the cardinality of `Employee` of ward *Maternity* of *Elizabeth* hospital was *(0)*, because nobody was employed.

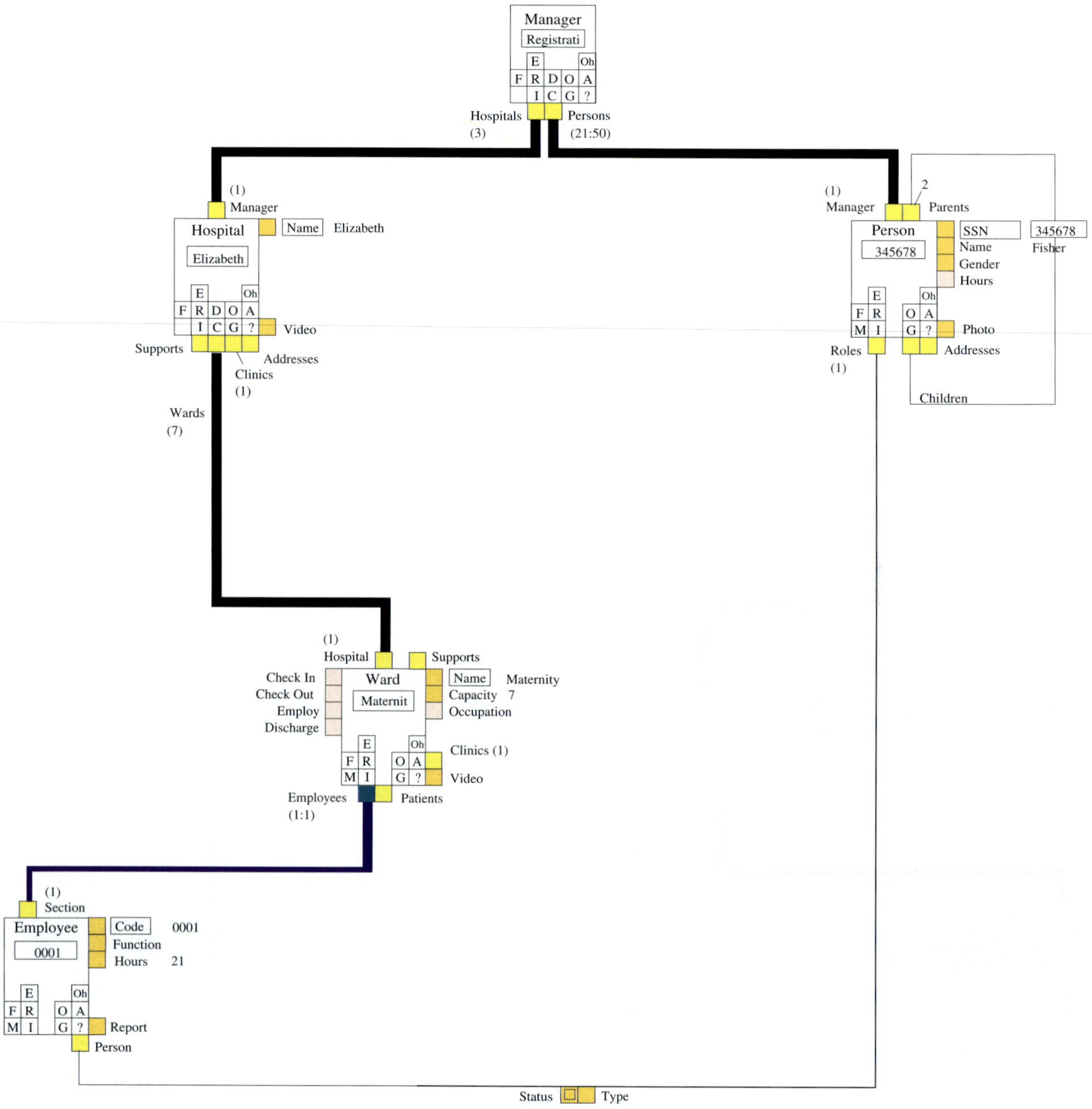

Figure 10.25: Activating the new instance of Employee of ward Maternity, *Elizabeth* hospital

Now one person is employed because the operation has created an instance of object type `Employee`. The special operation replaces the generic operation `Create` because the former requires more arguments than usual. This ensures that the created `Employee` is initialized with the `Hours` and the relation to `Person`. The generic operations `Create` and `Destroy` are not visible in the object type `Ward` which is also the case for `General Support`, `Medical Support`, `Clinic`, `Person`, `Patient` and `Employee`.

Figure 10.25 shows a situation where the newly created instance `Employee` with code *0001* is accessed. The `Function` value, for instance, can now be inserted.

Figure 10.26 illustrates another special operation; in this case `Person.Hours`. The operation computes the total number of hours a person is employed.

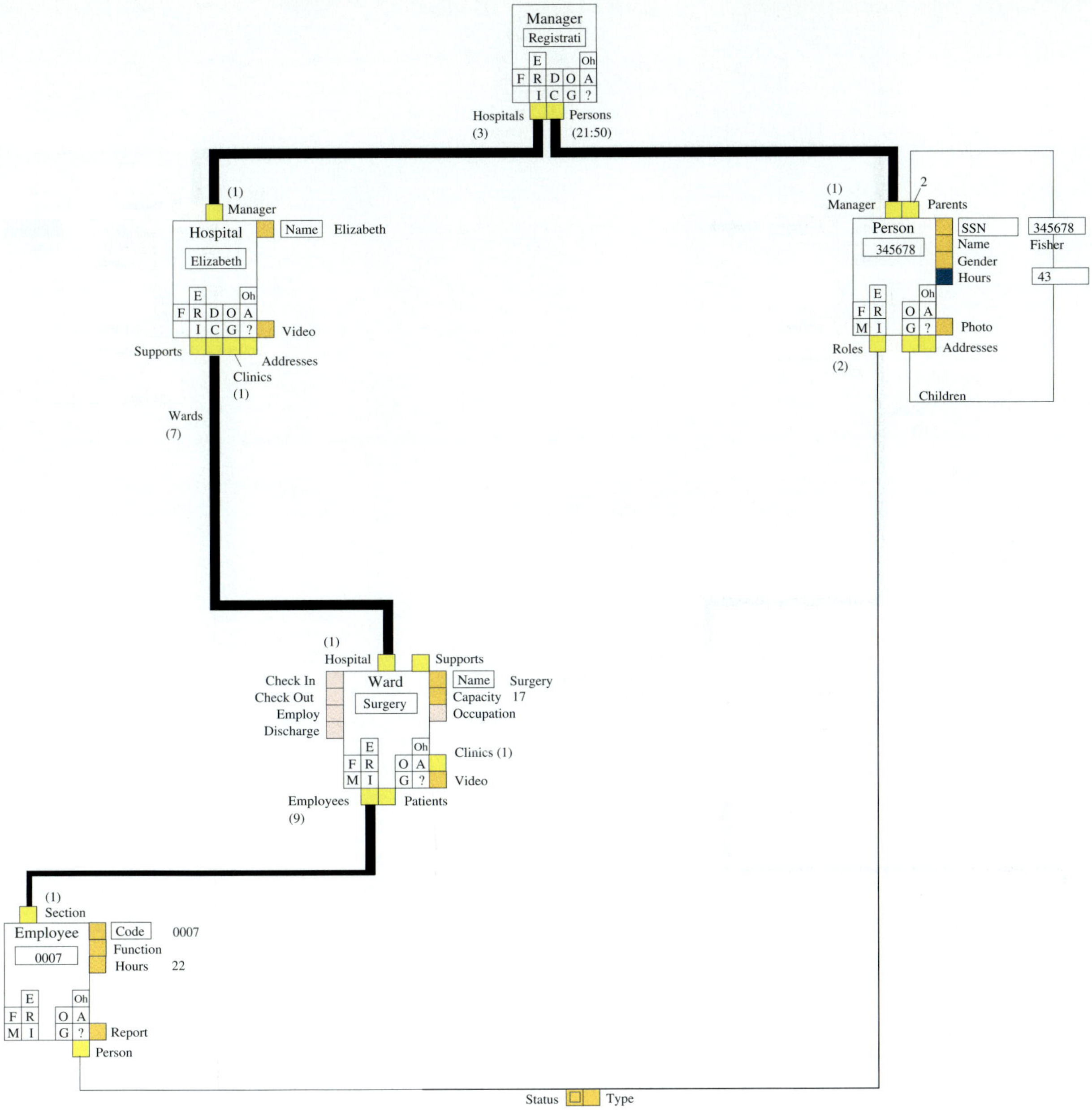

Figure 10.26: The result of the `Hours` operation

The person with `SSN` *345678*, who is employed at ward *Maternity* for *21* hours, and *Surgery* for *22* hours, works *43* hours in total. Here, the special operation needs no arguments from the user. The application sums up the hours of employment of the person at each relevant department.

Figures 10.27 and 10.28 illustrate the reaction of the system when the application logic is violated and show the system's reaction when a person is employed a second time at the same ward by mistake. The application logic disallows a double employment at the same department, even with a different Function. The application refuses to process the `Employ` operation for person with `SSN` *345678* at ward *Maternity* of *Elizabeth* hospital; see failure information in Figure 10.28.

From Figure 10.26 it is seen that person `SSN` *345678* works *43* hours in total. This is also the maximum number of hours a person may work.

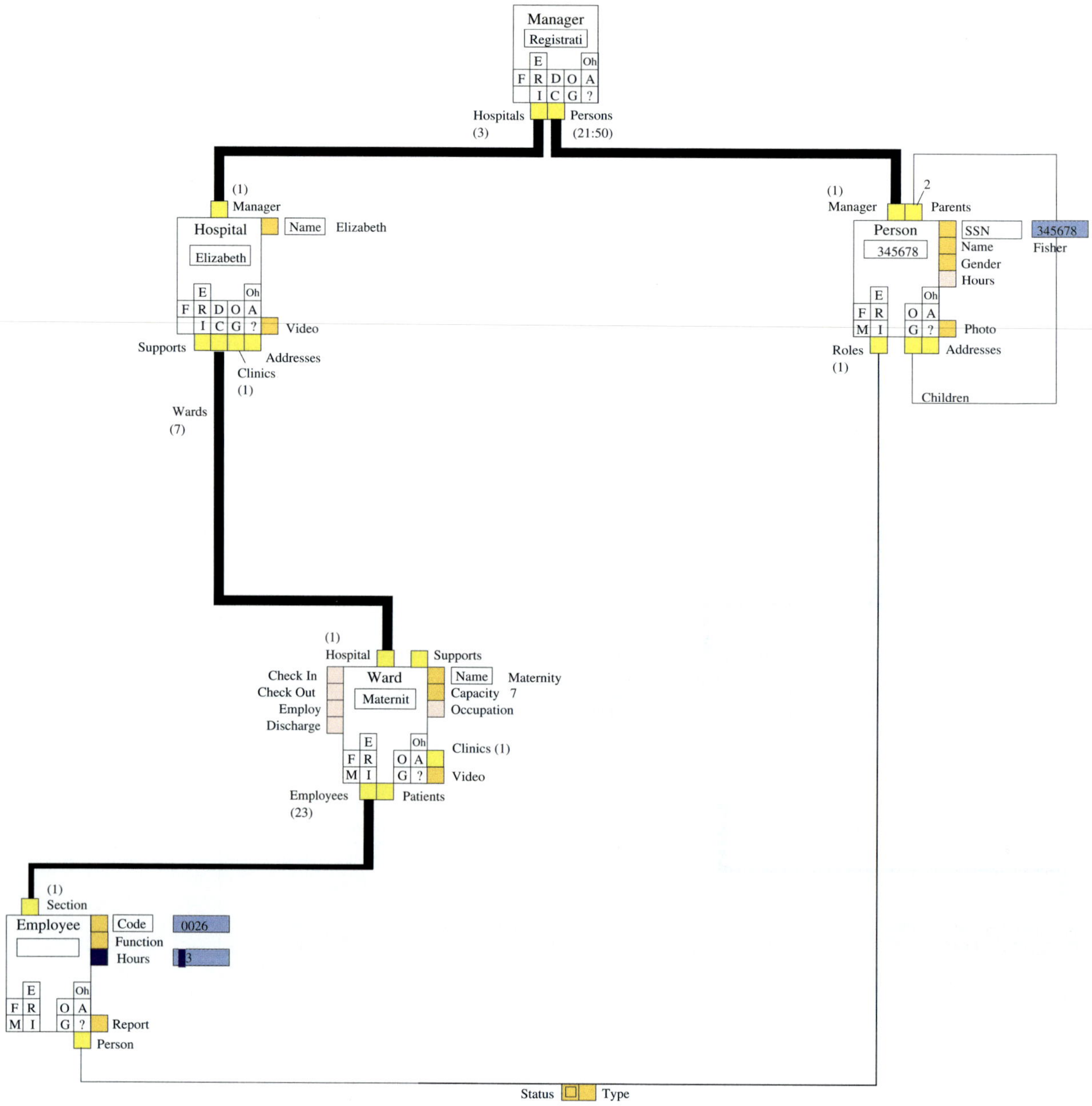

Figure 10.27: Attempting to `Employ` a `Person` already employed here

Figure 10.29 shows that the same person `SSN` *345678* is to be employed at an additional department, the ward *Pediatric* of *Elizabeth* hospital. The argument shows that the employment is for *5* hours. As soon as the operation is confirmed for processing, the situation of Figure 10.30 appears. The system checks and discovers that the maximum number of hours is exceeded. The employment at ward *Pediatric* is not allowed. The operation returns the value "failed" and an information window pops up, see Figure 10.30.

10.2.2 Aborting an Operation

If the operation is still in the argument collection phase (the user has not yet confirmed the last argument by pressing enter) the operation can be discontinued by clicking the operation once more.

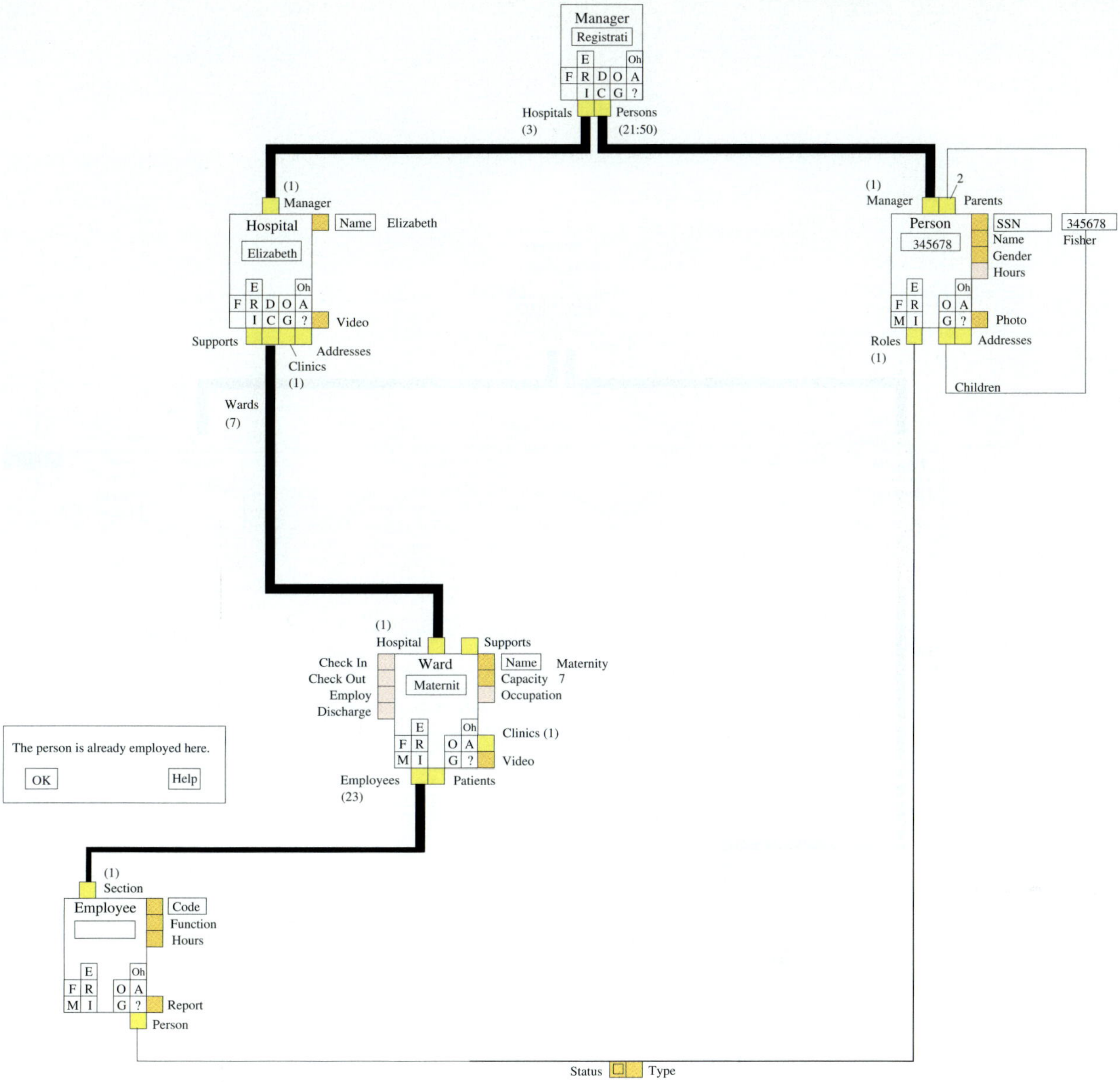

Figure 10.28: The system reaction to the fault: already employed here

If the operation is already executing, it can only be aborted by clicking a special **Stop** operation present in the object type Application_Manager which is visible in the `Application module`. The **Stop** operation may be added to other object types for convenience.

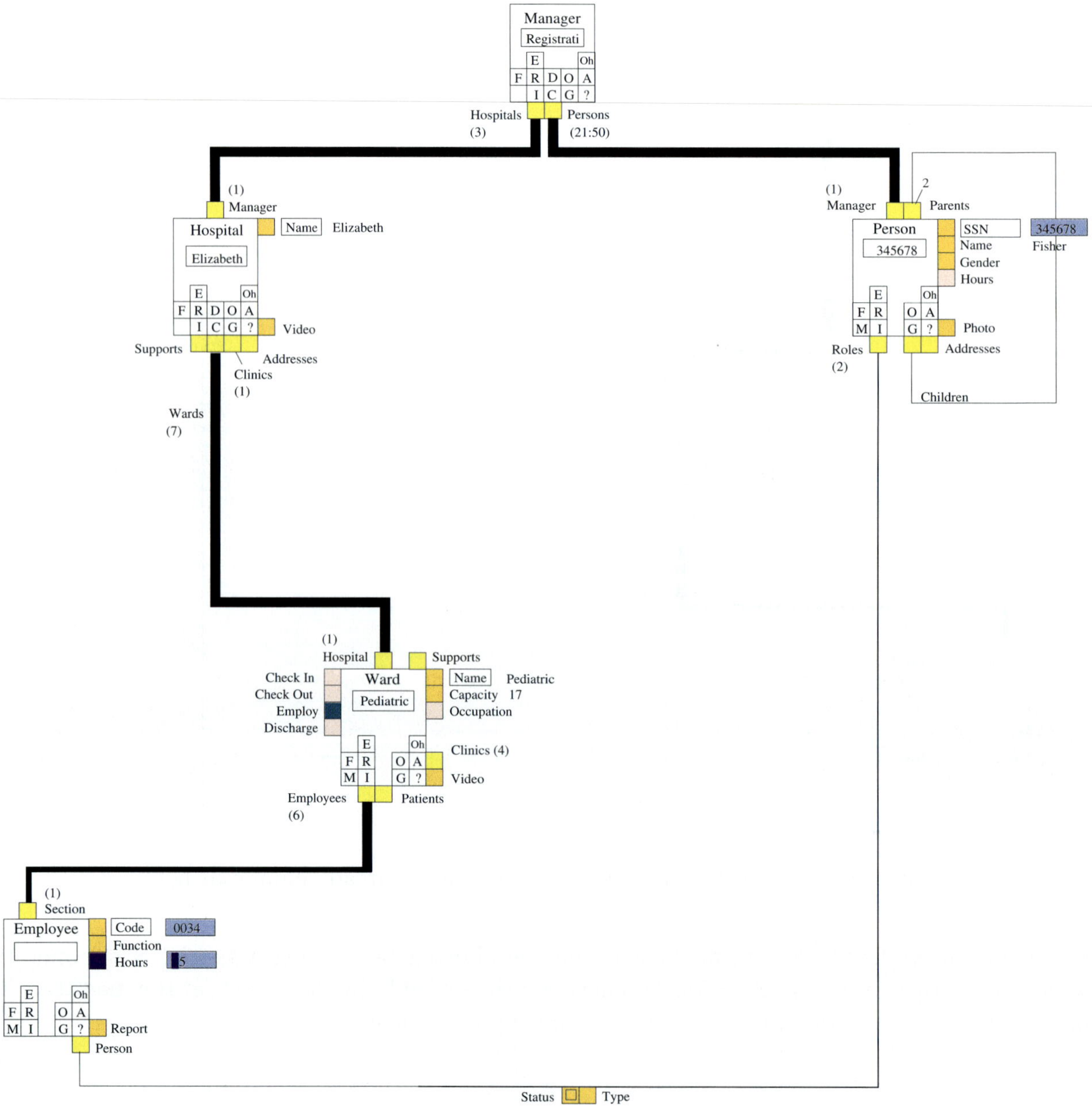

Figure 10.29: Violating a value constraint

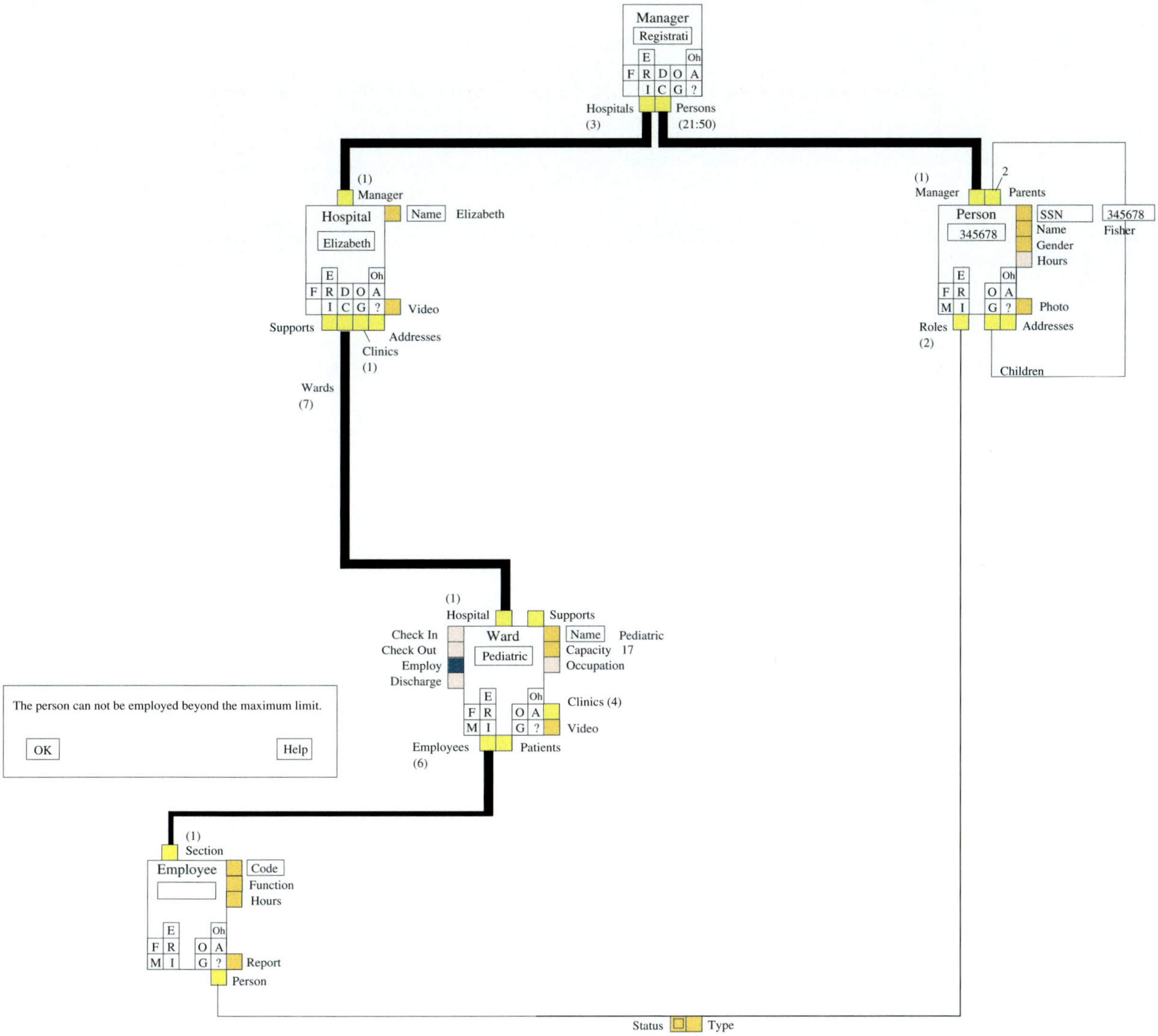

Figure 10.30: The system reaction to the fault: maximum hours exceeded

Chapter 11

Tabular Interaction: Forms

11.1 Structure of a Form View

A form view is the tabular equivalent of an object type in the schematic representation. It presents the members of the object type. If an instance of the object type is accessed in the form, the form presents its values. A form is constructed of two main parts, the **header** and the **body**. Figure 11.1 shows a form of ward *Surgery* of *Elizabeth* hospital.
The color coding is consistent with the schema.
The header of the form shows the context[1] of the object presented in the body:
All generic operations are given at the top (a Close operation is added). Below the top row the name of the source object type (on the left) and the identity of the source instance (on the right) appear. This is analogous to the navigation principle in the schema. Below the source object type name, the name of the selected (active) source relation appears, through which the accessed instance is reached. Below the selected (active) relation appears the name of the source object type once again (on the left), the key of the source instance (in the middle), and the cardinality index of its active relation (on the right).

The body of the form presents the information of the object in context:
It has two columns; the left contains the members of the object and the right contains the corresponding values of the members. Therefore a row contains the pair: member name, member value. In the case of a relation, the value indicates its cardinality and the key(s) of its instance(s). In the case of a method, clicking the member will execute the method. Where it has arguments, an argument value collection procedure precedes the execution.

11.2 Popping-up a Form

Figure 11.2 illustrates how to pop-up the form from the schema.

Open a form as follows:

- Access the source instance in the schema where the form is to be generated.
- Activate the generic operation `F` (Form) in the source instance:
    - The selectable relations turn green
    - Select the required relation by clicking it

[1]Via which object (source object) and relationship (source relation and target relation) was this object accessed?

Close	C D I R M F O A G ? E
Hospital >	Elizabeth
Wards	(6) Surgery, Pediatric, Intensive
Hospital:Elizabeth (1:6)	
Ward -	Surgery
Name -	Surgery
Capacity	17
Video	
Hospital -	(1) Elizabeth
Employees -	(45) 0001, 0002, 0004, 0005,
Supports >	(3) Kitchen, X-Ray, Pediatr
Patients -	(785) 0001, 0002, 0003, 000
Clinics >	(2) Orthopaedic, Pediatric
Employ >>	
Discharge >>	
Check In >>	
Check Out >>	
Occupation	

Figure 11.1: A Form

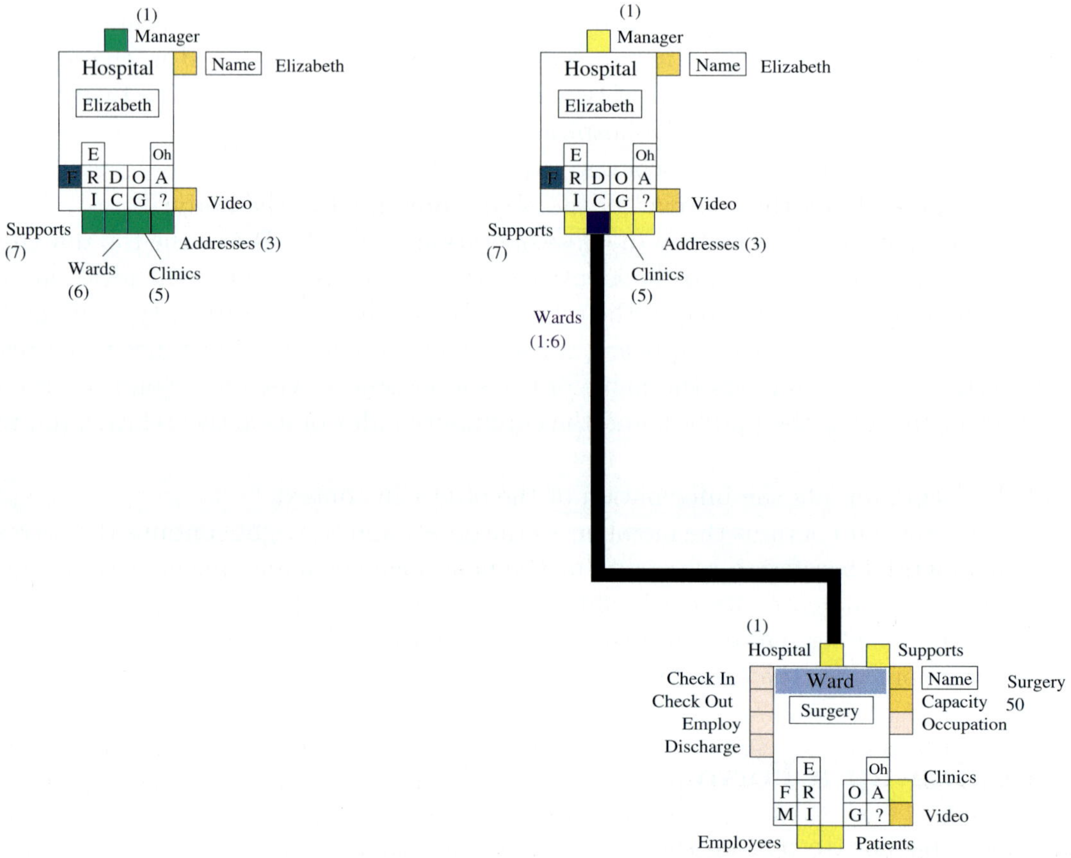

Figure 11.2: Popping-up a form: click the `F` button (left), select the relation (right).

- If the relationship is not split:
  - The relation turns blue
  - A window pops up displaying the form
- If the relationship is split:
  - The relation turns blue

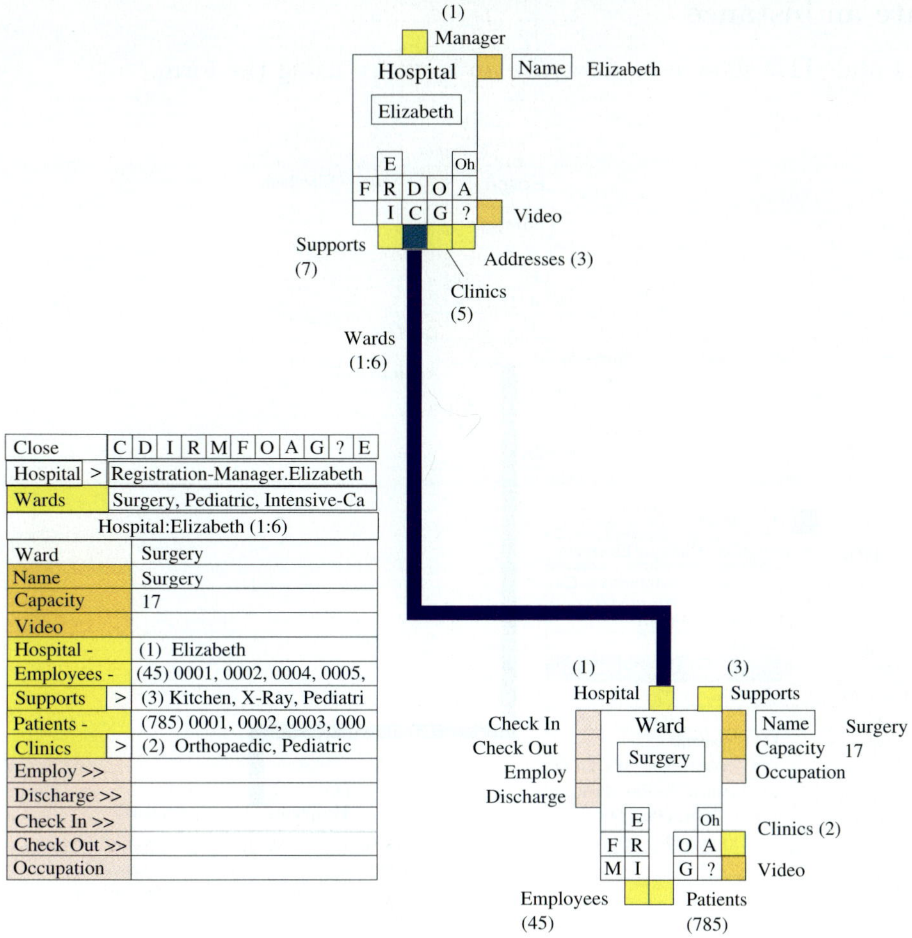

Figure 11.3: Popping-up the form (left), and the schematic presentation of the instance in context (right).

- The related selectable object types turn green
- Select one of the object types
- A window pops up displaying the form

The user can pop-up as many forms as required and can select the same source and target relations if necessary. A form can be popped up for both owner and secondary relations. The generic operations in the form are context sensitive to the relation type. For example, the Create and Destroy operations at the top of the form are not applicable to a form popped up through a secondary relation.

11.3 Exploiting the Form

11.3.1 Iterating the active relation

The form has one instance in access at a time. By pressing the Page-Up and Page-Down buttons, the user can iterate the instances in the relation forwards and backwards respectively. When a form of an empty relation is popped-up the source object's information is present and the members of the target object type are visible, but there is no target instance visible, i.e. the key value is empty (as well as the other members).

11.3.2 Create an instance

The Figures 11.4 and 11.5 show how to create an instance using the form.

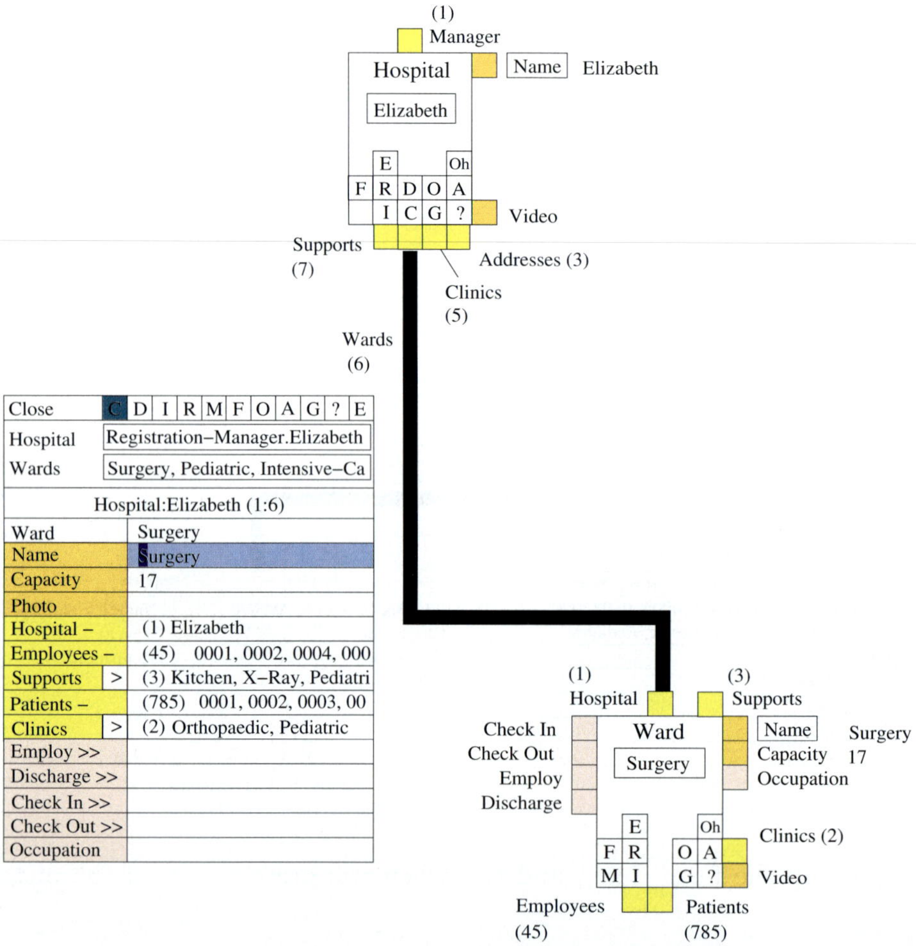

Figure 11.4: Creating an instance

The procedure for the creation of an instance is as follows:

- Activate the generic operation `C` in the first row of the form

  The key attribute becomes active (gray field, blue cursor)

- Insert the key value
- Press ENTER

  - The cardinality increases by one
  - The initial values of the new instance appear in the form

The creation operation is completed.
The cardinality value of the corresponding relation in the schematic likewise increases because the GUI keeps the state of the tabular and schematic presentations synchronized. Creation is only possible if the source instance (the instance from where the `F` was invoked) is a potential owner and the source relation is part of an owner relationhip of the target object type.
Figure 11.4 illustrates the situation in which the user invokes the `Create` operation in the form.

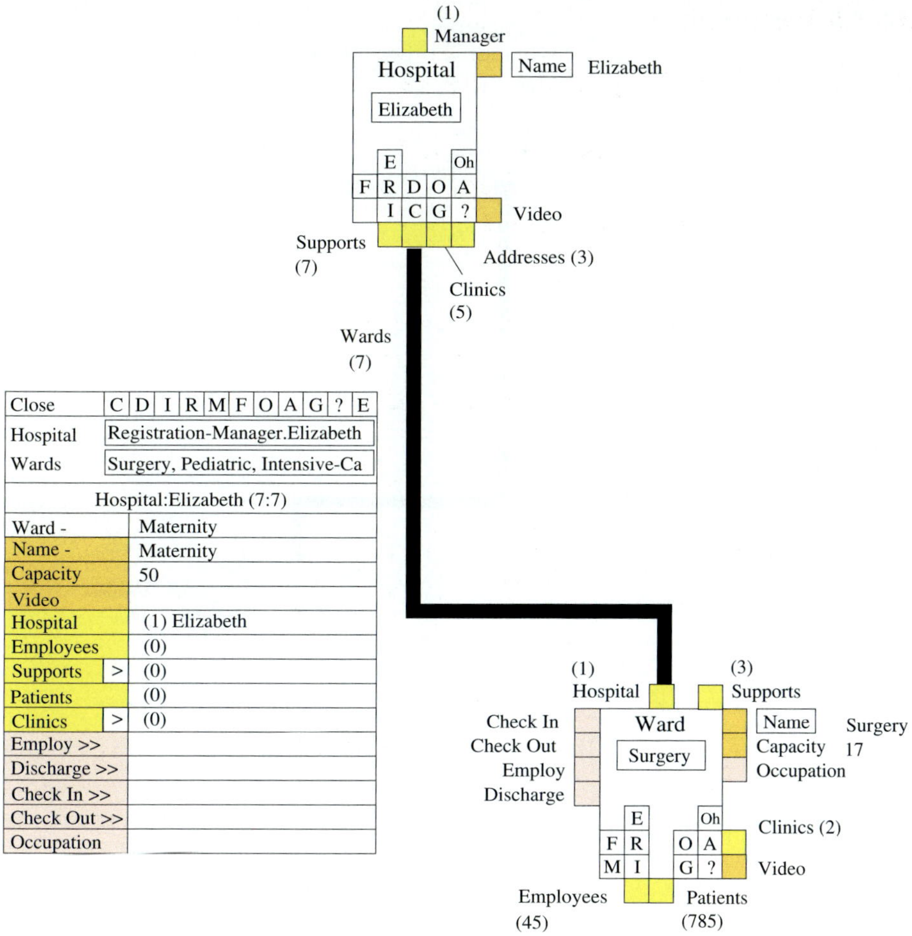

Figure 11.5: Creating an Instance

Initially the form and the schematic view both show the same instance within the activated relation i.e. ward *Surgery* of *Elizabeth* hospital. After clicking `C`, the cursor springs to the key field which turns blue. The user enters a key value and presses ENTER. Figure 11.5 shows that the instance *Maternity* has been created and appears in the form and the default values also appear. This is the same behavior as when invoking `Create` in the schematic.
The figure still shows the instance ward *Surgery* in the schematic. Note that the cardinality value of the active relation has increased by one.

Once an instance is created it is possible to apply to it the rest of the generic and the specific operations in the form.

11.3.3 Enter and modify attribute values for the created instance

In the following figures the instance in the form is also accessed in the schematic; see the colors of the relation and the connector. Figures 11.6, 11.7 show how to enter and modify attribute values of an instance.
For entering and modifying attribute values the generic operation `M` is used (as in the schematic). In the example, the value of the attribute `Capacity` is to be modified. In the present state it has the default value *50*. When `Capacity` is clicked a cursor appears in the value field. The new value can be entered.

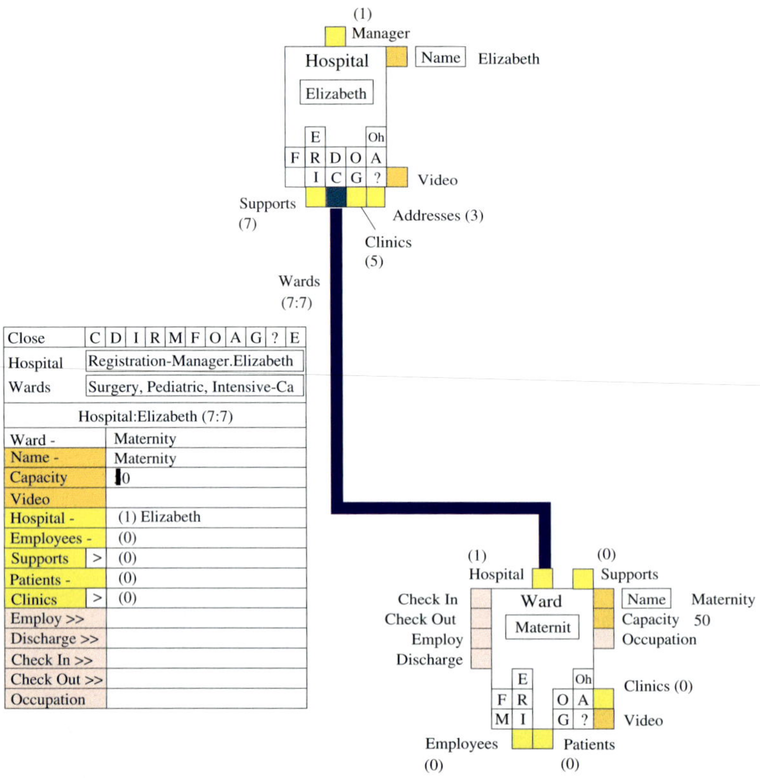

Figure 11.6: Enter and modify attribute values of an instance

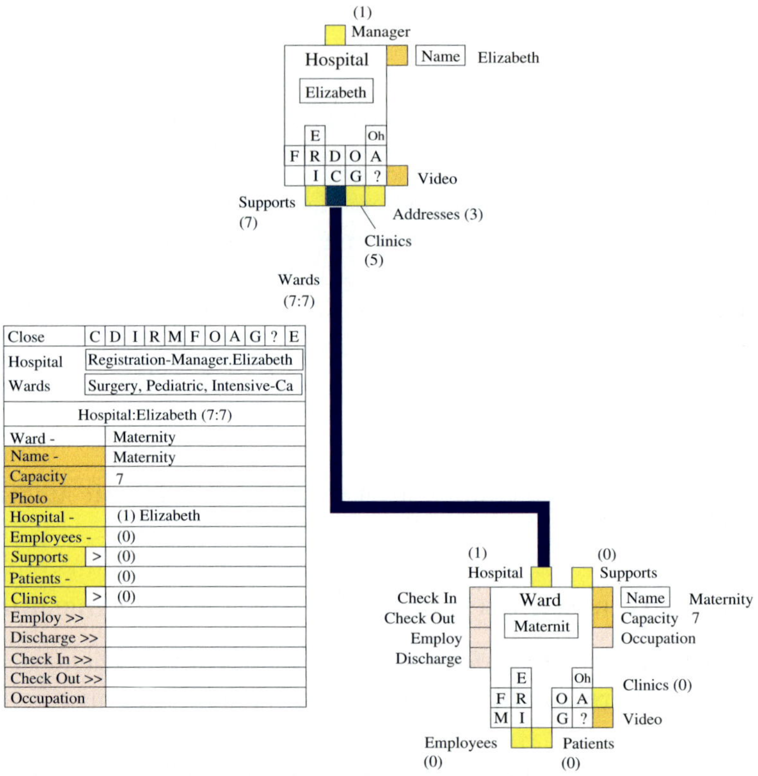

Figure 11.7: The attribute value is entered

It is also possible to modify an attribute directly by clicking the desired attribute row in the form as illustrated in *Figure 11.6* (`M` *is not invoked in the form otherwise the member would turn gray.* The steps described above and the appearance of the form are the same whether the operation `M` or the short cut is used.
Figure 11.7 shows the result of entering the new attribute value *7* for `Capacity`. `Ward` *Maternity* of *Elizabeth* is also active in the schema. For this reason the modification is also immediately visible in the schematic presentation.

11.3.4 Insert in a secondary relationship

Figures 11.8, 11.9, 11.10, 11.11, 11.12 show how to insert an instance in a secondary relationship.

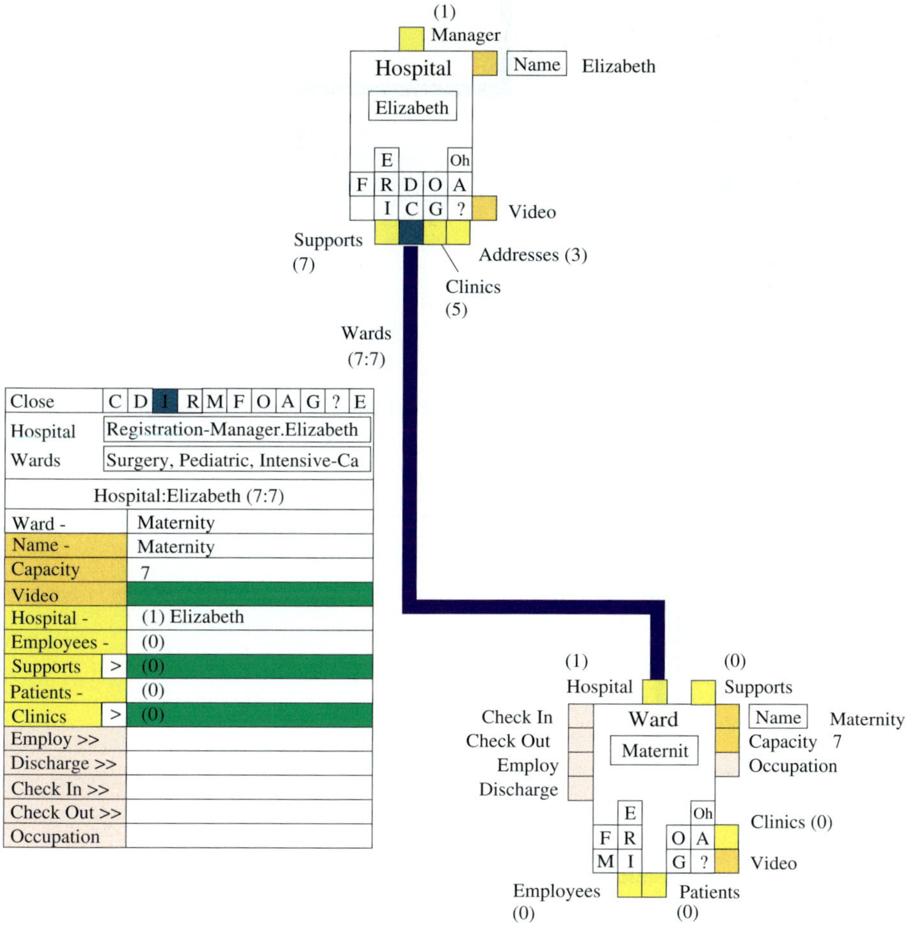

Figure 11.8: Inserting a secondary relationship, invoking the operation

In the example a secondary relationship to the clinic *Orthopaedic* of *Mother-Theresa* hospital is to be inserted. The generic operation `I` (`Insert`) is invoked within the form of ward *Maternity* of *Elizabeth* hospital. The choices colored green (see Figure 11.8) are the secondary relations `Supports` and `Clinics`.
`Clinics` is to be selected.
Figure 11.9 shows the situation after selecting `Clinics`. The blue of the value field and the cursor indicate that the instance to be related to ward *Maternity* must be entered.
To relate clinic *Orthopaedic* of *Mother Theresa* hospital, this instance is accessed in the schematic: First, *Mother-Theresa* hospital is accessed, then clinic Orthopaedic. The result is shown in Figure 11.10. The identity of the instance is entered in the value field of the form.

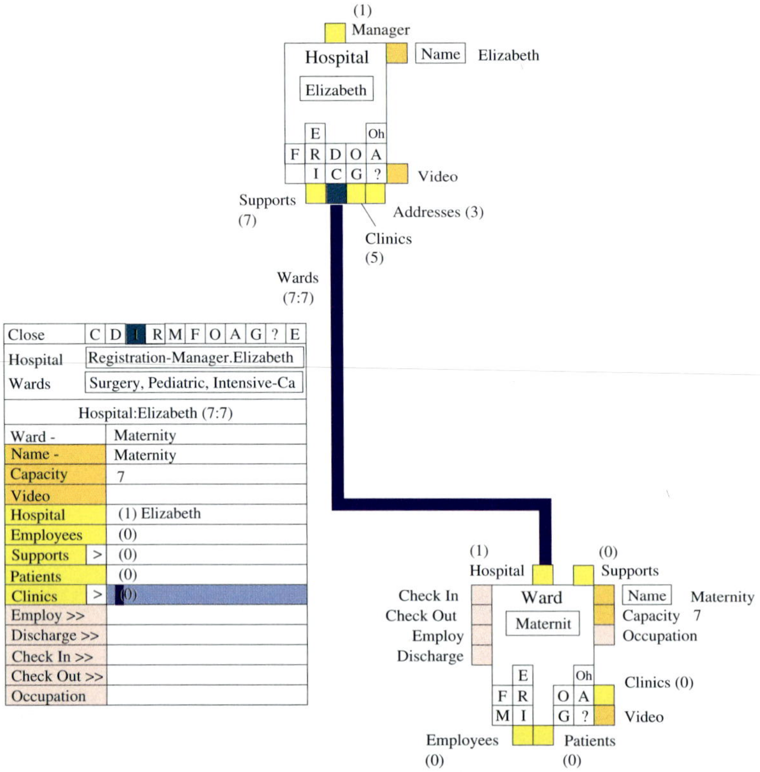

Figure 11.9: The related instance is to be entered

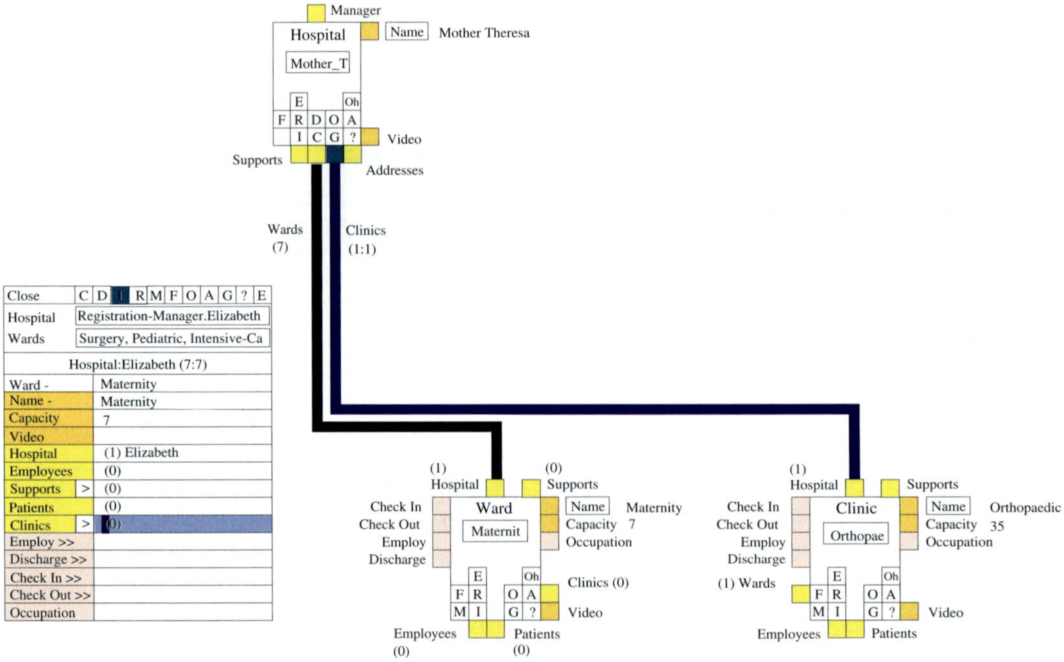

Figure 11.10: Accessing the instance (in the schematic) to be related

This is done by positioning the cursor on the object-ID, pressing down the left mouse button, dragging the object-ID value to the form and dropping it on the value field (i.e. by using the drag-drop function). The identifier of the related instance now appears in the value field of relation `Clinics` in the form, see Figure 11.11.

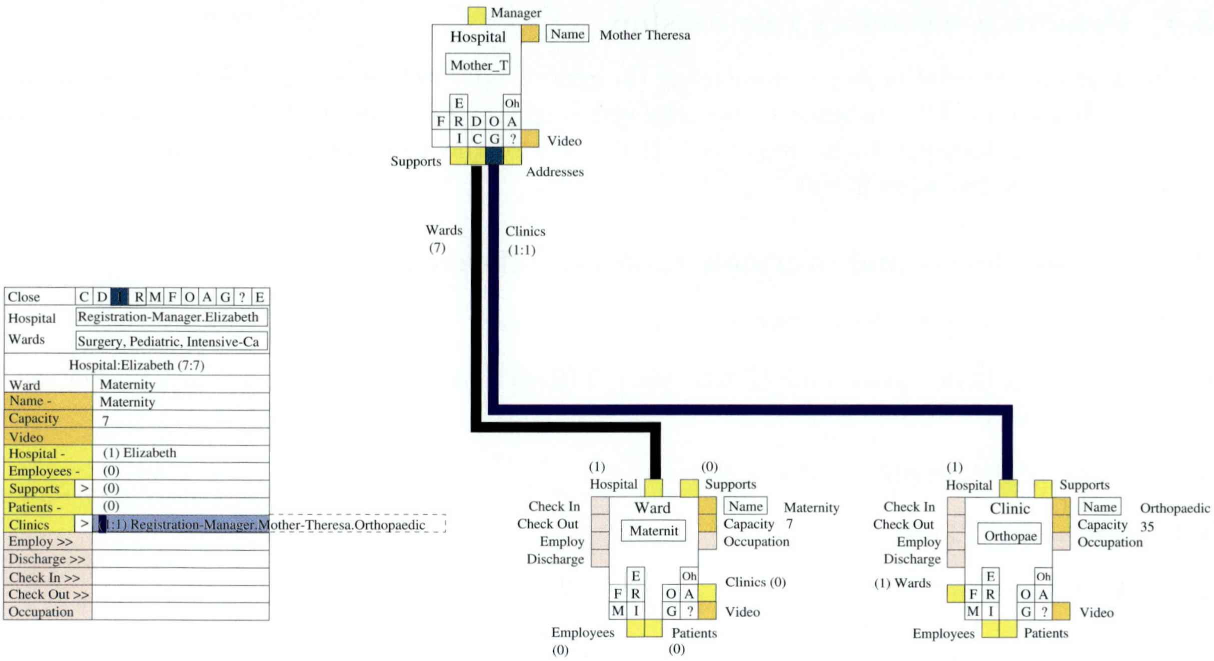

Figure 11.11: Inserting the instance in the secondary relationship

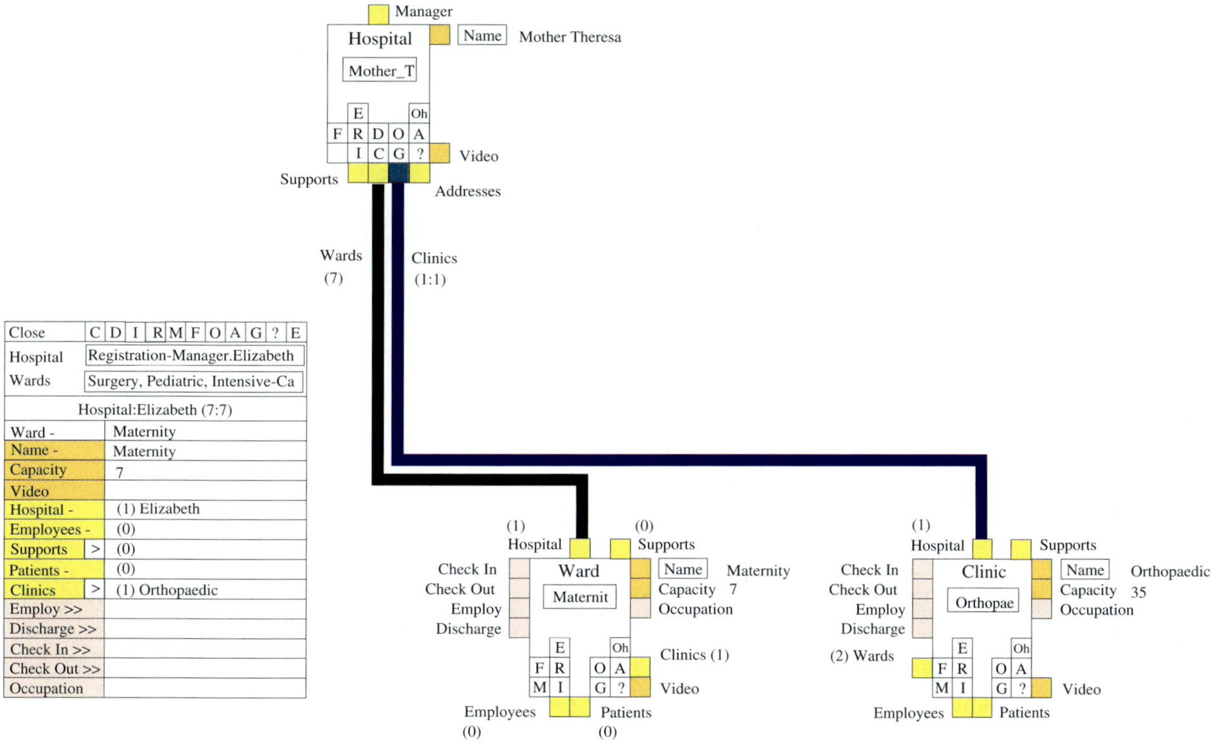

Figure 11.12: The instance is inserted

After confirming with ENTER, the insert operation is executed, the cardinality increases by one and the instance name appears in the value of the relation, see Figure 11.12. As expected, in the schematic the cardinality value of the relevant relation in both instances has increased by one (`Clinics` *1*, `Wards` *2*).

11.3.5 Remove a secondary relationship

Removing a secondary relationship is done using the generic operation `R` (`Remove`) in the form. Removal is similar to Insertion. The instance to be removed is set in the value field of the relation, pressing ENTER causes the instance to be removed. If the key of the instance is unique in the secondary relation entering the key is sufficient.

11.3.6 Pop-up forms and overview tables of related instances

The following steps are always the same:

- Activate the generic operation `F` (`Form` view), `O` (`Overview`) or `A` (`Association` View) in the top row of the header of the form
- Select one of the possible relations (green)
- Confirm with ENTER
- The table pops up

Information on the Overview and Association View tables is given in the next chapter. It is possible for an end-user to manipulate the application solely through tables, because the tabular representation describes the complete object model. In practice to be most effective the end-user combines the tabular and schematic representations.

11.3.7 Destroy the active instance:

- Activate the generic operation `D` (Destroy) in the first row of the form
  The ID (first) field turns blue
- Confirm with ENTER

The active instance is destroyed and the form becomes empty of target values[2]. By iterating, eg by pressing Page-Up or Page-Down the next or previous instance in the relation is accessed.

11.3.8 Invoke specific operations

The Figures 11.13, 11.14, 11.15 illustrate how to invoke specific operations in a form.
The same example is used as in the schematic.

`Ward` *Maternity* is to employ an additional person: the specific operation `Employ` is clicked in the form of ward *Maternity* of *Elizabeth* hospital. The invoked operation name turns gray. In addition an argument collection form pops up containing the argument list of `Employ`. In Figure 11.13 the first member row of the popped-up form shows the name of the invoked operation followed by the arguments. In the example the `SSN` value is (to be) set to the *person* to be employed. The `Person` therefore must be made active in the schematic (right side of Figure 11.14). The attribute value `SSN` is set by dragging and dropping the `Person`, the other attributes are then filled in. The `Code` is generated automatically if left empty.

[2]Actually, if the target object contains owning relations, invoking the Destroy operation causes the ID field and owning relations to become selectable, i.e. turn green. If the ID field is selected, the procedure is as described previously. If an owning relation is selected the user can enter the key of the instance to be destroyed, then confirm with ENTER. In the case of the Form with the type Ward, the fields Ward, Employees and Patients turn green.

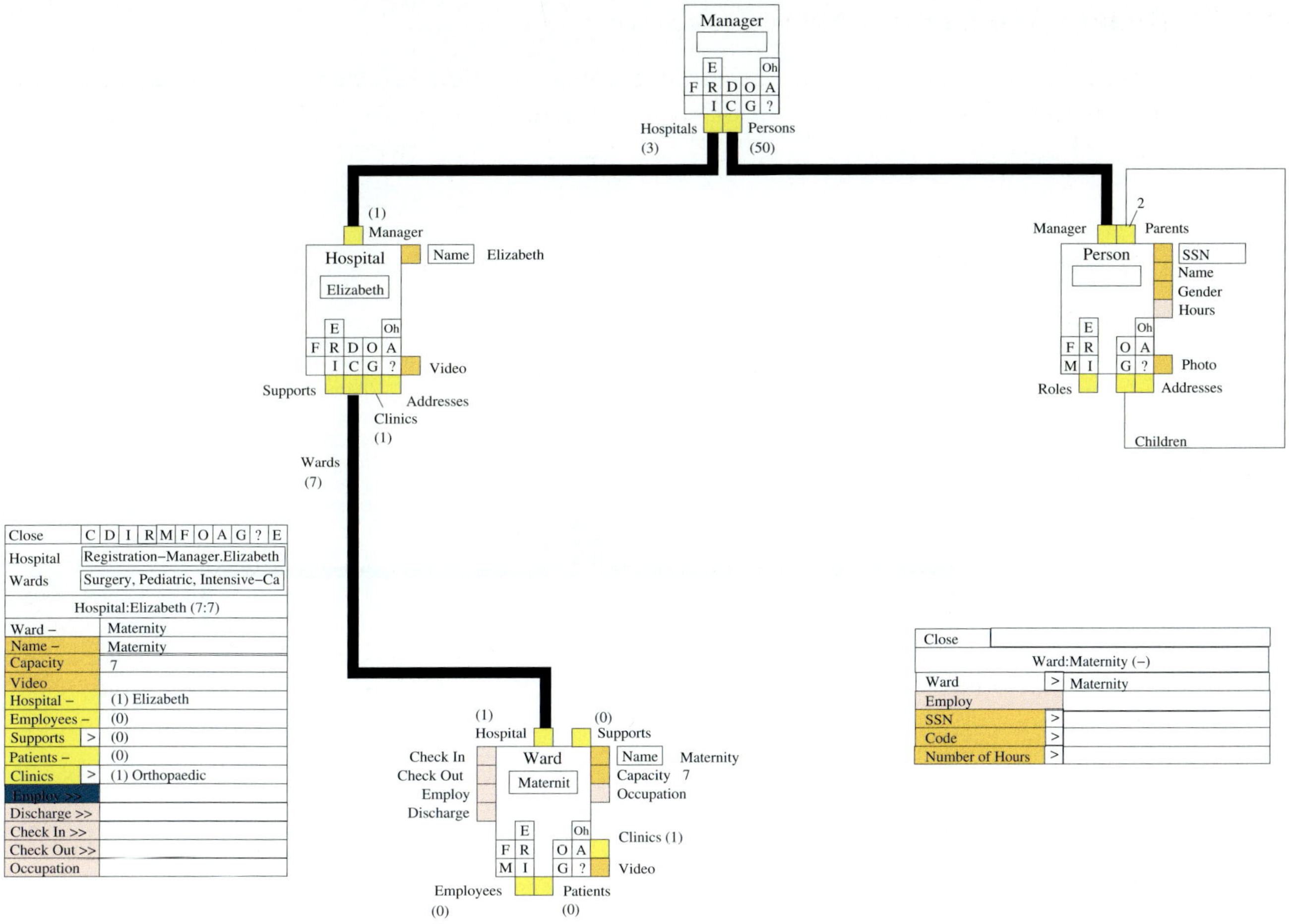

Figure 11.13: Invoke a specific operation; the operation is invoked

Figure 11.14 illustrates the situation after entering the operation arguments. Once all arguments are filled in the user invokes the `Execute` operation, see top row in the header of the argument collection form. Figure 11.15 shows the result of the operation `Employ`. An `Employee` instance is created as a result of the `Employ` operation. In the form the cardinality of `Employees` of ward `Maternity` is increased by one and the key of the `Person` instance is visible in the value field of the relation. The cardinality of the relation `Employees` of ward *Maternity* in the schematic increases accordingly. Figure 11.15 also illustrates that the newly created `Employee` instance is connected to the appropriate `Person`, the routine behavior of the `Employ` operation.

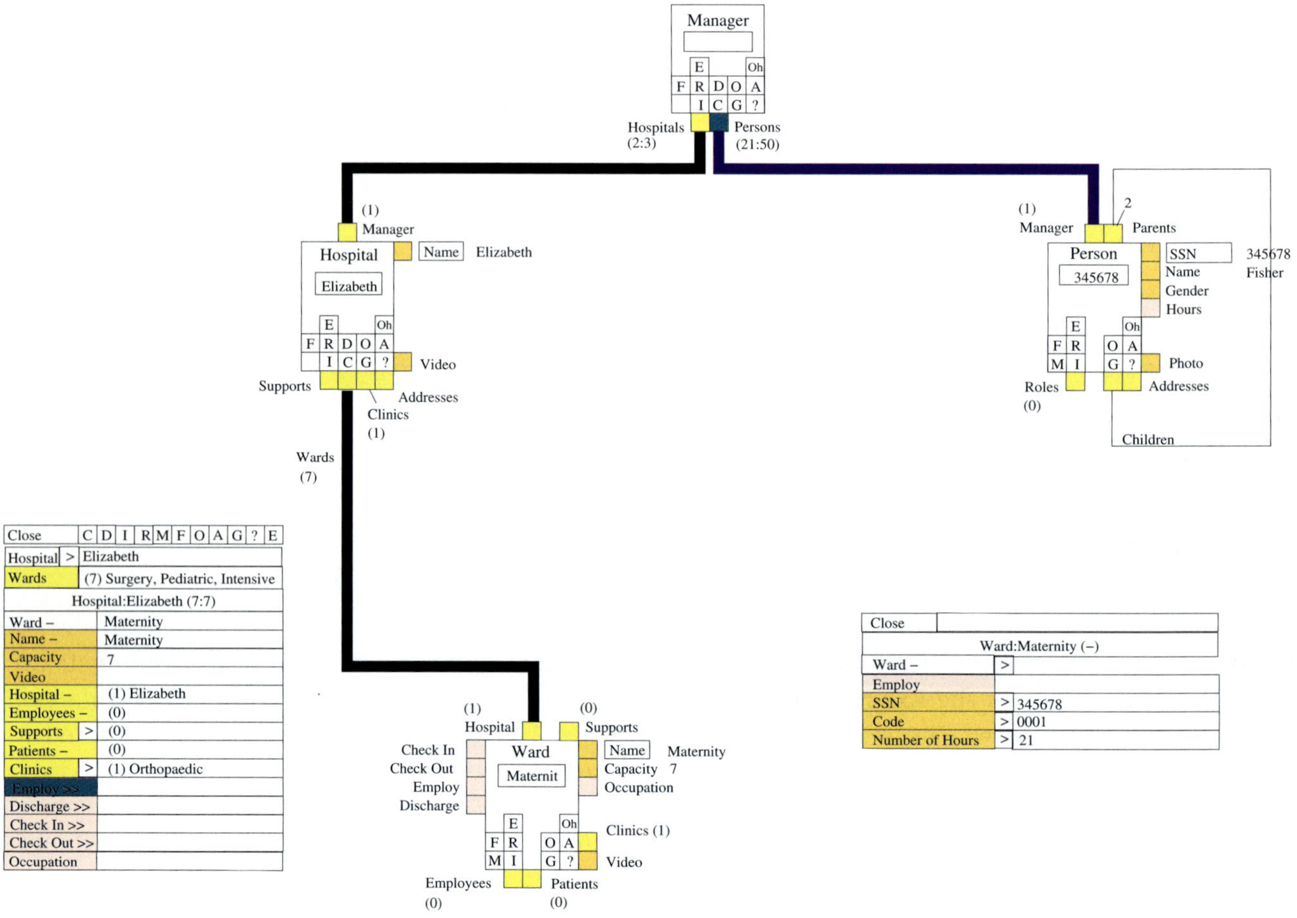

Figure 11.14: Invoke a specific operation; entering the arguments

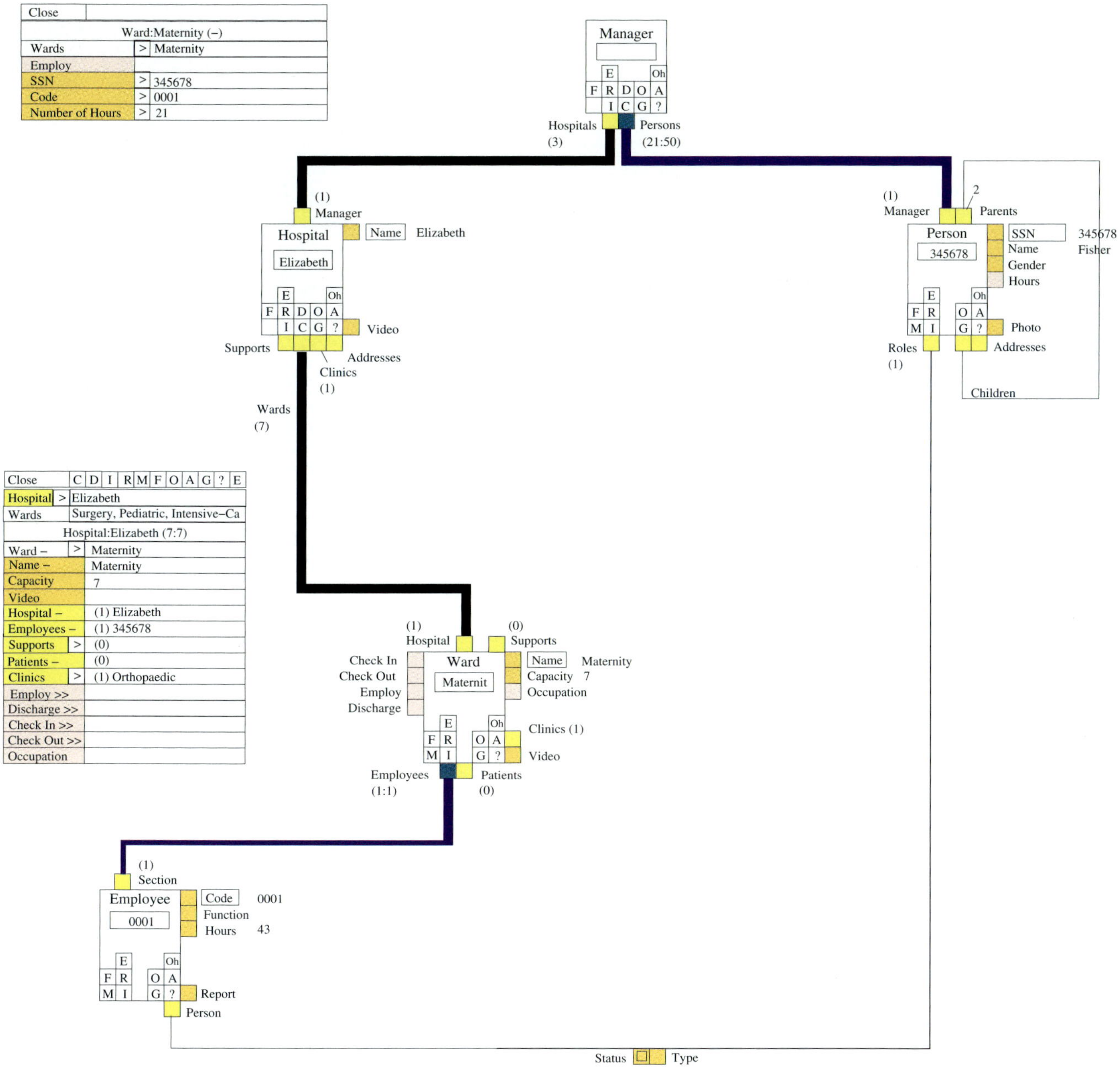

Figure 11.15: The specific operation is executed

Chapter 12

Tabular Interaction: Ancillary Views

12.1 Overviews

12.1.1 Structure of an Overview

An overview shows a list of all instances related to a particular instance through a particular relation. The attributes of each instance are also displayed. The color coding is consistent with the schema.

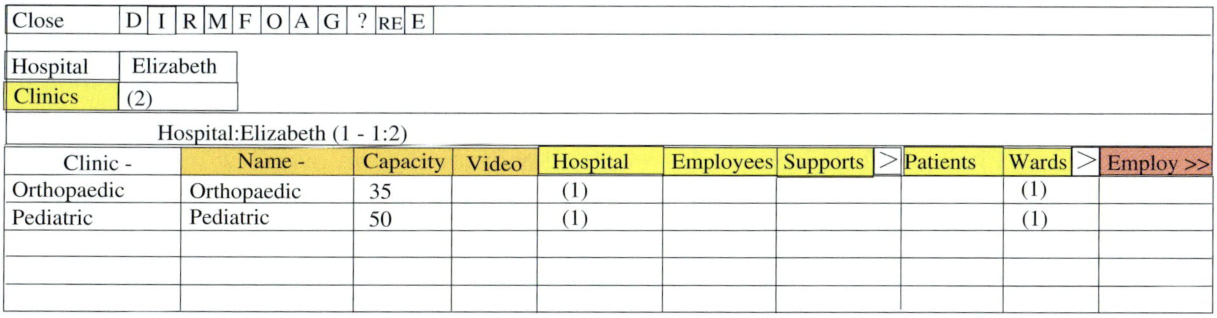

Figure 12.1: An overview

An example of an overview is shown in figure 12.1. It is constructed of two main parts, the **header** and the **body**.

The header shows the context of the objects presented in the body, and is similar to the header of the form view. At the top all relevant generic operations are given. Immediately below them the source object type (on the left) and the identity of the source instance (on the right) appear. Below the source object type name, the name appears of the active source relation through which the instances in the view are reached (left) and the cardinality index of the selected relation (right) indicating which instances in the list are currently visible. Below the active relation, the name appears of the source object type (left), the key of the source instance (middle), and the cardinality index of its active relation (right), indicating which instances in the list are visible.

The body of the overview is a table. The first row shows the column headers; the name of the target object type followed by the names of its attributes. Each subsequent row displays the key of an instance followed by the values of the attribute (corresponding to the attribute name in the respective column).

12.1.2 Popping-up an overview

Figures 12.2, 12.3 show how to pop-up an overview. In the `examples`, the overview is of the clinics with which ward *Surgery* of *Elizabeth* hospital cooperates.

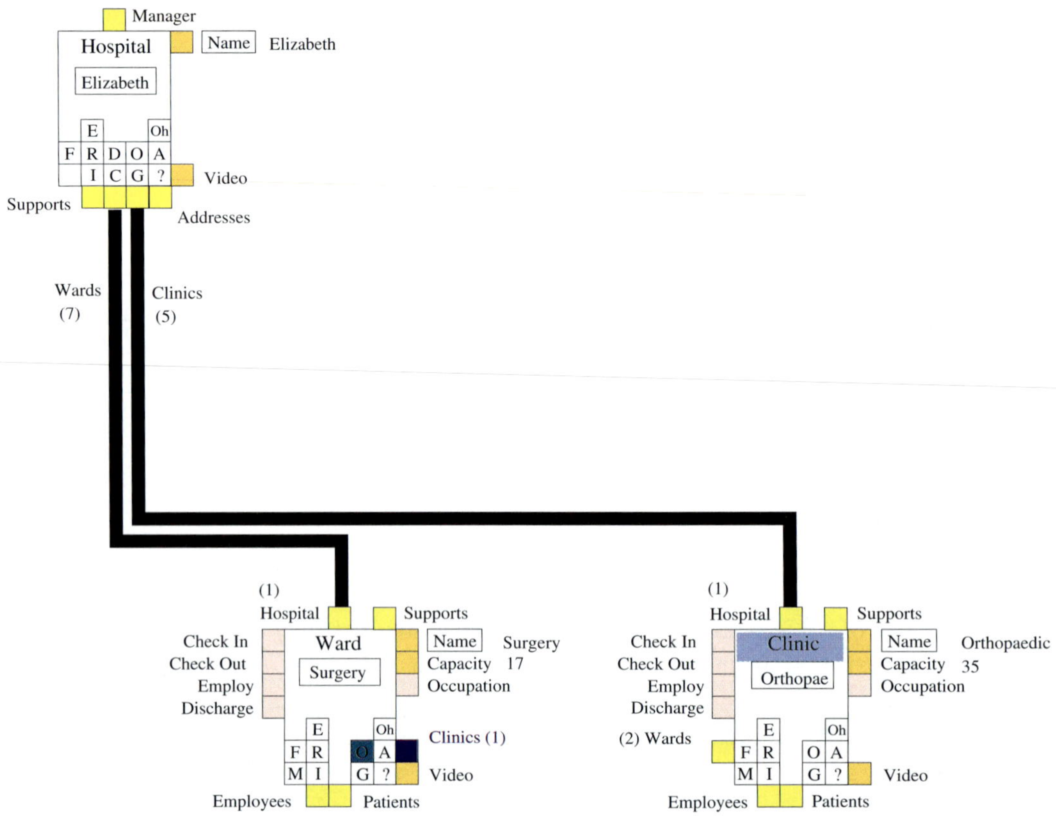

Figure 12.2: Selection of a relation for producing an overview

The procedure to open a form is as follows:

- In the schema, access the source instance where the overview is to be generated
- Activate the generic operation `O` in the instance
  - The operation turns bright and the selectable relations turn green
  - Select the required relation by clicking it
  - The relation turns blue
- If the relationship is not split:
  - A window pops up displaying the overview
  - the operation and the relation turn back to the original state
- If the relationship is split:
  - The related selectable object types turn green to be selected
  - Select one of the object types
  - A window pops up displaying the overview
  - The operation, the relation and the selectable object types turn back to the original state

Figure 12.2 shows the situation in which the generic operation `O` (`Overview`) is selected in ward *Surgery* of *Elizabeth* hospital and where the relation `Clinics` is selected. The relation, its name and its cardinality have turned blue.

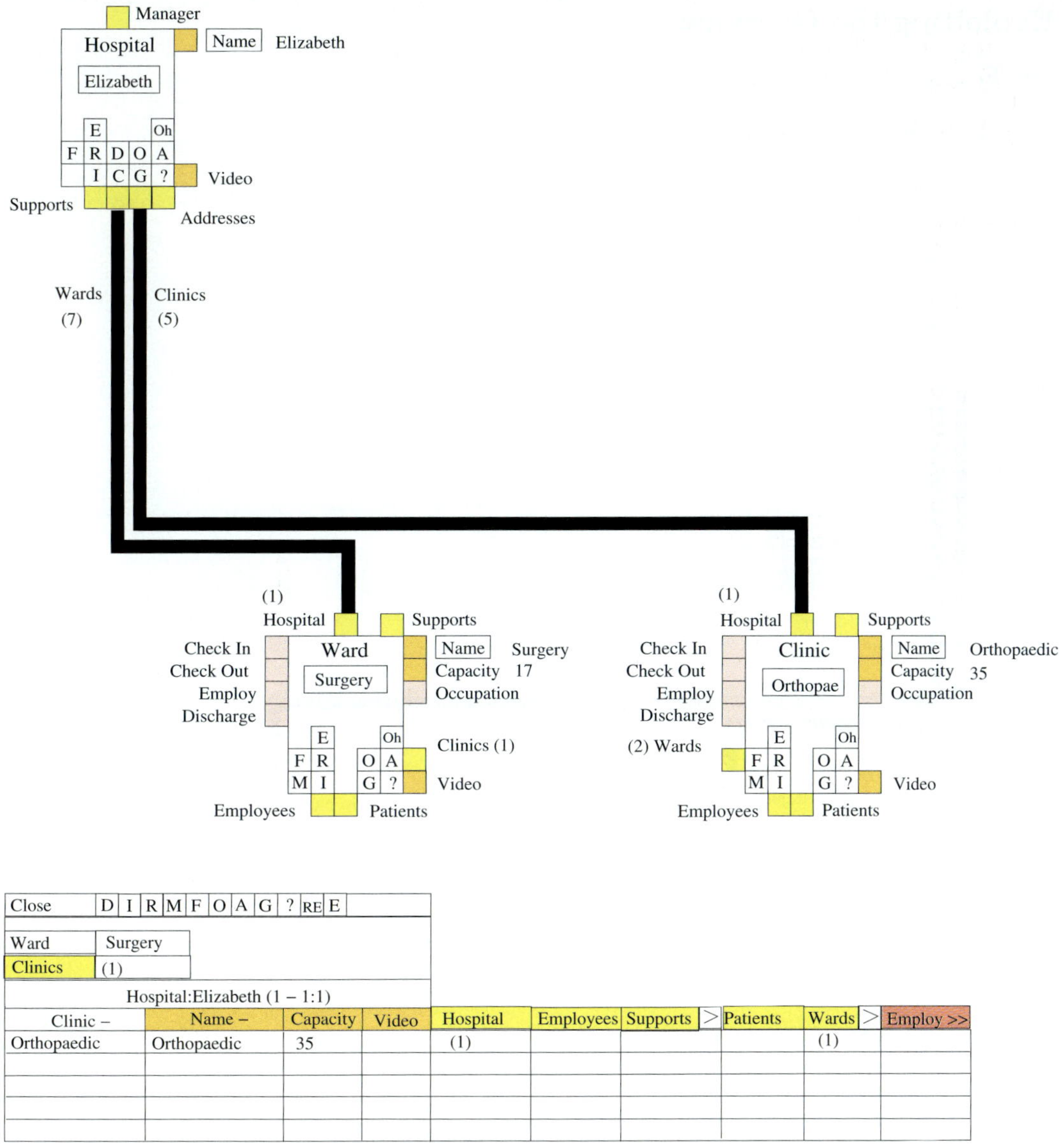

Figure 12.3: A popped-up overview

Because the relationship type is not split, the related object type becomes active immediately as recognizable by the blue background of the object type's name.
Figure 12.3 shows the popped-up overview. `Clinics` relates to only one instance in the example. Producing an overview from a `form` or from another ancillary view is analogous.
The user can pop-up as many overviews as required and can select the same source relations and target object types if necessary. An overview can be popped-up for both owner and secondary relations. The generic operations in the overview are context sensitive; for example, if the user activiates an Insert operation, the items in the left column become selectable, and if the user activates the Modify operation, the items in the other columns become selectable. The Create and Destroy operations cannot be activated because `Ward` is not the owner of `Clinic`.

12.1.3 Exploiting the Overview

Popping-up Forms, Overviews

Figures 12.4, 12.5 show how to pop-up a form from an overview.

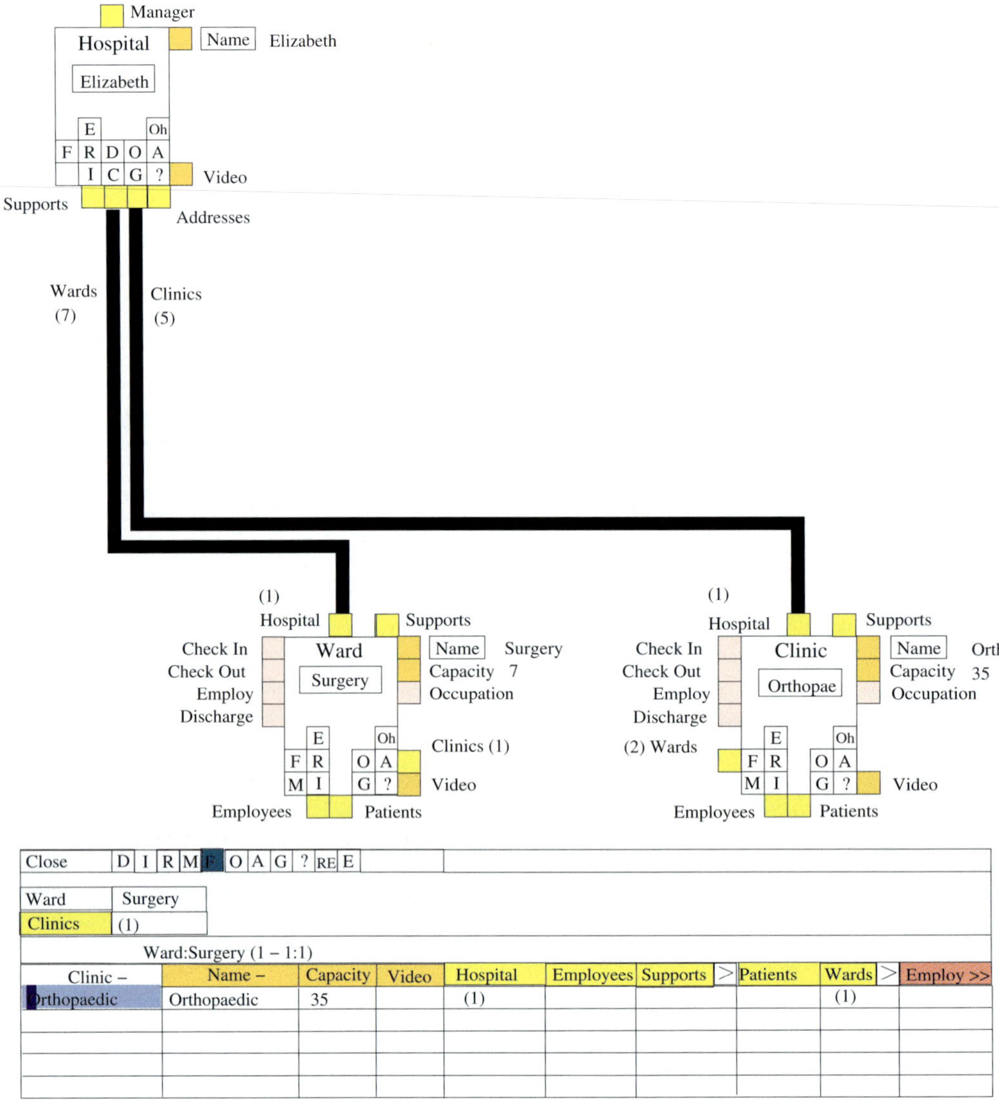

Figure 12.4: Popping-up a form from an overview

Figure 12.4 shows the situation in which the generic operation `F` (`Form`) is activated. The instances in selectable relations turn green. In the example, there is only one relation column and it contains one instance, therefore only the left column becomes activated, in this case the instance Orthopaedic (see the blue color and the cursor).
After confirming with `ENTER`, the form pops up. This is shown in Figure 12.5 in which the form contains the information on the sole instance in the relation, clinic *Orthopaedic*.

Popping up other views is similar, e.g. to pop-up another overview, select the `O` (`Overview`) button.

Remove a relationship

The procedure to remove a relationship from the overview is as follows:

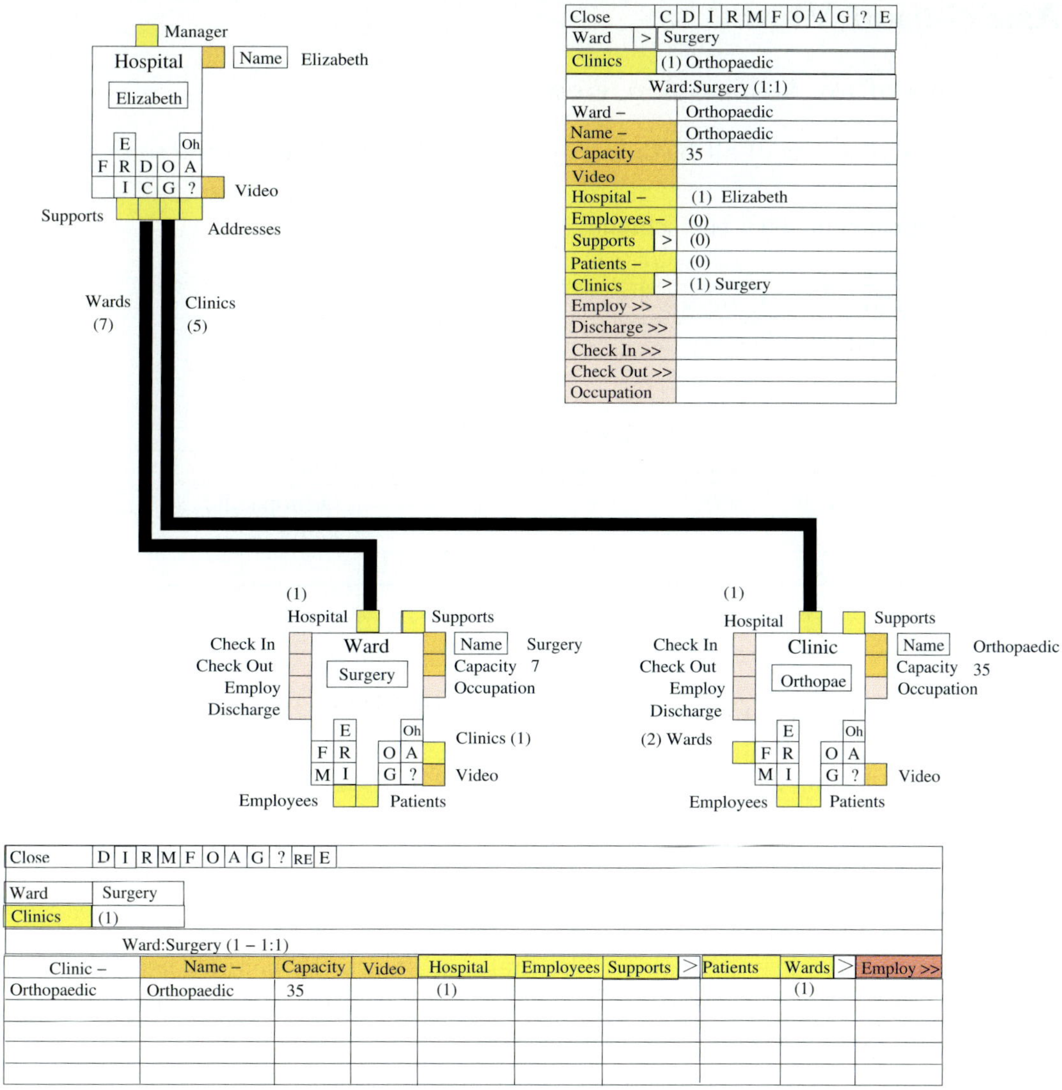

Figure 12.5: The form popped-up from an overview

- Pop-up an overview of the relation from which an instance is to be removed
- Activate the generic operation `R` (`Remove`) in the overview:
  - All fields of the identity column turn green, they are selectable
- Select the required related instance by clicking it in the green identity field:
  - The identity field turns blue (being the active relationship now)
  - Press `ENTER` to confirm
  - The instance will disappear since it is no longer an element of the set of related instances; only the relationship is removed (the instance itself still exists because this is a secondary relationship)
  - The cardinality decreases by one

The remove procedure can be carried out from both sides of the relationship.

12.2 Association View

12.2.1 Structure of an Association view

An Association view shows lists of all instances (their identities) related to the source instance.

The color coding is consistent with the schema.

Close	Refresh	?
Ward	Surgery	

Ward:Surgery (1-1:1)

Hospital	Employees	Supports	Patients	Clinics
Elizabeth	0001			Orthopaedic
				Pediatric

Figure 12.6: An Association view

An example of an association view is shown in Figure 12.6. It is constructed of 2 main parts, the **header** and the **body**:
The header of the association view shows the context of the objects presented in the body. At the top all relevant generic operations are given. Below the top row the source object type (left) and the identity of the source instance (right) appear.
The body of the association view is a table. The first row shows the column headers. Each column header presents a relation of the source instance. The elements under each column header display the keys of the instances related through that relation[1].
Columns vary in length according to the number of related instances.

12.2.2 Popping-up an Association view

Figure 12.7 shows how to pop-up an association view. The procedure is as follows:

- In the schema, access the source instance where the association view is to be generated
- Activate the generic operation `A` in the instance:

    - A window will pop-up displaying the association view

Figure 12.7 shows an association view of *Surgery* ward of *Elizabeth* hospital. The association view shows: ward *Surgery* is related to hospital *Elizabeth*, to `Employee` *0001* and to clinic *Orthopaedic*. The other relations are still empty[2].

[1]A major difference between an Association and an Overview is that each row in an Overview contains the data of one instance, whereas in an Association each element represents one instance. Another difference is that an Overview displays information on all instances in one relation, whereas an Association displays the instances of all relations.

[2]Currently there are only three relevant generic operations in the association view, `Close`, `Refresh` and `?` (help)

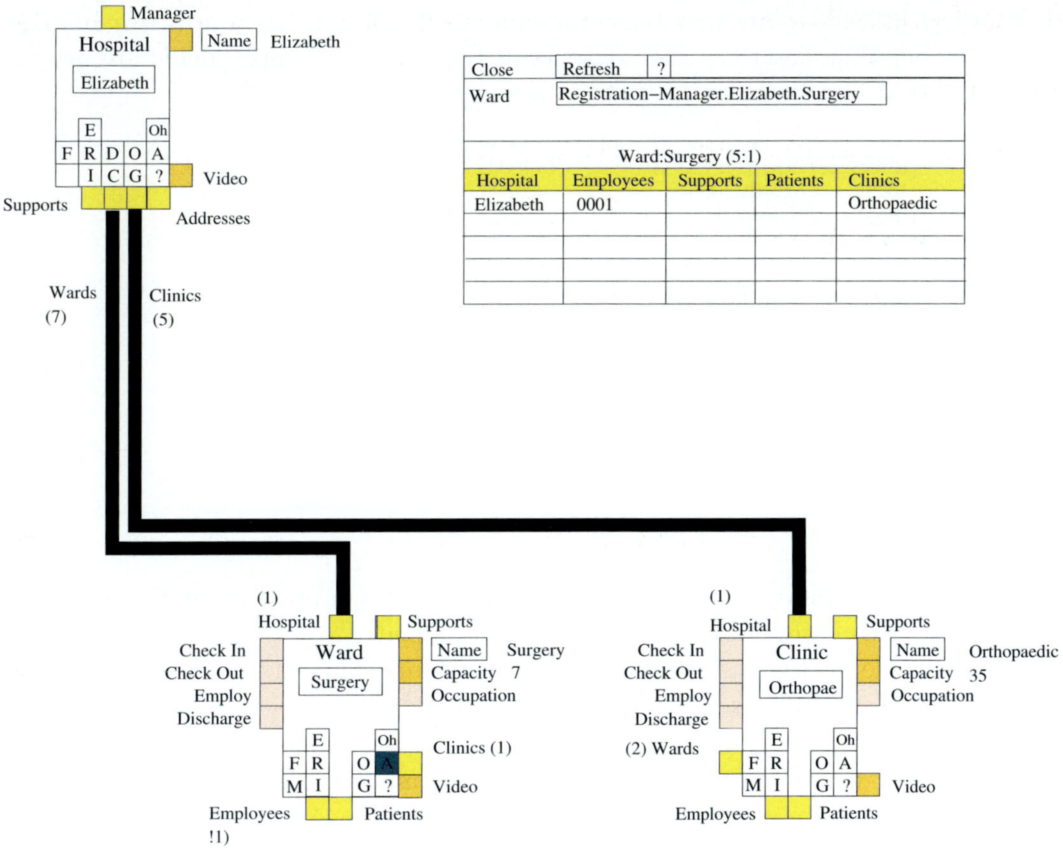

Figure 12.7: Popping-up an Association overview

12.2.3 Exploiting the Association view

The purpose of this view is to have all instances related to the source instance in one table. A common practice is to find a particular instance in the assocation table and manipulate it by dragging the field containing the instance to its object type in the schema, the instance becomes active in the schema. By clicking the field containing the instance a form view pops up containing the instance[3].

12.3 Query view

12.3.1 Structure of a query view

A query is designed to collect data needed for a specific task. A query view shows data extracted from the object base by executing a query. The data depends on the instance from which the query view is popped up, called the source (or root) instance, and on the query itself. A list of named queries may be defined for every object type.

The query view is composed of the **title bar** and the **query table**. The title bar of the query view shows the root instance and the name of the query. Data items are stored in **fields** of the **query table**, fields are organized in `columns` and `rows`. Each **row** of a query table shows related data that belongs to one or more instances. Each **column** of a query table shows related data; either instances reached by traversing a relation, or object attribute values.

[3]There is a slight difference between invoking the association view in the schema or in a table. In the schema the association view gives all objects related to the source object. In the table, it gives those objects present in the table.

Relations and object attributes are members, therefore each column has a **column header** showing the name of a member that describes the contents of the column. Empty fields are used to prevent repetitions or show that a value or an instance is missing.

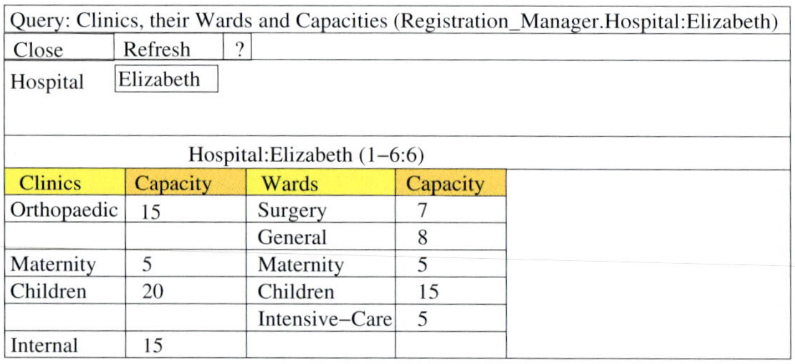

Figure 12.8: A query view

Figure 12.8 shows a query view. The title bar shows that it was popped up at the instance *Registration-Manager.Hospitals:Elizabeth*, by the query named *Clinics, their Wards and Capacities*. The query view shows the `Clinic` instances belonging to *Elizabeth* hospital instance, the `Ward` instances belonging to each of these `Clinic` instances, and the `Capacity` values of these `Clinic` and `Ward` instances.

The column headers show member names; `Clinics` is a member of `Hospital`, `Wards` is a member of `Clinic`, the first `Capacity` a member of `Clinic`, the second `Capacity` a member of `Ward`. Thus, the first column shows `Clinic` instances, the second and fourth columns show `Capacity` values, and the third column shows `Ward` instances.

Each row of this query table shows logically related data: the data in the first row belongs to the instances *Orthopaedic* and *Surgery*, the data in the second belongs to the instances *Orthopaedic* and *General*, the data in the third belongs to the instances *Maternity* `Clinic` and *Maternity* `Ward`, and so on. The first row shows that the *Surgery* instance is reachable by the `Wards` relation from the *Orthopaedic* instance. Since the field under *Orthopaedic* is empty, the second row shows that the *General* instance is also reachable by the `Wards` relation from the *Orthopaedic* instance. The empty fields in the row of the *Internal* instance show there is no `Ward` instance connected to the *Internal* `Clinic` instance.

12.3.2 Popping up a query view

Figure 12.9 shows how to pop-up a query view. The procedure to pop-up a query view is as follows:

- In the schema, access the root instance where the query view is to be generated
- Activate the special operation `Query` attached to the right side of the instance:
  - A list of query names appears
- Choose the name of the query to be executed:
  - A window pops up displaying the query view

The example shows the execution of the query *Wards Without Employees*, which may be used to check consistency of data.

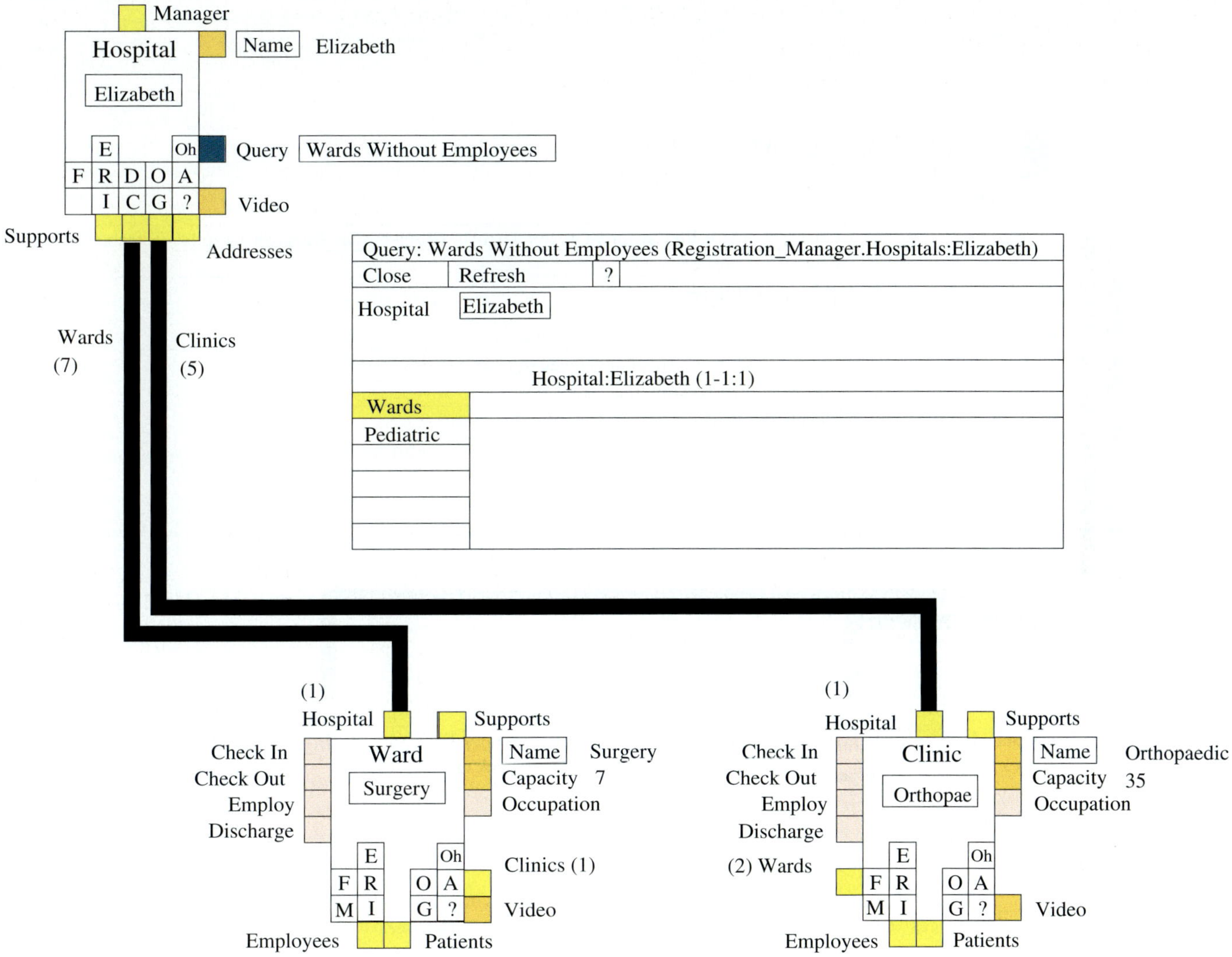

Figure 12.9: Popping up a query view

12.3.3 Exploiting a query view

The intention of the query view is to show the instances and related data needed for a specific task. The common usage is to inspect the table, and to find a particular instance in the table in order to activate it in the schema or to pop up a form view. By dragging the field containing the instance to its object type in the schema where upon the instance becomes active in the schema. Clicking the field containing the instance a pops up a form view containing the instance.

12.3.4 Popping up a query view with parameters

`Query` is a special operation. Some queries do not need arguments, so they can be popped up as described in 12.3.2.
Other queries need arguments. The arguments for queries are collected along the `collection path` as described in 10.2.
An example of parameterized query usage is shown in Figure 12.10. The procedure to pop-up the query view shown is as follows:

- In the schema, access the root instance where the query view is to be generated

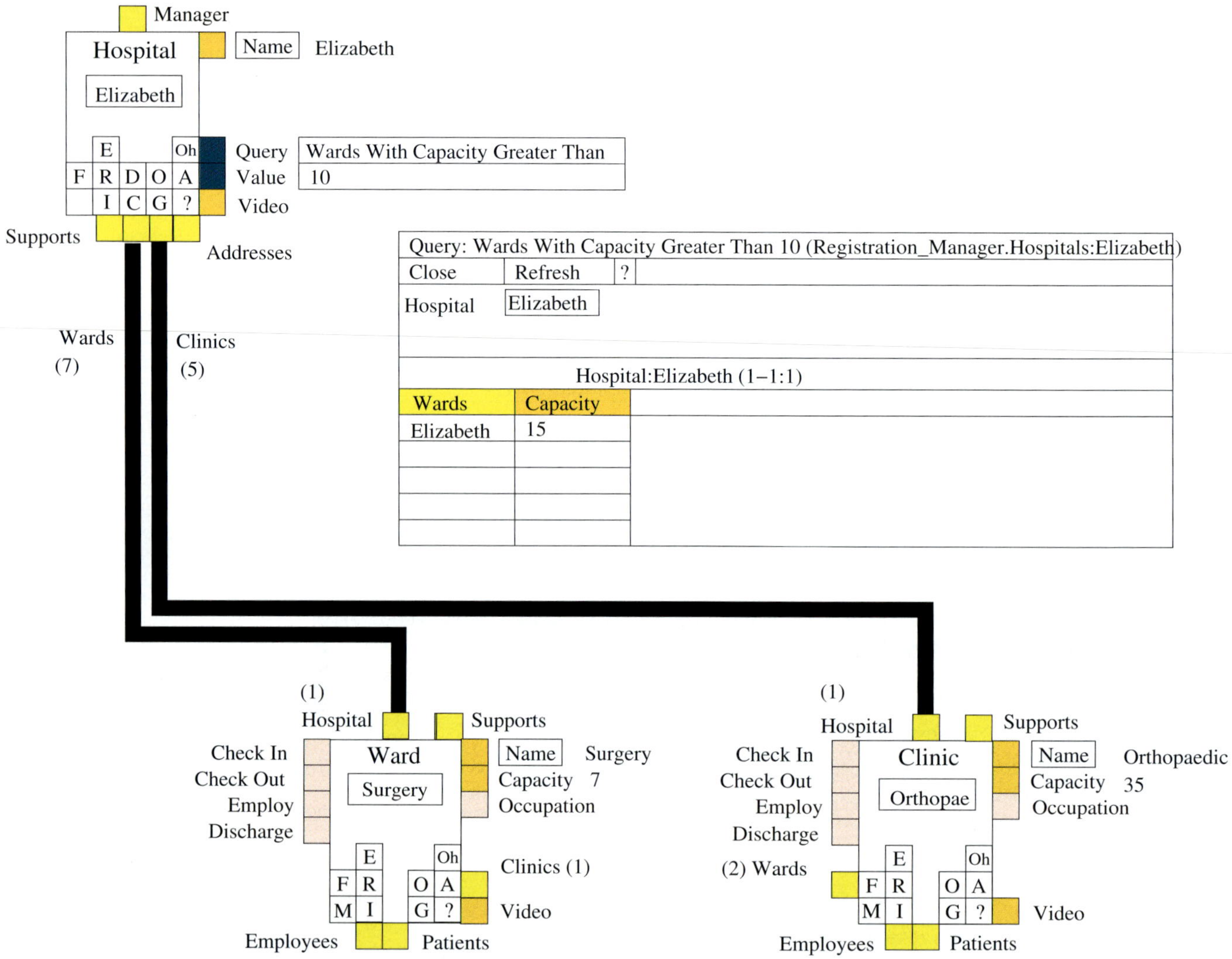

Figure 12.10: A query with a parameter

- Activate the operation `Query` attached to the right side of the instance
  - A list of query names appears
- Choose the name of the query to be executed:
  - The hidden instance member `Value` appears and turns blue
- Insert the value in the value field:
  - A window pops up displaying the query view

12.3.5 Defining New Queries

The end-user may define new queries.
The procedure to define a new query is as follows:

- In the schema, find the object type of the root instance
- Find the manager of the module where this object type is located

- Activate the special operation `Update Query` attached to the right side of the manager:
  - A number of object types in the module turn blue
- Choose the object type of the root instance:
  - The selected object type turns blue, the others turn back to their original color
  - A list of query names appears
- Type the name of the new query:
  - A window with an editor pops up for editing the query string
- Type the query string
- Exit the editor

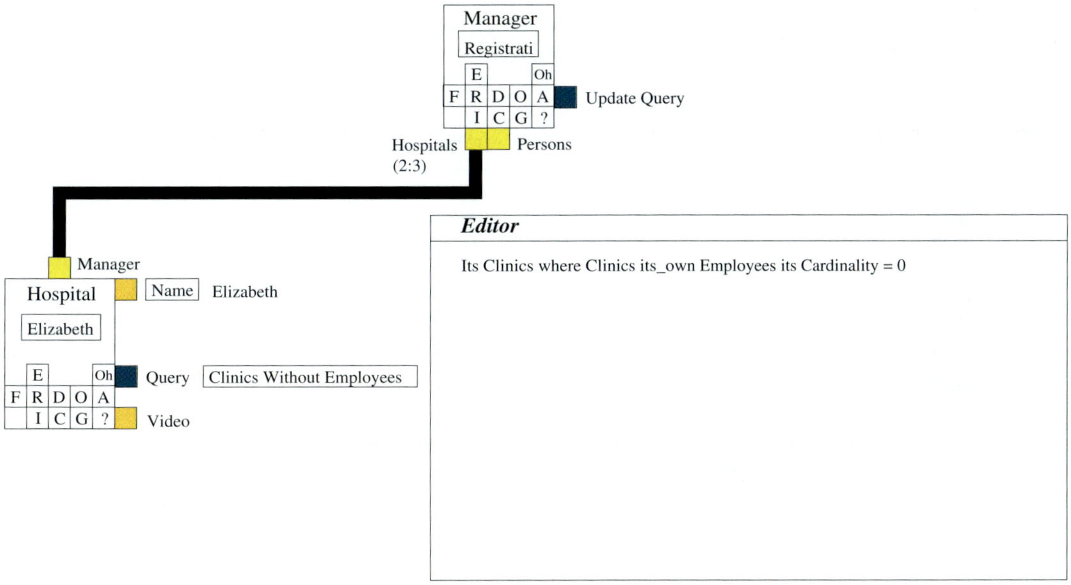

Figure 12.11: Defining a new query

An example of the definition of a new query is shown in Figure 12.11. The explanation of the query string and the query syntax are found in the next section. After defining the query, it can be invoked in the same way as the predefined queries (see Figure 12.12).

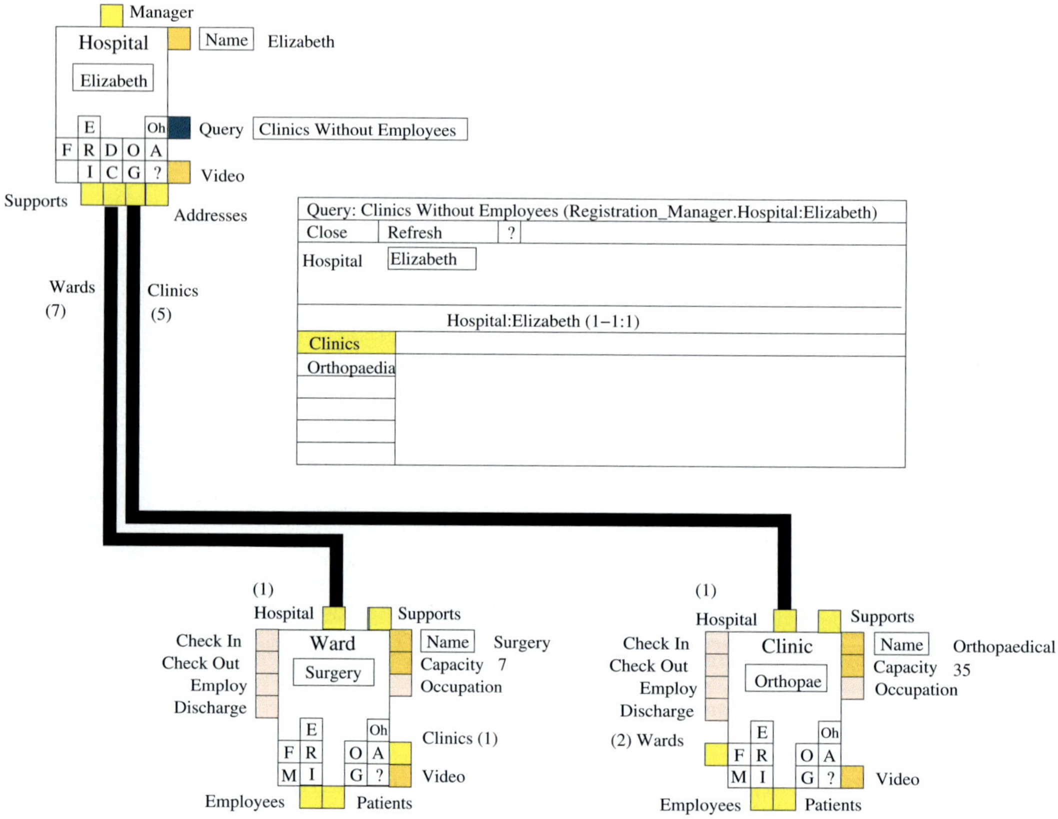

Figure 12.12: Popping up a query view for a newly defined query

Chapter 13

Query Principles

13.1 Basic Querying

13.1.1 Meaning of Query

Querying means to find and to retrieve instances and values in the object base by describing what is required.

Querying can be imagined as traversing an ownership hierarchy of instances and if necessary, crossing to another via a secondary relationship (or several) to continue the traversal as it was done during navigation. In contrast to navigation, the `traversal path` is described by the end-user but the traversal is done by Perspective-DB, not the end-user. Perspective-DB is guided by the required result as specified in the query, the answer being gathered during the traversal.
The query principles are described in detail in [Szántó, 2004]. When defining a new query, the user enters a query string that describes the traversal path. The query string must adhere to the query syntax that is explained below using examples.
The query string is interpreted in the context of the object type of the root instance. The query string is composed of a `selection clause` and an optional `WHERE clause`.
A **query item** is the part of a query string that describes one step on the traversal path. A query item is composed of a navigator and a member name. The navigator `its` requests navigation over the member that follows it.
A query item is a selection item if it is followed by a comma or if it is at the end of the selection clause. The other query items are `traversal items`. A query item appears in the query result only if it is a selection item.

13.1.2 Query items: selection and traversal items

Get the `Ward` instances of the `Hospital` *Elizabeth*.

```
Example 2.1a (query)
```

```
its Wards
```

The query consists of one query item: `its Wards`. It requests navigation to the instances from a Hospital instance over its relation `Wards`.

```
Example 2.1b (result)

  Wards
 Surgery
 General
 Maternity
 Pediatric
 Intensive-Care
```

The query result is a query table containing the `Ward` instances. The first row in the query table is the header that contains the column headers corresponding to the query items.
The query string is relative to the root object, in this case the `Hospital` *Elizabeth.* The following example illustrates that the root instance can also be a `Clinic` instance:

Get the `Ward` instances of the `Clinic` instance *Orthopaedic.*

```
Example 2.1c (query)

its Wards
```

```
Example 2.1d (result)

  Wards
 Surgery
 General
```

Hereafter, the root instance of the queries is the `Hospital` *Elizabeth*, unless stated otherwise.

Get the capacities of the `Ward` instances of the `Hospital` *Elizabeth.*

```
Example 2.2a (query)

its Wards its Capacity
```

The query consists of two query items: `its Wards` and `its Capacity`. The first query item requests navigation from a `Hospital` instance over its relation `Wards`. The second query item requests to continue navigation from the reached instances over their attribute `Capacity` to the capacity values.

```
Example 2.2b (result)

  Capacity
     7
     8
     5
    15
     5
```

The query result is a query table containing the capacity values.
Nothing in the query string indicates whether the traversal is of a relation or an attribute; no distinction is made between `Wards` and `Capacity`. Similarly, nothing in the query string indicates if the destination of the traversal is an instance or a value.
The `Ward` instances are not present in the query result 2.2b, because `Wards` is a traversal item. The following query requests both the `Ward` instances and their capacity values to appear in the query result.

Example 2.3a (query)

```
its Wards, its Wards its Capacity
```

Example 2.3b (result)

Wards	Capacity
Surgery	7
General	8
Maternity	5
Pediatric	15
Intensive-Care	5

In Example 2.3a, the first query item is `its Wards`, followed by a comma, and is therefore included in the query result (selection item), as opposed to the first query item in Example 2.2a, which is also `its Wards`, but is followed by a navigator and therefore not included in the query result (traversal item).

13.1.3 Traversing several relations

A query may traverse several relations and may gather data along the traversal path.

Get the clinics of the `Hospital` *Elizabeth*, their capacities, the wards of these clinics, the capacities of these wards.

Example 3.1a (query)

```
its Clinics,
its Clinics its Capacity,
its Clinics its Wards,
its Clinics its Wards its Capacity
```

Example 3.1b (result)

Clinics	Capacity	Wards	Capacity
Orthopaedic	15	Surgery	7
		General	8
Maternity	5	Maternity	5
Pediatric	20	Pediatric	15
		Intensive-Care	5
Internal	15		

The query result table indicates that the *Orthopaedic* clinic has two wards, *Surgery* and *General*, since *Surgery* is in the same row as *Orthopaedic*, *General* is one row below, but its corresponding `Clinics` field is empty, indicating that the value is to be found above. The table places related values near to each other (this is the same table as that shown in Figure 12.8).
In order to minimize user typing, already mentioned traversal items may be omitted from the query string in accordance with the following rule: if a selection item is followed by a comma, the traversal continues either at the root instance, or at the query item that leads to the current selection item. In order to continue at the root instance, the comma must be followed by a navigator; in order to continue at the query item that leads to the current selection item, the comma must be followed by the next member name.

So the query in Example 3.1a can be formulated shorter:

```
Example 3.1c (query)

its Clinics,
    Clinics its Capacity,
                Wards,
                Wards its Capacity
```

The query in example 3.1c produces the same result as 3.1a, i.e. the query table shown in 3.1b. In 3.1a the whole traversal route is described from the root instance to the selection items, but in 3.1c portions of the route are omitted. In 3.1a every comma is followed by the navigator `its`, which indicates that the traversal continues at the root instance. In 3.1c a comma is not followed by the navigator, instead every comma is followed by a member name, indicating that the traversal continues at the query item leading to the selection item before the comma. For example the query item `Wards` continues the traversal at the Clinics query item, because it is the query item leading to `Capacity`, which is the selection item before the comma.
Whitespace is insignificant in query strings, so 3.1c can also be formulated as:

```
Example 3.1d (query)

its Clinics, Clinics its Capacity, Wards, Wards its Capacity
```

13.2 Advanced Querying

13.2.1 Applying filters

If a query string contains a WHERE-clause, the latter is used to contain filter criteria to filter out rows from the query table. One filter criterion applies to one relation, in other words it filters the instances of one relation. Filter criteria may be combined in the WHERE-clause by using the logical operators AND and OR.
A filter criterion is a comparison of a member value to a constant or to an expression of constants and member values. The comparison may compare numbers or strings. For comparing numbers, the following comparison operators are used: =, != , <, >, <=, >=. For comparing strings, only = and ! = are permitted, but the wildcard $*$ may also be used.

Get the wards with capacity greater than 6.

```
Example 1.1a (query)

its Wards where its Wards its Capacity > 6
```

```
Example 1.1b (result)

  Wards
 Surgery
 General
 Pediatric
```

In this example there is one filter criterion that applies to the Wards relation. The Ward instances Maternity and Intensive-Care are filtered out, because they do not meet the filter criterion.

Get the wards with capacity greater than 6, and also get the capacity values, so that we can see that they meet the filter criterion.

Example 1.2a (query)

```
its Wards, Wards its Capacity  where its Wards its Capacity > 6
```

Example 1.2b (result)

Wards	Capacity
Surgery	7
General	8
Pediatric	15

The following query is an example of combining two filter criteria.

Get the wards and their capacity values with a capacity greater than 6 but smaller than 10.

Example 1.3a (query)

```
its Wards, Wards its Capacity
where its Wards its Capacity > 6 and its Wards its Capacity < 10
```

Example 1.3b (result)

Wards	Capacity
Surgery	7
General	8

A shorter version is also possible.

Example 1.3c (query)

```
its Wards, Wards its Capacity where Capacity > 6 and Capacity < 10
```

The query shown in 1.3c is equivalent to that shown in 1.3a, so its result is the same as the query table shown in 1.3b. The traversal items can be omitted after the `where`, `and`, `or` keywords using the same rules as after the comma.
When traversing and filtering several relations, the filter does not only affect the instances in the relation that it applies to. The following queries illustrate this with two relations.

Get the `Clinics`, their `Wards` and the capacities of the `Wards`, but only for the `Clinics` that have a `Name` beginning with the letter *P*.

Example 1.4a (query)

```
its Clinics, Clinics its Wards, Wards its Capacity where its Clinics its Name = P*
```

The filter applies to the relation `Clinics`, but `Ward` instances are also filtered out, since the traversal does not reach the `Ward` instances not connected to the `Clinic` Pedriatric. This is also an example for using a wildcard.

Example 1.4b (result)

Clinics	Wards	Capacity
Pedriatric	Pediatric	15
	Intensive-Care	5

Get the `Clinics`, their `Wards` and the capacities of the `Wards`, but only those `Clinics` with `Wards` that have a capacity greater than *6*.

Example 1.5a (query)

```
its Clinics, Clinics its Wards, Wards its Capacity where Capacity > 6
```

Example 1.5b (result)

Clinics	Wards	Capacity
Orthopaedic	Surgery	7
	General	8
Pediatric	Pediatric	15

The filter applies to the `Ward` instances, but the `Clinic` instances are also filtered out, since only those `Clinic` instances are shown that have a `Ward` with a capacity greater than *6*.
The same principle applies when the filter applies to a relation that is a traversal item and does not appear in the query result.

Get the `Wards` of the `Clinics` and the capacities of the `Wards`, but only for the `Clinics` that have a Name beginning with the letter *P* (variation of Example 1.4a).

Example 1.6a (query)

```
its Clinics its Wards, Wards its Capacity where its Clinics its Name = P*
```

The filter applies to the relation `Clinics` and indirectly to `Ward` instances as in example 1.4a, but here, `Clinic` instances are not retrieved.

Example 1.6b (result)

Wards	Capacity
Pediatric	15
Intensive-Care	5

Get the `Clinics` that have at least one `Ward` with capacity greater than *6* (variation of Example 1.5a).

Example 1.7a (query)

```
its Clinics where Clinics its Wards its Capacity > 6
```

Example 1.7b (result)

Clinics
Orthopaedic
Pediatric

Only those `Clinic` instances are shown that have a `Ward` with a capacity greater than *6*.

13.2.2 Applying type selectors

Heterogeneous relations may be traversed in the same way as homogeneous relations. A query item that instructs the query to traverse a heterogeneous relation may also instruct the query to select instances of a particular type only.

Traverse the `Supports` relation of `Hospital` *Elizabeth*.

```
Example 2.1a (query)

its Supports
```

```
Example 2.1b (result)

  Supports
 Kitchen
 Laundry
 X-Ray
```

Get the `Supports` of `Hospital` *Elizabeth*, but only those of type `General-Service`[1].

```
Example 2.2a (query)

its Supports type Hosp_General_Support
```

```
Example 2.2b (result)

  Supports
 Kitchen
 Laundry
```

13.2.3 Using meta-members

The object model includes the following notions:

- object key
- object type
- object id
- object owner

These notions can also be used in query items to describe the traversal in the place of the member name. They are not members but represent a kind of meta-information about members, so they are called meta-members.

Get the `key`, `type`, `id` and `owner` of a `Hospital` instance.

```
Example 3.1a (query)

its key, type, id, owner
```

[1]If the object type name is aliased, the alias can be used as an alternative.

Example 3.1b (result)

key	type	id	owner
Mother-Theresa	Hospital	Reg-Manager.Hospitals:Mother-Theresa	Reg-Manager

(Reg-Manager is Registration-Manager.)

Get the objects that are owned by a `Hospital` instance.

Example 3.2a (query)

```
its owned
```

Example 3.2b (result)

Supports	Wards	Clinics	Address
Kitchen	Surgery	Orthopaedic	987654321
Laundry	General	Maternity	
X-Ray	Maternity	Pediatric	
	Pediatric	Internal	
	Intensive-Care		

13.2.4 Recursive queries

Recursive relationships can be traversed by non-recursive and by recursive query items. A non-recursive query item instructs the query to traverse the relation once; a recursive query item instructs the query to traverse a recursive relation several times, i.e. as many times as is necessary. In order to make a query item recursive, the navigator `its_recursive` must be used.

Get all the descendants of the `Person` *345678* (the root instance is the `Person` *345678*).

Example 4.1a (query)

```
its_recursive Children
```

The navigator `its_recursive` may also be used in combination with meta-members. This is useful in the case of the meta-members `owner` and `owned`. `Its_recursive owner` requests all the instances that are above the root instance in the ownership hierarchy, up to the manager object. `Its_recursive owned` requests the ownership hierarchy of instances starting at the root object.

Get the ownership hierarchy of objects for `Hospital` *Elizabeth*.

Example 4.2a (query)

```
its_recursive owned
```

A recursive hierarchy of instances may be also regarded as a tree of instances. In some cases, the leaves of this tree are required.

Get the leaves of the tree of descendant's of the `Person` *345678* (the root instance is the `Person` *345678*). In other words, those descendants not having children are requested.

Example 4.3a (query)

```
its_recursive_leaves Children
```

13.2.5 Querying relation cardinality

The cardinality of a relation is the number of instances in the relation. To query the cardinality of a relation, the special navigator `its_own` must be used to prevent the query traversing the relation to the instances at the other end, so `its_own` means to navigate to the relation itself.

Get the number of `Employees` of each `Ward`.

```
Example 5.1a (query)

its Wards its_own Employees its Cardinality
```

```
Example 5.1b (result)

  Wards            Cardinality
 Surgery               3
 General               0
 Maternity            14
 Pediatric            20
 Intensive-Care       10
```

The cardinality is sometimes useful in finding inconsistencies in the object base.

Get the `Wards` that have no `Employees`.

```
Example 5.2a (query)

its Wards where Wards its_own Employees its Cardinality = 0
```

```
Example 5.2b (result)

  Wards
 General
```

13.2.6 Aggregating a number of values

Aggregation is computing the maximum, the minimum, the count, the sum, or the average of a number of values. Aggregation is achieved by requesting the type of aggregation (max, min, count, sum, or avg) and by indicating the beginning and end of the query items to be aggregated.

Get the maximum number of `Hours` worked by each `Employee` at each `Ward` where she or he is employed.

```
Example 6.1a (query)

its Wards its max(Employees its Hours)
```

```
Example 6.1b (result)

  Wards                 max
 Surgery                 8
 General                 0
 Maternity              10
 Pediatric              12
 Intensive-Care          8
```

Get the total number of `Hours` the `Employees` work at each `Ward`.

Example 6.2a (query)

```
its Wards its sum(Employees its Hours)
```

Example 6.2b (result)

Wards	sum
Surgery	24
General	0
Maternity	120
Pediatric	110
Intensive-Care	72

Get the `Wards` with no `Employees`. This is an alternative to query 5.2a.

Example 6.3a (query)

```
its Wards where Wards its count(Employees) = 0
```

Example 6.3b (result)

Wards
General

For every `Hospital`, get the number of `Employees` that work at the `Wards`.

Example 6.4a (query)

```
its Hospitals, Hospitals its count(Wards its Employees)
```

Example 6.3b (result)

Hospitals	count
Elizabeth	47
Mother-Theresa	30

13.2.7 Executing methods from queries

`Operations` can be executed from queries by making query items composed of the name and arguments of the requested operation. This way, the query can also be used for data manipulation operations other than for extracting and restructuring data, e.g. for object creation and for setting attribute values.

Set the `Name` attribute of the `Ward` called *Surgery* to *Surgery1*.

Example 7.1a (query)

```
its Wards its Set_Data("Name", Surgery1) where Name = Surgery
```

Example 7.1b (result)

```
  Set_Data
 Surgery1
```

Subtract 2 (two) from the Hours attribute of the `Employees` of the *Wards*.

Example 7.2a (query)

```
its Wards its Employees its Set_Data("Hours", Hours-2)
```

Example 7.2b (result)

```
  Set_Data
      6
      2
      3
      4
      0
      8
      7
      8
      3
      8
     10
      8
     10
      9
      6
      4
      3
      5
```

Chapter 14

The GOML Domain

14.1 Introduction

The `GOML` domain is the textual equivalent of the schematic end-user view. GOML stands for Graphical Object Management Language because it configures the graphical presentation of objects. One `GOML` file contains the configuration information for one module.
The configuration of graphical objects and the run-time management of the GUI is done by objects of the GOMS layer, the graphical layer of Perspective-DB, described in Chapter 19.
The value of the `View` field is always *GUI*.
The value of the `Manager` field is always *Template*, indicating that it manages templates for the graphical presentation of objects. Re-using the templates is an important task of the `Template Manager`. The **Metatype** field has the range: *Object, Position, Member, Network, Create,* and *Copy.* The semantics of the `Metatype-, Type-` and `Key-`values are explained using examples from the `GOML` file of the hospital case study.

14.2 Spatial placement of objects

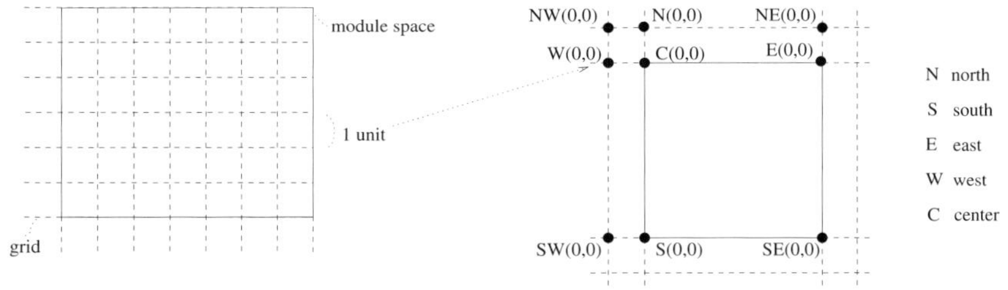

Figure 14.1: A grid and a compass for graphical presentation

An application representation consists of one or more **Windows**, each containing a (sub)system. For example, the Hospital application is represented in a Main Window and the additional framework services available to the end-user are represented in an Ancillary Window. Therefore the application has two windows, each with its own object schema.
The **canvas** is the area inside a window where objects are drawn.
The position of an object on a canvas is defined using a **Grid**, see Figure 14.1, left side. A position on the grid is given by "counting" the horizontal and vertical grid units starting from another position, the reference point. The position can be defined absolutely or relatively. If the reference point is the coordinate 0,0 it is absolute. If the reference point is another item (object, member etc) it is relative.

The default is that the GOML object is positioned relative to its owner GOML object.

A **system grid** places each module in a unique position on the canvas.
The **module grid** places each object type within the module in a unique position relative to the module. The module grids are owned by (children of) the system grids.

The object type `grid` places each member of an object type in a unique position relative to the object type. The members can be placed using an absolute object type grid coordinate, or using a coordinate relative to another member of the object type.

In addition to the horizontal and vertical "counting" of units, a compass position indicates how to orient the target position with respect to the reference point. The compass positions are shown on the right side of Figure 14.1. *C(0,0)* is the top left corner of an object. *W(0,0)* is one unit left of *C(0,0)*. *NW(0,0)* is one unit left of, and one unit above *C(0,0)*. *S(0,0)* is the bottom left corner of an object. *SW(0,0)* is one unit left of *S(0,0)*. *E(0,0)* is the top right corner of the object. *NE(0,0)* is one unit above *E(0,0)*. *SE(0,0)* is the bottom right corner of the object. This combined compass-coordinate notation simplifies the placement of members.
When several modules belong to an application, the modules are placed on the system grid in a way that makes the semantics of the whole object schema clear. The placement of the modules should take various factors into account. Primarily that object types related across modules should be in close proximity. Secondarily, that the position of relations should keep connectors short and avoid unnecessary crossing of connectors.

14.3 Configuring an object type and its members

14.3.1 Configuring object types

```
Person "Center 65 16" Position Template GUI { }
  (1)       (2)                      (1)
```

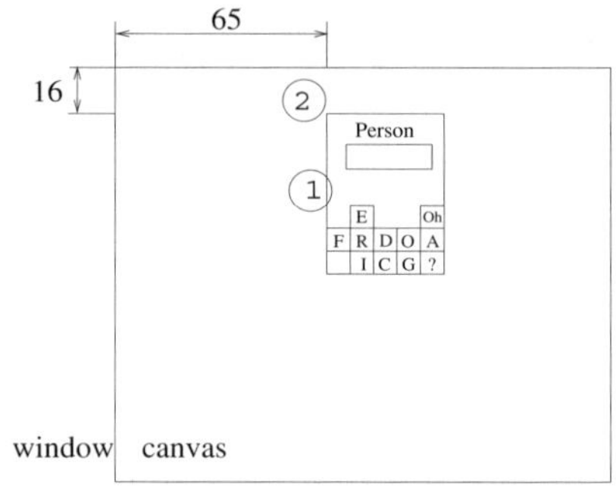

Figure 14.2: Configuring an object type

The left side of Figure 14.2 shows the `GOML` configuration for presenting an object type on the canvas. `Person`, the object type name, is the `Key` value of the GOML object. Mark 1 implies that a GUI object type template is selected describing the standard rectangle size, the positioning of the generic operations, etc. The template is used to define the object type `Person`.

The `Metatype` value *Position* indicates that position information is given.
The position information (Mark 2) is the `Type` value of the GOML object. In this case `Person` is placed 65 units to the right of and 16 units below the central position (top left corner) of the module grid. The right side of the figure shows the graphic effect of the configuration.

14.3.2 Configuring members

```
    Person "Center 65 16" Position Template GUI
    {
(1)   SSN "East 0 0" Position { }
      Name "East 0 1" Position { }
      Gender "East 0 2" Position { }
(2)   Hours "East 0 3" Position { }
      Photo "East 0 6" Position { }
(3)   Manager "North 2 0" Position { }
      Parents "North_East -2 0" Position { }
      Roles "South 1 0" Position { }
(4)   Children "South_East -1 0" Position { }
      Addresses "South_East 0 0" Position { }
    }
```

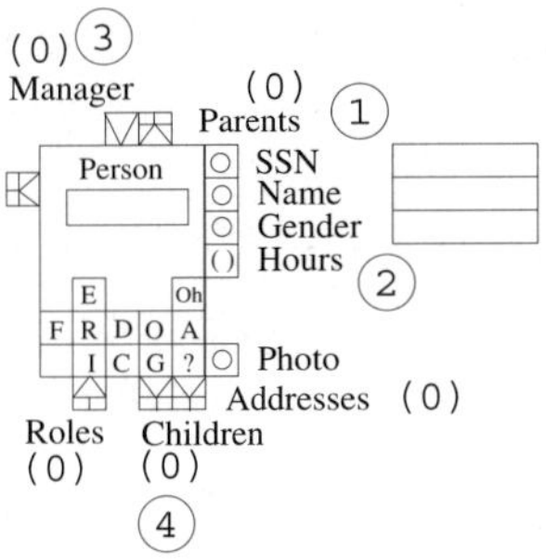

Figure 14.3: Configuring members

The configuration information for each member is basically the same, independent of its role. The configuration describes the position of the rectangle denoting the member. The default position of the corresponding text and value fields are automatically regulated by the system. The text field contains the name of the member. The semantics of the value field depend on the member's role.

The positioning of members is configured within the body of their object-type GOML object. Figure 14.3 shows the member configuration of the GOML object `Person`.

Each member is a GOML object (the tail rule is applied).

The values of the `Metatype, Type` and `Key` have semantics analogous to the object type and the positioning is now given relative to the object type.

- Attribute (Mark 1):
  The attribute `SSN` is positioned at "East 0 0". The value field contains the attribute value (when an instance is in access).

- Operation (Mark 2):
  The operation `Hours` is positioned at "East 0 3". The value field is used to contain the return value of the operation (e.g. succeeded or failed, true or false, etc). This field is invisible by default. It becomes visible when the operation terminates.

- Relation (Marks 3, 4):
  The relation `Manager` is positioned at "North 2 0". The value field contains the cardinality index. The default cardinality value is *(0)*. When an object is in access, the value switches to the actual cardinality.

14.3.3 Modifying the default position of text and value fields

Configuring the position of text and value fields is achieved similarly to that of object types and their members. Marks 2-5 of Figure 14.4 are examples. Mark 3 shows that the cardinality index of `Parents` has been placed above the member `SSN` so as not to obstruct the connectors leading out of the relations `Parents` and `Manager`.

```
     Person "Center 65 16" Position Template GUI
     {
      SSN "East 0 0" Position
       {
(1)      Text.Display_Bitmap "Gui_Intensity 3" Member { }
       } Value.Display_Bitmap "Gui_Intensity 3" Member { }
      Name "East 0 1" Position { }
      Gender "East 0 2" Position { }
      Hours "East 0 3" Position { }
      Photo "East 0 6" Position { }
      Manager "North 2 0" Position
       {
(2)      Text "West 0 0" Position { }
       } Value "North 0 0" Position { }
      Parents "North_East -1 0" Position
       {
(3)    } Value "East 5 0" Position { }
      Roles "South 1 0" Position
       {
(4)      Text "South_East 0 4" Position { }
       } Value "South_East 0 5" Position { }
      Children "South_East -1 0" Position
       {
(5)      Text "South_East 0 2" Position { }
       } Value "South_East 5 2" Position { }
      Address "South_East 0 0" Position { }
     }
```

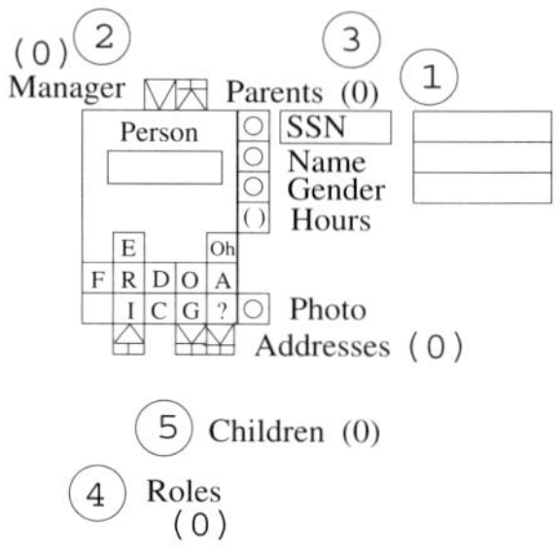

Figure 14.4: Text and value field positioning

14.3.4 Highlighting members

It is possible to configure the intensity[1] of text and value fields within the body of the GOML object. This `GOML` object contains two members, `Text` and `Value` which contain information on the configuration of the text and value fields of the owner, in this example for the member `SSN` see Figure 14.4 Mark 1[2].

The `Metatype` value is *Member*, the `Type` value is a parameter for the color intensity of the rectangle surface, and the `Key` value denotes that it refers to the display bitmap of the text field on the first line and the display bitmap of the value field on the second line. The display bitmap contains various display parameters concerning its owner.

14.4 Configuring Connectors and Nodes

14.4.1 Building a network between relations

A node is a GOML object that denotes a point on the canvas. A connector line is a GOML object contained within the body of a relation or a node which is its starting point. The destination of a connector line is generally a node or a relation[3]. A network is constructed by connecting a series of connector and node GOML objects.

[1]There are currently 4 grades: erased, normal, highlighted, faded.

[2]This configuration is actually done automatically by the GUI, because it detects that the member is the key.

[3]The destination can also be an object type (if the connector represents a pointer) and a relation attribute.

```
    Person "Center 65 16" Position Template GUI
    {
     .....
     Roles "South 1 0" Position
      {
       Text "South_East 0 4" Position { }
       Value "South_East 0 5" Position { }
(1)    Connector "Node" Network
        {
(2)      Node "South -7 25 Roles" Position
          {
(3)        Connector "Patient.Person" Network { }
(4)        Connector1 "Splitter" Network
            {
(5)          Splitter "South -10 25 Roles" Position
              {
(6)            Connector "Hosp_Status" Network { }
(7)            Monitor: "Splitter.Connector" Member { }
(8)            Connector1 "Employee.Person" Network { }
              }
            }
          }
        }
      }
     ....
    }
```

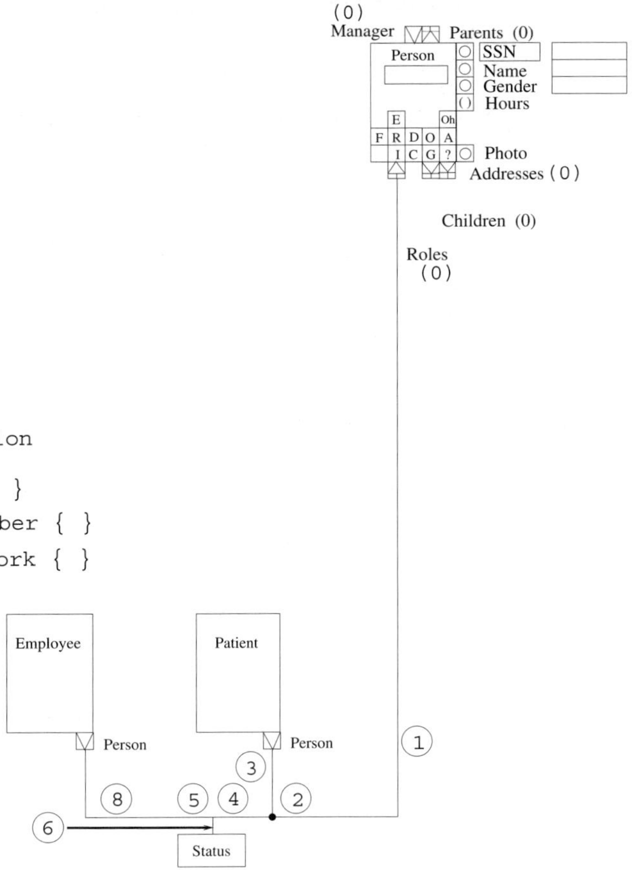

Figure 14.5: Configuring connector lines

Figure 14.5 illustrates the network of connectors and nodes necessary to visualize the relationship between the object types `Person, Employee` and `Patient`, taking into consideration the relation attribute `Status`[4].
In Figure 14.5, two categories of node are applied:

1. A `Node` is used to guide the connector to a specific point on the canvas, change the direction of a connector or to split up one connector line into several.

2. A `Splitter` is a special node used to attach a relationship attribute to a connector.

The positioning of the `GOML` objects `Node` and `Splitter` are configured similarly to the positioning of other `GOML` objects, see Examples Mark 2 and Mark 5. Node and Splitter are the `Key` values, the position is given in the `Type` value relative to the relation `Person.Roles` (see section 14.4.3).
A `Connector` GOML object has the `Metatype` value *Network* (Mark 1). This Metatype means that the connector line is to be drawn to the destination defined in the `Type` field.
The GOML objects (connectors) must be identified uniquely within the scope of their owner (the node with Mark 2), therefore the connector lines must have different names. For `example` node with Mark 2 is the owner of two connector lines (Marks 3, 4).
The GOML object `Monitor` (Mark 7) is added to indicate to the GUI system that it must take the relation attribute into account.

[4]Giving the position of the Text field (of member Role) is only required to overrule the automatic placement. The Value field follows the Text field as a rule, therefore the placement of the Text field (of member Role) also overrules the automatic placement.

14.4.2 Minimizing the number of nodes

The drawing manager automatically chooses the direction of a connector to the destination (another node or a relation). If the choice is not satisfactory a node must be configured. For example, the connector line between the relation `Person.Roles` and the node with Mark 2 in Figure 14.5 has automatically been placed correctly, therefore no additional node is required to guide it.

14.4.3 Configuring reference points

The position of a GOML object is by default relative to its owner GOML object as mentioned in 14.2. For example, the position of `Person.Roles` is relative to the position of `Person` and the position of `Roles.Text` is relative to `Person.Roles`.
It is sometimes necessary to position an object relative to an object other than its owner. For example, a position relative to a connector is ambiguous (is it the beginning or the end?). The node marked 2 in Figure 14.5 is owned by the connector marked 1 but the positioning of the node is given relative the owner of its connector, `Roles`.
Another example is when a node is far from its GOML object owner, making it difficult to figure out the right position coordinates.

14.4.4 Configuring the width of a connector line

```
Person "Center 65 16" Position Template GUI
{
 .....
 Roles "South 1 0" Position
  {
   ....
   Connector "Node" Network
    {
 (1)    Form.Width "3" Member { }
        Node "South -7 25 Roles" Position
        {
         Connector "Patient.Person" Network { }
         Connector1 "Splitter" Network
         ....
        }
    }
  }
  ....
}
```

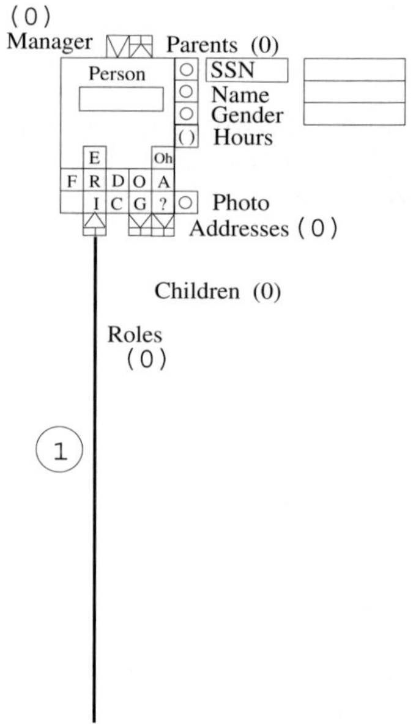

Figure 14.6: Configuring the width of a connector line

Figure 14.6 adds the configuration of the width of a connector line.
The value for the `Metatype` is *Member*, the `Type` value is the numerical value for the width, and the `Key` value is the term *Form.Width*. The member `Form` of the connector contains various members including the width.

```
Person "Center 65 16" Position Template GUI
{
 .....
 Roles "South 1 0" Position
  {
   .....
   Connector "Node" Network
    {
     .....

        {
         Splitter "South -10 25 Roles" Position
          {
           Connector "Hosp_Status" Network { }
            {
       (1)   Apparition_Bitmap "Gui_Orientation 5" Member { }
            }
           ....
          }
        }
      ....
    }
  }
 ....
}
```

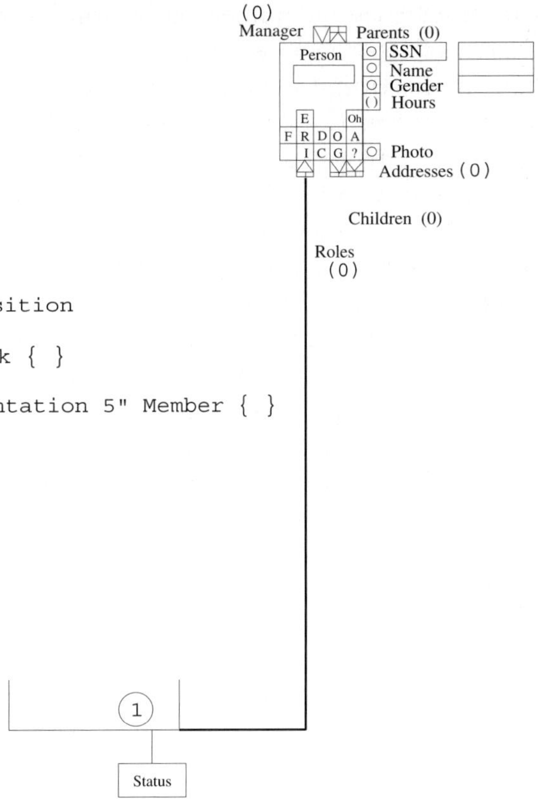

Figure 14.7: Configuring a hint

14.4.5 Configuring a hint for the drawing manager

Hints are intended to help the drawing manager perform a more optimal placement, or to reduce the processing time it needs to calculate a placement. Figure 14.7 shows how a hint is applied. The connector leading from the relation `Roles` branches and changes direction. The drawing manager is hinted how to orient the connector to the relation attribute `Status`. In this example the orientation is *5* which implies South (the other options are *1* North, *2* North-East, *3* East, *4* South-East, *6* South-West, *7* West, *8* North-West and *9* Center).

14.4.6 Configuring a constraint

```
Person "Center 65 16" Position Template GUI
{
 .....
 Roles "South 1 0" Position
  {
(1) Kernel_Bitmap "Gui_May_Insert 0 Gui_May_Remove 0" Member { }
    Text "South_East 0 4" Position { }
    Value "South_East 0 5" Position { }
    Connector "Node" Network
     ....
  }
 ....
}
```

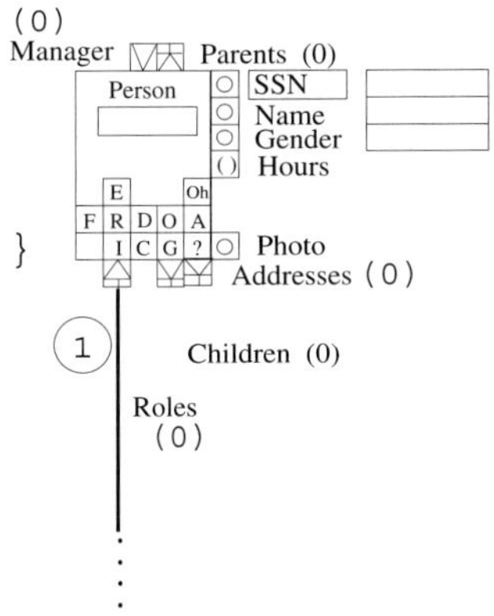

Figure 14.8: Configuring a constraint for relation behavior

Application logic can be influenced by configuring constraints. An `example` is disabling the insertion and removal of relationships[5].

The logic of the Hospital case study forbids the end-user to insert and remove roles of a particular person by applying the `Insert` and `Remove` operations to the relationship type `Person.Roles`: A person will be employed and discharged in the role of employee by the specific operations `Employ` and `Discharge`. A person will be checked in and out as patient by using the specific operations `Check_In` and `Check_Out`. These operations collect the `SSN` value for the particular person as input argument for the operation, see Figure 10.21. The relation between `Person.Roles` and `Employee.Person` or `Patient.Person` is managed by the respective operation. As a consequence, the generic operations `I` (`Insert`) and `R` (`Remove`) must be disabled for `Person.Roles, Employee.Person` and `Patient.Person`. This is achieved with the addition (Mark 1) shown in Figure 14.8.

In this example, it is only necessary to constrain the `Insert` and `Remove` of the relation `Roles`. The generic operations `Insert` and `Remove` in `Person` remain applicable to its other relations (`Parents, Children`). The `Insert` and `Remove` of `Employee.Person` and `Patient.Person` are constrained in a similar manner (not shown).

14.4.7 Configuring a recursive connector

```
Person "Center 65 16" Position Template GUI
{
 .....
(1) Children "South_East -1 0" Position
  {
    Text "South_East 0 2" Position { }
    Value "South_East 5 2" Position { }
    Connector "Node" Network Template GUI
     {
(2)     Node "North_East 12 -4 Person" Position
        {
          Connector "Person.Parents" Network Template GUI { }
        }
     }
  }
  .....
}
```

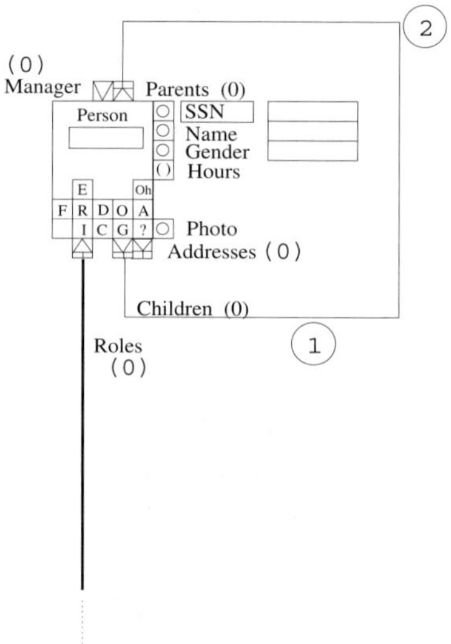

Figure 14.9: Configuring a recursive connector

The configuration of a recursive and a non-recursive connector is the same, see Figure 14.9. The example shows that it is sufficient to position one node in this case[6].

14.4.8 Configuring the visibility of a member

A member that is not relevant for the end user has to be made invisible. For `example`, in the Hospital application, `Person` has no owned relations therefore the create and destroy operations are not relevant. Figure 14.10 shows how the generic operations `C` (`Create`) and `D` (`Destroy`) in the object type `Person` are made invisible (Mark 1).

[5]This is a GUI constraint and applies to the end-user therefore it does not apply to the application code.

[6]In Figure 14.9, "Template GUI" can be left out in the second and third occurrences since the system already recognizes that this configuration is a template from the first occurrence.

```
Person "Center 65 16" Position Template GUI
  {
   .....
(1)   Create.Apparition_Bitmap "Gui_Should_Be_Visible 0" Member { }
      Destroy.Apparition_Bitmap "Gui_Should_Be_Visible 0" Member { }
  }
```

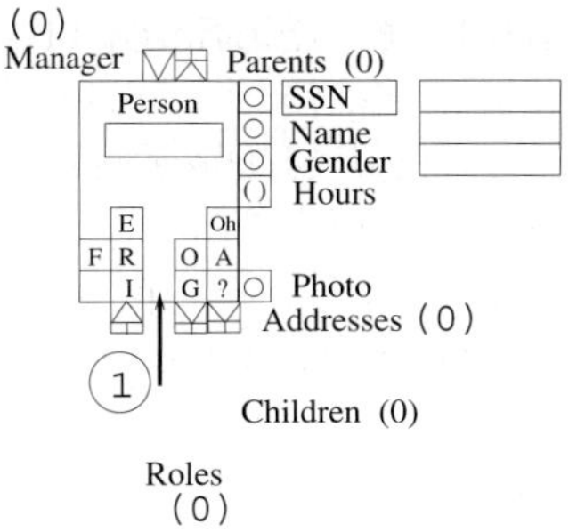

Figure 14.10: Making generic operations invisible

14.4.9 Configuring visibility in the form view

A member is normally displayed in both the schematic and the form view. It is possible to overrule this behavior by explicitly making the member invisible in the schematic or the form[7]. Figure 14.11 shows how an operation is explicitly set on (Mark 1); to set the display of the operation Hours on in the Form View of Person the type field is: *Gui_Part_Of_Form_View 1.* To set the display off, the type field should be: *Gui_Part_Of_Form_View 0.*

```
 Person "Center 65 16" Position Template GUI
 {
   ....
  Hours "East 0 3" Position
    {
(1)   Kernel_Bitmap "Gui_Part_Of_Form_View 1" Member { }
    }
  ....
 }
```

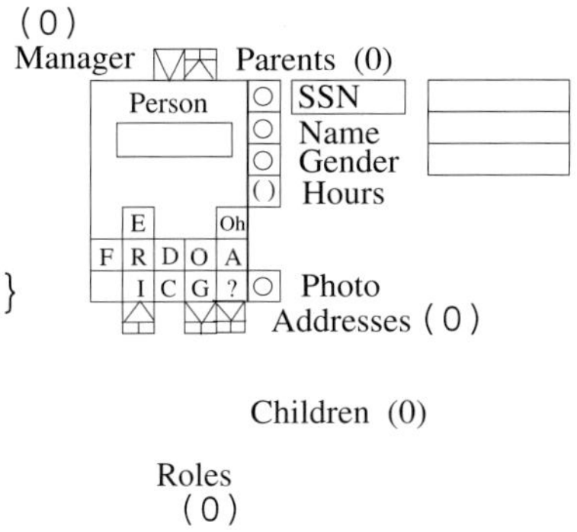

Figure 14.11: Making an operation visible in the form view

14.4.10 Reconfiguring the size of an object type

Figure 14.12 shows how to resize the object type. By default, it is a rectangle 6 (horizontal) by 9 (vertical). The `example` shows the resizing of object type `Hosp_Manager` (Mark 1).

```
   Hosp_Manager "Center 45 2" Position Template GUI
    {
     GUI_External_Position.GUI_External_Position GUI_Position_Object Create
      {
(1)     GUI_MT_Position "5 7 GUI_Size" Member { }
      }
(2)  Object_Bitmap "Gui_Secondary_Role 1" Member { }
     ......
    }
```

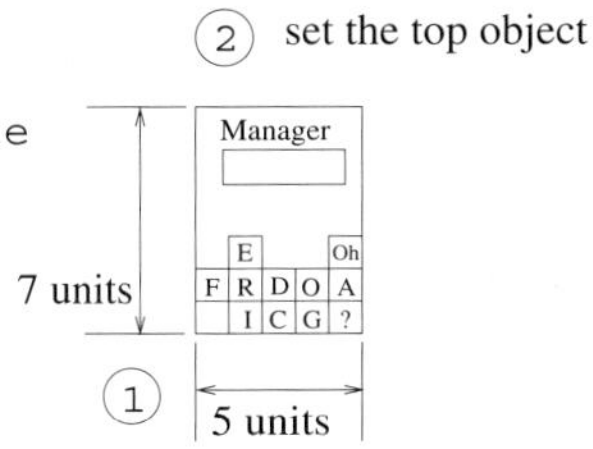

Figure 14.12: Configuring the size of an object type and setting the top object

[7]The same object model concepts apply to schematic and tabular views, therefore in principle both representations should contain the same information. In practice, situations may arise where it is not practical to display all members in a table, or in the schema.

14.4.11 Setting the top object

Setting the top object is a hint to the drawing manager that an object is the root of the ownership hierarchy. This example is for illustration purposes because the setting is done once for the base type of all the managers (*OMS_Object_Manager*); the specialized managers therefore inherit the property of being top objects. Thus, application developers need not set managers to be top objects. Figure 14.12 shows this hint (Mark 2).

14.5 Inheritance of configurations

14.5.1 Configuring a generalization

```
Department Department Object Template GUI
 {
  Name "East 0 0" Position
   {
    Text.Dispplay_Bitmap "Gui_Intensity 3" Member { }
    Value.Display_Bitmap "Gui_Intensity 3" Member { }
   }
  Capacity "East 0 1" Position { }
  Occupation "East 0 2" Position { }
(1) Video "South_East 0 -1" Position
   {
    Text "East 0 0 Video" Position { }
    Value "East 5 0 Video" Position { }
   }
  Hospital "North 2 0" Position
   {
(2)  Text "West 0 -5 Hospital" Position { }
    Value "West -1 -5 Hospital" Position { }
   }
  Employees "South 0 1" Position
   {
(3)  Text "West 0 0 Employees" Position { }
    Value "West 0 1 Employees" Position { }
   }
  Employ "West 0 2" Position { }
  Discharge "West 0 3" Position { }
  Create.Apparition_Bitmap "Gui_Should_Be_Visible 0" Member { }
  Destroy.Apparition_Bitmap "Gui_Should_Be_Visible 0" Member { }
 }
```

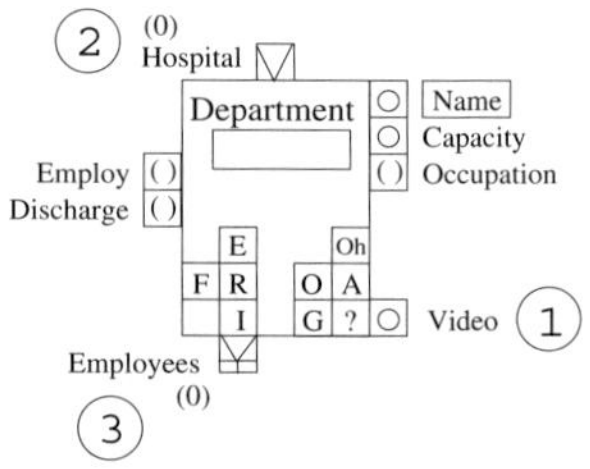

Figure 14.13: Configuring a generalization

Configuring generalization object types is the same as configuring object types which are visible in the user view, with the exception that it is not necessary to position them on the canvas (generalizations are not visible in the user view). Therefore:

1. The value of the `Metatype` is *Object*, instead of *Position*.

2. The value of the `Type` is the object type name instead of the coordinates.

See Figure 14.13 first line. The generalization `Department` is known from the developer view (Figure 6.3). It is not visible in the user view (Figure 6.1).

Configuration values for generalizations should be chosen carefully to fulfill the positioning requirements of as many specialization objects as possible, otherwise the positioning has to be overruled too often, making it difficult to ensure that members present in several specializations remain in the same position. Irregularity is confusing for the end-user. For `example`, Figure 14.13 shows the positioning (Mark 1) of the member `Video` in the generalization `Department`, hence all four of its visible (indirect) specializations (`General_Support, Medical_Support, Ward, Clinic`) show member `Video` in that position[89].

14.5.2 Adding additional members to a specialization

```
    Support Support Object Template GUI
     {
(1)    Services "North_East -1 0" Position
        {
          Text "East 0 0 Services" Position { }
          Value "East 0 -1 Services" Position { }
        }
     }
```

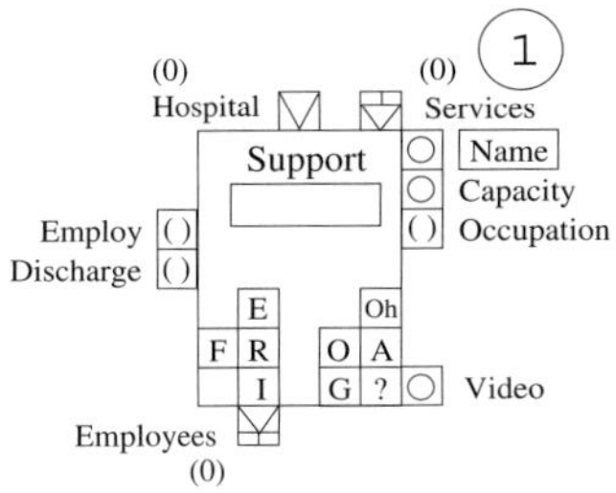

Figure 14.14: Adding a member to a specialization

Figure 14.14 illustrates the configuration of the object type `Support`. The object type is a specialization of `Department`. It adds the relation `Services` to its inherited members. `Support` is the generalization of `General_Support` and `Medical_Support` Department, therefore the specializations indirectly inherit the configuration of `Services`.

14.6 Configuring the collection path for operation arguments

To configure the collection path of arguments a virtual connector is defined to the collection places. Virtual implies that it is not visible but tells the drawing manager where to collect the next argument. Figure 14.15 shows the configuration of a collection path.

`Employ` (Mark 1) is an operation of `Department`. `Employ` assigns a person identified by a social security number to a particular role within a department for a given number of hours.
Its first argument is `SSN`. It collects the argument in `Person.SSN` so this is where the first connector is directed. The next argument is `Code` of `Employee`, therefore the second connector leads to `Employee.Code`. The third argument is `Hours`, therefore the third connector leads to `Employee.Hours`.

The operation `Discharge` has only one input argument that specifies the employee role to be discharged.

The behavioral effects of this configuration are demonstrated in Chapter 10.

```
    Department Department Object Template GUI
     {
       .....
(1)    Employ "West 0 2" Position
        {
         SSN GUI_Argument Object
          {
           Connector "Person.SSN" Network { }
           Code GUI_Argument Object
            {
             Connector "Employee.Code" Network { }
             Hours GUI_Argument Object
              {
               Connector "Employee.Hours" Network { }
              }
            }
          }
        }
(2)    Discharge "West 0 3" Position
        {
         Code GUI_Argument Object
          {
           Connector "Employee.Code" Network { }
          }
        }
       .....
     }
```

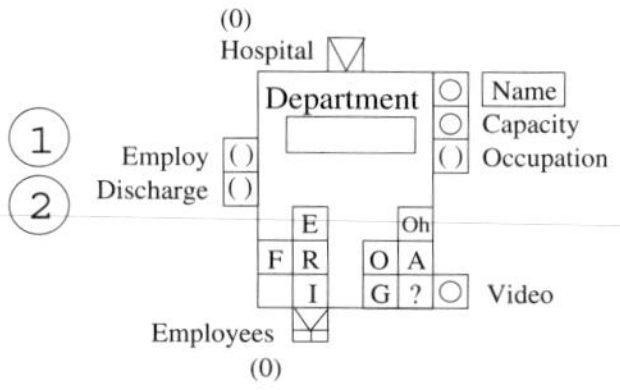

Figure 14.15: Configuring an argument collection path

```
   Patient "Center 45 50"  Position Template GUI
    {
     ...
(1)  Department.Connector "Source Ward.Patients.Connector.Node" Network
      {
       Form.Width "8" Member { }
      }
    }
```

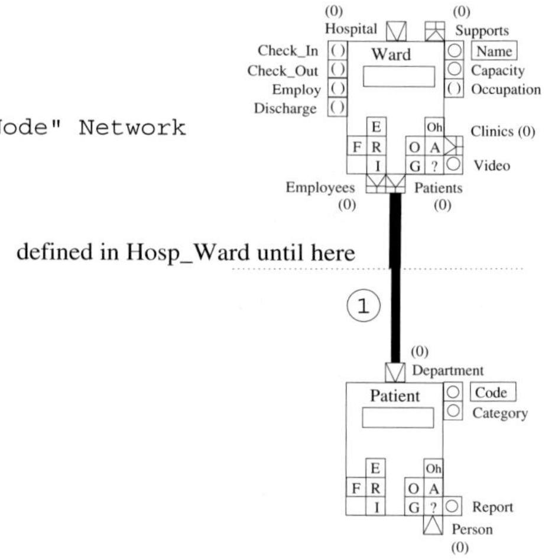

Figure 14.16: Illustration of coupling separately defined connector parts

14.7 Applying configuration to the Hospital case study

14.7.1 Coupling separately defined connector parts

Figure 14.16 illustrates how separately configured connector lines are coupled. In this case the connector of member `Department` of `Patient` is coupled to the node of the connector of the member `Patients` of the object `Ward` which is located in the figure at the meeting point of the thick and the thin connectors, indicated by the dotted line.

---

[8]Actually, it is not necessary to configure the intensity of member `Name` because the GUI recognizes that it is the key and will adjust the intensity automatically.

[9]`Video` can also be positioned as `East` rather than `South_East`, in which case configuring `Text` and `Value` is not necessary since the GUI can automatically position them correctly.

14.7.2 Illustration of inheritance of positioning

```
      Patient "Center 45 50"  Position Template GUI
       {
(1)      Category "East 0 1" Position { }
         Department.Connector "Ward.Patients.Connector.Node" Network
          {
           Form.Width "8" Member { }
          }
       }
```

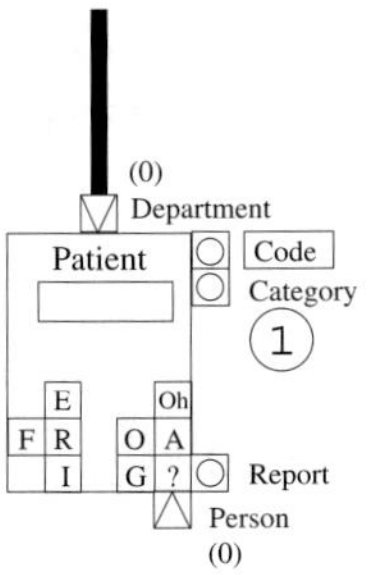

The rest of the object type Patient is inherited from Role:

```
Role Role Object Template
 {
   Code "East 0 0" Position
    {
      Text.Display_Bitmap "Gui_Intensity 3" Member { }
      Value.Display_Bitmap "Gui_Intensity 3" Member { }
    }
   Report "South_East 0 -1" Position
    {
      Text "East 0 0 Report" Position { }
      Value "East 5 0 Report" Position { }
    }
   Department "North 2 0" Position
    {
      Text "West 0 0 Department" Position { }
      Value "West 0 1 Department" Position { }
    }
   Person "South_East -1 0" Position
    {
      Text "West 0 0 Person" Position { }
      Value "West 0 1" Person Position { }
    }
   Create.Apparition_Bitmap "Gui_Should_Be_Visible 0" Member { }
   Destroy.Apparition_Bitmap "Gui_Should_Be_Visible 0" Member { }
 }
```

Figure 14.17: Illustration of inheritance

Figure 14.17 illustrates the effect of inheritance for positioning. The first part of the figure shows the additional member in the specialization `Patient`. The lower part of the figure shows the configuration for the generalization object type (`Role`), so that the reader can see the impact of the configuration.

14.7.3 The object type Service (Service Department)

`Service` department (Figure 14.18) is a specialization of `Department` and inherits the configurations of `Department`, therefore it is sufficient to configure the additional members. There are four marked members: the relation `Supports`, the relation `Patients`, and the operations `Check_In` and `Check_Out`.

```
    Service Service Object Template GUI
    {
(1)   Supports "North_East -1 0" Position
      {
        Text "East 0 0 Supports" Position { }
        Value "East 0 -1 Supports" Position { }
      }
(2)   Patients "South 2 0" Position
      {
        Text "East 0 0 Patients" Position { }
        Value "East 0 -1 Patients" Position { }
      }
(3)   Check_In "West 0 0" Position
      {
        Kernel_Bitmap "Gui_Part_Of_Form_View 1" Member { }
        SSN GUI_Argument Object
         {
          Connector "Person.SSN" Network { }
          Code GUI_Argument Object
           {
            Connector "Patient.Code" Network { }
           }
         }
      }
(4)   Check_Out "West 0 1" Position
      {
        Kernel_Bitmap "Gui_Part_Of_Form_View 1" Member { }
        Code GUI_Argument Object
         {
          Connector "Patient.Code" Network { }
         }
      }
    }
```

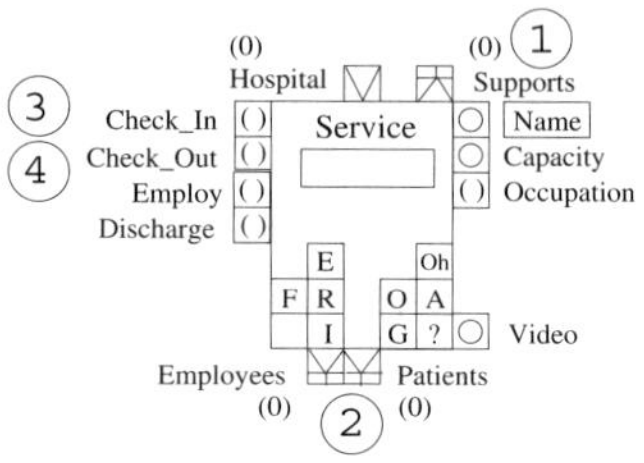

Figure 14.18: Example object type Service department

Check_In collects its arguments from **Person.SSN** in order to know which person is to be checked in, and from **Patient.Code** in order to find out the patient's code. **Check_Out** collects its single argument from **Patient.Code**, to know which person is to be checked out[10].

14.7.4 The object type Ward

Figure 14.19 shows the configuration of the object type Ward.

The relation **Clinics** is added to the inherited members with text and value field positioning (Mark 1).

The connector is configured directly to its destination relation (Mark 2). A node is not necessary because it is a direct connection and only one line has to be drawn.

The hint helps the drawing manager to find the right placement to the destination (Mark 3).

[10]Actually, it is not necessary to configure that the methods Check_In and Check_Out are visible in the **Form_View** since this is automatic. This configuration is useful to overrule the situation whereby a method is configured not to be visible in the base object type (because in most of its specializations the member should not be visible).

```
    Ward "Center 45 32"  Position Template GUI
     {
(1)   Clinics "East 0 5" Position
       {
        Text "East 0 -1 Clinics" Position { }
        Value "East 5 -1 Supports" Position { }
(2)     Connector "Clinic.Wards" Network Template GUI
         {
(3)       Apparition_Bitmap "Gui_Orientation 3" Member { }
         }
       }
(4)   Supports.Connector "Node" Network
       {
        Node "North 0 -2 Supports" Position
         { Connector "Medical_Support.Services.Connector.Node" Network { }
(5)
         }
       }
(6)   Employees.Connector "Node" Network
       {
        Form*Width "10" Member { }
        Node "South 0 4 Employees" Position { }
       }
(7)-> Patients.Connector "Clinic.Patients.Connector.Node" Network
       {
        Form*Width "10" Member { }
       }
     }
```

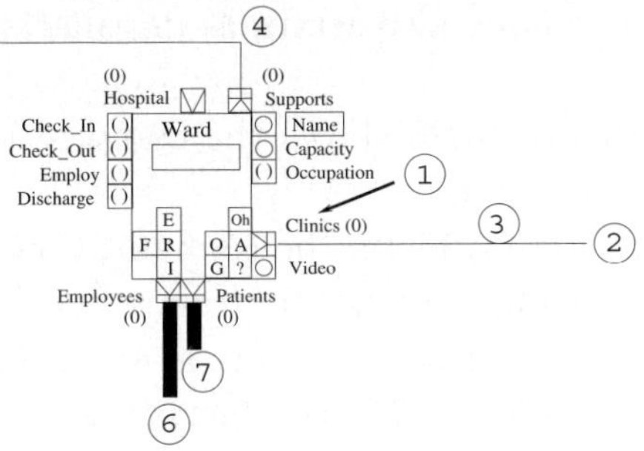

Figure 14.19: Example object type Ward

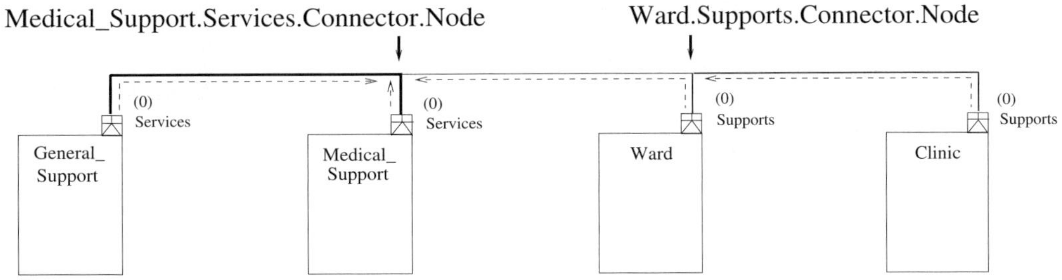

legend:
the arrows illustrate how the connector is configured (from – to)

Figure 14.20: Illustration of composing a split connector

Because the relation `Supports` (Mark 4) is already configured in the generalization object type `Service` department, the connector drawn from there is directly referred to, from the (inherited) owning relation (Mark 5).

The configured part of the connector needs two lines.

- The first configures a node (following Mark 4) positioned north (North 0) of the relation `Supports`, two units higher above `Supports`.
- From this node, the second line is drawn to a further node (Mark 5) configured in `Medical_Support` for the relation `Services`, where it becomes the first node in the connector.

The node *"North 0 -2 Supports"* is the origin of the connector to the destination node *Medical_Support.Services.Connector.Node.*

The node also serves as destination for the connector starting at *Clinic.Supports*.

Figure 14.20 shows the composition and direction of the connectors and nodes leading from the departments.
In Figure 14.19, the configuration of the connector starting at `Ward.Employees` (Mark 6) is telling the drawing manager to draw a line to a node with a position given ("South 0 4") relative to `Employees`. The connector starting at `Ward.Patients` (Mark 7) has to be drawn to the node of the connector of the relation `Clinic.Patients`.

There is no connector configured starting from `Ward.Hospital`. This relation is the destination of a connector line which is configured in another object type's relation, here `Hospital.Wards` (shown in Figure 14.21).

```
Hospital "Center 45 16" Position Template GUI
 {
   .....
   Wards "South 0 2" Position
    {
      Text "South_West -3 3" Position { }
      Value "South_West -3 4" Position { }
(1)   Connector "Node" Network
       {
         Form.Width "10" Member { }
(2)      Node "South 0 15 Wards" Position
          {
(3) (4)     Connector "Ward.Hospital" Network
             {
               Form.Width "10" Member { }
             }
          }
       }
    }
   .....
 }
```

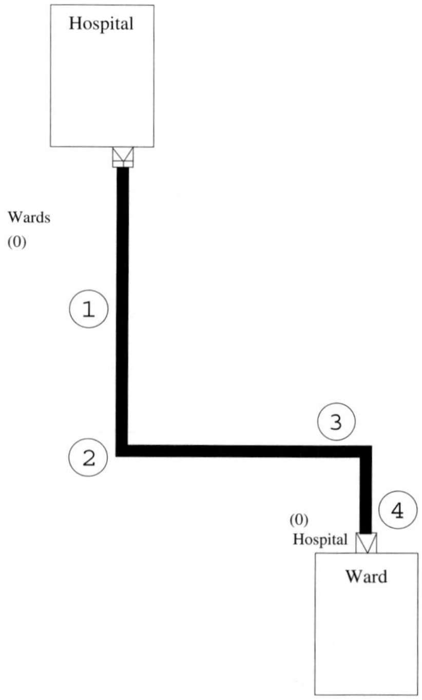

Figure 14.21: Configuring the connector "missed" in Ward

14.7.5 The object type Clinic

The other specialization object type of Service department is configured in Figure 14.22.

14.8 Additional configurations

14.8.1 Configuring a relationship attribute

A relationship attribute is configured similarly to other object types. It is an object type in the role of an attribute of a relationship type. The convention is to attach it to the connector as illustrated in Figure 14.23. Mark 1 concerns the configuration of the relationship attribute. Mark 2 refers to the attribute of the relationship attribute.

```
    Clinic "Center 75 32"  Position Template GUI
    {
(1)   Wards "West 0 5" Position
      {
        Text "West 0 -1 Wards" Position { }
        Value "West 5 -1 Wards" Position { }
      }
(2)   Supports.Connector "Ward.Supports.Connector.Node" Network { }
(3)   Employees.Connector "Node" Network
      {
        Form*Width "10" Member { }
        Node "South 0 4 Employees" Position
        {
(4)       Connector "Ward.Employees.Connector.Node" Network
          {
            Form*Width "10" Member { }
          }
        }
      }
(5)   Patients.Connector "Node" Network
      {
        Form.Width "10" Member { }
        Node "South 0 2 Patients" Position
        {
(6)       Connector "Ward.Patients.Connector.Node" Network
          {
            Form.Width "10" Member { }
          }
        }
      }
    }
```

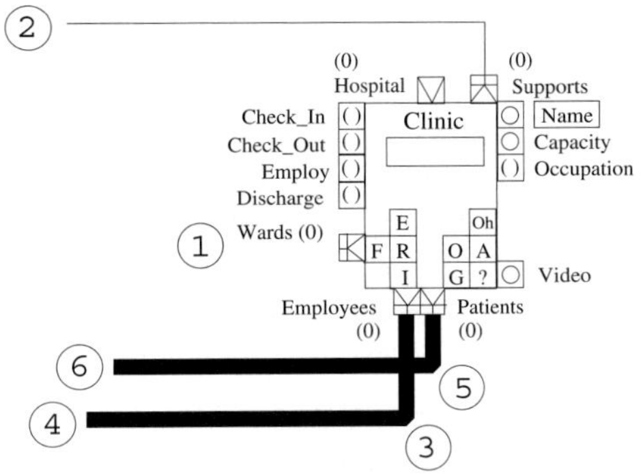

Figure 14.22: The object type Clinic

```
(1) Hosp_Status "Center 11 7 Employee" Position Template GUI
    {
(2)   Hosp_Type "East 0 0" Position { }
(3)   Kernel_Bitmap "Gui_Is_Shared 1 Gui_Hide_Inactive 1" Member { }
    }
```

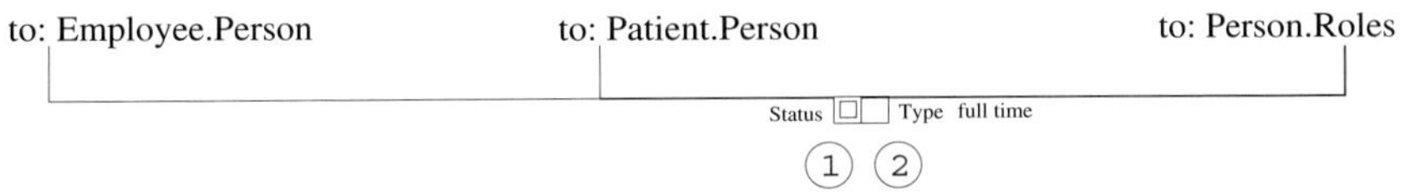

Figure 14.23: Configuring a relationship attribute

The `Splitter` connector (see Figure 14.7) connects the relationship attribute with the `Splitter` node, however being so short it is invisible.

The Kernel_Bitmap (Mark 3) configures two aspects. The relationship attribute is shared and visible.

14.8.2 Configuring the application window

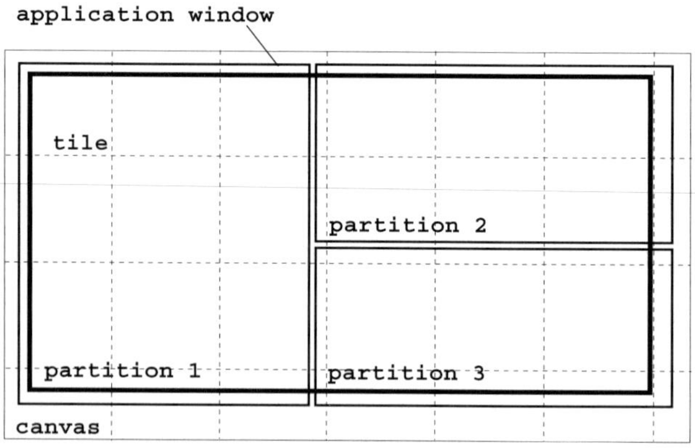

Figure 14.24: Illustration of the window, canvas, partitions and tiles

Figure 14.24 illustrates the configuration of window, canvas, partitions and tiles. These objects are configured in the following definitions. The figure shows three partitions, although in the hospital case study there is only one, covering the whole canvas.

```
(1)  Hospital_Window GUI_Application_Window Copy Template GUI
      {
(2)     Window_Name "Hospital" Member { }
(3)     Physical_Display.Rectangle "0 0 2200 1400" Member { }
(4)     Scale_Factor "75" Member { }
(5)     Canvas GUI_Goml_Canvas Object
         {
(6)        Canvas_Display.Rectangle "0 0 2440 1640" Member { }
(7)        Canvas_Display.Width "1600" Member { }
(8)        Hosp_Hospital_Partition GUI_Partition Object Template GUI
            {
(9)           GUI_External_Position GUI_Position_Object Create
               {
(10)             GUI_MT_Position "20 20 GUI_Absolute" Member { }
                 GUI_External_Position GUI_Position_Object Create
                  {
(11)                GUI_MT_Position "2400 1600 GUI_Absolute GUI_Size" Member { }
                  }
               }
(12)          Hosp_Manager          Hosp_Manager          Copy { }
              Hospital              Hospital              Copy { }
              Person                Person                Copy { }
              Address               Address               Copy { }
              General_Support       General_Support       Copy { }
              Medical_Support       Medical_Support       Copy { }
              Ward                  Ward                  Copy { }
              Clinic                Clinic                Copy { }
              Employee              Employee              Copy { }
              Patient               Patient               Copy { }
              Hosp_Status           Hosp_Status           Copy { }
            }
         }
      }
```

Figure 14.25: Definition of the window, canvas, partition and tiles

Marks 1 - 7 of Figure 14.25 refer to objects which configure the appearance of the application window. The canvas (Mark 5) contains the partitions. Each partition defines the area reserved for its corresponding module. The case study application canvas contains a sole partition.
The application window (here *Hospital_Window*) is a copy of a template object called *GUI_Application_Window* (Mark 1).
An application window has a title bar. The content of the title bar is configured in Mark 2. The window's rectangle starts at position 0,0 (left upper corner of the canvas) and counts 2200 units in x-direction, and 1400 units in y-direction (Mark 3). Within the window all objects are shown with a magnification of 75 percent when the window is opened (Mark 4). This magnification will change when a user zooms in and out according to the configurations of the compass. Thus during interaction with the user, the window's coordinates will change size to enable zooming and moving about on the canvas. Below two canvas display objects are configured:

- Marked 6, the size of the canvas surface itself, measured from its left upper corner, 2440 units in x-direction and 1640 units in y-direction.
- Marked 7, the size of the tiles. In the example, a tile is a square of 1600 units.

The tiles form a grid. Each tile is an area in which the drawing manager first looks for objects to be handled after an event in the graphical user interface.
The objects with Mark 8 and higher define the content of the module, as explained in the next section.

14.8.3 Configuring the appearance of the application module

Marks 8 - 12 of Figure 14.25 show how to configure the appearance of the module. The module is placed on the canvas in a partition.

The object `Hosp_Hospital_Partition` (Mark 8) is defined as a template of `GUI_Partition`.

It is necessary to configure where the partition is to be placed on the canvas and how large it should be to accommodate all objects of the module.

Mark 10 indicates the placement, Mark 11 the size which is almost as large as the canvas. Both configurations are given in pixels and absolutely; the positioning is the absolute position of the left upper corner of the partition on the canvas (Mark 10). The size is determined by the bottom right corner ("2400 1600 Absolute") see Mark 11.

Once the partition has been defined the object types belonging to the corresponding module are copied into the partition as shown at Mark 12 and beyond. Only the visible object types are copied, therefore the drawing manager will not display any generalizations.

Chapter 15

The Language Domain

15.1 Introduction

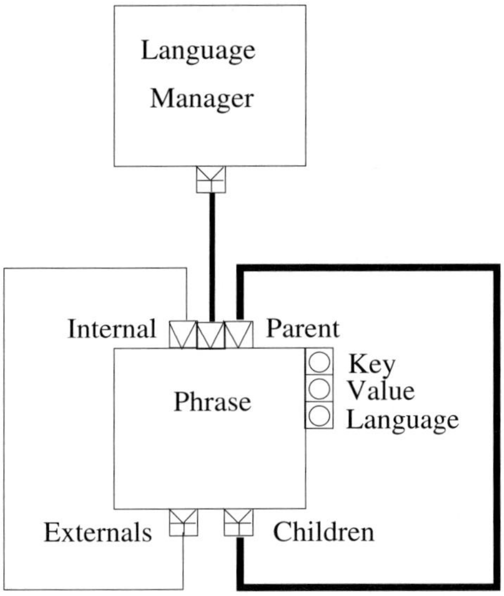

Figure 15.1: Schema of the Thesaurus module

15.1.1 Separating developer and end-user language

In Perspective-DB the language related aspects of an object are configurable by means of the `TOML Language` domain. The language aspects concern the naming of object-types, members, values and any additional information that appears to the end-user in natural language. The advantage of configuring language related aspects is that the functionality of a system can be developed independently, meaning that only one realization of the system is necessary. Consequently the same system can operate in various languages, and the language of a running system can be switched dynamically.

15.1.2 One Internal and Many External Languages

There is one language that serves as the fixed translation reference point to and from any other language. Called `Internal`, the language is the one in which the system is realized by the developers.

The task of an `External` language is to provide a translation of the terms defined in the internal language to equivalent terms most appropriate to a native speaker end-user of a particular language, such as English. It is common practice for the system developers to use English as the basis for the internal language. Developers often use jargon that is too technical for end-users, consequently the end-user's external English will differ from the internal.
An external language can also be used to provide a variant in the same external language. This happens when end-users in the same country use different, organization specific terminology.

15.2 The Thesaurus module

The language management is a service provided by the OMS layer (see Chapter 19, section Object Management System). The service is contained in the module called `Thesaurus`. The primary object-type in this module is the first order object-type Phrase.
Figure 15.1 shows a simplified schema of the `Thesaurus` module having the structure of the generic object-type `Phrase`. The recursive ownership relationship consisting of the relations `Children` and `Parent` enables the construction of instance hierarchies.

```
(1)   Person OMS_Type_Phrase Object Internal_Thesaurus Instantiation
       {
        ....
       }

(2)   Person OMS_Type_Phrase Object English_Thesaurus Instantiation
       {
        Internal: Person Member { }
        ....
       }
```

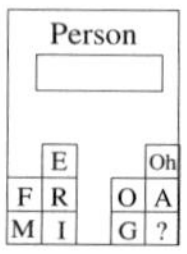

Figure 15.2: Defining a phrase for an object-type

15.2.1 The Phrase Object Type

The key attribute of `Phrase` is named *Key*. The value of the key is a term in a particular language. The attribute `Value` enables provision of an alias for the term used in the key. If circumstances permit, the system uses the term defined in the `Value`. `Phrase` can be used to define all the terms in any language, including the internal. Attribute `Language` is the language used by `Phrase`.
`Phrase` also has a secondary relationship consisting of the relations `Internal` and `Externals`. The relationship enables the capture of the references between an internal term and its corresponding external terms and vice versa.
The schema is simplified because object type `Phrase` is the generalization of a set of specialized object types each dedicated to a particular kind of translation, for object type names, member names and values, dictionary words and messages etc.

15.2.2 The Language Controllers

The `Phrase` instance hierarchies are split according to language and each language is managed by a dedicated controller (layer administrator).
Each controller is responsible for all phrases and the translation of terms for the names, ranges, arguments, and messages necessary to input and output information in that particular language.
Currently it is possible to use languages written from left to right and using Latin characters including German letters such as ä, ü, ö and French and Spanish accents.

```
    Person OMS_Type_Phrase Object English_Thesaurus Instantiation
     {
      Internal: Person Member { }
(1)   SSN OMS_Member_Phrase
       {
        Internal: SSN Member { }
(2)
       }
(3)   Name OMS_Member_Phrase
       {
        Internal: Name Member { }
       }
(4)   Gender OMS_Member_Phrase
       {
        Internal: Gender Member { }
(5)     Values OMS_Value_Phrase
         {
(6)       Internal: Values Member { }
(7)       Value: "Male!Female!Unknown" Member { }
         }
       }
(8)   Photo OMS_Member_Phrase
       {
        Internal: Photo Member { }
       }
      ....
     }
```

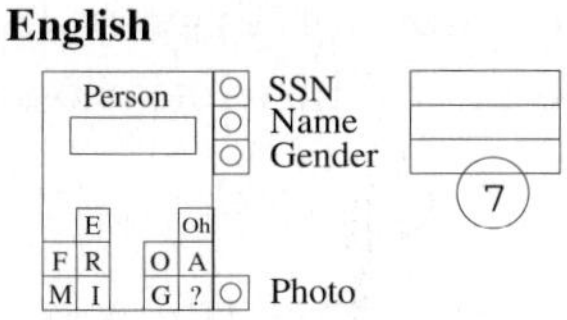

Figure 15.3: English translation for attributes

15.3 Configuring the phrases using TOML

Perspective-DB supports a set of language configuration files structured similarly to other configuration files.
The TOML configuration files are split by module and by language. The naming convention for a file is *Language_[aLanguage].toml*, for `example` Language_UK.toml is the language file for UK English. The file containing the internal terminology is named *Language_INT.toml*.

15.3.1 Applying Inheritance to terms

The configuration of the language used in a system conforms to the same design principles as other aspects of the system. This improves the consistency and maintainability of language. For `example`, the term used for an attribute in a generalized object-type is inherited by, and can be overruled in, the specializations.
It is good practice to translate the members and values in the object-type that corresponds best with the Designers view. It is better to define the translation once in the generalization object-type where the member is defined, than to repeat the process in each specialized object-type. Take for example the member *Name* in Figure 3.18. It must be translated once if defined in object-type *Department*, twice if defined in the specializations *Service* and *Support* and four times if defined in the specializations *Ward*, *Clinic*, *General_Support* and *Medical_Support*. In case one of the names must be changed in a specialization, it can be re-defined in that specialization and thereby overrule the translation of the base object-type.

15.3.2 The TOML View field

The value for `View` is *Instantiation*, see first line of Figure 15.2. The Language domain is a special case of the Instantiation domain (explained in the following chapter).

15.3.3 The TOML Manager field

The value for **Manager** (first line of Figure 15.2) is one of the following:

- *Internal_Thesaurus*: if the file is Language_INT.toml.
- *aLanguage_Thesaurus*: if the file is Language_aLanguage.toml, for example English_Thesaurus.

15.4 Defining translations for an object-type and its members

```
      Persoon OMS_Type_Phrase Object Dutch_Thesaurus Instantiation
       {
        Internal: Person Member { }
(1)     SOFI OMS_Member_Phrase
         {
(2)       Internal: SSN Member { }
         }
        ....
(4)     Geslacht OMS_Member_Phrase
         {
          Internal: Gender Member { }
(5)       Values OMS_Value_Phrase
           {
(6)         Internal: Values Member { }
(7)         Value: "Man!Vrouw!Onbekend" Member { }
           }
         }
        ....
       }
```

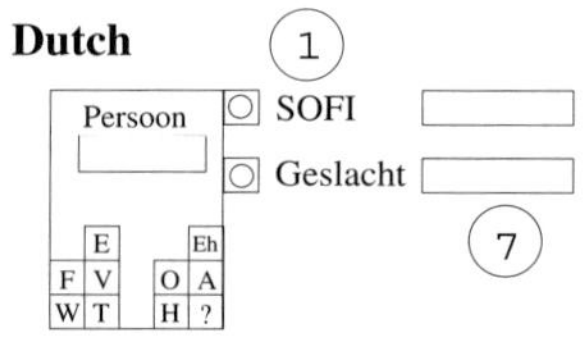

Figure 15.4: Dutch translation for attributes

15.4.1 Defining translation for an object-type

The `Metatype` Object is used to define a phrase object, the `Type` is *OMS_Type_Phrase* indicating that it is the phrase used to translate an object-type. OMS_Type_Phrase is a specialization of OMS_Phrase. `Key` is the name of the object-type. The name of the object-type is translated into the relevant language. The upper part of Figure 15.2 shows the Internal language definition. Here the development name is given as key, therefore the object-type name is prefixed with the system name (Hosp), see Mark 1.

The lower part of Figure 15.2 shows the English translation. For the English end-user presentation, the prefix is not necessary, see Mark 2. The link between the external and its internal phrase is given in the body of the external object-type's phrase definition. The `Key` value is *Internal* (optionally followed by a :), indicating the reference to the internal. The internal name is given in the `Type` value. The internal expression for the phrase has the `Metatype` *Member*.

```
    Person OMS_Type_Phrase Object English_Thesaurus Instantiation
     {
      Internal: Person Member { }
      ....
(1)   Roles OMS_Member_Phrase
       {
        Internal: Roles Member { }
       }
(2)   Manager OMS_Member_Phrase
       {
        Internal: Manager Member { }
       }
(3)   Parents OMS_Manager_Phrase
       {
        Internal: Parents Member { }
       }
(4)   Children OMS_Manager_Phrase
       {
        Internal: Children Member { }
       }
      ....

     }
```

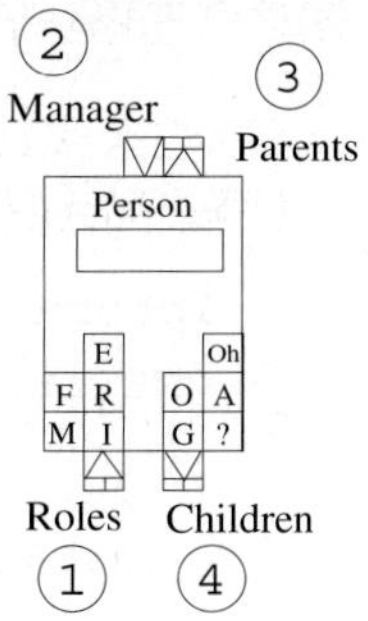

Figure 15.5: Translations for relations

The internal expression is commonly the first object within the body (the objects within the curly bracket, see Mark 2) of an external phrase. An important constraint is that object-type names are unique within the scope of the language.

15.4.2 Defining translation for an attribute

Figure 15.3 shows English attribute translations while Figure 15.4 shows the corresponding Dutch attribute translations.
As with object-type phrases, external attribute phrases refer to the corresponding internal expression, see Mark 1 and 2. The tail rule is applied, therefore only the `Key` and the `Type` values are given for the attribute. The `Type` value is *OMS_Member_Phrase*, a specialization of OMS_Phrase. The `Key` value is the translation of the internal expression in the external language, see Marks 1, 3, 4 and 8. An important constraint is that the attribute's name is unique within the scope of its owning object-type and the language.

15.4.3 Defining a value range for an attribute

Figures 15.3 and 15.4 illustrate the definition of the value range for an attribute, see Marks 5 -7.
The attribute `Gender` in English (`Geslacht` in Dutch) is indicated by Mark 4. The required English values are: *Man, Woman, Unknown* (the Dutch: *Man Vrouw* and *Onbekend*).
The translation is achieved with an object contained within the attribute (Mark 5). The `Key` is *Values* and the `Type` is *OMS_Value_Phrase*, a specialization of OMS_Phrase.

```
Department OMS_Type_Phrase Object English_Thesaurus Instantiation
 { ....
   Employ OMS_Method_Phrase
    {
     Internal: Employ Member { }
(1)  OMS_Errors OMS_Message_Phrase
      {
       Internal: OMS_Errors Member { }
(2)    Value: "A system error has occurred.(#1)!
(3)     There is no Person with social security number %s. (# 2)!
        The Person is already employed here. (#3)!
        The Person can not be employed beyond the maximum limit. (# 4)!
        Not enough Capacity to employ an extra Person. (# 5)!
        An Employee with this Code probably exists. (# 6)"
                                  Member { }
      }
    }
   Discharge OMS_Method_Phrase
    {
     Internal: Discharge Member { }
     OMS_Errors OMS_Message_Phrase Object { }
      {
       Internal: OMS_Errors Member { }
      }
    }
   ....
 }
```

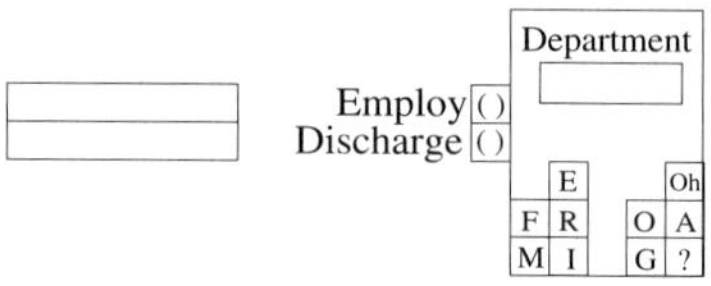

Figure 15.6: Translations for operations

```
Person OMS_Type_Phrase Object Internal_Thesaurus Instantiation
    {
     ....
(1)  Hours OMS_Method_Phrase
      {
       Internal: Hours Member { }
      }
    }
```

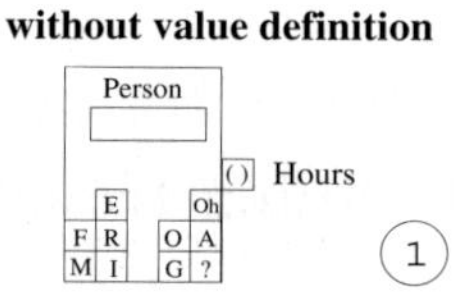


```
Person OMS_Type_Phrase Object English_Thesaurus Instantiation
 {
  Internal: Person Member { }
  ....
  Hours OMS_Method_Phrase
   {
    Internal: Hours Member { }
(2) Value: "Total number of hours" Member { }
    OMS_Errors OMS_Message_Phrase
     {
      Internal: OMS_Errors Member { }
      ....
     }
   }
  ....
 }
```

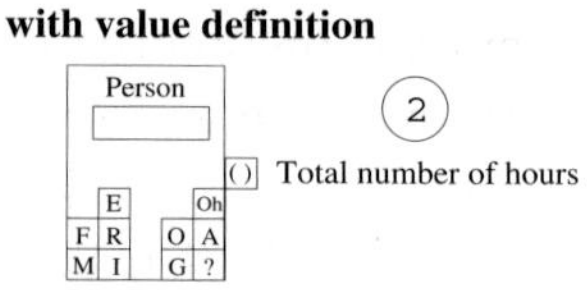

Figure 15.7: Aliasing a translation

The external Values object is connected to its corresponding internal Values object (Mark 6) via the Internal member[1].

Values contains the value range (Mark 7). This is the object with `Key` Value. The translated values appear in the `Type` field.
The first value within the range is the default. Each value is separated from the next by a !. The string is given within quotes.

In the case of `Gender`, the internal range definition is: 1 0 2 (not shown). The range values are translated to suitable end-user terms. In the example, 1 becomes Male, 0 Female, and 2 Unknown, in the English translation while 1 becomes Man, 0 Vrouw and 2 Onbekend, in the Dutch translation. The sequence of the values in the range must correspond to the sequence in the internal Values phrase. The internal range itself is also sometimes defined in the `Meta TOML` to ensure correct functionality of the system, independent of language considerations. In the case of `Gender`, it is *Simple "Equals: 1 0 2" Range OMS Behavior*, see Figure 8.8. The range in the internal language must be identical to the range in the `Meta`.

15.4.4 Defining translation for a relation

The translation of relations is done in the same manner as attributes, as shown in Figure 15.5. The `Type` is also *OMS_Member_Phrase* and the translation is the `Key` value. The corresponding internal expression is defined using Internal within the body of the phrase object.
Figure 15.5 shows that there is no difference in the translation between ownership and secondary relations. `Roles` (Mark 1) is a secondary relation, `Manager` (Mark 2) is an ownership relation, `Parents` (Mark 3) and `Children` (Mark 4) are secondary relations. The last two relations form a recursive relationship which has no impact on the translation.

15.4.5 Defining a translation for an operation

The `Type` value for the phrase which translates operations is *OMS_Method_Phrase* (a specialization of OMS_Phrase), see Figure 15.6. The Figure shows the translations for the operations `Employ` and `Discharge` of object-type `Department`. The `Key` values are the translations of the operation names. Analogous to the other phrase objects, the internal expression is given within the body of the operation phrase.
An operation may contain an error message object. An appropriate message will be displayed to the end-user if the operation execution fails. An error message is of `Type` *OMS_Message_Phrase* and the `Key` value is *OMS_Errors*. The reference to the internal expression is the `Type` value *OMS_Errors* of `Metatype` *Member*. The translation of the internal expression is done in the standard manner using the member `Value`. In this example, the case of the operation Discharge, there is no external message translation so the internal message will be displayed. In the case of the operation `Employ`, the external messages are translated (Mark 2) in the `Type` field of `Key` Value. There are 6 messages, separated by a !. The system displays the appropriate message according to the situation. Additional values can be placed in the message, see Mark 3. In this case the social security number will be substituted in the place of %s.

15.5 Aliasing the Key of a phrase

The use of the Value member of a phrase for translation has been mentioned and demonstrated in the previous sections. One of the functions of the `Value` member is to act as an alias for the `Key`.

[1] Values is not translated, it only has a supporting role and is not a required translation.

In this section we explain when this becomes necessary.

The translation for an object-type or member is normally given in the `Key` value. The name of an object-type must be unique within the scope of all object-types in the system. This also applies to the translation in a particular language. The language manager will complain when it encounters the same translation for different object-types. In order not to restrict the end-user interface the Value member can be used, in which case it appears instead of the `Key` value. Similar uniqueness requirement problems can occur among the members of an object type[2].
Another limitation is that spaces are not allowed in the `Key` value. When the `Key` value is composed of several natural language words, they are usually coupled using a "-" or "_" for example. The `Value` phrase object can be used to alias the translation to one with spaces. For `example`, in Figure 15.7, the operation with the internal name `Hours` is normally translated to `Hours` (Mark 1). However, the translation appears as "Total number of hours" (Mark 2). This is due to the usage of the `Value` phrase object[3].

```
Dictionary OMS_Word_Phrase Object Internal_Thesaurus Instantia
 {
   Address OMS_Word_Phrase { }
   Capacity OMS_Word_Phrase { }
   ....
 }

Dictionary OMS_Word_Phrase Object English_Thesaurus Instantiat
 {
   ....
   Check-In OMS_Word_Phrase
    {
     Internal: "Check_In" Member { }
 (1) Value: "Check In" Member { }
    }
   ....
   "Total number of hours" OMS_Word_Phrase
    {
     Internal: "Hours" Member { }
    }
   ....
 }
```

Figure 15.8: A dictionary

15.6 Defining and referencing the dictionary

It is important that the translation of a term remains consistent throughout the system. Good practice requires building a dictionary. The thesaurus module provides the means to define such a dictionary.

15.6.1 Defining the dictionary

Figure 15.8 shows how a dictionary phrase object is configured.

[2] Translating one member to the name of another member within the same object type can cause confusion and should only be done when there are no better alternatives.

[3] In the Hospital Case Study in order to keep things simple the alias is not applied.

The `Metatype` is *Object*. The `Type` value is *OMS_Word_Phrase*, indicating the translation of a string. The `Key` value is *Dictionary*.
The `body` contains the list of words to be translated.
The difference of the interpretation depends on whether it is the `Internal` language or a translation:

- Manager **Internal_Thesaurus**[4] (upper part of Figure 15.8):
  `Type` is *OMS_Word_Phrase*.
  `Key` is the word as defined internally.

- Manager **[aLanguage]_Thesaurus** (lower part of Figure 15.8):
  The notation [aLanguage] implies the name of a natural language, the English_Thesaurus[5] for example.
  `Type` is *OMS_Word_Phrase*.
  `Key` is the translation. The external translation can be aliased when necessary using the phrase object `Value` (see Mark 1). The `body` contains the reference to corresponding internal expression and if necessary the `Value` phrase. The `Metatype` in both cases is *Member*.

```
    Role OMS_Type_Phrase Object English_Thesaurus Instantiation
     {
      Internal: Role Member { }
      ....
(1)   <Department> OMS_Member_Phrase Object
       {
        Internal: Department Member { }
       }
      ....
     }
```

with inclusion of the dictionary term

(1)

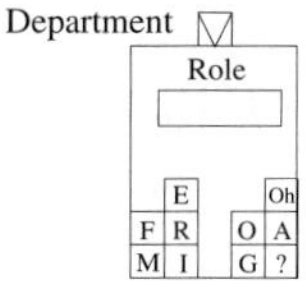


```
    Role OMS_Type_Phrase Object English_Thesaurus Instantiation
     {
      Internal: Role Member { }
      ....
      <Department> OMS_Member_Phrase Object
       {
        Internal: Department Member { }
(2)     Value: Section Member { }
       }
      ....
     }
```

overwriting the dictionary term

(2)

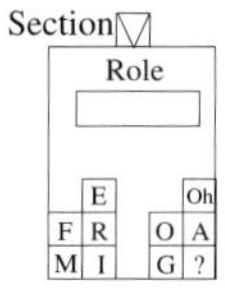

Figure 15.9: Referencing a dictionary term

15.6.2 Referencing the Dictionary

To reuse a term from the dictionary it is sufficient to reference the term. A dictionary reference is denoted as follows at the place of substitution:

```
<internal_term>.
```

[4]The abbreviation Internal can be used alternatively.
[5]The abbreviation English can also be used.

The <> implies substitute the internal term for its corresponding external term in the dictionary. A dictionary reference can be used in both the `Key` and `Value` attributes of a phrase.
The upper part of Figure 15.9 (Mark 1) shows how the reference is made. The use of a reference does not influence the value of the `Type` and `Metatype` fields[6].
An alias for the reference can be added by using the `Value` phrase object. This is shown in the lower part of Figure 15.9 (Mark 2).

```
Hosp_Controller OMS_Controller_Phrase Object English_Thesaurus Instantiation
 {
  Internal: Hosp_Controller Member { }
  Instantiation OMS_Viewtype_Phrase
   {
    Internal: Instantiation Member { }
    Object OMS_Metatype_Phrase
     {
      Internal: Object member { }
     }
    Attribute OMS_Metatype_Phrase
     {
      Internal: Member Member { }
     }
   }
 }
```

Figure 15.10: Hosp_Controller translation

15.7 Configuring a Controller

Configuring the `Controller` (layer administrator) provides the means to translate the name of a layer and also to modify if necessary the terms of the object model, such as `Object` and `Member`. This enables the definition of TOML files which use translations for the names of fields. Figure 15.10 shows the English translation of the `Hosp_Controller`.

`Type` is *OMS_Controller_Phrase*.
`Key` is the name of the layer controller, here *Hosp_Controller*.

The `body` describes the Internal object and owns the object with `Key` Instantiation.
`Type` is OMS_Viewtype_Phrase. It is possible to translate the name of the view type; in the example it remains the same as the Internal.

Instantiation owns two objects:
The first ownership is with `Key` *Object* of `Type` *OMS_Metatype_Phrase*. As in the case of the view type, the term remains the same as the `Internal`.
The second is with `Key` *Attribute* of `Type` *OMS_Metatype_Phrase*. *Attribute* is given here to illustrate a possible translation for the corresponding internal term, *Member*.

15.8 Configuring a Manager

The managers (module administrators) also require language configuration. The manager is an object-type with an additional important role; an instance of the manager of a particular object type can be replaced with an instance of a specialization of that object type.

[6]The translation of the internal term in the dictionary should be defined prior to the use of the reference.

```
Manager OMS_Manager_Phrase Object English_Thesaurus Instantiation
 {
  Internal: Hosp_Manager Member { }
 }

Hospital_Manager OMS_Type_Phrase Object English_Thesaurus Instantiation
 {
  Internal: Hosp_Hosp_Manager Member { }
  Value: "Manager" Member { }
  ....
 }
```

Figure 15.11: Manager translation

The object-type name changes to the name of the specialization but the manager name remains the same. This leads to two translations; for the object-type name of the specialized manager and for the manager name. Figure 15.11 shows both configurations for the English translation.

15.8.1 Manager role

The `Key` is the English translation of the inherent manager name, here *Manager*.
`Type` is *OMS_Manager_Phrase*.

15.8.2 Object-type role

The `Key` is the English translation of the object type, here *Hospital_Manager*.
`Type` is *OMS_Type_Phrase*.
`Value` is used to alias the the object type translation to *Manager*. The value is used to resolve a uniqueness conflict in this example because the English translation *Manager* is the same for both roles.

The `body` contains the owned objects such as the members of the `Manager`, and follows the normal translation rules which apply to the body of any object-type.

15.9 The Abbreviated Form of Translation

The additional abbreviated form reduces repetition in the external language definitions, by introducing the construct `Translate` in `Meta-type` field. The internal value is then given as the `Type` field instead of as a separate line. The `Type` and `Meta-type` information conform to the definition given in the `Internal` language. Since the name of each object-type is unique within the scope of all object types and the members they contain are unique within, this information can be extracted from the `Internal` language consistently.
For example, the English translation of object type *Person* as described in Figure 15.3 becomes:

```
Person Person Translate English_Thesaurus Instantiation
  {
    SSN SSN { }
    Gender Gender {
    Values Values {
      Value: "Male!Female!Unknown" { }
    }
  }
```

The Dutch translation of object type *Person* as described in Figure 15.4 now becomes:

```
Persoon Person Translate Dutch_Thesaurus Instantiation
  {
    SOFI SSN { }
    Geslacht Gender {
    Values Values {
      Value: "Man!Vrouw!Onbekend" { }
    }
  }
```

Chapter 16

The Instantiation Domain

16.1 Introduction

The TOML Instantiation domain concerns the manipulation of the application object instances. It is used to import instances from a file into the object base of a running application or to export instances from the running application to a file, as illustrated in Chapter 7 Figure 7.1.

16.1.1 Instantiation

The Instantiation TOML file (Instance TOML for short) contains OML objects describing application object type instances. When imported, the OML objects are converted into instances of an object type. The operation to import an Instance TOML file is called Instantiation.
The OML Parser first converts the data in the file into an OML Tree of OML instances. These instances are then processed by the relevant Controller and converted into application object type instances. The controller and other managers that participate in converting the OML instances to application object type instances consult the object schema information (primarily the data concerning the structure and behavior of the objects)[1].

16.1.2 Roles of the Instantiation TOML format

The Instantiation operation is applied in several situations and can be triggered automatically or invoked manually.

Initializing an object base: Instantiation is triggered automatically to initialize the object base when the system is started up for the first time. This ensures that all instances required for the system to operate correctly are in place.

Loading an object base: Instantiation is triggered automatically or invoked manually to populate the object base of the application with the persistent objects stored in the form of Instance TOML files. This is the user's data. The Run_Site (explained briefly in Chapter 19) is the standard location of the persistent object bases. Each object base has a set of versions. Each version is a set of Instance TOML files containing the user's data. Normally each file represents an application module.

[1]The structure and behavior information are derived from the Meta TOML file.
The presentation (GUI) information is derived from the GOML and Language TOML files. For this reason the Meta, GOML and Language files containing information required to process the Instantiation file must be imported and processed before the processing of the Instantiation file begins.

Saving an object base: Instantiation is triggered automatically or invoked manually to save the object base of the application. This is the reverse operation to populating the object base. The object base is converted into persistent OML objects stored in the Instance TOML files. A new object base version is created or an existing one is modified depending on the situation.

Manipulating a populated object base: Instantiation is applied to manipulate an existing object base by creating or modifying instances and is commonly used to export objects from one object base and import them into another object base. Instantiation can be triggered automatically as in the case of OML based information transfer between a client and a server application in which case the OML objects are not exported to a file, but to a buffer. This buffer is passed by means of an Inter-Process Communication (IPC) procedure from one running application (the client) to the other (the server) or vice versa.

Replacing an object base version: Instantiation is applied to replace the object base version of a running application with a different version and is often invoked manually.

16.2 Hierarchical Instantiation

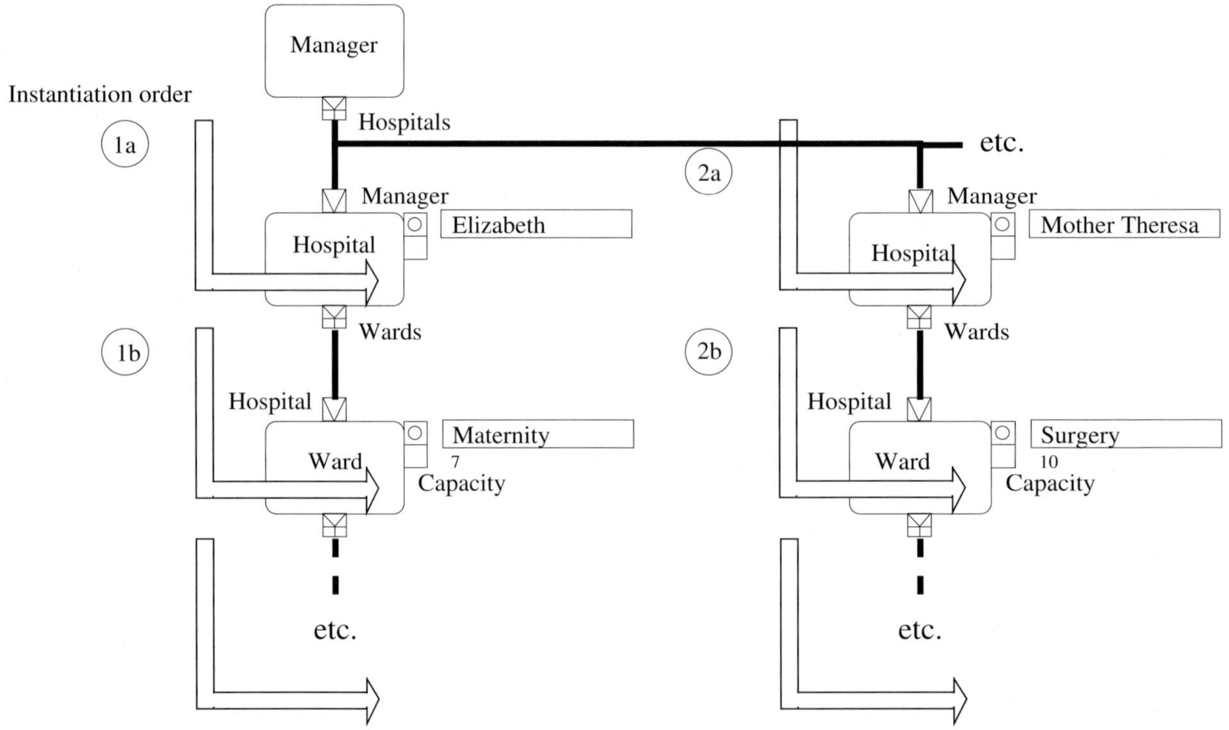

Figure 16.1: Principle of hierarchical instantiation

Figure 16.1 illustrates the hierarchical instantiation procedure[2]. With the exception of the manager, an instance can only be created if its owner exists. This existential integrity constraint implies that instantiation should start at the manager of a module and proceed systematically down the ownership hierarchy. This ensures that the owner of an instance is created first.

[2] An instantiation procedure can also occur in a different order. In this figure, the Hospital *Elizabeth* instance is created, then its Ward *Maternity* followed by the objects it owns, this is a vertical form of instantiation. Another example is for all Hospitals to be created first, then the Wards of each Hospital etc, this is a horizontal form of instantiation.

A manager has no owner and is created automatically when the system starts up[3]. First *Elizabeth Hospital* is instantiated, followed by its *Maternity* `Ward` and by its `Employees` and `Patients` (not shown)[4]. The remaining wards of *Elizabeth* `Hospital` are then instantiated in the same fashion (not shown). The same procedure is repeated for *Mother-Theresa* `Hospital`.

16.3 Instantiating a manager

```
Hosp_Manager Hosp_Hosp_Manager Object Hosp Instantiation
 {
  (1)   Hospitals ...
        Persons ...
 }
```

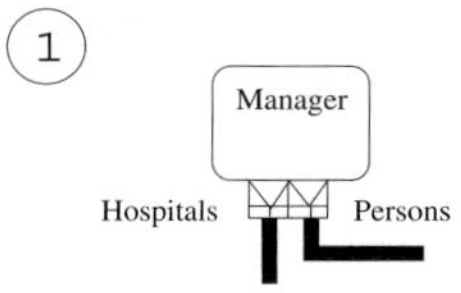

Figure 16.2: Manager instantiation

Figure 16.2 shows the instantiation of the manager.
The OML `View` field value is Instantiation as is the case for all OML objects in the Instantiation domain.
The `Controller/Manager` field value is *Hosp* as it is the name of the controller of the Hospital system.
The `Metatype` field value is *Object*. This is the `Metatype` for all OML objects that represent instances of application object types.
The `Type` field value is the manager's object type name, *Hosp_Hosp_Manager*. The `Key` field value is the manager's name, *Hosp_Manager*.
The controller checks whether the manager exists and generates a message if it does not. In any case, it will not create a new manager. The reason for defining the manager instance (despite the fact that it already exists) is to provide the context for the instantiation of other instances belonging to the module and to set its attributes if necessary. All other instances of the module are contained in the body of the manager, see Mark 1.

16.4 Instantiating an object instance

The instantiation of an object type is similar to that of the manager with the exception that it must be instantiated within the context of its owner. The controller creates an instance of the object type given in the `Instance TOML` file with the given key. The create operation ensures that the instance is inserted into the relevant relation, which is the ownership relation through which its owner instance owns it.
Figure 16.3 shows the Instance TOML of the person instances with the codes *123456* and *345678*.

The `View` field value is *Instantiation*.
The `Manager` field value is the name of the controller, here *Hosp*.
The `Metatype` field value is *Object*.
The tail rule is applied to the last two fields because an instance has the same values for the `View` and the `Manager` fields as its owner instance.

[3]This is how it is perceived by application developers and end-users. Actually, the managers are owned by the object base and are created automatically at start-up.

[4]The employees and patients of *Maternity* will be instantiated on condition that *Maternity*, which is the owner, has already been instantiated (or created by some other means).

```
Hosp_Manager Hosp_Hosp_Manager Object Hosp Instantiation {
  (1) Persons:123456 Person Object { }
  (2) Persons:345678 Person Object { }
      etc.
}
```

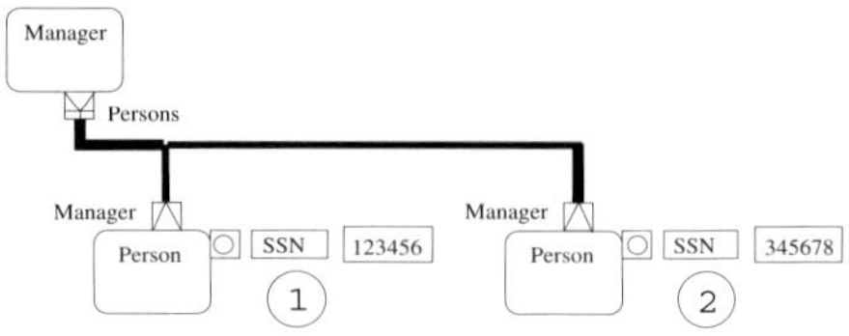

Figure 16.3: Instances of an object type

The tail rule could also have been applied to the Metatype value (*Object*) but the tail has been kept for clarity.

The Type field value is the name of the object type, in this case Person. The Key field value is a combination of the name of the owner relation (in this case Persons) and the value of the object instance's key attribute (in this case *123456* and *345678*). Relation names and instance keys are separated by a :.

This provides the controller with a unique identification of the instance. The relation Persons is a unique member of the manager and the keys (attribute SSN) *123456* and *345678* are unique within the owning relation Persons. This ensures that an instance will not be created more than once. Suppose the instance *123456* already existed in the object base of the running application. The controller first looks for the instance and if found, does not attempt to create the instance again but continues the instantiation procedure as if the instance had just been created[5].

This protocol makes it possible to update parts of an existing object base by loading an Instance TOML file containing additional instances or modifications to existing ones. This process is also called **merging**.

16.5 Instantiating the attributes of an object instance

```
Hosp_Manager Hosp_Hosp_Manager Object Hosp Instantiation
 {
     Person:123456 Person Object
      {
(1)     Name: Lasker Member { }
        Gender: Female Member { }
        Photo: "/tmp/Lasker.tif" Member { }
      }

     Person:345678 Person Object
      {
(2)     Name: Fisher Member { }
        Gender: Male Member { }
        Photo: "/tmp/Fisher.tif" Member { }
      }
 }
```

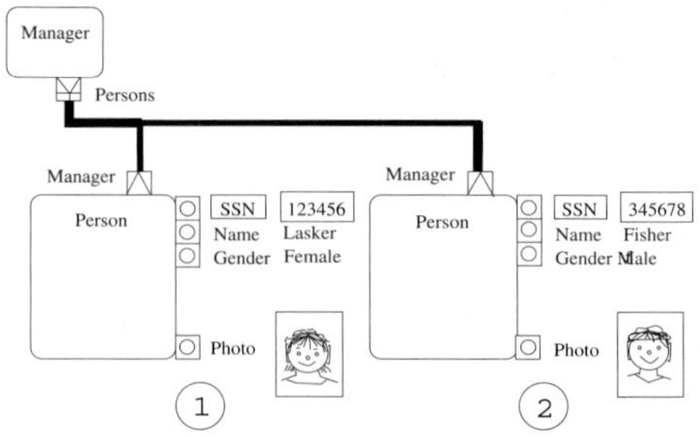

Figure 16.4: Attribute instantiation

The controller modifies the value of the attribute of the relevant instance to the value given in the Instance TOML file. Figure 16.4 shows how the attributes of the two Persons are set.
The tail rule is applied to the last two fields because an attribute has the same values for the View and the Manager fields as its owner instance.

[5]The current member values are retained. If a member is present in the Instance TOML file, the member will be modified to the new value.

The Metatype field value is *Member.*
The Type field value is the attribute's value.
The Key field is the attribute's name, optionally followed by a :.

The figure shows that the Name of Person *123456* is set to *Lasker* and the Gender to *Female.* Member Photo refers to the file system path where the photo is located. Photo is a member of type OMS_Image_File, therefore the file Fisher.tif located at path /tmp will be imported into the system [6].

```
Person:789234 Person Object
{
  Name: Taylor Member { }
  Gender: Male Member { }
  Photo: "/tmp/Taylor.tif" Member { }
(1) Children: "Hosp_Manager.Persons:987654" Member { }
}
```

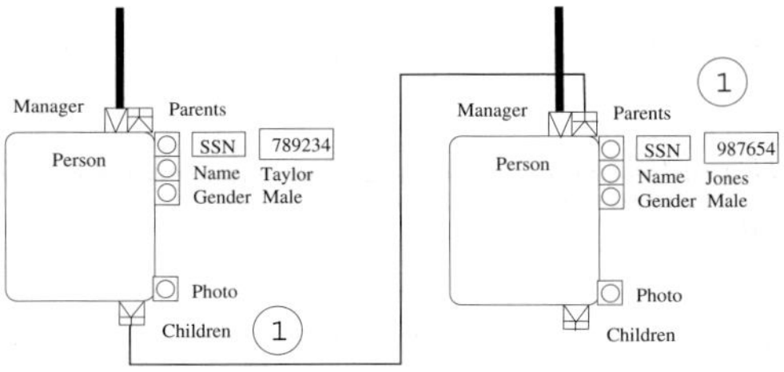

Figure 16.5: Secondary Relation instantiation between two Persons

16.6 Instantiating a secondary relation

The controller finds the relevant (target) instance and inserts it in the relation of the relevant (source) instance.
The Instance TOML for a secondary relation is illustrated in Figure 16.5.
In Instance TOML, a secondary relation has the same values for the View and the Manager fields as its owner OML instance, therefore the tail rule is applied.
The Metatype field value is *Member.*
The Type field value is the Canonical-ID (see section 4.5) of the related instance[7]. In the case that the relation contains several instances, the Canonical-ID of each instance appears in the Type field, separated by an empty space.
The Key field is assigned the relation's name, optionally followed by a :.

In the figure, the person with SSN *987654* is inserted into the secondary relation Children of the person *789234* named *Taylor.* Since a relation is bi-directional, the person *789234* is also present in the relation Parents of person *987654.*
If there is no instance ID ambiguity problem, ID forms other than the Canonical-ID can be used. There is no ambiguity as to which relation is implied (in this case Parents). The controller consults the Meta TOML information to find out which is the relevant relation on the target side. In this example the only possibility of relating one Person instance with another is through the relationship Person.Children and Person.Parents.

[6] A copy of the file is made and stored in the file-system of the database.

[7] The Canonical-ID begins with an instance key of the manager, then comes a . separator, then the relation name, then a : separator, then the next instance key, then a . etc. This pattern is repeated depending on the depth of the ownership hierarchy.

```
Wards:Orthopaedic Ward Object {
  Clinics: "Hosp_Manager.Hospitals:Mother-Theresa.Clinics:Orthopaedic" Member { }
 }  (1)                                                              (2)
```

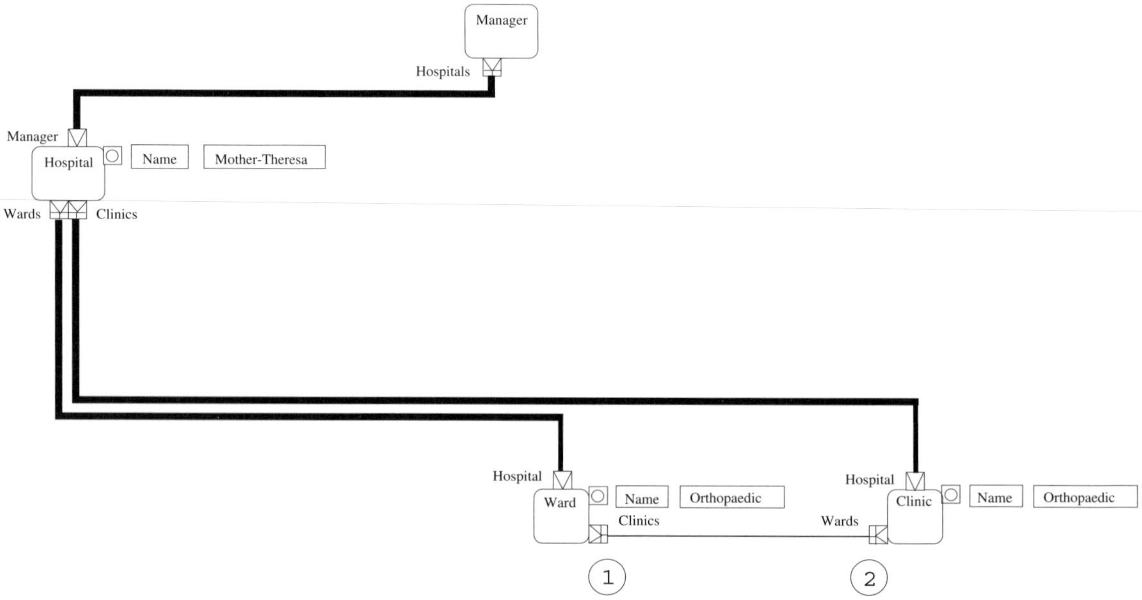

Figure 16.6: Secondary Relation instantiation between Clinic and Ward

Since the relation `Children` is already given (as the Key field value) and since a relationship may not exist between a relation and itself, the only possibility is `Parents`.

Figure 16.6 contains an additional example of a secondary relation instantiation. The secondary relation `Clinics` of *Orthopaedic Ward* (of *Mother-Theresa* `Hospital`) is instantiated. The relation on the other side of the relationship is `Wards` of instance *Orthopaedic* `Clinic` (of *Mother-Theresa* `Hospital`).

16.7 Instantiating an operation

The controller invokes the owner instance of the operation to execute the operation.
The value of the OML `View` field is *Manipulation* and the `Manager` field is *OMS*. *Hosp* can also be used, in which case the Hosp controller delegates the handling to the OMS manager which is its (indirect) generalization. The `Metatype` field value is *()*.
The `Type` field value is the name of the operation. The `Key` field value is user definable. If the same operation is to be executed more than once, the convention is to append the sequence number in order to distinguish between the executions[8].

Figure 16.8 shows the Instance TOML of the operation `Hours` for `Person` with `SSN` *345678*. The operation has no arguments.

Another example in Figure 16.9 illustrates how arguments are defined and how the same operation is instantiated more than once.

[8]Because in OML, the members of an instance must be unique.

```
(1) Hosp_Manager.Hospitals:Mother-Theresa Hosp_Hospital Object Hosp Instantiation
     {
       Wards:Surgery Hosp_Ward Object
        {
          Capacity:17 Member { }
(2)       chil Check_In () OMS Manipulation
           {
             args "345123!000002" Arguments { }
           }
(3)       Patients:000002.Category:NHF Member { }
          .....
        }
       .....

     }
```

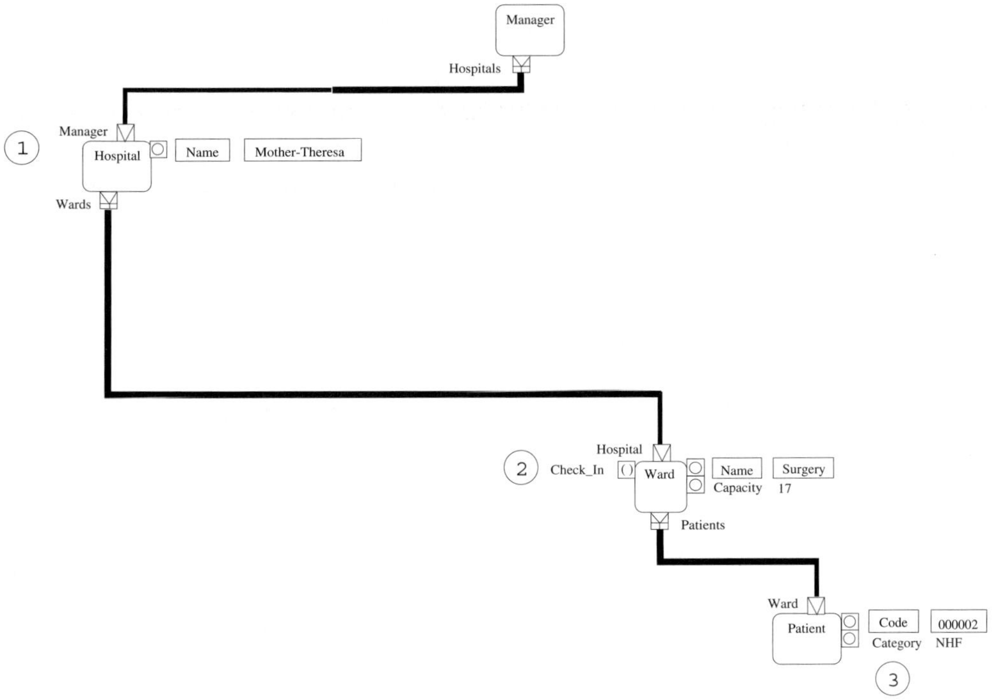

Figure 16.7: Instantiation with the Instance ID

```
    Person:345678 Person Object
     {
       .....
(1)    hours1 Hours () OMS Manipulation { }
     }
```

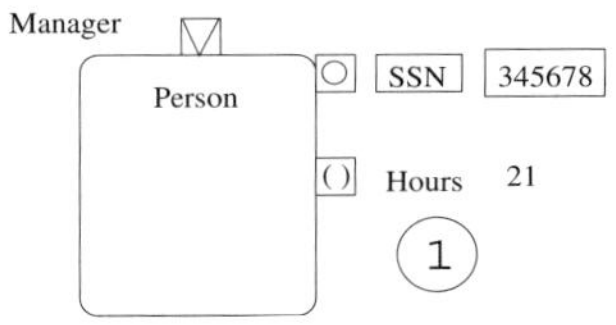

Figure 16.8: Operation instantiation

The argument object has the same values for the OML `View` and `Manager` fields as its owner (the operation), therefore the tail rule is applied. The `Metatype` field is *Arguments*.
The `Type` field defines the argument values. The `Key` field is *args*.

The `Employ` operation (Mark 1) has several arguments which are separated by a !. They appear in the same order as defined in the Meta TOML definition of this operation (see subsection 8.1.4).

```
Ward:Surgery Ward Object
 {
   .....
(1) empl0001 Employ () OMS Manipulation
     {
      args "123456!0003!23" Arguments { }
     }
(2) empl0002 Employ () OMS Manipulation
     {
      args "123457!0007!20" Arguments { }
     }
(3) empl0003 Employ () OMS Manipulation
     {
      args "345123!0023!15" Arguments { }
     }
   .....
 }
```

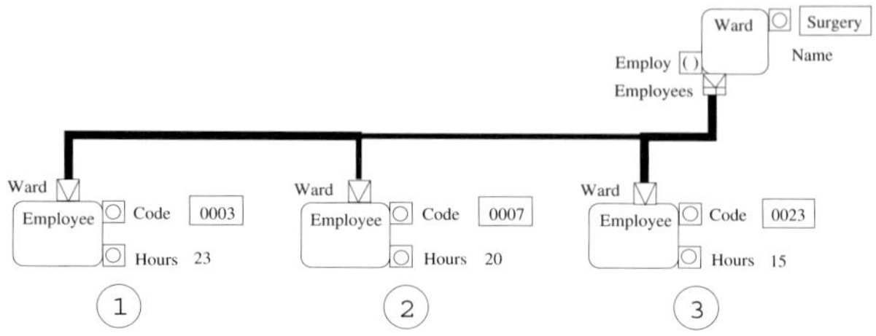

Figure 16.9: Operation instantiation, several arguments, several invocations

In the example, the operation `Employ` is instructed to hire the employees of *Surgery* `Ward` of the *Mother-Theresa* `Hospital`. These are the three invocations of the operation `Employ`, see Marks 1, 2 and 3. The invocations, identified here as *empl0001, empl0002* and *empl0003*, are unique within the scope of the owner, as required.

16.8 Instantiation Using the Instance ID

It is also possible to instantiate objects in a non-hierarchical or semi-hierarchical fashion. In this case, the Canonical-ID of the instance is assigned to the `Key` field value. An `example` is given in Figure 16.7, Mark 1. In the example, *Mother-Theresa* `Hospital` is instantiated. The ID is therefore *Hosp_Manager.Hospitals:Mother_Theresa.* The `Type` field value is `Hospital` and the `Metatype` field value is `Object`. The `Manager` and the `View` fields are also given because the tail rule cannot be applied.

The body of *Mother-Theresa* `Hospital` retains the normal hierarchical construction, while in this case the *Surgery* `Ward` is instantiated. Its body assigns *17* to the member `Capacity`, and invokes the operation `Check_In`, with the arguments *345123* and *000002.* The first argument implies that `Person` *345123* is to be checked-in as a `Patient` in the *Surgery* `Ward`, with the `Code` *000002* (Mark 2). Note that the method is invoked before the controller proceeds with the instantiation. As a result, the newly created `Patient` can now be found and its `Category` assigned the value *NHF* (Mark 3). In the example, the Truncated-ID of the member of the instance is used (see 4.7).

16.9 Using the instantiation constructs together

This example shows a part of an instantiation of the Hospital system. Only the key attributes and some of the operations and secondary relations are given to demonstrate the concepts. Figure 16.10 shows a part of the Instance TOML file. The corresponding graphical representation is given in Figure 16.11.

`Patient` *000002* is instantiated indirectly (Mark 1) by invoking the `Check_In` operation and `Patient` *000034* is instantiated directly (Mark 2). When simulating the result of an operation by means of a direct instantiation it is important to maintain consistency. In the example the relation `Person` (Mark 2) must also be instantiated.

```
Hosp_Manager Hosp_Hosp_Manager Object Hosp Instantiation
 {
  Persons:789234 Person Object
   {
    ....
   }
  Persons:123457 Person Object
   {
    ...
    Children: "Hosp_Manager.Persons:789234" Member { }
   }
  Persons:345123 Person Object
   {
    ...
   }
  Hospitals:Mother-Theresa Hospital Object
   { ....
    Supports:Laundry General_Support Object
     {
      ....
     }
    Supports:Blood-Lab Medical_Support Object
     {
      ....
     }
    Wards:Surgery Ward Object
     {
      ....
(1)   chi34 Check_In () OMS Manipulation
       {
        args "789234!000002" Arguments { }
       }
       ....
      Emloyees:0023 Employee Object
       {
        ....
        Person: "Hosp_Manager.Persons:345123" Member { }
       }
(2)   Patients:000034 Patient Object
       {
        ....
        Person: "Hosp_Manager.Persons:345123" Member { }
       }
      ....
      Supports: "Hosp_Manager.Hospitals:Mother-Theresa.Supports:Blood-Lab" Member { }
     }
    Wards:Pediatric Ward Object
     {
      ....
      Supports: "Hosp_Manager.Hospitals:Mother-Theresa.Supports:Blood-Lab" Member { }
     }
   }
  Hospitals:Elizabeth Hospital Object {
    ....
   }
 }
```

Figure 16.10: Instance TOML example for Hospital

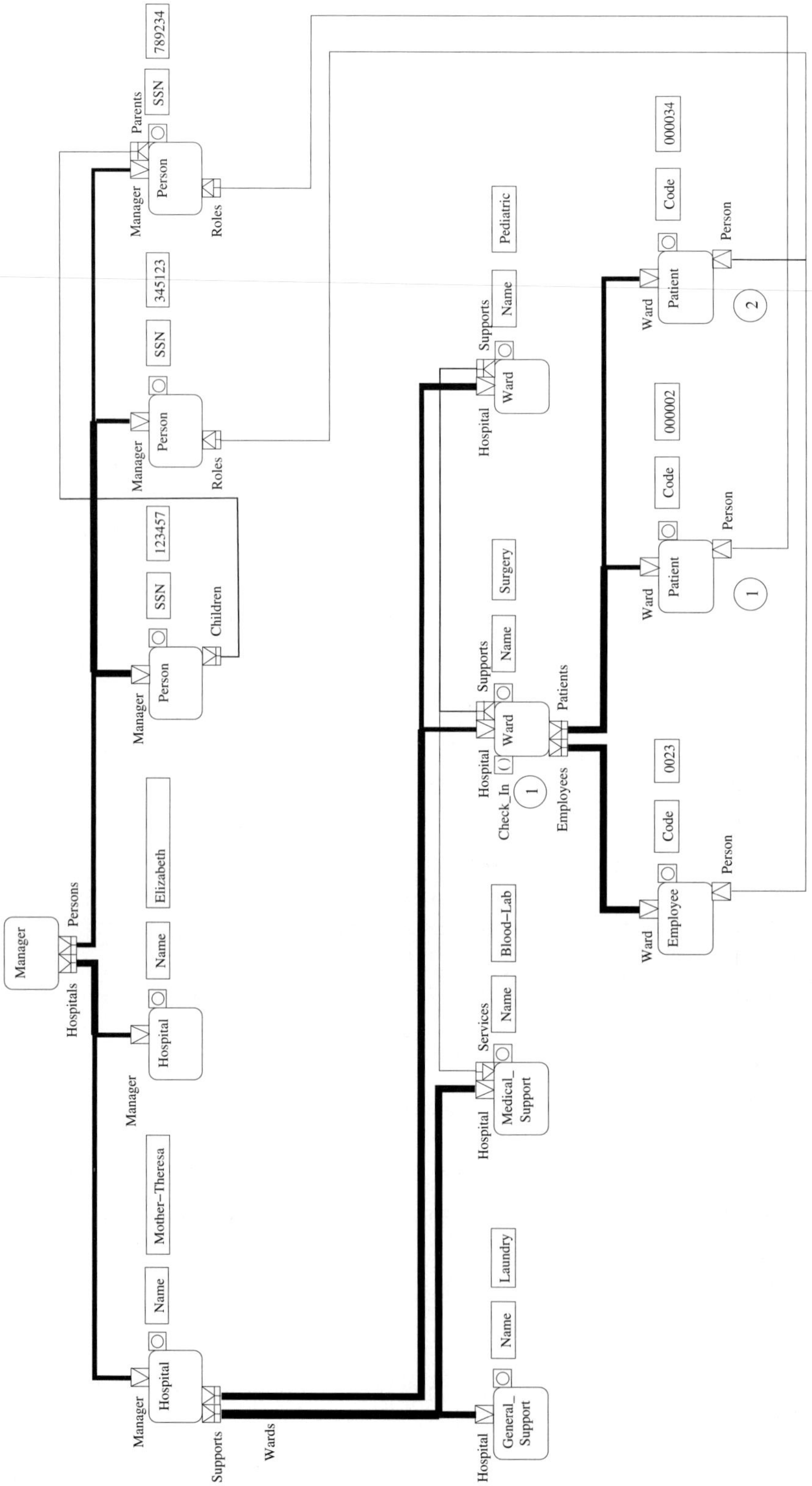

Figure 16.11: Corresponding Instance schema of Hospital Instance TOML

Chapter 17

The Instance Domain: Set By Query

17.1 Introduction

`Set by query` is an extension of the *Instantiation* view of the `Instance Domain`. The role of the `Set` Controller is to manipulate a populated object base. The term `Set by query` is used because the `Controller` calls upon the query module to assist in selecting which objects in the object-base are to be affected. Using `Set` it is possible to:

- select and modify objects in the object-base that satisfy a particular condition.
- determine under which conditions an object should or should not be created.

The Manager/Controller field has the value Set. The View field has the value Instantiation. The other fields use the same values as the *Instantiation* view whenever possible. In any case the extent of the deviation from those values is minimal. Since the `Instantiation` view is the basis for the `Set` manager, it is possible to substitute the manager field with `Set` in an *Instantiation* TOML file. When the file is imported it produces the same result in the object base.
The `Set` manager operates differently from the standard controller of the *Instantiation* view which is `OMS Controller` or one of its specializations, such as Hosp, the controller of the Hospital application. The `TOML` file is converted to an OML-tree according to standard procedure but then the OML-tree is processed by the **Query_Controller**. The `Query_Controller` builds a new OML-tree with view *Instantiation* which is then processed by the `OMS Controller` in the standard way. This conversion process is also called **expansion**, since a compact description of which object to select, is converted into an explicit OML-tree containing those objects.

17.1.1 Creating and modifying an instance using standard controller

We start with an example showing that Set can do the same thing as the standard controller. Suppose the user wants to set the `Gender` of a person in the object base to *Female*. Using the standard controller this can be achieved as follows:

```
Example 1.1

Hosp_Manager Hosp_Manager Object Hosp Instantiation Instance
  {
    Persons:123457 Person Object
      {
        Gender:  Female Member { }
      }
  }
```

17.1.2 Creating and modifying an instance using Set controller

In the following example, although the controller is `Set` the result is the same as with the standard controller.

Example 1.2

```
Hosp_Manager Hosp_Manager Object Set Instantiation Instance
  {
    Persons:123457 Person Object
      {
        Gender:  Female Member { }
      }
  }
```

17.2 Selecting instances via the Ownership Relation

With the standard controller, navigation via ownership relations is performed by specifying the name of the relation and the key of the object. `Set` controller can do the same in a more compact fashion since it can handle a list of keys.

17.2.1 Selecting using standard controller

Suppose it is necessary to modify the `Gender` of a set of persons in the object base to *Female*. The instances are *123457 789234 345678 987654 987123*. With the standard controller it is done as follows:

Example 2.1

```
Hosp_Manager Hosp_Manager Object Hosp Instantiation Instance
{
  Persons:123457 Person Object
    {
      Gender:  Female Member { }
    }
  Persons:789234 Person Object
    {
      Gender:  Female Member { }
    }
  Persons:345678 Person Object
    {
      Gender:  Female Member { }
    }
  Persons:987654 Person Object
    {
      Gender: Female  Member { }
    }
  Persons:987123 Person Object
    {
      Gender:  Female Member { }
    }
}
```

17.2.2 Selecting using a list of keys

The above result is achieved in a more compact manner using the `Set` controller:

```
Example 2.2

Hosp_Manager Hosp_Manager Object Set Instantiation Instance
  {
    Persons:"123457 789234 345678 987654 987123" Person Object
    {
      Gender:  Female Member { }
    }
  }
```

The `Metatype` *Object* implies that if the object is not found it will be created. This is consistent with the standard controller. Therefore any person in the list who did not previously exist is created by the controller and the final result is that all persons in the list exist and their `Gender` value is set to *Female.*

17.2.3 Selecting existing instances only

In some cases it is not desirable to create instances that do not already exist. With the `Set` controller it is possible to modify members of existing objects only.
Suppose it is necessary to set the `Gender` of the persons *123457 789234 345678 987654 987123* to *Female.* An additional condition is that they should only be modified if already existing in the object base. This extra control can be achieved using the `Set` controller:

```
Example 2.3

Hosp_Manager Hosp_Manager Object Set Instantiation Instance
  {
    Persons:"123457 789234 345678 987654 987123" Person Filter_Object
      {
        Gender:  Female Member { }
      }
  }
```

The `Metatype` **Filter_Object** indicates to the `Query Controller` that it may only select existing objects from the list[1].

17.2.4 Selecting a list of existing instances hierarchically

Suppose it is necessary to set the `Capacity` of the `Wards` with the keys *Maternity* and *Pediatric* in the `Hospitals` *Elizabeth* and *Mother-Theresa* to *10*, on condition that those `Wards` exist. The *Filter_Object* applies to all the objects mentioned in the navigation path. The result can be achieved as follows:

[1] The system also checks whether the objects are of the proper type.

```
Example 2.4

Hosp_Manager Hosp_Manager Object Set Instantiation Instance
  {
    Hospitals:"Elizabeth Mother-Theresa".Wards:"Maternity Pediatric"
    Ward Filter_Object
      {
        Capacity: 10 Member { }
      }
  }
```

The `Metatype` *Object* works the same way. Example 2.5 creates the `Hospitals` *Elizabeth* and *Mother-Theresa* and their `Wards` *Maternity* and *Pediatric*, if they do not already exist. In addition it sets their `Capacity` to *10*.

```
Example 2.5

Hosp_Manager Hosp_Manager Object Set Instantiation Instance
  {
    Hospitals:"Elizabeth Mother-Theresa".Wards:"Maternity Pediatric" Ward Object
      {
        Capacity: 10 Member { }
      }
  }
```

17.2.5 Selecting all instances by relation name

Specifying the relation without appending any keys implies that all instances in the relation are selected.
Setting the `Gender` of all of the instances specified by the relation `Persons` to *Female* is done as follows:

```
Example 2.6

Hosp_Manager Hosp_Manager Object Set Instantiation Instance
  {
    Persons: Person Filter_Object
    {
      Gender:  Female Member { }
    }
  }
```

In order to achieve the same result with the standard controller it is necessary to name all the persons in the relation[2].

17.2.6 Selecting all instances using a wild-card key

Alternatively it is possible to use a wild-card key '*', meaning all instances[3].

[2]If Object is specified instead of Filter_Object the system will default to Filter_Object in order to be lenient.

[3]In case Metatype Object is specified instead of Filter_Object, the system will default to Filter_Object because the * is disallowed as a key value.

Example 2.7

```
Hosp_Manager Hosp_Manager Object Set Instantiation Instance
  {
    Persons:* Person Filter_Object
      {
        Gender:  Female Member { }
      }
  }
```

All instances of a relation can also be defined hierarchically in the ID field. In Example 2.8 all `Wards` of all `Hospitals` are selected.

Example 2.8

```
Hosp_Manager Hosp_Manager Object Set Instantiation Instance
  {
    Hospitals:.Wards:* Ward Filter_Object
      {
        Capacity: 10 Member { }
      }
  }
```

Alternatively Example 2.9 achieves the same result.

Example 2.9

```
Hosp_Manager Hosp_Manager Object Set Instantiation Instance
  {
    Hospitals:*.Wards: Ward Filter_Object
      {
        Capacity: 10 Member { }
      }
  }
```

Set the `Gender` of persons having a key beginning with the numeral *1*. This is a wild-card combined with a numeral in the key.

```
Example 2.10
Hosp_Manager Hosp_Manager Object Set Instantiation Instance
  {
    Persons:1* Person Filter_Object
      {
        Gender:  Female     Member         { }
      }
  }
```

It is possible to combine several wild-cards with letters and numerals to achieve a list expansion in the key.
Set the Gender of persons having a key beginning with the numeral *1* or *3*.

Example 2.11

```
Hosp_Manager Hosp_Manager Object Set Instantiation Instance
  {
    Persons:"1* 3*" Person Filter_Object
      {
        Gender:  Female Member        { }
      }
  }
```

Set the `Capacity` of the `Wards` of all `Hospitals` that have a key beginning with letter *E* to *10*.

Example 2.12

```
Hosp_Manager Hosp_Manager Object Set Instantiation Instance
  {
    Hospitals:E*.Wards: Ward Filter_Object
      {
        Capacity: 10 Member { }
      }
  }
```

Set the `Capacity` of the `Wards` of all `Hospitals` that have a key beginning with letter *E* or *M* to *10*.

Example 2.13

```
Hosp_Manager Hosp_Manager Object Set Instantiation Instance
  {
    Hospitals:"E* M*".Wards: Ward Filter_Object
      {
        Capacity: 10 Member { }
      }
  }
```

17.3 Selecting instances by filtering attribute values

We may also want to filter the instances of a relation based on the values of their members.

17.3.1 Selecting by filtering one attribute value

In Example 3.1 the `Gender` of every person born on *1949-01-23* should be set to *Female*.

Example 3.1

```
Hosp_Manager Hosp_Manager Object Set Instantiation Instance
  {
    Persons: Person Filter_Object
      {
        Birthdate: 1949-01-23  Filter_Member { }
        Gender:    Female             Member { }
      }
  }
```

17.3.2 Selecting using a wild-card filter

In Example 3.2 the `Gender` of every person with a `Name` beginning with the letter *F* should be set to *Female*. A wild-card can be used as follows:

```
Example 3.2

Hosp_Manager Hosp_Manager Object Set Instantiation Instance
{
  Persons: Person Filter_Object
    {
      Name:    F*       Filter_Member { }
      Gender:  Female          Member { }
    }
}
```

Several wild-cards can be applied at the same time, as in Example 3.3. Set the `Gender` of those persons having a `Name` containing the string *"is"*[4].

```
Example 3.3

Hosp_Manager Hosp_Manager Object Set Instantiation Instance
  {
    Persons: Person Filter_Object
      {
        Name:    *is*     Filter_Member { }
        Gender:  Female   Member        { }
      }
  }
```

17.3.3 Selecting using a logical expression

Filtering the member values can be done by specifying a condition. The condition is described using logical operators such as >, <, = etc. Set the `Capacity` of the `Wards` of `Hospital` *Elizabeth* having an `Average_Occupation`[5] less than *15* to *20*.

```
Example 3.4

Hosp_Manager Hosp_Manager Object Set Instantiation Instance
  {
    Hospitals:Elizabeth Hospital Object
      {
        Wards: Ward Filter_Object
          {
            Average_Occupation: " < 15 " Filter_Member { }
            Capacity 20 Member { }
          }
      }
  }
```

[4]The position of the members Name and Gender can alternate, it makes no difference.

[5]The average occupation per month. This attribute is only introduced here for the example. For simplicity, the Hospital Case Study does not have this attribute.

Set the `Capacity` of the `Wards` of `Hospital` *Elizabeth* having an `Average_Occupation` greater than or equal to *15* to *30*.

```
Example 3.5

Hosp_Manager Hosp_Manager Object Set Instantiation Instance
{
  Hospitals:Elizabeth.Wards: Ward Filter_Object
    {
      Average_Occupation:   >=15   Filter_Member { }
      Capacity 30 Member { }
    }
}
```

17.3.4 Using control characters to differentiate list and verbatim expressions

The following three examples illustrate the two roles of double quotes. In Example 3.6, the double quotes are needed to indicate that both words belong to the same field (Type), and constitute a list of values.
Set the `Gender` of persons born either on *1949-01-23* or on *1955-05-24* to female.

```
Example 3.6

Hosp_Manager Hosp_Manager Object Set Instantiation Instance
  {
    Persons: Person Filter_Object
      {
        Birthdate: "1949-01-23 1955-05-24" Filter_Member { }
        Gender:    Female                          Member { }
      }
  }
```

The role of the *outer* double quotes in Example 3.7 is the same. By contrast, the role of the *inner* double quotes is to indicate that it is one verbatim expression. Thus the number of elements in the list in Example 3.7 is 1, while in Example 3.*8* it is *2*. Both roles of the double quotes are connected to the separating role of the space character: the double quotes remove that meaning from the space. The escaping back-slashes (Examples 3.7 and 3.8) are needed because without them the second double quote could be misinterpreted as the end sign for the list started by the first double quote.
Set the Gender of those persons called *Karen Fisher*.

```
Example 3.7

Hosp_Manager Hosp_Manager Object Set Instantiation Instance
  {
    Persons: Person Filter_Object
      {
        Name:    "\"Karen Fisher\"" Filter_Member { }
        Gender:  Female             Member        { }
      }
  }
```

Set the `Gender` of persons called "Karen Fisher" or "Betty Lasker".

Example 3.8

```
Hosp_Manager Hosp_Manager Object Set Instantiation Instance
  {
    Persons: Person Filter_Object
      {
        Name: "\"Karen Fisher\" \"Betty Lasker\"" Filter_Member { }
        Gender:  Female                           Member        { }
      }
  }
```

17.4 Filtering and setting the same Member

A special construct is required in the case where the filtering member is also the member whose value is to be set. This construct is the filter operator "?" that stands for *if*. The expression before the filter operator is the new value and after it comes the filter.
Set `Capacity` of `Wards` of `Hospital` *Elizabeth* to *20* if it is greater than or equal to *5*.

Example 4.1

```
Hosp_Manager Hosp_Manager Object Set Instantiation Instance
  {
    Hospitals:Elizabeth.Wards: Ward Filter_Object
      {
        Capacity:  " 20 ? >= 5 " Member { }
      }
  }
```

Set the `Capacity` of `Wards` of `Hospital` *Elizabeth* to *20* if it equals *5 7* or *9*.

Example 4.2

```
Hosp_Manager Hosp_Manager Object Set Instantiation Instance
  {
    Hospitals:Elizabeth.Wards: Ward Filter_Object
      {
        Capacity:  " 20 ? 5 7 9 " Member { }
      }
  }
```

Setting the key of filtered objects is similar, since the key is also a member.
Set the key to *Emergency* of the `Wards` of `Hospital` *Elizabeth* that have *Pediatric* as their key.

```
Example 4.3

Hosp_Manager Hosp_Manager Object Set Instantiation Instance
  {
    Hospitals:Elizabeth Hospital Filter_Object
      {
        Wards:"Emergency ? Pediatric" Ward Object { }
      }
  }
```

Set the key to *Emergency* of the Wards of Hospital *Elizabeth* that have a Capacity greater than or equal to *5* and their key is either *Maternity* or *Pediatric.*

```
Example 4.4

Hosp_Manager Hosp_Manager Object Set Instantiation Instance
  {
    Hospitals:Elizabeth Hospital Filter_Object
      {
        Wards:"Emergency ?  Maternity Pediatric" Ward Object
          {
            Capacity:   " >= 5 " Filter_Member { }
          }
      }
  }
```

The limitation that the key must be unique still holds, thus the key of only one of the Wards can be set to *Emergency* in the example[6].
Set the key to *Emergency* of the Wards of Hospital *Elizabeth* that have a Capacity greater than or equal to *5* and their key begins either with the letter *M* or *C.*

```
Example 4.5

Hosp_Manager Hosp_Manager Object Set Instantiation Instance
  {
    Hospitals:Elizabeth Hospital Filter_Object
      {
        Wards:"Emergency ? M* C*" Ward Object
          {
            Capacity:   " >= 5 " Filter_Member { }
          }
      }
  }
```

Set the key of the Ward *Pediatric* of Hospital *Elizabeth* to *Emergency* if its Capacity is greater than or equal to *5.*

[6] If an instance already exists with the key *Emergency*, the operation will fail. If both Wards fulfill the condition, the first, *Maternity* will be modified to the new key and *Pediatric* will remain unchanged because the key is no longer unique.

```
Example 4.6

Hosp_Manager Hosp_Manager Object Set Instantiation Instance
  {
    Hospitals:Elizabeth.Wards:Emergency?Pediatric Ward Object
      {
        Capacity:  " >= 5 " Filter_Member { }
      }
  }
```

17.5 Selecting instances based on object type filtering

As with filtering of the keys of instances in a relation, the Query controller can similarly filter the object type. This is advantageous when the object type is not known or not relevant.

17.5.1 Selecting any Object type

Set the `Gender` of all persons whose `Names` begin with the letter *F*, regardless of the type of the objects in the `Persons` relation.

```
Example 5.1

Hosp_Manager Hosp_Manager Object Set Instantiation Instance
  {
    Persons: "" Filter_Object
      {
        Name:    F*      Filter_Member { }
        Gender:  Female         Member { }
      }
  }
```

The Query controller substitutes the empty Type field with the appropriate object type.
Call the `Occupation` operation of all the `Supports` of the *Elizabeth* `Hospital`, regardless of their types.

```
Example 5.2

Hosp_Manager Hosp_Manager Object Set Instantiation Instance
  {
    Hospitals:Elizabeth Hospital Object
      {
        Supports: * Filter_Object
          {
            oml1 Occupation ()  OMS Manipulation { }
          }
      }
  }
```

The wild-card is expanded to `General_Support` and `Medical_Support`[7].

[7] A wildcard can also be placed in between . For example: *_Support.

17.5.2 Selection by filtering the general type

Alternatively, to achieve the same result, the object type generalization can be used.

```
Example 5.3

Hosp_Manager Hosp_Manager Object Set Instantiation Instance
  {
    Hospitals:Elizabeth Hospital Object
      {
        Supports: Support Filter_Object
          {
            oml1 Occupation ()  OMS Manipulation { }
          }
      }
  }
```

`Support` is the generalization of `Medical_Support` and `General_Support`.

17.6 Selecting instances via non-ownership relationships

17.6.1 Selecting based on Key

Connect Persons:789234 through the Roles relationship with Patient:123457.

```
Example 6.1

Hosp_Manager Hosp_Manager Object Set Instantiation Instance
  {
    Persons:789234 Person Object
      {
        Roles: 0007 Member { }
      }
  }
```

The above method of selection can be ambiguous since there is no guarantee that there is only one object that has the key *0007* among all the objects of type `Patient` and `Employee`.
There are three ways to express traversing a non-ownership relationship with the standard controller. All of them are valid with the `Set` controller. In all three cases the object to which we connect is specified in the `Type` field. The following three items may stand in the `Type` field:

- key
- short ID, without the manager and the names of the relations
- complete ID, manager and owner relations fully specified.

Example 6.1 used the key. Below are the other two cases:

17.6.2 Selecting based on ID

Connect `Person` *789234* through the `Roles` relationship with `Patient` *0007* using the ID. Example 6.2 shows the fully specified ID, which ensures unambiguity.

```
Example 6.2

Hosp_Manager Hosp_Manager Object Set Instantiation Instance
  {
    Persons:789234 Person Object
      {
        Roles:
        Hosp_Manager.Hospitals:Elizabeth.Wards:Intensive_Care.Patients:0007
                                                Member { }
      }
  }
```

17.6.3 Selecting based on short ID

Connect `Person` *789234* through the `Roles` relationship with `Patient` *0007* using the short ID.

```
Example 6.3

Hosp_Manager Hosp_Manager Object Set Instantiation Instance
  {
      Persons:789234 Person Object
        {
          Roles: Elizabeth.Intensive_Care.0007 Member { }
        }
  }
```

Chapter 18

The Instance Domain: Get By Query

18.1 Introduction

`Get by query` is an extension of the `Instantiation` view of the `Instance` domain. The role of the `Get` controller is to extract data selectively from an object base. The term `Get by query` is used because the query module is used to assist in selecting those objects of which data is required. The imported `TOML` file is converted into an OML-tree according to standard procedure. Since the domain is `Instance` and the controller is *Get* the OML-tree is considered a query. The Query controller produces a new OML-tree with the result of the query. The result is then exported as a `TOML` file of domain `Instance` and view *Instantiation.* The query results therefore contain the resulting objects and member values.
The syntax using the `Set` and `Get` controllers is similar since the selection criteria are the same. In the case of `Set`, objects are created and members modified whereas in the case of `Get`, objects and members are retrieved and no change in the object base occurs. The expansion and filtering mechanisms supported by `Set` are also supported by `Get`: expansion of keys using lists, wild-cards, expansion to the whole relation, expansion of navigation paths, expansion of the `Type` field. Filtering members using lists, wild-cards, and arithmetic comparison operators.
The domain field remains `Instance`, the view is `Instantiation` and the controller is `Get`.
The `Metatypes` *Member* and *Object* mean that the corresponding member value or object instance should be returned in the query results. In this chapter the queries are shown along with their results. The query is defined in `TOML` and in the `Perspective Query Language (PQL)` in addition (see 13.1) for comparison.
Both the `Instantiation TOML` and the tabular (`PQL`) representations of the results are shown.

18.2 Getting attribute values

The following queries ask for attribute values.

18.2.1 Getting by relation name

Get the `Names` of all `Persons`.
The `Metatype` *Member* is used to tell the Query controller to get the member values.

Example 2.1a (TOML query)

```
Hosp_Manager Hosp_Manager Filter_Object Get Instantiation Instance
  {
    Persons: Person Filter_Object
      {
        Name:  "" Member { }
      }
  }
```

Name: * Member { } produces the same result

Example 2.1b (PQL query)

```
Hosp_Manager its Persons its Name
```

Example 2.1c (TOML result)

```
Hosp_Manager Hosp_Manager Object Demo Instantiation Instance
  {
    Persons:123457  Person Object
      {
         Name:  "Karen Fisher" Member { }
      }
    Persons:789234  Person Object
      {
         Name:  "Betty Lasker" Member { }
      }
    Persons:345678  Person Object
      {
         Name:  "Peter Fisher" Member { }
      }
    Persons:987654  Person Object
      {
        Name:   "George Fisher" Member { }
      }
  }
```

The result is the `Name` of all instances in the `Persons` relation assuming that `Persons` *123457*, *789234*, *345678* and *987654* exist in the object base with the corresponding `Name` values.
In the `PQL` result, the first row of the table representation is the header while the following rows are the result values.

Example 2.1d (PQL result)

```
      Name
  Karen Fisher
  Betty Lasker
  Peter Fisher
  George Fisher
```

The TOML result differs slightly from the PQL result. The PQL result contains only requested values. The TOML result must however comply with the *Instantiation* view so that the result can be imported. Consequently, the complete path of the requested instances and members is present in the result.

18.2.2 Getting using a list of keys

Get the Names of all listed Persons.

Example 2.2a (TOML query)

```
Hosp_Manager Hosp_Manager Filter_Object Get Instantiation Instance
  {
    Persons:"123457 345678" Person Filter_Object
      {
        Name:  "" Member { }
      }
  }
```

Example 2.2b (PQL query)

```
  Hosp_Manager its Persons its Name
  where key = 123457 or key = 345678
```

The result is the Name of all listed Persons.

Example 2.2c (TOML result)

```
Hosp_Manager Hosp_Manager Object Demo Instantiation Instance
  {
    Persons:123457  Person Object
      {
        Name:  "Karen Fisher" Member { }
      }
    Persons:345678  Person Object
      {
        Name:  "Peter Fisher" Member { }
      }
  }
```

Example 2.2d (PQL result)

```
        Name
   Karen Fisher
   Peter Fisher
```

18.2.3 Getting using an attribute filter

Get the Name of all Persons having Gender *Female*.

Example 2.3a (TOML query)

```
Hosp_Manager Hosp_Manager Filter_Object Get Instantiation Instance
  {
    Persons: Person Filter_Object
      {
        Name:  ""         Member { }
        Gender:    Female Filter_Member { }
      }
  }
```

Example 2.3b (PQL query)

```
  Hosp_Manager its Persons its Name
  where Gender = Female
```

The result is the `Name` of all `Persons` having `Gender` *Female*, assuming that `Persons` *123457*, *789234* and *987654* have `Gender` *Female*.

Example 2.3c (TOML result)

```
Hosp_Manager Hosp_Manager Object Demo Instantiation Instance
  {
    Persons:123457  Person Object
      {
         Name:  "Karen Fisher" Member { }
      }
    Persons:789234  Person Object
      {
         Name:  "Betty Lasker" Member { }
      }
}
```

Example 2.3d (PQL result)

```
     Name
   Karen Fisher
   Betty Lasker
```

18.3 Filtering and getting the same attributes

18.3.1 Getting using a relation filter

Get the `Name` of all `Persons` called *Fisher*.

Example 3.1a (TOML query)

```
Hosp_Manager Hosp_Manager Filter_Object Get Instantiation Instance
  {
    Persons: Person Filter_Object
      {
        Name:  *Fisher* Member { }
      }
  }
```

A non-empty filter expression tells the Query controller to filter on the given member and include its value in the results (`Metatype` must be *Member*[1]).

Example 3.1b (PQL query)

```
  Hosp_Manager its Persons its Name
  where Name = *Fisher*
```

The result is the `Name` of all `Persons` called *Fisher*[2].

Example 3.1c (TOML result)

```
Hosp_Manager Hosp_Manager Object Demo Instantiation Instance
  {
    Persons:123457  Person Object
      {
         Name:   "Karen Fisher" Member { }
      }
    Persons:345678  Person Object
      {
         Name:   "Peter Fisher" Member { }
      }
    Persons:987654  Person Object
      {
        Name:    "George Fisher" Member { }
      }
  }
```

Example 3.1d (PQL result)

```
        Name
   Karen Fisher
   Peter Fisher
   George Fisher
```

[1]If Filter_Member were used the result would be empty.

[2]Actually, the result is all persons with the string Fisher contained in the name, such as Fisherman.

18.4 Getting objects

18.4.1 Getting using an attribute filter

Get all `Persons` with a `Name` that includes *Lasker*.

Example 4.1a (TOML query)

```
Hosp_Manager Hosp_Manager Filter_Object Get Instantiation Instance
  {
    Persons: Person Object
      {
        Name:  *Lasker* Filter_Member { }
      }
  }
```

Example 4.1b (PQL query)

```
  Hosp_Manager its Persons
  where Persons its Name = *Lasker*
```

The result is the `Person` named *Lasker*.

Example 4.1c (TOML result)

```
Hosp_Manager Hosp_Manager Object Demo Instantiation Instance
  {
    Persons:789234  Person Object { }
  }
```

Example 4.1d (PQL result)

```
   Person
   789234
```

18.4.2 Getting by relation name

Get all `Persons`.

Example 4.2a (TOML query)

```
Hosp_Manager Hosp_Manager Filter_Object Get Instantiation Instance
  {
    Persons: Person Object { }
  }
```

Example 4.2b (PQL query)

```
  Hosp_Manager its Persons
```

The result is all persons.

Example 4.2c (TOML result)

```
Hosp_Manager Hosp_Manager Object Demo Instantiation Instance
  {
    Persons:123457  Person Object { }
    Persons:789234  Person Object { }
    Persons:345678  Person Object { }
    Persons:987654  Person Object { }
  }
```

Example 4.2d (PQL result)

```
   Person
   123457
   789234
   345678
   987654
```

18.4.3 Getting using a list of keys

Get `Persons` *123457*, *345678*, and *987654*.

Example 4.3a (TOML query)

```
Hosp_Manager Hosp_Manager Filter_Object Get Instantiation Instance
  {
    Persons:"123457 345678 987654" Person Object { }
  }
```

Example 4.3b (PQL query)

```
  Hosp_Manager its Persons
  where Persons its key = 123457 or key = 789234 or key = 345678
```

A non-empty filter expression tells the Query controller to filter on the given objects and include them in the results (`Metatype` must be *Object*).
The result is the persons *123457*, *345678* and *987654*.

Example 4.3c (TOML result)

```
Hosp_Manager Hosp_Manager Object Demo Instantiation Instance
  {
    Persons:123457  Person Object { }
    Persons:345678  Person Object { }
    Persons:987654  Person Object { }
  }
```

Example 4.3d (TOML result)

```
    Person
    123457
    345678
    987654
```

18.5 Getting via non-ownership relationships

It is possible to traverse non-ownership relationships as with the `Set` controller.

18.5.1 Getting by secondary relation name

Get the `Persons` who are `Patients` at the *Intensive-Care* `Ward` of the *Elizabeth* `Hospital`.

```
Example 5.1a (TOML query)
```

```
Hosp_Manager Hosp_Manager Filter_Object Get Instantiation Instance
  {
    Hospitals:Elizabeth Hospital Filter_Object
      {
        Wards:Intensive-Care Ward Filter_Object
         {
           Patients: Patient Filter_Object
             {
               Person: "" Object { }
             }
         }
      }
  }
```

```
Example 5.1b (PQL query)
```

```
  Hosp_Manager its Hospitals its Wards its Patients its Person
  where its Hospitals its key = Elizabeth
  and Wards its key = Intensive-Care
```

The result is the persons *123457* and *345678*.

```
Example 5.1c (TOML result)
```

```
Hosp_Manager Hosp_Manager Object Demo Instantiation Instance
  {
    Persons:123457  Person Object { }
    Persons:345678  Person Object { }
  }
```

```
Example 5.1d (PQL result)
```

```
      Person
      123457
      345678
```

18.5.2 Getting by attribute name

Get the `Persons` who are `Patients` in the *Intensive-Care* `Ward` of the *Elizabeth* `Hospital`. Also get the `Gender` of those `Persons`.

Example 5.2a (TOML query)

```
Hosp_Manager Hosp_Manager Filter_Object Get Instantiation Instance
  {
    Hospitals:Elizabeth Hospital Filter_Object
      {
        Wards:Intensive-Care Ward Filter_Object
          {
            Patients: Patient Filter_Object
              {
                Person: "" Object
                  {
                    Gender "" Member { }
                  }
              }
          }
      }
  }
```

Example 5.2b (PQL query)

```
  Hosp_Manager its Hospitals its Wards its Patients its Person,
  Person its Gender
  where its Hospitals its key = Elizabeth
  and Wards its key = Intensive-Care
```

The result is the persons *123457* and *345678* both with `Gender` *Female.*

Example 5.2c (TOML result)

```
Hosp_Manager Hosp_Manager Object Demo Instantiation Instance
  {
    Persons:123457  Person Object
      {
        Gender Female Member { }
      }
    Persons:345678  Person Object
      {
        Gender Female Member { }
      }
  }
```

Example 5.2d (PQL result)

```
  Person  Gender
  123457  Female
  345678  Female
```

Chapter 19

System Building Object Types

Perspective-DB object types are, as previously mentioned, also used to build the information system architecture. In this chapter we introduce some of the object types necessary to understand application building and exploitation.

19.1 System Architecture

Complex systems are best constructed in a modular fashion by dividing the system into subsystems. A subsystem may also incorporate other subsystems. A specialized system or subsystem can be constructed by incorporating a generic subsystem and adding necessary services. When a specialized system is designed in this manner it is done by stacking subsystems on top of each other in layers. A layer describes all object types of an object schema on a similar abstraction level concerning the commonality of the objects.

19.1.1 Layer Roles

Layers are distinguished by the various roles they play in a system. The layer which a user deals with is the **application layer**. The application layer describes all objects carrying application semantics. The application layer can use one or more **application domain layers** beneath it (lower in the system inheritance hierarchy). In general, an application domain layer is not intended to be used directly but to provide basic services for specialized systems. These layers carry semantics of an application domain. For example, a `Hospital application layer` could be a more specific layer of a `Health-care organization domain layer`, and this could be more specific of an `Organization domain layer`. In this case, `Hospital` would have a generalization `Health-care_Organization` which would have the generalization `Organization`.

The layers beneath the application (domain) layer(s) are simply called **system layers**. The role assigned to a layer is relative. For example, we could decide to add an additional layer `University Hospital` on top of `Hospital`. From the point of view of `University Hospital`, `Hospital` may be considered an `Application domain layer`.

The object types of an upper layer are specializations of generalized object types of lower layers. In principle, an object type of an upper layer can specialize any object in any one of its lower layers.

Layers are further decomposed into **Modules** which are explained later on in this chapter.

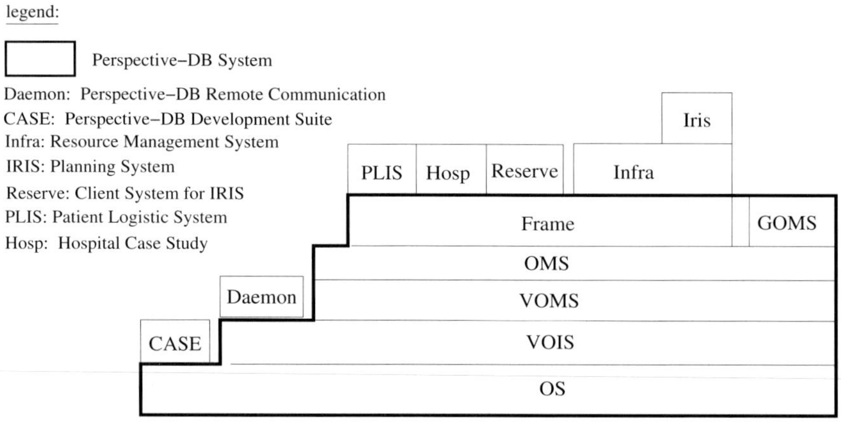

Figure 19.1: Principle of re-use of layers

19.1.2 Perspective-DB Architecture

Perspective DB is also built in layers as illustrated in Figure 19.1.
In the following list of layers the names are abbreviated and we provide a short explanation. A more comprehensive explanation follows in the next section.
The system layers of Perspective-DB, starting with the most basic:

- `OS` provides basic services such as computer resource management, file system management, and basic object types such as for time management.

- `VOIS` provides services such as object persistence, information on object types (meta data), networking, and more advanced object types such as various collections.

- `VOMS` provides services such as object relations and query.

- `OMS` provides services for extended object management such as owner and secondary relationships, constraints on ranges, object identity and language support. **At this level the object type evolves into a first order object**, i.e. possesses the full range of characteristics and capabilities of the Perspective-DB object model.

- `GOMS` provides generic services for the presentation of objects, window interfacing, user interface, and activity flow configuration.

- `Frame` provides enhanced coupling for data exchange with external systems such as mailers and spreadsheets, and run site management, i.e. a file system location where all the information related to an application instance is stored.

19.1.3 Layer Re-use

The purpose of layering is mainly re-use of object definition and implementation. Re-use increases the efficiency of processes, reduces programming errors and improves maintainability. The general idea is that functionality although used several times is defined and realized only once. If an error is made, it occurs in one place, and only there needs to be corrected so that maintenance is localized.
In addition to re-use, there is a clear effect of the layering on simplifying the object structure by separating abstraction levels and with this, also separating orthogonal semantic aspects of objects. The simplification of the object structure improves understanding of the objects during their design and use which reduces errors and improves maintainability.
How to re-use the already designed and implemented object types depends on the layer above.

We can imagine several layers side by side re-using the same layer below, each with its own interpretation and extension. In other words, the layer below is a relative root of those layers above it, which are able to build their own specialized branches in the abstraction hierarchy. This means that layering also offers flexibility in the sense of different re-use. We refer to Figure 19.1 for the remainder of the section. The figure shows the general situation for layering Perspective-DB.
Applications are normally built using layer `Frame` as the foundation, because this enables using the all services of Perspective-DB.
An application layer can also serve as a generalization for additional application layers, which also define more specialized object bases and with them more specialized applications.
In special cases it is possible to build an application using deeper layers as the foundation. For example, layer `OS` is used to build so-called **light-weight** applications. In the figure, the `CASE` system re-uses `OS` layer directly[1]. Another special case is the Perspective-DB `Daemon`, built on `VOIS`[2].

- `GOMS` is re-used by all layers above `OMS`, including `Frame`. Re-use in this case is transitive through `OMS`. `GOMS` adds the graphical representation and behavioral properties to the `OMS` objects.

- The `OMS` layer offers `OMS_Object` with its characteristics, in particular the member roles attribute and operation, and extends relations to the relationship categories ownership and secondary. Basic relationship management is already introduced in `VOMS`. Thus, the `OMS` layer mainly consolidates the concepts of the Perspective-DB object model.

- The applications `PLIS`, `Hosp` and `Infra` are built on the layer `Frame` which means that they specialize the generalization object types of `Frame` for their own purposes.

- An example of an application layer on top of Frame is `Hosp` which is used for training and realizes the hospital case study application.

- `PLIS` is a commercial Patient Logistic Information System, that provides a wide range of services to various departments of a large hospital.

- `Infra` is an existing commercial layer containing particular organizational object types describing an organizational infra-structure, personal infra-structure, activity infra-structure etc.
  The `Iris` application re-uses `Infra`[3].

- `Iris` is an existing commercial application layer. `Infra` provides `Iris` with the objects needed for its task; making reservations and scheduling organizational resources (rooms, personal, equipment, activities and events)[4].

---

[1] `CASE` is a tool suite used for software development.

[2] The daemon is the system that enables Perspective-DB applications to communicate.

[3] `Infra` for example can be used to `provide information on persons` who perform a particular function, rooms that belong to particular room types, equipment placed in a particular room, etc. This information is re-used for `formulation of schedule requirements`.

[4] In `Iris` for example, activity A should be scheduled on each Monday during the months October and November, for 2 consecutive hours between 8 and 12 a.m. in a room with video conferencing equipment. The same room should be scheduled for the entire period. Participants are staff members who function as department managers. `Infra` is also re-used for `scheduling` in `Iris`. For example, selecting a free room with video conferencing equipment according to the time constraints etc. `Infra` is also re-used for `solving conflicts` with `Iris`. For example, there is only one room with video conferencing equipment and it is already booked for the required hours. In this case, the requirements must be made more realistic by asking for the free time units of this video conferencing room. `Iris` also re-uses `Infra` to `inform people` about the schedule result, in this case to inform all department managers about the meeting times and rooms.

19.2 Layer Architecture

19.2.1 Layer Notation

The layer name is prefixed to the object type name, and separated by a '_', e.g. Hosp_Department for the object type Department of the layer Hosp (Hospital).
This convention ensures that it is always possible to identify the layer to which an object type belongs and also enables re-use of object type names, e.g. OMS_Object, Frame_Object etc[5].

Graphical notation:

The layer name is placed above the object type name, see Figure 19.2.

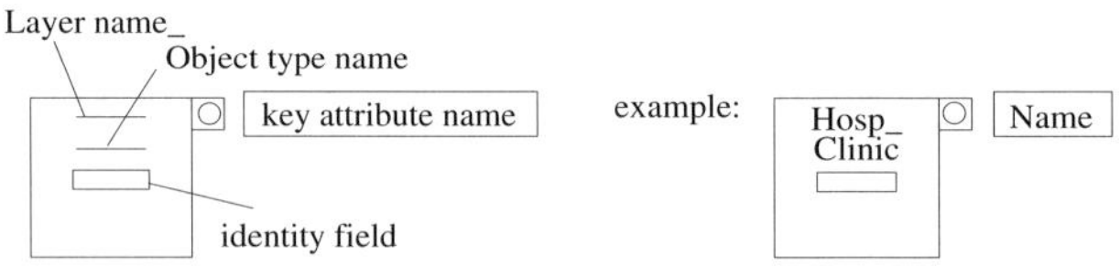

Figure 19.2: Placement of the layer name on an object type

19.2.2 Layer Components

Inherited objects across the layers:

Figure 19.3 shows the main objects inherited across the Perspective-DB layers and supplementary information that configures the layer. The four main branches of the system's inheritance hierarchy are: the base objects, the layer controllers, the layer managers and the layer initializers (not shown). The configuration information and object types are explained below.

- **TOML files**: The configuration files are commonly called TOML files. TOML is the name given to the special format used to define the information contained in the files and stands for Textual Object Model Language. The TOML format recognizes 4 domains: metadata, language, graphics and instantiation. The **metadata** domain contains structure, behavior, constraints and integrity information. The **language domain** contains the translations necessary to present the textual information in various natural languages. The **graphics domain** configures the appearance of the user-interface. The **instantiation domain** enables creation and manipulation of various object instances that are required for a running system to be operational and thereafter to be manipulated. Chapters 7, 8, 14, 15, 16, 17 and 18 are dedicated to the TOML format. Every module in the layer has a set of TOML files, usually one file per domain[6].

- **Base objects**: Every layer has a base layer object type. The base layer object type is a specialization of the base layer object type of its underlying layer. In general, new object types are specialized on this base. This is not enforced and in many situations it may be useful to specialize other object types, such as OS_Object.

- **Layer controller**: Starting at VOIS, every layer has a Controller object type. In general there is one controller per layer. The controller specializes the controller of its underlying layer. It is sometimes unnecessary to specialize a new controller for a layer.

[5]The layer prefix is usually removed from the end-user interface. This is accomplished in the external language translation. For example, the object type Hosp_Clinic is translated to Clinic.

[6]It is also possible to include several domains in one file.

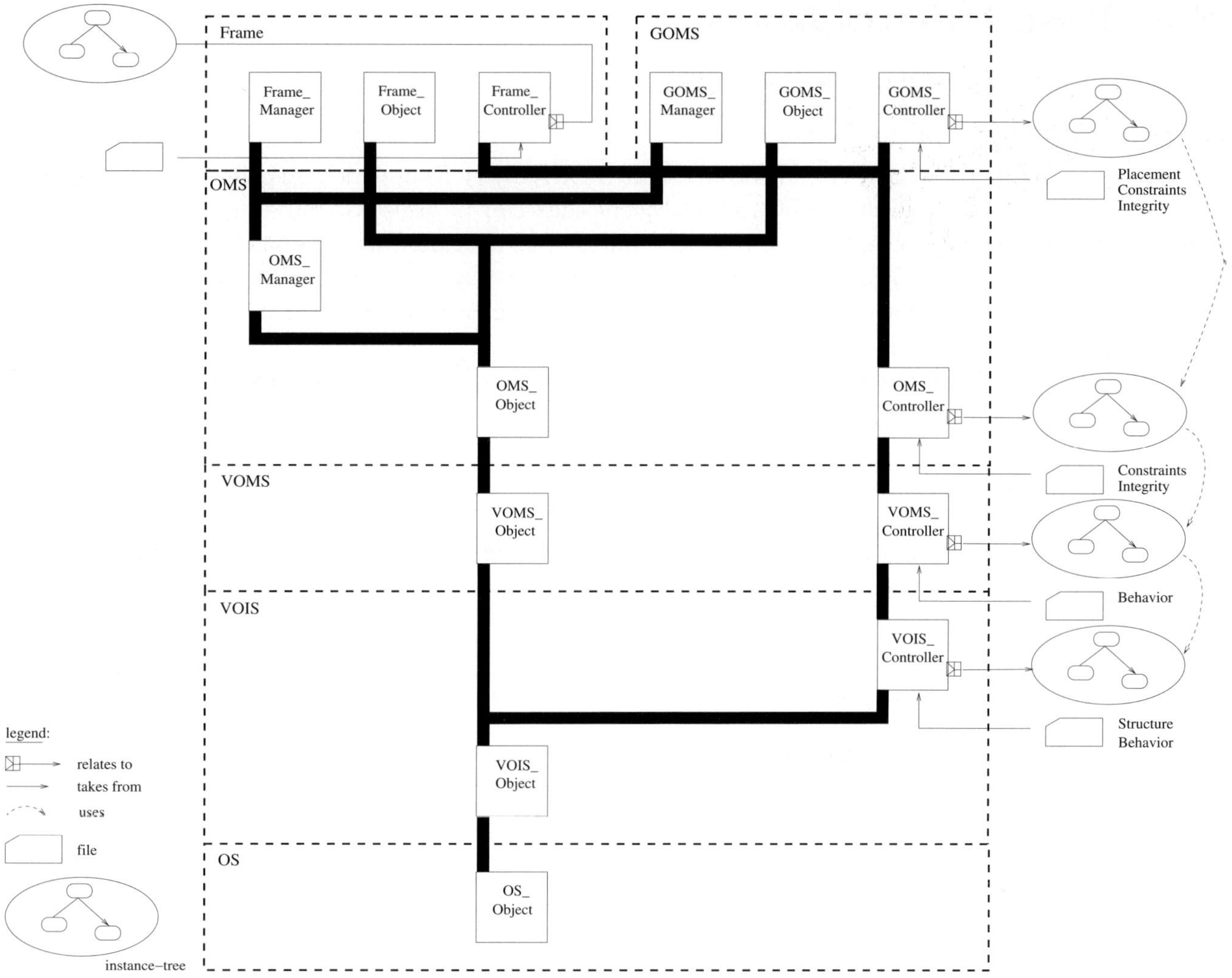

Figure 19.3: Main inheritance hierarchy between the layers of Perspective-DB

In that case the base controller provides the service. The task of the controller is to convert the information stored in the `TOML` files into objects in the application, shown in Figure 19.3 as `instance trees`.

- **Layer manager**: Starting at OMS, each layer has a base manager object type. In general there is one base manager per layer. The manager specializes the base manager of its underlying layer. The base manager is the general object type used to define specialized managers responsible for managing a module. `Modules` are used to partition layers into smaller components, as explained in the next section.

- **Layer initializer**: Every layer has a `layer initializer object type`. Its task is to ensure that its layer is properly initialized. When an application instance is started-up, each layer beginning with the lowest, undergoes an initialization procedure which ensures that all information the layer requires in order to function properly is in place. The Layer Initializer delegates the initialization task to the layer's modules. Every module has an **Initializer object type** that requests the layer controller to process its `TOML` information.

19.3 Perspective-DB Layers

19.3.1 Operating System Layer (OS)

OS Object Types

The `OS` layer contains the most generic object, called OS_Object from which all other objects descend. It also contains various collections of useful objects that can be used for building, for example, the objects for storing and processing time information such as `OS_Time`, `OS_Date` and `OS_Calendar`. The objects of this layer are also called **lightweights** because they are designed to be small in size to save space in the computer's memory, and efficient in processing so that they can be called many times without causing too much delay.
A basic object type is provided with minimal knowledge about itself and its surroundings. For example, an instance knows its object type and owner.

OS Management

The `OS` management ensures that the layers built on top remain portable. This enables a single realization of a system to run on various operation systems, for example `UNIX` or `Windows`. An example is encapsulating file system access and manipulation. For example, file system paths on `UNIX` platforms look like this:

```
/a/b/c/d
```

while on a `Windows` platform they look like this:

```
a:\b\c\d\ or \\a\b\c\d
```

OS Services

The `OS` layer realizes various generic services used by the layers on top. An example of such a service is parsing of configuration information stored in `TOML` files that is loaded into every layer of the system when it starts running. This configuration data provides every layer with information on how it should behave. A special manager called the `Object Management Language` (`OML`) manager parses the information in the file and passes it on to a controller in every layer, in the form of an OML tree. The controller then builds instance trees by using the configuration data. This process is illustrated in Figure 19.3 on the right: for example, the structure and behavior information is parsed, the OML tree is processed by the VOIS_Controller to create an object base of meta data for the application. The `TOML` format is introduced in Chapter 7. Other important services include mechanisms to check for and deal with erroneous situations and monitor the use of resources by the application.

19.3.2 Virtual Object Interface System (VOIS)

VOIS Types

The `VOIS` layer contains various collections of useful objects. The object type `VOIS_Object` is the first object type that possesses the property of being virtual. The term `virtual` is given to the object in this layer because the user manipulating the objects in the object heap does not need to load objects explicitly. When an object in the object heap is **dereferenced**, i.e. pointed at because it is needed, the persistence services (explained below) will ensure it is there. `Virtual object types` have extended knowledge about themselves and their surroundings. For example, an object is aware of its members, i.e. it knows the type, name and size of its members.

VOIS Management

Two important services are `trigger` and `notification`.

- **Trigger** is the means to enable objects to automatically perform a particular action when a particular situation occurs. Common examples are the entry and exit triggers of an operation. When an operation of an object is invoked, the object can do certain things such as consistency checks before it embarks on executing the operation. When the operation is terminated the object can also perform various activities. The advantage of the trigger is that it is not necessary to explicitly program every operation to do these ancillary actions, because triggers are automatically inserted into the code by the compiler[7].

- **Notification** is the means to enable an object to notify other objects of changes in state. When object *a* wants to know whether the state of object *b* has changed, it can register itself by *b* to be notified of a particular type of change in situation. When this state occurs *b* will notify *a* and all other objects registered by *a*. One typical type of notification is that the object is to be destroyed. Another typical type is that the content is modified.

- At this layer the **meta object heap** is introduced. The **Meta objects** are special objects containing information about the object types and how they relate to each other. With the aid of this heap the `Virtual objects` extend their knowledge.

VOIS Services

- One important type of management is **Persistence** which ensures that objects residing in the object heap of the running application can be saved to files and similarly that these files can be re-loaded into the running application to restore the objects. The persistence services cover various situations.

- **Save** and **Load** versions: when the application is stopped the complete object heap is saved in various files that together comprise a database version. When the program is started the user can select and reload a database version. During a working session the user can save to new versions or overwrite an existing version. The previously mentioned `OML` manager is responsible for the conversion between the file information and the object heap.

- **Switch** versions: the user wants to switch from one database version to another without stopping the application. In this case the objects in the object heap are **purged**, i.e. removed from the heap. The selected version is then loaded.

- **Rewind** a version: the user wants to rewind a version to a previous state. In this case only that part of the object heap that has changed is purged and restored to the desired state.

19.3.3 Virtual Object Management System (VOMS)

VOMS Types

The object type `VOMS_Object` is the first object type which possesses the property of being able to connect to other object types through relationships. Various object types exist to provide this support. The VOMS_Object is also the first object type that can be queried. **Querying** is a means to extract information from an object or objects it relates to directly or indirectly. The query consists of two basic parts, a **select** part which determines the navigation path through the objects, and a **condition** part which determines the information required along the path.

[7]An example of an entry trigger is prompting a check on whether the object is still valid. An example of an exit trigger is calling the Notification mechanism in the case of a modification.

VOMS Management

The VOMS layer has ancillary object types for managing the various kinds of relationship (1:1, 1:many, many:many).

VOMS Services

Networking object types provide the basic functionality for an application to communicate directly with another application, either running on the same machine or remotely on another machine.

19.3.4 Object Management System (OMS)

OMS Types

The object type `OMS_Object` is the first object type of the first order. It contains the complete range of functionality associated with an object according to the Perspective-DB object model. `OMS` combines all services of base layers with functionality such as **`identification`**, **`transaction`**, **`ranges`** etc, to combine into `OMS_Object`. `OMS_Object_Manager` is a specialization of `OMS_Object` and the base of all managers. It provides the concept of replaceable managers and an entry point for data in partitions. Its relationship functionality is extended to distinguish between ownership and non-ownership relations. It possesses the full range of basic operations, a Key attribute, and an `object ID` which conforms to the object model. `OMS_Object` and its specializations can be displayed and manipulated according to the Perspective-DB graphical object model.

OMS Management

`OMS` provides several types of management of which the most important is integrity.
Integrity management diversifies into various forms of integrity necessary to uphold the concepts of the Perspective-DB object model in the running application. This layer has a special pool of objects containing meta information about the object types, i.e. knowledge about the characteristics of the object types and their interactions. For example, knowledge about the range of members and the conditions under which the values of the range can be set.
Some of the object model concepts managed here are listed below (the concepts were introduced in previous sections).

- **Basic operations**: `Create, Destroy, Insert, Remove, Copy, Move`, etc.
- **Ownership**: functionality that upholds the existence integrity of objects.
- **Object identity**: the various forms of object identity such as Key, ID and Alias identification.
- **Member ranges**: ensures that a value of a member (including e.g. key and alias) is consistent.

OMS Services

Coupling with the GUI layer enables the representation of the `first order` objects according to the object model.

- User Notification: enables the object types to generate messages to the end-user about their status.
- Instantiation: creates and manipulates instances (e.g. invokes special operations to connect instances through relations, etc) based on the `TOML` file input.

- Natural language translation: allows object types, members and member values to be translated from the internal system values into natural languages values appropriate for the representation and printing of information for end-user consumption. The translation module is also based on the object model and maps the object type hierarchy of the application.

19.3.5 Graphical Object Management System (GOMS)

The layer provides generic services for the representation of objects, window interfacing, user interface configuration and integrity configuration.

GOMS Types

Almost every object in the `GOMS` Layer is specialized from `GUI_Object` which is a specialization of `OMS_Object`. This provides the graphical object management system the same high level object management as is available to the application.

GOMS Management

The Primary goal of the `GOMS` is to provide a graphical user interface to the application. Two important types of management can be distinguished. The first type is responsible for interaction with the user and manages the graphical behavior such as windows, when and what to draw, and event handling. This is the foundation for the `GOMS`. The second type manages the interaction with the application data. This includes translation of members, values, ID's, interpretation of user input, and maintaining the integrity of the displayed data. It describes the object model. Object model management uses the foundation to interact with the user. Because the model has the knowledge of how to interact with first order objects, the application interface can be displayed without the need to add specific interface code.

GOMS Services

The Foundation uses the `Windowing System Services` to interact with the `Windowing system` (`X11` and `Windows`[8]). The service allows easy switching from one windowing system to another. The configuration of the user interface is based on `Template services` which use `Template-Instantiation services` to generate and configure the interface. This offers a flexible, expandable and familiar concept to application developers. Extended view services such as the various tabular view representations, includes Form, Overview and Ownership-hierarchy, for example.

19.3.6 Framework (Frame)

The task of this layer is to provide Perspective-DB application with high level services necessary for external communication.

Frame Types

The generalization object type and manager of `Framework` objects are `Frame_Object`, and `Frame_Object_Manager` respectively.

Frame Management

Messaging Management enables Perspective-DB applications to communicate with each other directly and interactively by means of invoking operations of remote objects.
`File System Management` enables the mapping of a tree of directories and files to Perspective-DB object types.

[8] X11 and Windows are the standard windowing systems for UNIX and Microsoft-Widows respectively.

It keeps the information in the application and the directories in sync which is necessary when the choice of the structure of information in the file system is determined by external circumstances.

`Run-Site Management` organizes all the relevant persistent information of a Perspective-DB application in a special hierarchy of directories and files called the **Run Site**. The run site stores versions of the application's information in various formats.

Frame Services

- Office Management enables the importing and exporting of information between the Perspective-DB application and a standard `Office` application e.g. `MS-Office` or `Star-Office`[9].
- Mail Management enables a Perspective-DB application to receive and send messages such as e-mail, similar to MS-Outlook or Netscape Messenger[10].
- Formatting Management enables formatting of information as overviews in various file formats, for example, HTML[11] and RTF[12].

19.4 Module Architecture

Modules are used to build layers and layers are used to build systems. Figure 19.4 gives an impression of the vertical placement of layers and the horizontal placement of modules inside a layer.

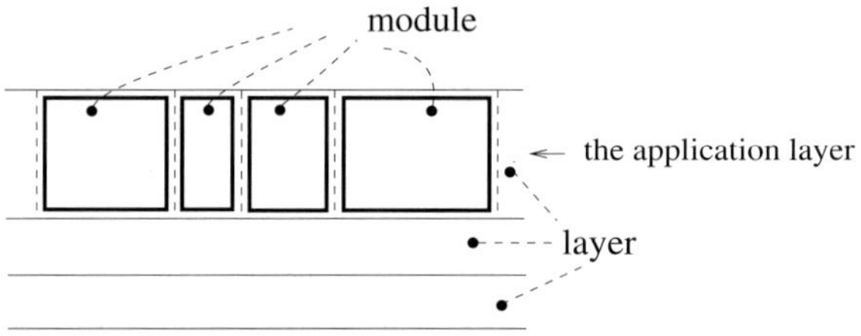

Figure 19.4: Layers and modules

The module itself is an abstraction. It can be considered the most abstract meaningful unit of information within a layer.
We associate the module with its representative object type, the module manager. A module in its entirety can be handled as an object by way of the module manager.

19.4.1 Module Characteristics

- Presence of a manager: every module has one `manager` which is the the owner of the module and as such is the root of the ownership hierarchy in the module. The manager provides the high level services that are expected of the module. It delegates the execution to the appropriate object types in the module. It is also possible to invoke the operations of an object type directly.
- Configuration of meta-data: every module has an associated meta data `TOML` file. The meta data configures the `structure` and `behavior` of the objects in the module, including configuration of the constraints concerning the objects within the module.

[9]MS-Office and Star-Office are the standard Office systems of Microsoft and Sun respectively. The `Office` packages are a collection of applications for normal office work such as a `word-processor`, `spreadsheet` etc.
[10]The standard e-mail client of Microsoft and the e-mail client accompanying the Netscape Web browser respectively.
[11]The format for defining Web pages.
[12]Rich Text Format, the format for the MS-Word word processor.

- Configuration of graphical representation: every module has an associated TOML file for graphical presentation. The file configures the user-interface of the objects in the module including information hiding.
- Configuration of language: every module has an associated `TOML` language file to configure the language in which the user-interface *works*, including the values of the instances.
- Configuration of instances: every module has an associated `TOML` instantiation file containing descriptions of all objects instances that should always be present in the module.
- Ownership hierarchies across modules are restricted: the characteristic follows from the first mentioned above. If a module has only one manager it can contain only one ownership hierarchy. If it contained just a part (only one object) of another ownership hierarchy, an object would be controlled by two managers. However, there are special cases where the restriction may be lifted, see section `Inter-Module Ownership`. However, even in this case an object instance is only owned by one of the optional managers.
- Manager Dynamism: it is sometimes necessary to replace the manager of an object type with a specialized manager, for example, when a module is re-used in a higher layer. In this case, the implementation in the lower layer cannot predict what modifications the upper layer will require. When the system is *starting up* the initialization procedure ensures that the managers will be switched so that the initialized module ends up with the most specialized manager.

19.4.2 Intra-Module Ownership

The main structure within a module is an ownership hierarchy. Chapter 6 (Case Study) makes clear that the semantics of an object is influenced by its location within the ownership hierarchy.
The root object of an ownership hierarchy can be seen as representing the semantics of the hierarchy as a whole. In Figure 6.1, the semantics of the ownership hierarchy is `Organization_of_Hospital`. A module exploits this fact for the purpose of building meaningful units of information. The border of such a unit is set by the integrity constraint related to the ownership relationship type. The point where the existential dependency ends defines the borders of the module.
The ownership relationship type hierarchies which can be contained within a particular module depends on the modeling situation. For example, `Hospital` and `Person` could each form a module with its separate ownership relationship hierarchy. In the case study we combine them and form a common module because there is only one administration unit for `Hospital` and `Person`. `Hospital` and `Person` are two branches of the same ownership relationship starting with `Hosp_Manager`. We keep orthogonality between object types concerning `Hospital` and object types concerning `Person`. Both hierarchies keep their semantic borders with respect to each other. Together, they also form the main concern of the hospital administration. `Hosp_Manager` is the common creator of all instances in the case study module.

In a real world situation of modeling a hospital organization it would be better to consider the organizational point of view; you would observe that there is a personnel organization within the hospital organization and there is a structural organization expressed through the departments. Both have their own existential dependencies which are orthogonal. They would belong to two separate ownership hierarchies, each with a manager as root.

As a consequence, we would organize the two ownership relationship types within two modules. The two modules would be related to each other through the secondary relationship types between the object types of each ownership hierarchy.

If we consider the information in the case study, there would be only one secondary relationship type bridging the modules, between `Person.Roles` in one module and `Employee.Person` and `Patient.Person` in the other.

19.4.3 Inter-Module Relations

As illustrated in the above example we see that secondary relationship types can function as *bridges* between ownership hierarchies. Modules are the means enabling flexibility and maintainability of applications.
The reason for enabling flexibility and simplifying maintainability by building modules is mainly to localize the effects of the following changes:

- Updating the object schema, including extension of the module, is simple because all semantic dependencies of the object model expressing the existential dependencies are well defined within the module. The module is maintainable without the involvement of outside objects.
- The secondary relationships to other modules can be dropped or re-interpreted and new ones added without seriously impacting the design and use of the modules.

Modularity is necessary to enable re-use. Through different combinations of modules, new applications can be *produced*. The combination occurs through defining new secondary relationship types between the modules in general.
In addition to flexibility, the horizontal object structure becomes simpler, as is the case with layers, although, with layers, the object structure is simplified vertically.

19.4.4 Module Interoperability

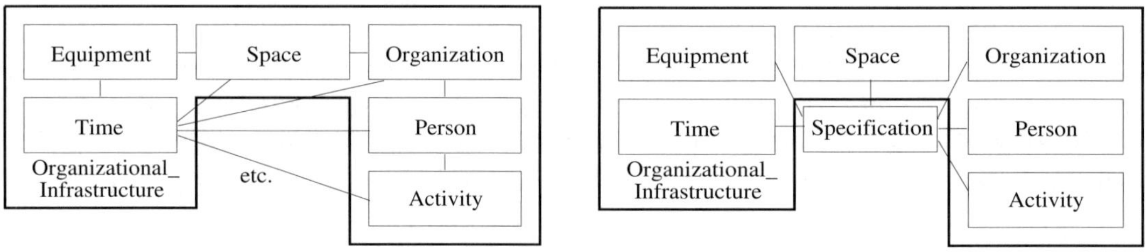

Figure 19.5: An example of several modules belonging to a more complex application

Figure 19.5 illustrates the principle of re-use of inter-operable modules. The figure reflects an existing application, called `Organizational_Infrastructure`[13].

The left side of the figure illustrates the modules belonging to the organizational infrastructure. The module names indicate that information on time, equipment, space, organization, persons and activities is modeled.

The `Time module` contains information on the calendar and time structure specific to the organization, e.g. particular periods, an academic year etc. The organizational time model and the calendar are mapped on each other.
The `Equipment module` informs on devices and device types. It can be extended to several categories of equipment belonging to facility management, for example.

[13]Two modules are presented in more detail in Figures 19.7 and 19.8 to illustrate inter-relations between modules.

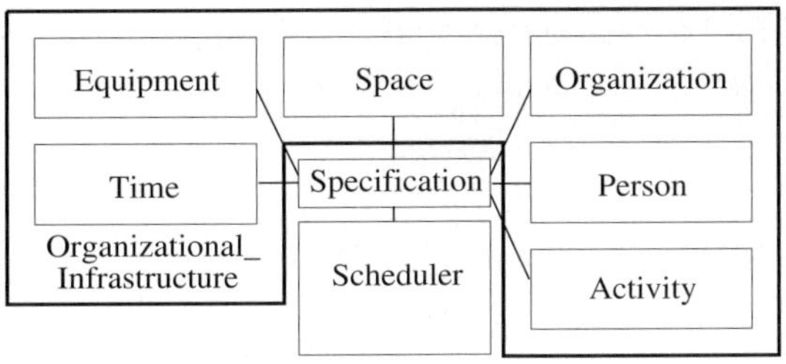

Figure 19.6: Example of reusing an application to build a new one by adding a module

The `Space module` informs on available buildings and rooms and gives related information, e.g. room types, to which particular rooms can be associated.
The `Organization module` describes the structure of the organization in terms of administrative units, e.g. the departments.
In the `Person module`, the real persons are modeled as well as the functions and function types offered by the organization. Persons and functions and function types are mapped on each other.
The `Activity module` models several categories of activities which are planned, managed, and realized by the organization e.g. a standard course with its characteristics, a curriculum, etc.

The modules are related to each other directly with secondary relationship types which the lines between the modules indicate. In Figure 19.5 only one line is drawn between two modules at a time. In reality several connectors would have to be used due to the great number of relationships. In fact, several object types in one module are connected with one or more other object types in other modules. For example, particular activities are related to the times at which they take place. Persons are related to the activities in which they participate.

The right side of Figure 19.5 demonstrates the same situation. However, the interoperability of the modules is extended with secondary relationship types between the infrastructure modules and a `Specification module`. Introducing the `Specification` module requires reconfiguring the interoperability between the infrastructure modules to specify the inter-module relations for this particular situation. Therefore, the introduction of the Specification module and the reconfiguration can be considered a new application, modeling a particular situation and information request. This new application re-uses the infrastructure modules. A reconfiguration of the Specification module would lead in turn to another application, in turn reusing the infrastructure modules.

Figure 19.6 illustrates how the orthogonally kept modules of Figure 19.5 are re-used for another application just by plugging in an additional module. In the example the module is a scheduler *engine.*
We do not explain the scheduler engine here. It is clear that a scheduler has to re-use the infrastructure within a particular configuration of inter-module operability.

19.4.5 Inter-Module Ownership

Inter-Module Ownership is necessary to ensure locality of object definition and manipulation. An example illustrates the issue as follows:
To administer facilities of an organization the available spaces have to be known, e.g. the buildings and their levels, the levels and their rooms. This situation is illustrated in the space module of Figure 19.7. The ownership hierarchy is controlled by `Space_Manager`. Let us assume there is a further application necessary for knowing which buildings are situated in which area of a particular town.

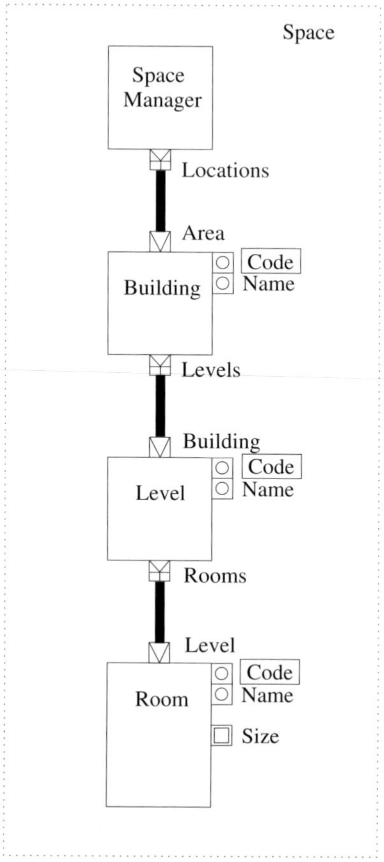

Figure 19.7: Space module

In addition it is necessary to compute the distances between rooms at several levels of several buildings; distances between buildings; between buildings in different areas of a town; or of different towns etc. It seems sensible to use the same distance computing operation with the same semantics and appearance between the relevant object types i.e. the smallest, being a particular room, and the biggest one, being a particular town. The relations between them are also important. For computing the distance between two rooms it is necessary to know if the rooms are situated at the same level within the same building. The object schema on the left side of Figure 19.8 which models the basic object types for this computation, shows that a part of the ownership hierarchy is the same as a part of Figure 19.7. Thus we could model the `Location` module to repeat the part `Building`, `Level`, `Room`. However this would violate a quality criterion of conceptual database design i.e. to avoid repetition of data. Applied to object modeling, we must avoid repetition of object types. This criterion is important to ensure consistency especially during manipulation operations. The reasons are the same as those mentioned above in relation to orthogonality; avoidance of repetition ensures localization of change. This means in its turn that we have to find a solution which violates neither the quality criterion of no repetition nor the integrity rules. The solution is to enable inter-module ownership. The method is illustrated as follows: we couple the two modules as shown on the right of Figure 19.8, resulting in the `Location` ownership hierarchy extending into the `Space` hierarchy.

The reader should be cautioned that the example given here for Inter-Module Ownership is used to explain the concept. It does not attempt to represent an optimal modeling of the situation. In general it is better to avoid very long ownership paths and to contain ownership within one module.

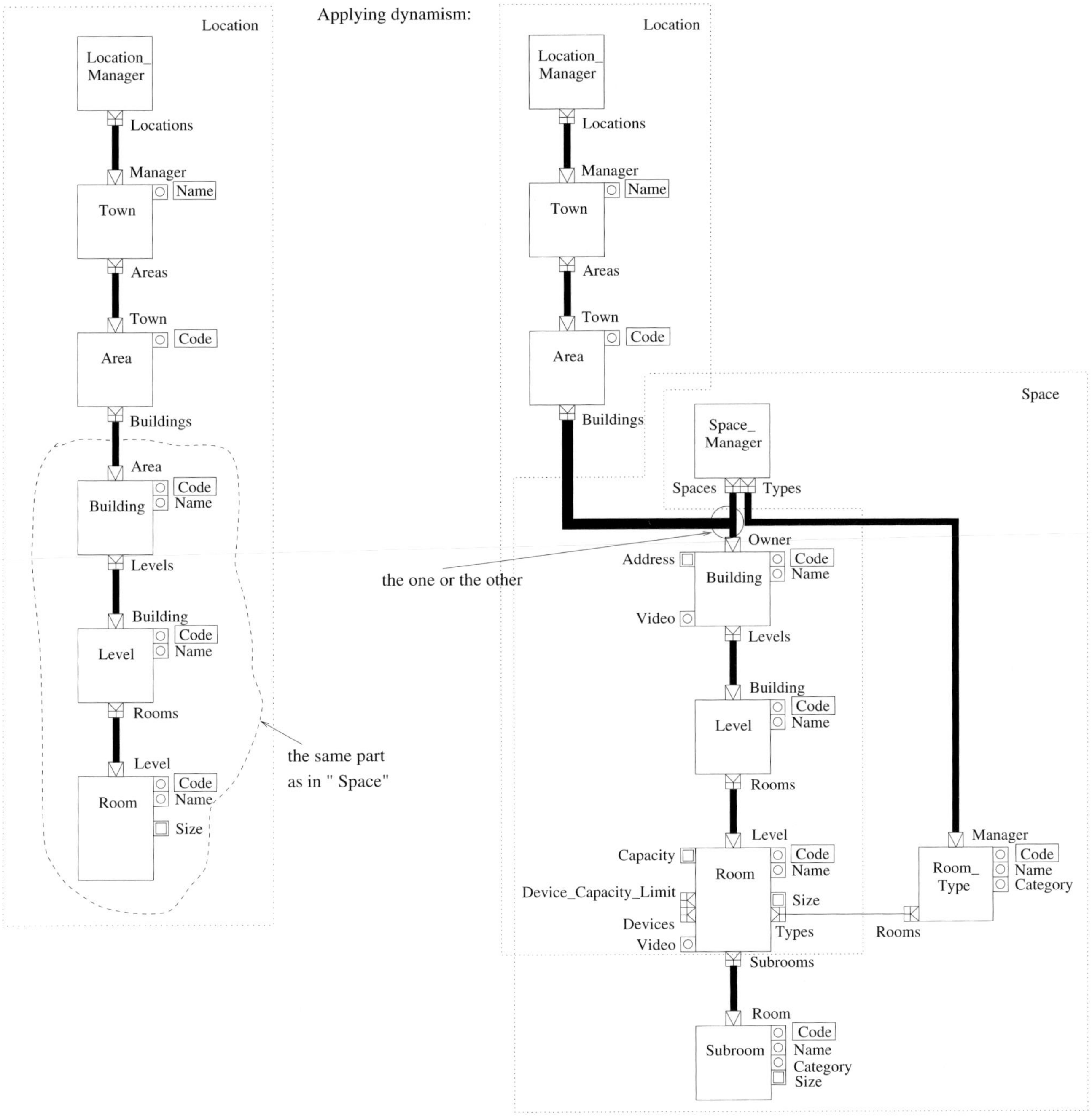

Figure 19.8: Illustration of Inter-Module Ownership

An alternative modeling solution is to connect the object `Area` in module `Location` with object `Building` in module `Space`, using a secondary relationship and selection of more complex `Code` values for the `Building` instances that consist of a code for the `Area` prefixed to the normal `Code` for `Building`. [Cattell and Barry, 2000]

Chapter 20

Comparison with state of the art object models, UML and ODMG

20.1 Introduction

20.1.1 Motivation of ODMG

The latest ODMG object model description is version 3.0 published in the year 2000.
The purpose of ODMG is to define a standard to be implemented by object database management systems and by object-relational mappings. Standardization (work) began in 1993. Over the years many major vendors of object database technology have joined the organization. Work has also been carried out on making the `OMG` standards compatible with the `ODMG` products.

The background and the goal of the ODMG work is described in [Cattell and Barry, 2000], Chapter 1. To illustrate the background, we quote from the ODMG document: "This document describes the continuing work by members of the Object Data Management Group (ODMG) on specifications for persistence of object-oriented programming language objects in databases 2.1. ... Before the ODMG specification, the lack of a standard for storing objects in databases was a major limitation to object application portability across database systems. ODMG enables many vendors to support and endorse a common object interface to which customers write their database applications... Our primary goal is to put forward a set of specifications allowing a developer to write portable applications, that is, applications that could run on more than one product. The data schema, programming language binding, and data manipulation and query languages must be portable. We are striving to bring programming languages and database systems to a new level of integration, moving the industry forward as a whole through the practical impetus of real products that conform to a comprehensive specification. The ODMG member companies, representing almost the entire ODMS industry, are supporting the specifications. Thus, our proposal has become a de facto standard for this industry. We have also used our specification in our work with standards efforts such as Java Community Process, OMG, and the INCITS X3H2 (SQL) committee..." The detailed standard description can be found in [Cattell and Barry, 2000].

Some aspects of the ODMG model will be discussed here in short, where necessary, to illustrate which characteristics of ODMG and Perspective-DB are shared and which are different in the two models. The comparison is made generally rather than in detail, because such a comparison is not the goal of the book[1].

[1] Certain information concerning UML and ODMG might be inaccurate or outdated in which case the documentation of the respective proprietary owner overrules.

20.1.2 A general comparison

Graphical configuration

Generally, the ODMG model does not deal with configuration aspects. All specifications are described within the (textual) object schema and the language bindings. There is a graphical legend of the object schema which does not play an important role in the design process, and is not mentioned in the application development or the exploitation of an application.

Language configuration

The ODMG model does not deal with natural language aspects such as the Language `TOMLs` of Perspective-DB, with one exception, called `naming`, see chapter 2.3.3 [Cattell and Barry, 2000].

Managers and Controllers

ODMG does not support the managers and controllers concept of Perspective-DB. There is no analog concept in ODMG.

Predefined types

The ODMG model specification has a more sophisticated predefined type and type constructor concept than Perspective-DB.

Language bindings

ODMG has well defined language bindings with Java and Smalltalk. These bindings are not specified yet in Perspective-DB. Both models have a C++ language binding.

Object type and instantiation

Both models uphold the concept of object type and instantiations of object types. The concepts are similar.

Inheritance

Both models uphold the concept of inheritance; the interpretation and realization are different as explained in 20.2.6.

Interface and Class

ODMG differentiates between interfaces and classes. According to Chapter 2.2 of [Cattell and Barry, 2000], an interface definition is a specification that defines the abstract behavior of an object type. A class definition is a specification that defines the abstract behavior and abstract state of an object type. Perspective-DB only supports the object type definition. Classes appear at language binding level. The Perspective-DB object type defines the abstract state and the abstract behavior of all objects of that type.

Implementation

ODMG defines that the implementation of an object type consists of a representation and a set of methods. The representation is a data structure derived from the abstract state by a language binding. The methods are procedure bodies that are derived from the abstract behavior by type definition. The principle is similar in Perspective-DB.
In both models, an object type can have more than one implementation.

System architecture

The only system architectural concept of ODMG, discussed in the 3.0 release, is the module concept.

In ODMG, modules define scopes, such as the object types and exceptions which together form a particular application. The module in Perspective-DB is formed by the semantic borders set by the `ownership hierarchy`. In ODMG, the module is a scope definition, open to the developer's interpretation and insights.

Exception handling
In ODMG, an exception is defined at the most general place of its occurrence, therefore the exceptions which are valid for a module are defined within it.
Perspective-DB currently does not support exception handling. A roll-back of the system to a previous consistent state is achieved programmatically and is closely coupled to the error handling mechanism.

Meta data
Concerning metadata, both object models are similar regarding the intentions and principles. However the difference between the two models is which information belongs to the metadata. This is the result of concepts of Perspective-DB have no analog in ODMG and vice versa, such as the role of the OML-object and the role of the ownership relations and its consequences for semantically based identification and maintaining consistency, including referential integrity, as well as the differences in inheritance interpretation and realization.

The syntax of metadata definition is also different. In ODMG, metadata involves scopes, visitors (double dispatch mechanism), meta object, module, operations, exceptions, constants, properties (attribute, relationship) and type (interface, class, collection, constructed type).

The metadata provides the model concepts itself and can be compared with the concepts of Perspective-DB which are explained as model building concepts in various chapters throughout this book. The metadata of ODMG are described in Chapter 2.8 of [Cattell and Barry, 2000]. The ODL (object definition language) of ODMG is similar to the Meta toml in Perspective-DB, on the general level. The OIF (object interchange format) of ODMG is similar to the Instance toml. The GOML and the Language TOML do not have an analog in ODMG.

Query
Perspective-DB has PQL, a query language based on path expressions (navigational), ODMG has an object query language (OQL) which is fairly similar to SQL3. OQL enables joins on two arbitrary extents. PQL enables navigational joins only, that is, joins through predefined relations. This query limitation in PQL is designed to ensure data consistency in query results and does not affect the information potential of the object base. Any information which is in accordance with the object model, can be queried. Queries not following the semantics of the object schema, cannot be formulated. This is an important requirement for a query language.

20.2 Comparing the object models

20.2.1 Basic modeling primitives

In ODMG, the concepts of object and literal exist side by side as modeling primitives. Objects have a unique identifier. Literals are identified by themselves, by their existence.

Object
The term object is explained by the aspects of an object: creation, identifier, name, lifetime and structure. These object aspects are discussed in Chapter 2.3 of [Cattell and Barry, 2000].

To create an object, the programmer invokes a create operation (new ()) on factory interfaces of a factory object. The factory object is supplied by the language binding. Via this object all user defined objects inherit an ODL (object definition language) interface.

The creation is similar in Perspective-DB. The difference lies in the ownership concept in Perspective-DB. The object identification is also comparable. In both models an object has an internal identifier which makes it uniquely identifiable within its storage domain. The identifier is immutable during the entire lifetime of the object.

Literals
The principle is the same in both object models. Literals cannot exist independently, they have to be embedded in objects. Objects and literals may be atomic or composed. Composed means that the object or literal consists of parts which in turn may be atomic or composed.

Object Naming
ODMG enables assigning of one or more meaningful names to an object instance. The names are mapped to the object by a function. This is done in Perspective-DB by the Language TOML. The assigning of meaningful names to objects are only one of the Language aspects of Perspective-DB.

Object lifetimes
The object lifetimes, transient and persistent, are the same in both models.

Predefined objects
ODMG supplies predefined object and literal collections: set, bag, list, array and dictionary. In Perspective-DB similar structures are provided in the form of ancillary modules rather than as part of the model[2].
Perspective-DB does not need the dictionary objects. The generic operations Overview and Association offer more generic but comparable functionality.
In ODMG, Date and Time are pre-defined and offered as part of the interface. In Perspective-DB these are not considered part of the model and are available as an ancillary object library.

20.2.2 Object type

In ODMG, objects and literals can be characterized by their types. All objects at application level belong to an object type in Perspective-DB: an object is either an object type or an instance of a type.

In both models, all elements of a given type have a common set of properties and a common set of operations.

20.2.3 Modeling state and behavior

The structuring of the characteristics of an object are similar in both models: Characteristics are separated into properties and operations.

State modeling

Properties are attributes and relationships. For details, see Chapter 2.6 of [Cattell and Barry, 2000].

[2] A pre-defined set as part of the model is too rigid and detailed.

To summarize:
"An attribute is of one type. A relationship is defined between two types, each of which must have instances that are referable by object identifiers." In Perspective-DB relationships can be established between more than two types i.e. heterogeneous relationships[3]

Attributes
In a class, an attribute defines the abstract state of its instances. The attributes are implemented as data structures. In an interface, an attribute defines only abstract behavior of its instances. The attributes are implemented as methods. As an example, the attribute age is described. The age of a person should be an attribute defined in an interface Person and not in the class Person. In the class, the attribute birth date is defined. The attribute age would use the attribute birthdate to compute the age of a person. Because an interface can not be instantiated, a class would have to inherit the attribute age to be usable within an application. If age were directly defined in a class as an attribute, it would be implemented as a data structure, which means it would not be computed, but rather represented by a value. The attribute, inherited from the interface, would represent the actual computed age; the attribute age defined in the class would have to be updated at each birthday of the person, or it would represent a particular value, valid for only one year of the person's lifetime.

In Perspective-DB, both variants are definable in the same object type if necessary, as well as the birthdate attribute. The age attribute which represents a value would get the name "age in time period ...", for example, and the other could be named "actual age" and would be better represented by an operation. For presentation purposes filtering can be applied to the user interface.
In both models, attributes can be composed of object types of different structure.

Example
The attributes of object type Person, see Chapter 8 of this book, would be defined in ODMG as shown in Figure 20.3 (case 1, right side).

Whereas the data type of an attribute is defined in the ODL declaration in ODMG, in Perspective-DB it can be within the language binding or configurable (using Meta TOML).

Media types
The ODMG standard does not define how to deal with the multi-media data types. Concerning the example, the attribute Photo cannot be defined here. It is not clear from the ODMG's specifications whether the concept of object-valued attribute can be used for multi-media data types.

Relationships
In both models only binary relationships are supported. The cardinality of participation of instances in a relationship is similar. Even the explicit declaration of the logical connection between the related object types is similar. The syntax is different. ODMG defines a traversal path and an inverse path, if the relationship is bi-directional (connects for bi-directional and connects_to for uni-directional in Perspective-DB).

In ODMG, the traversal paths can be ordered or unordered. When a traversal path connects to a set, the path is unordered. In Perspective-DB the relations can also be configured to be ordered or unordered.

[3] An instance can relate to instances of different object types through the same relation.

Perspective-DB fulfills the ODMG's requirement that the object database management system must maintain the referential integrity of relationships. This means that when an object participating in a relationship is deleted, any traversal path to that object must also be deleted.

There is no concept of a relationship member in ODMG, for Perspective-DB see Chapter 3 of this book. This means that the semantic of the member has to be defined in another way, e.g. as attribute of one of the related object types or as an additional object type.

Example 1
The connection between the relations Support.Services and Service.Supports (Figure 8.10 of this book) would be declared in ODMG as shown in the Figure 20.8 and 20.9 (relationships supports and services).
The cardinality many-to-many is expressed by the structure declaration "set" for both traversal paths. The first declaration means that the class Support has a relationship named services and it relates to the class Service. The inverse traversal path from the class Service is named supports.
The second declaration means that the class Service has a relationship named supports and it relates to the class Support. The inverse traversal path from the class Support is named services.

Example 2
The relations of object type Person would be defined in ODMG as shown in Figure 20.3, right side. There is no differentiation of relationship types in ODMG, such as the differentiation in ownership and secondary relations in Perspective-DB. There is also no explanation about the inheritance relationships, apart from the discussion of the types of inheritance. However this is not about the characterization of the relationships itself.

Behavior modeling

Behavior is specified as a set of operation signatures in both models.
Most of the operation characterization is similar. In ODMG, the name of an operation is unique within the object type. This is the same in Perspective-DB because the object type is the owner of the member. When two operations have the same name in ODMG, each belongs to a different object type. The operation can be overloaded due to the specialization of the object type. According to Chapter 2.7 of ODMG, "when an operation is invoked using an overloaded name, a specific operation must be selected for execution. This selection, sometimes called operation name resolution or operation dispatching, is based on the most specific type of the object supplied as the first argument of the actual call".

In Perspective-DB, overruling may take place for specializations, see section 3.3 of this book. The same principle is applied. However, it is clearly defined when overloading occurs.

20.2.4 Separation of specification and implementation

In both models an object type has an external specification and one or more implementations. The implementation is realized by a language binding. It contains the representations of the attributes and relations (relationships) as programming language terms. It also contains the method specifications which implement an operation. In addition, integrity conditions are represented by the programming language.
The language bindings are used to implement the specifications with a particular programming language. For this reason, there could be more than one implementation for one specification.

Concerning the names of the object types and their members, there is only one realization in Perspective-DB within a particular programming language. The names are applied in the Internal language. English, German, French or other languages are configured using the Language domain of the Perspective-DB object (Chapter 15). There is no such proposal in ODMG.

20.2.5 The key concept

Both models uphold the concept of a key (a semantic based identifier) additional to the system internal identifier. The main difference between the two is that ODMG chooses the scope of the extent for uniqueness. In Perspective-DB, the scope for uniqueness is the owner. Thus, semantic based identification is related to the existential dependency expressed by ownership and membership, (Chapter 3). It is an advantage that semantic based identification follows the semantics of the object schema. This seems the most natural method since it ensures the accessibility of the object within an application since the object is identified in its semantical context. This is a further aspect of ensuring consistency of a Persrpective-DB object base.

20.2.6 Inheritance

Inheritance is expressed as a relationship in ODMG.
ODMG separates the inheritance of behavior and state into different concepts. The two inheritance concepts are related to the interface and the class concept. Classes and interfaces may inherit behavior from one or more interface; classes may inherit state and behavior from one class only (only classes may inherit from a class). Only classes may inherit from a class. Inheritance applies only to object types; literals may not inherit.

Inheritance of behavior
The inheritance of behavior from interfaces is multiple but from classes it's single (name overloading is precluded during inheritance) while state inheritance is single. Inheritance is transitive. Behavior inheritance is polymorphic. An operation will be executed with those parameters which are valid for the particular specialized interface or class.
ODMG considers the inheritance of behavior as an inheritance-based type-subtype relationship. The specialized type is the subtype of the type it inherits from. This is the supertype or the generalization. For more details see Chapter 2.2.1 of [Cattell and Barry, 2000]. According to this explanation, "a subtype's interface may define characteristics in addition to those defined on its supertype. These new aspects of state and behavior apply only to the instances of the subtype (and any of its subtypes). A subtype interface can also be refined to specialize state and behavior".

Inheritance of state
`State` is defined by the values an object instance carries for a set of properties (attributes and relationships). Inheritance of state means the inheritance of the values of instances, thus the inheritance of the instance's properties.
As a consequence, a generalization class can be instantiated and its specialization classes inherit the instantiations and may specialize them (limit the domains and add additional properties). For this reason only classes can inherit state because interfaces cannot be instantiated. Mainly for this reason, inheritance is also represented by a relationship. The specialized state is related to that part of its state which it has in common with other specializations. To use a relationship for inheritance means to consider this kind of inheritance as a structural aspect of the object base. Relationships are a concept of structuring the object base and represent semantics through that structuring element.

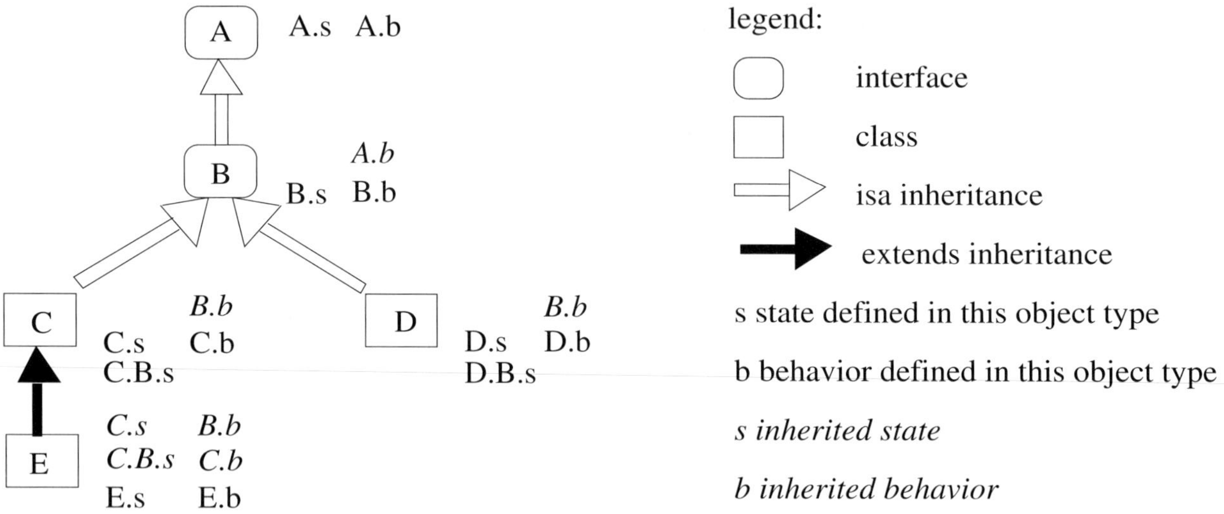

Figure 20.1: A Schema in ODMG

The advantage of representing inheritance by a relationship is that not only the leaves of a specialization hierarchy can build the application object. At the same time a more generic object can be part of an application without copying the object into an additional inheritance hierarchy where it forms a leaf. However to be able to exploit this advantage in practice requires running the applications with the same management system. It would be interesting to know whether the performance of the applications remains acceptable.

The sophisticated inheritance concepts of ODMG are introduced to support "fine grain" inheritance with opportunities of reusing characteristics from several (inheritance-)sources but excluding others from inheritance.

Figure 20.1 describes the principle in a general example: interface B is a subtype of interface A. That means B inherits all behavior from A via an isa relationship, and it may add specific state and behavior. Thus, it shows its own state and behavior in addition to the behavior of A. The classes C and D are subtypes of B. The classes C and D inherit the behavior from B (and with this also from A, transitively). The state specified in B is not inherited by C and D. However, the state is specified in B to express that the common supertype is characterized by such a state. When the classes C and D would have to "use" the common characteristics, the state characteristics have to be defined again in C and D. When another class E inherits from C this time via the extends-relationship it inherits all the state and behavior from C (and with it the behavior of B and A transitively).
The main differences between the ODMG inheritance concept and Perspective-DB are:

a) In ODMG inheritance is a relationship between object types. In Perspective-DB the inheriting object type includes the one inherited.
b) In ODMG there is a difference between behavior and state inheritance. In Perspective-DB there is only one concept which is transitive and selective for all object type characteristics. Those characteristics not to be presented to the end-user are filtered out by configuration.
c) In ODMG, behavior inheritance is multiple. Perspective-DB supports only single inheritance.
The inheritance concept of Perspective-DB is simpler and straightforward. The configurable filter mechanism gives flexibility with respect to the reuse of inherited characteristics at the user interface. It is not part of the object type definition itself and thus simple to adapt to changing application needs.

The effects of the inheritance concept of Perspective-DB can be compared mainly with the EXTENDS inheritance of ODMG. The only real limitation compared with ODMG is the exclusion of multiple inheritance. Multiple inheritance can be compensated for partly by introducing an additional common base object (generalization) which defines the characteristics of the multiple object types. Such a common base object does not always fit naturally into the inheritance hierarchy of the application layer which models the semantics of the Universe of Discourse. One can imagine cases where such a base object would have to be introduced fairly far from the place within the inheritance hierarchy where the common characteristics are needed within the specializations. This means that the characteristics will be inherited through several inheritance levels and have to be filtered out several times on their way.

However, such a situation is a rare exception because, from our experience, the semantics of the Universe of Discourse rarely requires multiple inheritance.
The support for multiple inheritance in Perspective-DB seems complicated, but then so it is with ODMG.
Thus we do not consider the lack of multiple inheritance as a real limitation of the inheritance concept in Perspective-DB.

20.2.7 Extents

In ODMG an extent of an object type is the set of all instances of the type within a particular object database system, i.e. the set of objects which fulfill the type characteristics and which belong to a particular application. The extent of a class is a means of maintaining the instances of a class automatically in an ODMG object base. The programmer decides if this maintenance should be done by the system or not. Creating and managing indexes is also related to the extent. Due to performance reasons, the programmer can specify that indexing and maintenance are supported separately by the extent, see Chapter 2.2.3 of [Cattell and Barry, 2000].

The extent is a concept which is unknown in Perspective-DB. Here the objects are clustered physically according to the structure of the ownership hierarchy. That means the objects are stored in accordance with their semantics making an extent unnecessary.

20.3 Applying the case study to ODMG

This section uses the ODMG object model to model the hospital case study in some detail in order to illustrate the similarities and differences between models more explicitly than in the textual description. Figure 20.2 describes the object schema with the graphical legend of ODMG, see Chapter 3.2.2 of [Cattell and Barry, 2000]. The schema of this figure is comparable to the developer's view of Perspective-DB of Figure 6.3 of this book. The ODMG schema does not contain the attributes and operations of the object types because the legend in ODMG3.0 does not define it.

Figures 20.3, 20.4, 20.5, 20.6, 20.7, 20.8, 20.9, 20.10, 20.11, describe the schema within ODL. To design the case study's semantics with the concepts of ODMG, it had to be decided which object types are defined as interfaces and which as classes. The object types are known from the analysis already made.
We took into account the roles of both concepts concerning inheritance (isa and extends). From the analysis we know that Role, Person, Address, Hospital and Department are basic object types in our hospital UoD. They do not have common properties.

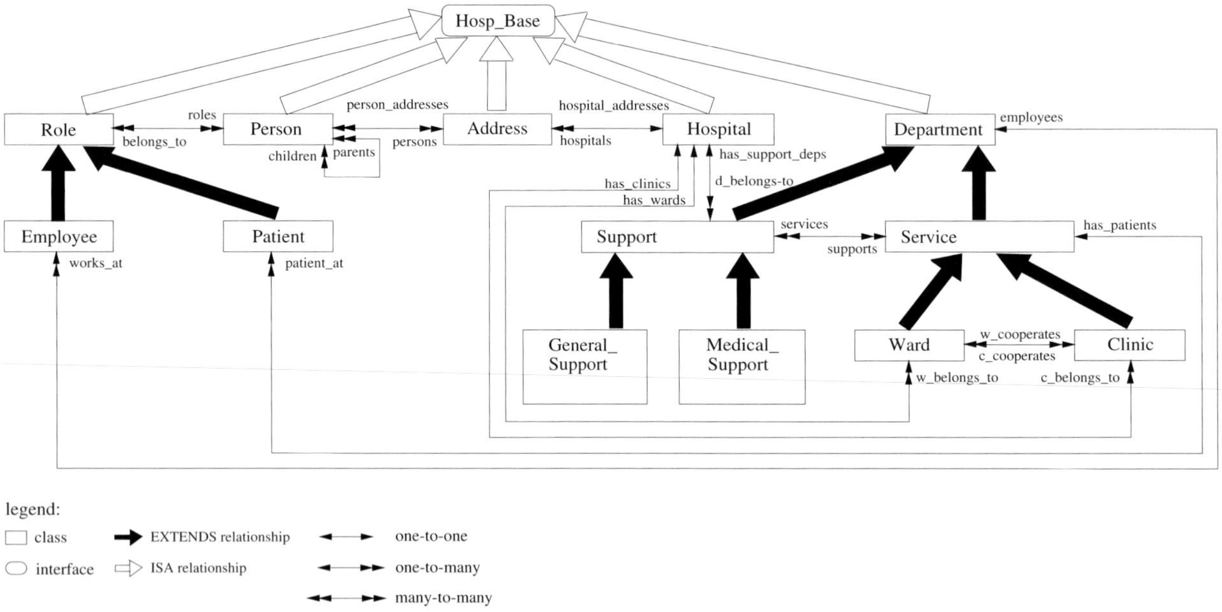

Figure 20.2: Modeling hospital in ODMG

```
module Hospital_Case
{
  ....
  exception AlreadyAtLimitOfOccupation();
  ......
  struct Report {Date date; string content;}
  interface Hosp_Base
    {
    };
  class Role : Hosp_Base
    ( extent roles )
    {
      attribute string code;
      attribute Report report;
      relationship list <Person> belongs_to
                        inverse Person::roles;
    };

class Person : Hosp_Base
  ( extent persons )
  {
    attribute string ssn;
    attribute string name;
    attribute enum gender {male, female, unknown};
    relationship set <Role> roles
                     inverse Role::belongs_to;
    relationship set <Person> parents
                     inverse Person::children;
    relationship set <Person> children
                     inverse Person::parents;
    relationship set <Address> person_addresses
                     inverse Address::persons;
    hours ( out short number_of_hours) raises (OverLimit);
  };
```

Figure 20.3: Hospital case in ODMG, 1: module Hospital

However we want to build a common base for the UoD to be able to define behavior which is dedicated to this universe which is why we model a Hosp_Base object as interface. The Hosp_Base object in ODMG inherits the behavior which is defined in the metadata's metatype, and *passes it* to the aforementioned object types of the case study.

The rest of the object types are modeled as classes. The motivation for this choice is that properties mainly have to be inherited. There was discussion whether to define Department and perhaps even Support and Service as interfaces because they have to inherit five operations to the four specializations. However in this case the properties would have to be inherited additionally e.g. by additional classes Dept_Support and Dept_Service. The advantage of inheritance compared with the increasing complexity of the schema did not justify this.

```
class Hospital : Hosp_Base
  ( extent hospitals )
  {
    attribute string name;
    relationship set <Support> has_support_deps
                     inverse Support::d_belongs_to;
    relationship set <Ward> has_wards
                     inverse Ward::w_belongs_to;
    relationship set <Clinic> has_clinics
                     inverse Clinic::c_belongs_to;
    relationship set <Address> hospital_addresses
                     inverse Address::hospitals;
  };
```

Figure 20.4: Hospital case in ODMG, 2: class Hospital

```
class Department : Hosp_Base
  ( extent departments )
  {
    attribute string name;
    attribute short capacity;
    relationship set <Employee> employees
                     inverse Employee::works_at;
    float occupation ()
    boolean employ ( in string ssn, in float hours, out string code )
            raises (PersonAlreadyEmployed);
    boolean discharge ( in string code ) raises (EmployeeAlreadyDischarged);
  };
```

Figure 20.5: Hospital case in ODMG, 3: class Department

There was also no need for multiple inheritance which would have forced us to apply the interface concept. Eventually, the simple and straightforward way of the EXTENDS inheritance was chosen.

In the schema, the thick arrows represent inheritance relationships.

```
class Address : Hosp_Base
  ( extent addresses)
  {
    attribute string code;
    attribute string town:
    attribute string street;
    attribute short number;
    ....
    relationship set <Person> persons
                     inverse Person::person_addresses;
    relationship set <Hospital> hospitals
                     inverse Hospital::hospital_addresses;
  }:
```

Figure 20.6: Hospital case in ODMG, 4: class Address

```
class Employee extends Role
  ( extent employees )
  {
    attribute string function;
    attribute short max_hours;
    relationship set <Department> works_at
                     inverse Department::employees;
  };
```

```
class Patient extends Role
  ( extent patients )
  {
    attribute string category;
    relationship set <Service> patient_at
                     inverse Support::has_patients;
  };
```

Figure 20.7: Hospital case in ODMG, 5: class Employee

```
class Support extends Department
  ( extent supports )
  {
    relationship <Hospital> d_belongs_to
                 inverse Hospital::has_support_deps;
    relationship set <Service> services
                 inverse Service::supports;
  };
```

Figure 20.8: Hospital case in ODMG, 6: class Support

The next step was to define the rest of the (non-inheritance) relationships. The following relationships were added:

- roles and belong_to between Role and Person,
- parents and children, recursive on Person,

```
class Service extends Department
  ( extent services )
  {
    relationship set <Support> supports
                     inverse Support::services;
    relationship set <Patient> has_patients
                     inverse Patient::patient_at;
    boolean check_in ( in string ssn, out string code )
            raises (PersonAlreadyPatient);
    boolean checkout ( in string code ) raises (PatientAlreadyCheckedOut);
  };
```

Figure 20.9: Hospital case in ODMG, 7: class Service

```
class General_Support extends Support
  ( extent general_supports )
  {
  };

class Medical_Support extends Support
  ( extent medical_supports )
  {
  };
```

Figure 20.10: Hospital case in ODMG, 8: Support classes

```
class Ward extends Service
  ( extent wards )
  {
    relationship set <Clinic> c_cooperates
                     inverse Clinic::w_cooperates;
    relationship set <Hospital> w_belongs_to
                     inverse Hospital::has_wards;
  };
```

```
class Clinic extends Service
  ( extent clinics )
  {
    relationship set <Ward> w_cooperates
                     inverse Ward::c_cooperates;
    relationship set <Hospital> c_belongs_to
                     inverse Hospital::has_clinics;
  };
```

Figure 20.11: Hospital case in ODMG, 9: class Ward

- person_addresses and persons between Person and Address,
- hospital_addresses and hospitals between Hospital and Address,
- patient_at and has_patients between Patients and Service,
- works_at and employees between Employee and Department,

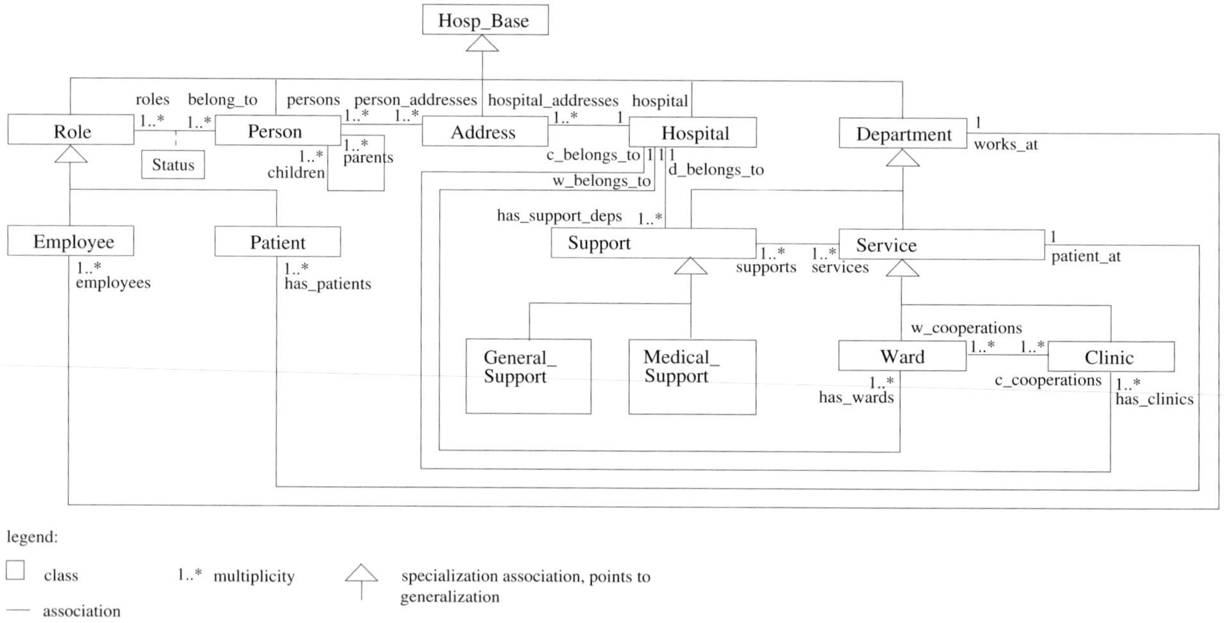

Figure 20.12: UML class schema designed in a static structure diagram

- w_cooperates and c_cooperates between Ward and Clinic,
- supports and services between Support and Service,
- d_belongs_to_hospital and has_support_deps between Hospital and Support,
- w_belongs_to_hospital and has_wards between Hospital and Ward,
- c_belongs_to_hospital and has_clinics between Hospital and Clinic.

The cardinality is represented by the number of points of the thin arrows, see the legend.
Because there is no concept of existential dependency nothing else has to be represented.
The ODMG schema looks simpler than that of Perspective-DB. However the Perspective-DB developer's schema of Figure 6.3 also describes the attributes, the keys, and differentiates between ownership and secondary relationships. In this schema it is already obvious which object types belong to a module represented by the manager.

These ODL definitions serve as a reference. ODMG compliant ODBMS's do not apply the definitions themselves in any way. The ODL definitions represent the object schema. The schema has to be mapped onto a language binding. We do not present such a mapping here because in the first place it would depend on the programming language.

20.4 Applying the case study to UML

Figures 20.12 and Figure 20.13 give an idea of how to describe the hospital case study using UML schematic. The textual notation is not addressed here.

Motivation

UML stands for Unified Modeling Language.

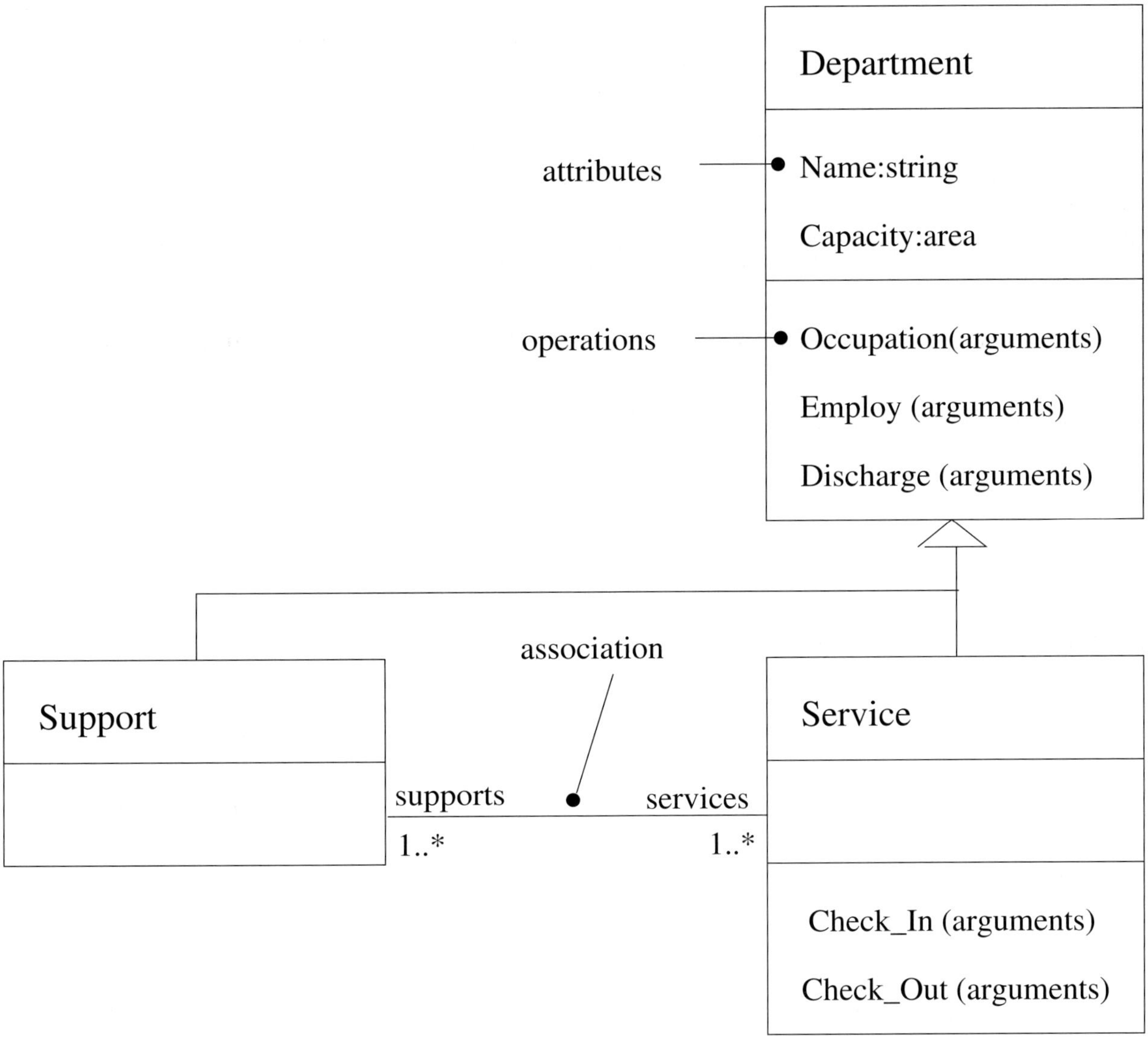

Figure 20.13: UML member representation for a part of the schema

"The language is the industry standard language for specifying, visualizing, constructing, and documenting the artifacts of software systems" according to the Rational website. "It simplifies the complex process of software design, making a 'blueprint' for construction." Rational is the leading commercial organization behind UML [4].
UML has been developed to support software engineering of complete applications. UML can also be used for the design of the databases. One of the arguments is that UML enables database design without any restrictions, e.g. compared to the well known Entity-Relationship Model (ERM). It is assumed by UML supporters that designing without restrictions makes the design more accurate and the communication easier. As set out in Chapter 1 Introduction, we believe that restrictions are necessary to ensure unambiguous design and database integrity. Lack of restrictions and accuracy of database design are to an extent contradictory.
UML is widely applied in software engineering. Within this process, database design is included mainly to supply the applications with data.

Only a short comparison between UML and Perspective-DB is made in this book. The main reason is that UML is not intended to be directly supported by a database management system. Neither is the structural language part of UML an ODL as in the case with ODMG for example. Nor as a consequence is manipulation and query language defined. In this sense it is comparable to ERM. A data schema designed with UML must be converted into a data schema of a data model supported by an implementation. Rational Rose supposes that this will be the relational data model. It has implemented a full set of rules to convert from a UML design to relational designs (see Chapter 1 Introduction).

A general comparison

UML upholds Static Structure Diagrams, Use Case Diagrams, Sequence Diagrams, Collaboration Diagrams, State-chart Diagrams, Activity Diagrams and Implementation Diagrams in order to represent the various aspects of software engineering. The strength of UML is based on this broad range of support.

The applied diagram techniques are not new. They are taken from well established former software engineering techniques and brought together. This is an additional strong point of UML. However, as is the case for the static structure design with UML, all the various diagrams are only specifications. The specifications are not supported by implementations in a 1 to 1 manner. By 1 to 1 we mean, to implement the specification without conversions. The conversion processes are automated up to several degrees by Rational (Rational Rose). This prevents loss of semantics, but even the best conversion program cannot prevent the loss of semantics caused by the nonexistence of a counterpart on the implementation side. Moreover it cannot prevent problems caused by updates in the implemented system. When there is no direct coupling between the implementation and the specification (as a kind of documentation of the system's semantics) one can be quite sure that both things start to go their own ways. To avoid these kind of problems, the implemented system would have to be coupled to reverse conversion tools to produce the actual specifications.

This discussion does not assume that the diagram techniques are not useful, however, they should be supported by implementations as far as possible and offer reverse conversion tools for other implementations.

[4] The UML-language and the logos are trademarks of the Object Management Group. Information can be found at http://www.rational.com/uml and http://www.omg.org. Version 1.1 of UML was published in 1997. The specifications of the actual version can be downloaded from the aforementioned web site of Rational.

Perspective-DB has the advantage of being an object model with an implementation. A disadvantage is that the behavioral aspects are not designed in an explicit way by diagram elements. However, behavioral aspects visible in the user view are supported by underlying modeling concepts such as representing the activity flow, i.e. only operations that may be invoked are visible and visibility of members is in accordance with the state (flow and visibility can be configured in the GOML domain). The UML diagram techniques such as sequence and activity diagrams can be used, of course, but then they too are only specifications without a direct implementation support. These aspects of Perspective-DB have also to be improved.

One of the main advantages of Perspective-DB is its clear modularization capability, based mainly on the strength of the ownership hierarchies. UML uses Packages as a means of modularizing applications including the databases. The borders of a package do not follow from understanding and maintaining the semantic integrity of the application's UoD. "A Package is a group of elements with a common theme. A package partitions a model, making it easier to understand and manage" (see [Blaha et al.,1998], p 61). Like a module, a package can be layered; the concepts of module and package are similar here. Blaha and Premerlani explain what is understood by a theme: "There are various themes for forming packages: dominant classes, dominant relationships, major aspects of functionality, and symmetry. For example, many business systems have a Customer package or a Part package;... The precise boundaries of a package are a matter of judgement..." Furthermore: "You can often use a class with a logical horizon as the nucleus for a package. The logical horizon [Feldman et al., 1986] of a class is the set of classes reachable by one or more paths terminating in a combined multiplicity of "one" or "zero or one"... etc". Combined multiplicity in UML can be interpreted as the maximum value of the cardinality range in Perspective-DB. This consideration is a matter of the direction in which a path is accessed. Furthermore, at a conceptual level, the cardinality is not a strong structuring concept as it is at the application level (a particular semantic view on the conceptual schema). It could be that the cardinality at a more general layer is "many" for the same object type participation in the relationship, and "one" for the layer of the considered application. Additionally, generalizations are relationships also in UML; packages can partition inheritance hierarchies. The consequences are not quite clear. The differences between the explicitness of the package building in UML and that of the module building in Perspective-DB are illustrated in [Gerhardt et al., 2000].

In general, the words commonly used in data and object modeling to name concepts are often used by UML but with rather different semantics. This leads to some confusion when a particular word stands for another term; the choice of the alternative word is not always justified by e.g. improved precision etc. In general, the Perspective-DB object types can be considered as UML classes, the relations as associations, the cardinality range as multiplicity, the connector as link. The terms attributes and operations are applied similarly. UML also upholds the concept of a relationship attribute. It supports relationship classes (called association class) additionally. UML can express conditions on the specialization association concerning participation of instances and disjointing of the participation in several specializations. It models aggregation and composition explicitly and separately. Here, UML is quite close to the so-called semantic data models. Unlike Perspective-DB or ODMG, UML does not support differences between operations expressing the generic database management functionality on the one hand and the application's functionality on the other. But this cannot be expected with regard to the goal of UML.

Figure 20.12 illustrates the class schema designed in a static structure diagram technique of UML. The main appearance is rather similar to that of the ODMG object schema. The members of the classes are not shown in this schema. Figure 20.13 illustrates the member representation for a part of the schema. The attributes and the operations appear within a particular part of the class rectangle.

The associations appear as named links between the class rectangles.

We must emphasize that in Figures 20.12 and 20.13 only some of the most generic modeling concepts of UML were used and not the more sophisticated concepts; these would have made a bigger difference not only to Perspective-DB but also to the ODMG schema. The reason is mainly because there are no suitable implementations for the more sophisticated concepts other than programming conditions which we do not deal with in this book.

Appendix A

Functional (Mathematical) Description

The purpose of this chapter is to give the reader an idea of the functional description of the Perspective object model. This appendix has been extracted from Chapter 11 of [Szántó, 2004] and is therefore not complete [1].

The functional description is achieved by a formal description of object types, and their properties, and of object instances.

We use the Hospital case study of Figure A.1 to help explain the functional description. This Hospital case study differs from the original Hospital case study used throughout the book [2].

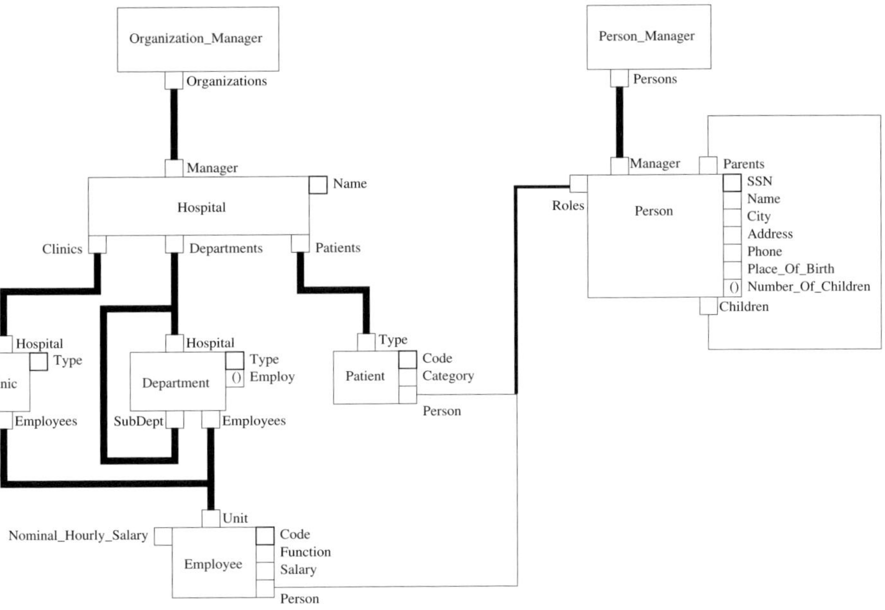

Figure A.1: Hospital Case Study (revised version)

The description will be presented in a top-down manner, accordingly, the first thing to describe is the database schema that is unique to each database. Every database schema is built on the set of atomic types, Θ, which is the same for each database.

[1]The functional description was defined with the help of Prof. T. P. van der Weide, Katholieke Universiteit Nijmegen and is to be published in a mathematical journal.

[2]The main differences are that object type `Person` has a different Manager than `Hospital`, object type `Department` has an additional recursive relationship, the specialization `Ward` of `Department` is not present, object type `Clinic` is not a specialization of `Department` and object type Patient is owned by `Hospital` rather than by `Department`.

A.1 Object types

The set S, a Perspective-DB schema, is a set of object types.
$S = \{O_1, O_2, \ldots\}$
The object types O are composite types. The Hospital schema will be used as running example, please refer to Figure A.1.

Example A.1 *In the Hospital schema, the object types are the following: Organization_Manager, Hospital, Clinic, Department, Patient, Employee, Person_Manager, and Person.*

Consistency criterion 1 *The set of object types and the set of atomic types are distinct.*
$S \bigcap \Theta = \emptyset$

□

Some of the object types are managers. Let
$M \subset S$
be the set of the manager object types.

Example A.2 *The managers are* ***Organization_Manager*** *and* ***Person_Manager****.*

In order to be able to define object types, the notations for attributes, relations and operations have to be introduced. Let $\mathbb{A}$ be the set of attributes in the database schema, let $\mathbb{R}$ be the set of relations in the database schema, and let Π be the set of operations in the database schema.

Definition 1 *An object type is defined as a 4-tuple.*
$O =< name, A, R, \Pi >$, *where*
name is the name of the object type,
$A \subset \mathbb{A}$ *is the set of attributes of the object type,*
$R \subset \mathbb{R}$ *is the set of relations of the object type, and*
$\pi \subset \Pi$ *is the set of operations of the object type.*

□

Following the top-down manner, attributes, relations and operations will be defined later.

Consistency criterion 2 *The name of the object type is unique.*
$name(O_1) = name(O_2) \Rightarrow O_1 = O_2$

□

It is now possible to introduce the relations *owner* and *owned*[3].

Definition 2 $owner : \mathbb{A} \bigcup \mathbb{R} \bigcup \Pi \bigcup S \rightarrow S$
$owned : S \rightarrow P(\mathbb{A} \bigcup \mathbb{R} \bigcup \Pi \bigcup S)$
$owned(O) = \{x \in \mathbb{A} \bigcup \mathbb{R} \bigcup \Pi \bigcup S \mid owner(x) = O\}$
$a \in \mathbb{A} \wedge a \in owned(O) \Leftrightarrow a \in O.A$
$r \in \mathbb{R} \wedge r \in owned(O) \Leftrightarrow r \in O.R$
$p \in \Pi \wedge p \in owned(O) \Leftrightarrow p \in O.\pi$
$\neg owner(x) \downarrow \Rightarrow x \in M$

□

[3] These relations are relations in the mathematical sense as opposed to the set of relations in the Perspective-DB schema, $\mathbb{R}$

The meaning of *owner* and *owned* is that each object type is the owner of its attributes, relations and operations, as well as some other object types. Additionally, manager object types are not owned by any other object types.

Example A.3 $owned(Hospital) = \{Name,$
$Manager, Clinics, Departments, Patients,$
$Compute\_ID, Get\_Data, Set\_Data,$
$Insert, Remove,$
$Create, Destroy, EOML\_Get,$
$Clinic, Department, Patient\},$

because
$Hospital.A = \{Name\},$
$Hospital.R = \{Manager, Clinics, Departments, Patients\},$
$Hospital.\pi = \{Compute\_ID, Get\_Data, Set\_Data,$
$Insert, Remove, Create, Destroy, EOML\_Get\}$, *and*
$Clinic, Department, Patient$, *are object types owned by the* $Hospital$ *object type.*
Furthermore,
$owner(Hospital) = Organization\_Manager.$

Attributes

Definition 3 *An attribute* $a \in \mathbb{A}$ *is a 2-tuple.*

$$a =< name, domain >, \text{ where}$$

name is the name of the attribute, and
domain is the domain of the attribute and it is an atomic type.

$$domain \in \Theta$$

Let

$$key : S \to \mathbb{A}$$

be the key of the object types, such that

$$key(O) \in O.A$$

□

Example A.4 *The object type* ***Employee*** *has the following attributes:*
`Code` $=< Code, integer >,$
`Function` $=< Function, string >,$
`Salary` $=< Salary, float >,$
`Nominal_Hourly_Salary` $=< Nominal\_Hourly\_Salary, float >.$
The key is `Code`.

Relations Relations are binary, and there exist both homogeneous and heterogeneous relations.

Definition 4 *A relation $r \in \mathbb{R}$ is a 3-tuple.*

$$r =< name, domain, dest >, \text{ where}$$

name is the name of the relation,
domain is the domain of the relation and it is a subset of the object types.

$$domain \subset S$$

The object types in domain are connected to $owner(r)$ via r.
$dest \subset \mathbb{R}$
is the destination of the relation, which is the set of relations connected to r.
$d \in dest \Rightarrow owner(d) \in domain$
$O \in domain \Rightarrow owned(O) \bigcap dest \neq \emptyset$
$d_1, d_2 \in dest \wedge owner(d_1) = owner(d_2) \Rightarrow d_1 = d_2$

□

Example A.5 *Hospital.Departments is a homogeneous relation.*

$$Hospital.Departments =< Departments, \{Department\}, \{Department.Hospital\} >$$

and Person.Roles is a heterogeneous relation.

$$Person.Roles =< Roles, \{Patient, Employee\}, \{Patient.Person, Employee.Person\} >$$

Relation types

Definition 5 *Each relation has one of three possible types:*

$\tau : \mathbb{R} \rightarrow \{owner, owned, secondary\}$

$\tau(r) = secondary \Rightarrow \forall_{d \in r.dest}[\tau(d) = secondary]$

$\tau(r) = owner \Rightarrow \forall_{d \in r.dest}[\tau(d) = owned] \wedge owned(owner(r)) \supset r.domain$

$\tau(r) = owned \Rightarrow \forall_{d \in r.dest}[\tau(d) = owner] \wedge owner(owner(r)) = r.domain$

□

Example A.6 *Relation types.*

- $\tau(Organization\_Manager.Organizations) = owner \Rightarrow$

  $\tau(Hospital.Manager) = owned \wedge$
  $owned(owner(Organization\_Manager.Organizations)) =$
  $= owned(Organization\_Manager) \supset \{Hospital\} =$
  $= Organization\_Manager.Organizations.domain$

- $\tau(Employee.Unit) = owned \Rightarrow$

  $\tau(Clinic.Employees) = owner \wedge \tau(Department.Employees) = owner \wedge$
  $Employee.Unit.domain = \{Clinic, Department\}$

- $\tau(Person.Roles) = secondary \Rightarrow$

  $\tau(Patient.Person) = secondary \wedge \tau(Employee.Person) = secondary$

Abbreviation 1 *A relation whose owner is element of its domain is a recursive relation.*

$recursive \subset R$

$r \in recursive \equiv owner(r) \in r.domain$

□

Example A.7 *Department.SubDept is a recursive relation.*

Operations

Definition 6 *An operation is a 3-tuple.*

$p =< name, domain, arguments >$

name is the name of the operation,
domain is the domain of the (result of the) operation and it is either an atomic type or an object type.

$domain \in \Theta \bigcup S$

arguments is the sequence of arguments.

Each argument is a 2-tuple.

$argument =< domain, category >$, *where*

$domain \in \Theta \bigcup S$, *and*

$category \in \{input, output, input - output\}$

□

Example A.8 *Person.Number_Of_Children and Department.Employ are operations to calculate the Number of Children a Person has, and to Employ a Person as a new Employee at a Department.*

$Person.Number\_Of\_Children =< Number\_Of\_Children, integer, \emptyset >$ *computes the number of children of the given Person.*

$Department.Employ =< Employ, integer, arguments >$ *creates a new Employee object, where*

$Department.Employ.arguments[1] =< integer, input >$ *is the argument to specify the SSN of the Person to be employed,*

$Department.Employ.arguments[2] =< integer, input >$ *is the argument to specify the Code of the new Employee object, and*

$Department.Employ.arguments[3] =< string, input >$ *is the argument to specify the Function of the new Employee object.*

Generic and specific operations Operations are classified as generic and specific operations. In addition to the generic operations Compute_ID, Get_Data, Set_Data, Insert, Remove, Create, Destroy, EOML_Get, each object type has its own set of specific operations.

Example A.9 *Person.Number_Of_Children and Department.Employ are specific operations.*
The generic operation Set_Data is used to set an attribute to a value, and it is defined as
$< Set\_Data, boolean, arguments >$, *where the domain is boolean to indicate success or error,*
$Set\_Data.arguments[1] =< string, input >$ *for the name of the attribute, and*
$Set\_Data.arguments[2] =< string, input >$ *for the new value of the attribute.*

Names are unique

Consistency criterion 3 *Names of attributes, relations and operations must be unique within an object type.*

$x_1, x_2 \in O.A \bigcup O.R \bigcup O.\pi \wedge x_1.name = x_2.name \Rightarrow x_1 = x_2$

□

Managers

Consistency criterion 4 *Managers have no owned relations, because their instances (see later) cannot be owned by any other object types.*

$$O \in M \wedge r \in O.R \Rightarrow \tau(r) \neq owned$$

□

Example A.10 *The two managers,* ***Organization_Manager*** *and* ***Person_Manager*** *have only owner relations.*
$\tau(Organization\_Manager.Organizations) = owner$

$\tau(Person\_Manager.Persons) = owner$

Summary of object type notations To conclude this section, here is a summary of the notations mentioned.
Θ : set of atomic types

S : database schema, set of all object types, $S \bigcap \Theta = \emptyset$

M : set of manager object types, $M \subset S$

$\mathbb{A}$: set of all attributes within a database schema

$\mathbb{R}$: set of all relations within a database schema

Π : set of all operations within a database schema

$O =< name, A, R, \pi >$: object type, where $A \subset \mathbb{A}$, $R \subset \mathbb{R}$, and $\pi \subset \Pi$

$a =< name, domain >$: attribute, $key : S \rightarrow \mathbb{A}$

$r =< name, domain, dest >$: relation, $\tau : \mathbb{R} \rightarrow \{owner, owned, secondary\}$

$p =< name, domain, sequence\ of\ arguments >$: operation

$argument =< domain, category >$

A.2 Object instances

A database instance for the database schema S is a set of object instances.
$\mathbb{I}(S) = \{I_1, I_2, \ldots\}$

Definition 7 *An object instance is the 3-tuple.*
$I =< O, As, Rs >$, *where*
As *is the attribute assignment.*
$As : O.A \rightarrow values$, *such that* $I.As(a) \in a.domain$
Rs *is the relation assignment.*
$Rs : O.R \rightarrow instances$, *such that* $i \in I.Rs(r) \Rightarrow i.objtype \in r.domain$

□

Example A.11 *In these examples, only the non-empty relations are shown.*
$< Organization\_Manager, \emptyset, Organizations = \{Mother\_Theresa\} >$
$< Hospital, Name = Mother\_Theresa, Manager = \{Organization\_Manager\} >$

Definition 8 *The set of currently existing instances of object type* O *is*
$\iota(O) = \{I \in \mathbb{I}(S) \mid I.objtype = O\}$
This set is also called the extent of the object type.

□

Consistency criterion 5 *There is exactly one instance in the extent of each manager object type.*
$x \in M \Rightarrow \exists!_{I \in \mathbb{I}(S)}[I.objtype = x]$

□

Example A.12 $\iota(Organization\_Manager) = \{Organization\_Manager\}$

Consequently, the minimal database instance contains only the manager object instances.
$\mathbb{I}_{minimal}(S) = \{I \mid I.objtype \in M\}$
The reader might wonder why operations were not mentioned in Definition 7. The reason is that Operations are instantiated only when the need arises.

Definition 9 *Operation instantiation*
In order to instantiate an operation, an object instance of the proper type and arguments are necessary. Consequently, an operation instantiation is defined as the four-tuple.
$ps =< p, I, args, result >$, *where*
$p \in O.\pi$,
$I \in \iota(O)$,
args is the arguments assignment that conforms the arguments definition of p, *and*
result is the result of the operation, and it must be of type domain.

□

Example A.13 $< Set\_Data,$
$Organization\_Manager.Hospitals : Mother\_Theresa, Name, MT, true >$[4]
is the instantiation of the generic operation Set_Data *on the object instance* $Organization\_Manager.Hospitals$ $Mother\_Theresa$. *The operation sets the* $Name$ *attribute of this object instance to the value* MT *successfully.*

Definition 10 *The value of the key attribute is said to be the key value.*
$key(I) \equiv I.As(key(I.objtype))$

□

[4]The id of the object instance is used already in this section to refer to the object instance, even though it is only introduced at the end of the next section

Connection of objects through relations

Definition 11 *The relation "connected to" indicates that an object instance is connected to another.*

I_1 *connected to* I_2 *via* $r \equiv I_2 \in I_1.Rs(r)$

I_1 *connected to* $I_2 \equiv \exists_{r \in \mathbb{R}}[I_1$ *connected to* I_2 *via* $r]$

□

Consistency criterion 6 *The relation "connected to" is symmetric.*

□

Example A.14 $Person\_Manager.Persons : 111$ *connected to* $Person\_Manager.Persons : 222 \Rightarrow$

$Person\_Manager.Persons : 222$ *connected to* $Person\_Manager.Persons : 111$

Insert and Remove The generic operations *Insert* and *Remove* connect and disconnect objects via secondary relations.
$< Insert, boolean, arguments >$
$< Remove, boolean, arguments >$
The domain is boolean to indicate success or error.
Both operations take three arguments that are the object instance to which or from which the current object instance is to be connected or disconnected and the names of the relations.
Here we give examples of instantiations of these operations.

Example A.15 $< Insert, Person\_Manager.Persons : 222,$
$Person\_Manager.Persons : 111,\ Children,\ Parents, true >$
is a successful connection of the two instances.
$< Remove, Person\_Manager.Persons : 222,$
$Person\_Manager.Persons : 111,\ Children,\ Parents, false >$
is an attempt to disconnect the two instances. The attempt is unsuccessful, because the two instances were not connected.

Owner objects

Definition 12 *If a first object is connected to a second object through an owner relation the first object is said to be the owner of the second object and the second object is said to be owned by the first object.*

I_1 *owns* $I_2 \equiv \exists_{r \in \mathbb{R}}[I_1$ *connected to* I_2 *via* $r \wedge \tau(r) = owner]$

Alternative notations are

$I_1 = owner(I_2) \Leftrightarrow I_1$ *owns* I_2*, and*

$I_2 \in owned(I_1) \Leftrightarrow I_1$ *owns* I_2*, where*

$owned(I_1) = \{I \mid owner(I) = I_1\}$

□

Example A.16 $Organization\_Manager.Hospitals : Mother\_Theresa$ *owns* $Organization\_Manager.Hospitals : Mother\_Theresa.Clinics : Surgery.$

Existential dependency

Consistency criterion 7 *For an object instance to exist, either it has to be a manager, or its unique owner has to exist.*
$\forall_{I \in \mathbb{I}(S)}[I.objtype \in M \vee \exists_{I' \in \mathbb{I}(S)}[I' \ owns \ I]]$

□

Example A.17 *The object instance* $Person\_Manager$ *exists without any precondition, but for the object instance*
$Organization\_Manager.Hospitals : Mother\_Theresa.Clinics : Surgery$
to exist, it is a precondition that
$Organization\_Manager.Hospitals : Mother\_Theresa$ *also exists.*

Key values are unique

Consistency criterion 8 *The values of keys of instances are unique within the owner relation.*
Provided that $\tau(r) = owner$ *and* $I_1, I_2 \in I.Rs(r)$, *then*
$key(I_1) = key(I_2) \Rightarrow I_1 = I_2$

□

A.3 Object creation

Existential dependency (see Consistency criterion 7) must hold for all database instances. Consequently, an object instance can only be created by an existing object instance through one of its owner relations. Similarly, an object instance can only be destroyed by its owner object instance through its owner relation. Here follows the example when the first non-manager object instance is created.
Recall that for the database schema S, the minimal database instance $\mathbb{I}$ is the set of the manager object instances.
$\mathbb{I}_{minimal} = \{I \mid I.objtype \in M\}$
For the minimal database instance, it also holds that
$I \in \mathbb{I}_{minimal}, r \in I.objtype.R \Rightarrow I.Rs(r) = \emptyset$
that is, no relations of these instances contain any instances.
A new object instance can only be created by one of the existing instances,
$I \in \mathbb{I}_{minimal}$
through one of its owner relations.
$r \in I.Rs, \tau(r) = owner$
As the result of the creation, the new object instance I' will be the element of the r relation of the I object instance.
$I' \in I.Rs(r), I'.objtype \in S \backslash M$

Example A.18 *In our example, the minimal database instance contains the two managers.*
$\mathbb{I}_{minimal} = \{Organization\_Manager, Person\_Manager\}$.
The only owner relation of $Organization\_Manager$ *is* $Organizations$. *Through this relation, a* $Hospital$ *object instance, e.g.* $Organization\_Manager.Hospitals : Mother\_Theresa$ *can be created as the first non-manager object instance of the new database instance.*
$$\mathbb{I}_{new} = \{Organization\_Manager, Person\_Manager, \\ Organization\_Manager.Hospitals : Mother\_Theresa\}.$$

Create and Destroy The generic operations *Create* and *Destroy* create and destroy objects via primary relations.
$< Create, boolean, arguments >$
$< Destroy, boolean, arguments >$
The domain is boolean to indicate success or error.
Both operations take two arguments that are the name of the owner relation and the key of the owned object.
Here we give examples of instantiations of these operations.

Example A.19 $< Create, Organization\_Manager,$ $Organizations, Mother\_Theresa, true >$
is a successful creation of the object instance $Organization\_Manager.Hospitals : Mother\_Theresa$.
$< Destroy, Organization\_Manager, Organizations, Theresa, false >$
is an attempt to destroy the object instances $Organization\_Manager.Hospitals : Theresa$. *The attempt is unsuccessful, because this object does not exist.*

Any valid database instance $\mathbb{I}(\mathbb{S})$ can be reached by applying the generic operations *Create*, *Insert*, and *Set_Data* to the minimal database instance $\mathbb{I}_{minimal}(S)$. Any database instance that can not be reached this way, is not a valid database instance.

Object identity Consequently, the object identity of any of the object instances can be constructed as follows.

$$id(I) = \begin{cases} key(I) & if\ I.objtype \in M \\ id(owner(I)).(r.name) : key(I) & otherwise \end{cases}$$

In the latter case, r is such that $owner(I)$ *connected to* I *via* r.

The generic operation $Compute\_ID$ computes the id for the object instance.
$< Compute\_ID, string, \emptyset >$
The result of the operation is the id (in string format).

Index

Glossary

GUI Graphical User Interface. A subsystem that enables end-users to interact with the application., 13

Information System An Information System, commonly abbreviated to **IS** is a system composed of various components such as database management systems, application programs and user interfaces, which together provide the functionality that the various users of the system require., 2

Instantiation, TOML The Instantiation TOML file (Instance TOML for short) contains OML objects describing application object type instances. When imported, the OML objects are converted into instances of an object type., 203

ODBMS An ODBMS is a generic software system that is used as the foundation upon which a specific software system can be built., 2

ODMG implementation, state of the art ODMG defines that the implementation of an object type consists of a representation and a set of methods. The representation is a data structure derived from the abstract state by a language binding. The methods are procedure bodies that are derived from the abstract behavior by type definition., 254

ODMG interface, state of the art ODMG differentiates between interfaces and classes. An interface definition is a specification that defines the abstract behavior of an object type. A class definition is a specification that defines the abstract behavior and abstract state of an object type., 254

ODMG, extents In ODMG an extent of an object type is the set of all instances of the type within a particular object database system, i.e. the set of objects which fulfill the type characteristics and which belong to a particular application., 261

ODMG, state of the art The purpose of ODMG is to define a standard to be implemented by object database management systems and by object-relational mappings. Standardization (work) began in 1993. Over the years many major vendors of object database technology have joined the organization., 253

OML manager The OML manager is responsible for the conversion between the file information and the object heap. It interprets the information in the `TOML` file and passes it on to a controller in each layer., 79

OML object The OML-Tree is constructed of instances of one type only, the OML_Object., 79

OML tree mapping Data in TOML format can be converted to an OML-Tree and vice-versa., 82

OML tree The OML manager manages its own object heap called the OML-Tree., 79

TOML configuration, language Perspective-DB supports a set of language configuration files structured similarly to other configuration files., 193

TOML files The configuration files are commonly called TOML files. TOML is the name given to the special format used to define the information contained in the files., 240

TOML, meta The Meta TOML is the textual equivalent of the schematic developer view., 85

UML UML stands for Unified Modeling Language. The language is the industry standard language for specifying, visualizing, constructing, and documenting the artifacts of software systems, according to the Rational website., 266

aggregating values, query Aggregation is computing the maximum, the minimum, the count, the sum, or the average of a number of values. Aggregation is achieved by requesting the type of aggregation (max, min, count, sum, or avg) and by indicating the beginning and end of the query items to be aggregated., 167

application layer, architecture The application layer describes all objects carrying application semantics. The application layer can use one or more application domain layers beneath it (lower in the system inheritance hierarchy)., 237

application An Application encapsulates an object base into one single object that fulfills the principle needs of various users. Applications can be associated with each other for the purpose of fulfilling user requests on several object bases., 12

applying filters, query If a query string contains a WHERE-clause, the latter is used to contain filter criteria to filter out rows from the query table. One filter criterion applies to one relation, in other words it filters the instances of one relation. Filter criteria may be combined in the WHERE-clause by using the logical operators AND and OR, 162

applying type selectors, query Heterogeneous relations may be traversed in the same way as homogeneous relations. A query item that instructs the query to traverse a heterogeneous relation may also instruct the query to select instances of a particular type only., 165

atomic attribute Atomic attributes can store integers, characters, strings, floating points etc., 25

attribute member The purpose of the member attribute is to store values. An attribute is constructed from fundamental literal and array object types by applying inheritance and membership. It represents a semantic unit of information., 25

behavior view, meta The Behavior view specifies the dynamic aspects of objects., 89

bi-directional relationship A bi-directional relationship type implies that both object types possess the relation member., 29

canonical-ID identification Starting from the manager, the keys and relationships along the ownership hierarchy are concatenated to form an application wide unique identifier of the instance., 48

cardinality of a relationship The cardinality of a relationship type indicates the number of instances actually associated with each other in a relationship of the considered relationship type., 30

cardinality range of a relationship type The cardinality range of a relationship type is composed of the cardinality ranges of the participating relations., 29

collection attribute Collection attributes represent various sorts of lists, arrays, sets, bags etc., 25

composite attribute Composite attributes contain various members but do not represent a collection., 25

connector and node, GOML A node is a GOML object that denotes a point on the canvas. A connector line is a GOML object contained within the body of a relation or a node which is its starting point. The destination of a connector line is generally a node or a relation., 174

controller, language The `Phrase` instance hierarchies are split according to language and each language is managed by a dedicated controller (layer administrator). Each controller is responsible for all phrases and the translation of terms for the names, ranges, arguments, and messages necessary to input and output information in that particular language., 192

default ownership A default ownership is a particular branch in the ownership hierarchy which is the most dominant, i.e. which will be used most. The identification of instances within such a branch can use a short form for the notation., 50

developer view The developer view describes how the application is constructed., 58

developer We use the term developer for a person who specifies the object schemas and applications., 12

draw hint, GOML Hints are intended to help the drawing manager perform a more optimal placement, or to reduce the processing time it needs to calculate a placement., 177

end-user language, TOML In Perspective-DB the language related aspects of an object are configurable by means of the TOML Language domain. The language aspects concern the naming of object-types, members, values and any additional information that appears to the end-user in natural language., 191

end-user We use the term end-user for a person who uses applications., 12

entity type An entity type is a template for a semantic categorization of entities., 5

entity An entity is a unique identifiable unit carrying semantics within the UoD., 3

executing methods, query Operations can be executed from queries by making query items composed of the name and arguments of the requested operation., 168

exploiting, association view, GUI The purpose of this view is to have all instances related to the source instance in one table., 153

exploiting, query view, GUI The common usage is to inspect the table, and to find a particular instance in the table in order to activate it in the schema or to pop up a form view., 155

external language The task of an External language is to provide a translation of the terms defined in the internal language to equivalent terms most appropriate to a native speaker end-user of a particular language, such as English., 191

first order object The characteristics of the object type must be suitable to express the semantics of the UoD in terms which are familiar to the human user. This object type has evolved through an inheritance hierarchy in order to acquire its current interface. We categorize this type and its specializations as first order object types., 25

form view visibility, GOML A member is normally displayed in both the schematic and the form view. It is possible to overrule this behavior by explicitly making the member invisible in the schematic or the form., 179

get by query, instantiation, TOML The role of the Get controller is to extract data selectively from an object base. The term Get by query is used because the query module is used to assist in selecting those objects of which data is required., 227

global identification of an instance Instances are globally identified by an identification path. The identification path is called the identity of an instance., 48

global member identification of object At object type level the global identification is the same as the local because the object type name is globally unique. At instance level the global identification of a member is given through the combination of the identity of the instance and the member name concatenated to the identification path and separated by a dot., 52

instance alias identification The alias is an arbitrary (also atomic) attribute which functions as a nick-name for the key. A constraint on the alias is that it must not conflict with another alias or key within the same owner relation. This ensures that the system can at all times identify the object by its key or by its alias so that both are legitimate local identifiers., 47

instantiation view The object base changes with each operation performed by the application as instances are created and destroyed, relations between instances inserted and removed and the values of attributes modified. The instantiation schema is therefore a snap-shot of a selected part of the application., 76

internal language There is one language that serves as the fixed translation reference point to and from any other language. Called Internal, the language is the one in which the system is realized by the developers., 191

key identification An instance is locally identified semantically by its key. Local means within the scope of its owner_relation., 46

loading an object base, instantiation Instantiation is triggered automatically or invoked manually to populate the object base of the application with the persistent objects stored in the form of Instance TOML files., 203

local member identification The local identification of a member happens according to the existential dependencies defined by membership. The local member identification is given by: `object_type_name.member_name`., 52

manipulating an object base, instantiation TOML Instantiation is applied to manipulate an existing object base by creating or modifying instances and is commonly used to export objects from one object base and import them into another object base., 204

model The semantics of the object base have to be a model. A model is a simplified description of a system used in explanations, calculations, etc., 11

module grid, GOML The object type grid places each member of an object type in a unique position relative to the object type., 172

object base management An object base management system is a structured collection of objects that enable and support the definition and manipulation of object bases., 12

object base An object base is used to store objects, if necessary persistently, commonly in file format on a hard disk., 11

object instance Any object fulfilling the definition of an object type is an **instance** of that object type., 15

object model An object model is a collection of constructs that enable one to express the semantics and functionality of a UoD by means of an object schema., 12

object schema An object schema defines the semantics and functionality of an object base that models the UoD. An object schema consists of objects that define other objects. An object base consists of objects., 11

object type grid, GOML The members can be placed using an absolute object type grid coordinate, or using a coordinate relative to another member of the object type., 172

object type identification An object type is semantically identified by its name. Names of object types must be unique within the application., 46

object type Object which defines a collection of objects sharing the same characteristics. The object type is assigned a unique name., 14

object An object is a unique identifiable unit carrying semantics which can be expressed in a formal way by unambiguous characteristics., 11

operation generic A generic operation is an operation shared by each object type in the object base in principle., 37

operation member An operation is an object type which characterizes another object type by means of processing particular activities on the object type it characterizes and on other object types., 37

persistence Persistence ensures that objects residing in the object heap of the running application can be saved to files and likewise, such files can be loaded in the running application to restore the objects., 79

polymorphism An operation is polymorphic when several object type have a different implementation (behavior) yet the signature of the operation remains the same., 42

primary ownership The rest of the ownership hierarchy that is not primary. The canonical form of the identification path has to be given to identify an instance., 50

private relationship member Any relationship extending from one relation instance has its own relationship member., 33

query meaning, model Querying can be imagined as traversing an ownership hierarchy of instances and if necessary, crossing to another via a secondary relationship (or several) to continue the traversal as it was done during navigation., 159

recursive relationship type A recursive relationship type has the same object type at both ends of the relationship., 32

recursive, query A recursive query item instructs the query to traverse a recursive relation several times, i.e. as many times as is necessary. In order to make a query item recursive, the navigator its recursive-clause must be used., 166

reference point, GOML The position of a GOML object is by default relative to its owner GOML object., 176

relation member A relation is an object type characterizing its owner by associating the owner object type to one or more object types. The name of the relation is generally the name or role of the object type it refers to in singular or plural form., 28

relational database This is a well thought-out and widely used technology with a sound underlying theoretical basis. The available data structure is a relation, represented as a table., 5

relationship member Relationship types may have members. They are called relationship members. Normally these members are attributes, hence the term relationship attribute., 33

relationship type, ownership Ownership expresses and maintains existential dependency between instances of the related object types., 34

relationship type, secondary Secondary relationship types can associate object types from several abstraction levels of the same ownership hierarchy, either the same branch or different branches of it, as well as of different ownership hierarchy., 36

relationship type A relationship type represents an association between object types. This can be an association with other object types outside the considered object type or with the considered object type itself (recursive relationship type)., 28

relationship, heterogeneous An ownership relationship is heterogeneous if the owner relation can relate to instances of two or more object types., 36

relationship A relationship is an instance of a relationship type. A relationship may be created if and only if the instances of the associated object types already exist and the relationship type exists., 28

replacing an object base, instantiation Instantiation is applied to replace the object base version of a running application with a different version and is often invoked manually., 204

road-map A set of generic constructs of a comprehensive graphical object model can be compared to the legend of a road map. An object base developer can apply the graphical object model, according to the generic object model rules, to produce a canonical object schema that can be interpreted by colleagues and other users., 12

saving an object base, instantiation TOML Instantiation is triggered automatically or invoked manually to save the object base of the application. This is the reverse operation to populating the object base., 204

schema mapping instances, GUI With several additions, the static End-user schema is transformed into an interactive GUI that can be used to manipulate the system and the object base it maintains., 99

schema navigation, GUI Navigation enables the end-user to access selected instances by traversing step by step through the object base from one instance to another., 99

semantic identification Identification on a semantic basis means that the identification of an object is associated with the meaning of the object. An object is recognizable by a user through its characteristics or a particular part of its characteristics., 45

set by query Set by query is an extension of the Instantiation view of the Instance Domain. Using Set it is possible to select and modify objects in the object-base that satisfy a particular condition., 213

shared relationship member All relationships extending from one relation instance share the same relationship member., 33

short-ID identification When an instance is part of a default ownership hierarchy it can also be uniquely identified using an abbreviated form of the canonical-ID. The short-ID is a concatenation the of the keys along the ownership hierarchy., 49

structure view, meta The Structure View specifies the static aspects of object types., 85

structure, form view, GUI A form view is the tabular equivalent of an object type in the schematic representation. It presents the members of the object type. If an instance of the object type is accessed in the form, the form presents its values., 133

structure, overview, GUI An overview shows a list of all instances related to a particular instance through a particular relation. The attributes of each instance are also displayed., 147

structure, query view, GUI The query view is composed of the title bar and the query table. The title bar of the query view shows the root instance and the name of the query. Data items are stored in fields of the query table, fields are organized in columns and rows., 153

structured collection A structured collection means the objects have to be associated with each other in terms of the semantics of the UoD and the functionality they offer to their users (and to each other)., 11

syntactic identification Identification on a syntactic basis means that an identifier exists for each object which is part of the object definition and known to the system which manages the object. The management system can find and access the object based on this identifier and it can refer to the object through this identifier., 45

system architecture Complex systems are best constructed in a modular fashion by dividing the system into subsystems. A subsystem may also incorporate other subsystems., 237

system grid, GOML A system grid places each module in a unique position on the canvas., 172

system layer, architecture The object types of an upper layer are specializations of generalized object types of lower layers. In principle, an object type of an upper layer can specialize any object in any one of its lower layers., 237

thesaurus module, language The language management is a service provided by the OMS layer. The service is contained in the module called Thesaurus., 192

traversing relations, query A query may traverse several relations and may gather data along the traversal path, by means of the ITS-clause., 161

truncated-ID identification When an object needs to be identified within a particular context it is enough to provide sufficient identity to locate the object. This

ID is identical to the complete ID, with one or more of the keys beginning with the root, truncated. Depending on whether the object is along a default ownership path or not, the Truncated-ID can be in the Canonical-ID form or the Short-ID form., 51

uni-directional relationship A uni-directional relationship type implies that only one of the object types possesses the relation member., 29

universe of discourse A Universe of Discourse or UoD for short is the limited field of interest of the users of a particular object base. It is a part of a real or imaginary world or a mix of both., 11

user view The end-user view describes the object types visible at the interface., 58

view, schema A different observation angle shows different aspects of the object schema. A view can also present the same aspects using different appearances. For example, suppose we are observing instances of object types. We can view these in canonical schematic form or in tabular form., 57

window, GOML An application representation consists of one or more Windows, each containing a (sub)system., 171

Bibliography

[Abiteboul et al., 1997] Abiteboul, S., Quass, D., McHugh, J., Widom, J., and Weiner, J. L. (1997). The lorel query language for semistructured data. *Journal of Digital Libraries*, 1(1):68–88.

[Abiteboul and Vianu, 1997] Abiteboul, S. and Vianu, V. (1997). Regular path queries with constraints. In *Proceedings of the Sixteenth ACM SIGACT-SIGMOD-SIGART Symposium on Principles of Database Systems, May 12-14, 1997, Tucson, Arizona*, pages 122–133. ACM Press.

[Batini et al.,1992] Batini C., Ceri S. and Navathe S.B. (1992) Conceptual Database Design- an Entity-Relationship Approach Benjamin/Cummings, 1992 ISBN 0-8053-0244-1

[Blaha et al.,1998] Blaha M. and Premerlani W. (1998) Object-Oriented Modeling and Design for Database Applications (includes UML) Prentice Hall/Upper Saddle River, NJ, 1998

[Buneman et al., 1995] Buneman P., Davidson, S. B., and Suciu, D. (1995). Programming constructs for unstructured data. In Atzeni, P. and Tannen, V., editors, *Database Programming Languages (DBPL-5), Proceedings of the Fifth International Workshop on Database Programming Languages, Gubbio, Umbria, Italy, 6-8 September 1995*, Electronic Workshops in Computing, page 12. Springer.

[Cattell and Barry, 2000] Cattell R. and Barry D. (2000). *The Object Data Standard: ODMG 3.0.* Morgan Kaufmann.

[Christophides et al., 1996] Christophides V., Cluet S., and Moerkotte G. (1996). Evaluating queries with generalized path expressions. In Jagadish, H. V. and Mumick, I. S., editors, *Proceedings of the 1996 ACM SIGMOD International Conference on Management of Data, Montreal, Quebec, Canada, June 4-6, 1996*, pages 413–422. ACM Press.

[Date, 1995] Date C. J. An Introduction to Database Systems Vol. 1 Addison-Wesley, 1995. 6th edition ISBN 0-201-82458-2

[Deutsch et al., 1999] Deutsch A., Fernandez M. F., Florescu D., Levy A. Y., and Suciu D. (1999). Xml-ql: A query language for xml. In *Proceedings of the Eighth International World Wide Web Conference, Toronto, Canada, May 1999.*

[Elmasri, 89] Elmasri R. Navathe Fundamentals of Database Systems The Benjamin/Cummings Publishing Company, Inc. 1989 ISBN 0-8053-0145-3

[Essenius et al., 1998] Essenius E., Sim M., Kist P., Simon N., and Gerhardt W. (1998). A working generic canonical schematic uims for an odbms. In Ioannidis Y. E. and Klas W., editors, *Visual Database Systems 4 (VDB4), IFIP TC2/WG 2.6 Fourth Working Conference on Visual Database Systems, L'Aquila, Italy, 27-29 May 1998*, pages 168–174. Chapman and Hall.

[Feldman et al., 1986] Feldman P, and Miller D. (august 1986). Entity model clustering: Structuring a data model by abstraction. *Computer Journal*, 29, 4.

[Fernandez et al., 1997] Fernandez M. F., Florescu D., Levy A. Y., and Suciu, D. (1997). A query language for a web-site management system. *SIGMOD Record*, 26(3):4–11.

[Fernandez and Suciu, 1998] Fernandez M. F. and Suciu D. (1998). Optimizing regular path expressions using graph schemas. In *Proceedings of the Fourteenth International Conference on Data Engineering, February 23-27, 1998, Orlando, Florida, USA*, pages 14–23. IEEE Computer Society.

[Gerhardt and Simon, 1999] Gerhardt W. and Simon N. (1999). Characteristics of an object model and object management to support decision processes. In *InterSymp'99, 11th International Conference on System Research, Informatics and Cybernetics, Baden-Baden, Germany, August 2-7, 1999.* International Institute for Advanced Studies in Systems Research and Cybernetics.

[Gerhardt et al., 2000] Gerhardt W., van Katwijk J., and Essenius E. (2000). Design orthogonal concepts orthogonally - a contribution to maintainability of enterprise information systems. In Thoma H., Mayr H. C., and Erkollar A., editors, *ReTIS 2000, Preparing to E-Business, Sixth International Conference on Re-Technologies for Information Systems, Basel, Switzerland, 29 February - 3 March 2000*, pages 21–33. Österreichische Computer Gesellschaft.

[OMG] http://www.omg.org

[Rational Rose] http://www.rational.com

[Sim, 1993] Sim (1993). *Tool and Database Interfacing based on Virtual Objects.* PhD thesis, Delft University of Technology, Delft.

[Sim, Gerhardt, Kist and Simon, 1994] The Specification of a Seamless O-O Programming Interface for CAD Tools, TOOLS 13, Prentice Hall International, UK, 1994.

[sql, 1992] (1992). Iso/iec sql revision. iso-ansi working draft database language sql (sql3). Technical Report document ISO/IEC JTC1/SC21 N6931, New York, NY 10036.

[Szántó, 2001] Szántó I. (2001). Recursive path queries in an ownership-hierarchy based object model. In *Proceedings of "The White Object Oriented Nights" (WOON), St. Petersburg, Russia, 14-15 June 2001.*

[Szántó, 2004] Szántó I. (2004). *Design, Optimization and Evaluation of a Path Query System.* PhD thesis, Delft University of Technology, Delft (to appear).

[Szántó and Kist, 2000] Szántó I. and Kist P. (2000). A partial view maintenance variant for the perspective-db odbms. In *InterSymp'00, 12th International Conference on System Research, Informatics and Cybernetics, Baden-Baden, Germany, August 1-4, 2000.* International Institute for Advanced Studies in Systems Research and Cybernetics.

[ter Bekke, 1992] ter Bekke J. H. (1992). *Semantic Data Modeling.* Prentice Hall, New York.

[UML] http://www.uml.org http://www.rational.com/uml

[van der Wolf, 1993] van der Wolf P. (1993). *Architecture of an open and efficient CAD framework.* Delft University of Technology, Delft.